D1070590

GARRICK V. ALLEN is a Lecturer in New
Testament at Dublin City University and a
research associate of the School of Ancient
Languages, University of Pretoria. He is
the author of multiple articles, including
pieces in the *Journal of Biblical Literature*,
Zeitschrift für die neutestamentliche Wissenschaft,
and *Catholic Biblical Quarterly*. He has edited
numerous volumes dealing with ancient
biblical interpretation and with the Book of
Revelation.

THE BOOK OF REVELATION AND EARLY JEWISH TEXTUAL CULTURE

Volume 168

The Book of Revelation and Early Jewish Textual Culture explores the relationship between the writing of Revelation and its early audience, especially its interaction with Jewish scripture. It touches on several areas of scholarly enquiry in biblical studies, including modes of literary production, the use of allusions, practices of exegesis, and early engagements with the book of Revelation. Garrick V. Allen brings the book of Revelation into the broader context of early Jewish literature, including the Dead Sea Scrolls and other important works. Arguing that the author of the New Testament Apocalypse was a scribal expert, someone who was well versed in the content of Jewish scripture and its interpretation, he demonstrates that John was not only a seer and prophet, but also an erudite reader of scripture.

GARRICK V. ALLEN is a Lecturer in New Testament at Dublin City University and a research associate of the School of Ancient Languages, University of Pretoria. He is the author of multiple articles, including pieces in the *Journal of Biblical Literature, Zeitschrift für die neutestamentliche Wissenschaft*, and *Catholic Biblical Quarterly*. He has edited numerous volumes dealing with ancient biblical interpretation and with the book of Revelation.

SOCIETY FOR NEW TESTAMENT STUDIES

MONOGRAPH SERIES

General Editor: Paul Trebilco

168

THE BOOK OF REVELATION AND EARLY JEWISH
TEXTUAL CULTURE

SOCIETY FOR NEW TESTAMENT STUDIES
MONOGRAPH SERIES

Recent Titles In The Series:

The Book of Revelation and Early Jewish Textual Culture

GARRICK V. ALLEN
Dublin City University, Ireland

CAMBRIDGE
UNIVERSITY PRESS

CAMBRIDGE
UNIVERSITY PRESS

University Printing House, Cambridge CB2 8BS, United Kingdom

One Liberty Plaza, 20th Floor, New York, NY 10006, USA

477 Williamstown Road, Port Melbourne, VIC 3207, Australia

4843/24, 2nd Floor, Ansari Road, Daryaganj, Delhi - 110002, India

79 Anson Road, #06-04/06, Singapore 079906

Cambridge University Press is part of the University of Cambridge.

It furthers the University's mission by disseminating knowledge in the pursuit of education, learning, and research at the highest international levels of excellence.

www.cambridge.org
Information on this title: www.cambridge.org/9781107198128
DOI: 10.1017/9781108182157

© Garrick V. Allen 2017

First published 2017

Printed in the United States of America by Sheridan Books, Inc.

A catalogue record for this publication is available from the British Library.

Library of Congress Cataloging-in-Publication Data
Names: Allen, Garrick V., author.
Title: The Book of Revelation and early Jewish textual culture / Garrick V. Allen, University of Wuppertal, Germany.
Description: New York : Cambridge University Press, 2017. | Series: Society for New Testament studies monograph series ; 168 | Includes bibliographical references and index.
Identifiers: LCCN 2017003102 | ISBN 9781107198128 (hardback)
Subjects: LCSH: Bible. Revelation – Criticism, interpretation, etc. | Bible. Revelation – Criticism, interpretation, etc., Jewish. | Bible. Revelation – Criticism, Textual.
Classification: LCC BS2825.52 .A45 2017 | DDC 228/.06 – dc23
LC record available at https://lccn.loc.gov/2017003102

ISBN 978-1-107-19812-8 Hardback

For Andrea and Eloise

CONTENTS

TABLES

ACKNOWLEDGEMENTS

I am indeed grateful for the many people who have contributed to this book, both directly and indirectly. And there are many. First, my gratitude goes to Bill Tooman who supervised an earlier form of this book as my PhD thesis at the University of St Andrews. Sitting around his kitchen table, drinking red wine, and talking shop was deeply formative for me. The ease with which he was able to recall obscure (at least to me) secondary texts and the details of equally obscure (at least to me) Hebrew lexemes is a skill that I'm sure I will never have. Thanks also to the other members of the *Yaḥad* who sat around this table with me, including Sheree Lear, Allen Jones, Sean Cook, Penny Barter, Madhavi Nevader, and Adam Harger.

This book also benefitted from many conversations around the Roundel, particularly with Jesse Nickel and Chris Brewer. Discussions with Paul Sloan, Denny Kinlaw, Raymond Morehouse, and the denizens of the Black Room also shaped the book. The final phase of this project took place in beautiful Wuppertal, Germany under the shadow of the Schwebebahn. To my colleagues at the ISBTF, Martin Karrer, Marcus Sigismund, Darius Müller, and Matthias Geigenfeind, thank you for your grace and patience during my time there. I also want to thank my colleagues at Dublin City University in advance for what I'm sure will be many years of collaboration and discourse. Thanks also goes to Ron Herms, who introduced the book of Revelation to me as an undergraduate. Both Ron and Brad Embry greatly encouraged my academic pursuits at an early stage and for that I am grateful. This book received financial support from the Faculty of Humanities and Social Sciences Book Publication Scheme at Dublin City University, which covered the costs associated with indexing.

Parts of Chapter 3 were originally published as 'Textual Pluriformity and Allusion in the Book of Revelation. The Text of Zechariah 4 in the Apocalypse', *ZNW* 106 (2015): 136–145; parts of Chapter 4 were initially published as 'Reusing Scripture in the Book of Revelation: Techniques of Reuse and Habits of Reading', in *The Book of Revelation: Currents in British Research on the Apocalypse* (ed. G. V. Allen, I. Paul, and S. Woodman; WUNT 2.411; Tübingen: Mohr Siebeck, 2015), 1–17; and a small portion of Chapter 5 was recently published as 'Zechariah's Horse Vision and Angelic Intermediaries: Translation, Allusion, and Transmission in Early Judaism', *Catholic Biblical Quarterly* (2017). Many thanks to Walter de Gruyter, Mohr Siebeck and the Catholic Biblical Association of America for their kind permission to use reworked portions of these articles here.

Finally, I thank my family, especially my wife Andrea and our daughter Eloise, for being constant sources of encouragement and joy through the many transitions periods of the past five years. I am smitten. I dedicated my thesis to the 1995 Seattle Mariners, but I dedicate this book to them.

GVA
19 September 2016

ABBREVIATIONS

AB	Anchor Bible
ABG	Arbeiten zur Bibel und Ihrer Geschichte
AcBib	Academia Biblica
ANESsup	Ancient Near Eastern Studies Supplement
ANTC	Abingdon New Testament Commentaries
ANTF	Arbeiten zur neutestamentlichen Textforschung
AOTC	Abingdon Old Testament Commentaries
AUSDDS	Andrews University Seminary Doctoral Dissertations Series
AUSS	*Andrews University Seminary Studies*
AYB	Anchor Yale Bible
BBC	Blackwell Bible Commentaries
BDAG	W. Bauer, F. W. Danker, F. W. Arndt, and F. W. Gingrich, eds. *Greek-English Lexicon of the New Testament and Other Early Christian Literature*. 3rd edn. Chicago: Chicago University Press, 1999.
BDB	F. Brown, S. R. Driver, and C. A. Briggs, eds. *A Hebrew and English Lexicon*
BECNT	Baker Exegetical Commentary on the New Testament
BETL	Bibliotheca Ephemeridum Theologicarum Lovaniensium
BHQ	*Biblia Hebraica Quinta*
BIOSCS	*Bulletin of the International Organization for Septuagint and Cognate Studies*
BNTC	Black's New Testament Commentaries
BO	Berit Olam
BQ	Biblia Qumranica
BR	*Biblical Research*
BT	Biblical Tools and Studies

BTS	Biblisch-Theologische Studien
BZAW	Beihefte zur Zeitschrift für die alttestamentliche Wissenschaft
BZHT	Beiträge zur historischen Theologie
BZNW	Beihefte zur Zeitschrift für die neutestamentliche Wissenschaft
CBC	Cambridge Bible Commentary
CBET	Contributions to Biblical Exegesis and Theology
CBIEJ	M. Henze, ed. *A Companion to Biblical Interpretation in Early Judaism*. Grand Rapids: Eerdmans, 2011.
CBQ	*Catholic Biblical Quarterly*
CBR	*Currents in Biblical Research*
CEJL	Commentaries on Early Jewish Literature
CRINT	Compendia Rerum Iudaicarum ad Novum Testamentum
DCLS	Deuterocanonical and Cognate Literature Studies
DJD	Discoveries in the Judean Desert
DSD	*Dead Sea Discoveries*
DSI	De Septuaginta Investigationes
EDSS	L. Schiffman and J. VanderKam, eds. *Encyclopedia of the Dead Sea Scrolls.* 2 vols. Oxford: Oxford University Press, 2000.
EJL	Early Judaism and Its Literature
ET	*Expository Times*
FAT	Forschungen zum Alten Testament
FRLANT	Forschungen zur Religion und Literatur des Alten und Neuen Testaments
GAP	Guides to the Apocrypha & Pseudepigrapha
HALOT	L. Koehler, W. Baumgartner, and J. J. Stamm, eds. *The Hebrew and Aramaic Lexicon of the Old Testament*. 2 vols. Leiden: Brill, 2001.
HBM	Hebrew Bible Monographs
HB/OT	M. Sæbø, ed. *Hebrew Bible/Old Testament: The History of its Interpretation Volume 1: From the Beginnings to the Middle Ages Part 1: Antiquity.* Göttingen: Vandenhoeck & Ruprecht, 1996.
HdO	Handbuch der Orientalistik
HDR	Harvard Dissertations in Religion

HRCS	E. Hatch and H. A. Redpath, eds. *Concordance to the Septuagint and Other Greek Versions of the Old Testament*. Reprinted by Grand Rapids: Baker, 2001.
HTA	Historisch-Theologische Auslegung
HZNT	Handbuch zum Neuen Testament
ICC	International Critical Commentary
IEJ	*Israel Exploration Journal*
IJTS	*International Journal of Transpersonal Studies*
JAJ	*Journal of Ancient Judaism*
JAJsup	Journal of Ancient Judaism Supplements
JATS	*Journal of Adventist Theological Society*
JBL	*Journal of Biblical Literature*
JCP	Jewish & Christian Perspectives
JECH	*Journal of Early Christian History*
JECS	*Journal of Early Christian Studies*
JETS	*Journal of the Evangelical Theology Society*
JHS	*Journal of Hebrew Scriptures*
JJS	*Journal of Jewish Studies*
JPT	*Journal of Pentecostal Theology*
JSBLE	*Journal of the Society of Biblical Literature and Exegesis*
JSHZ	Jüdische Schriften aus hellenisitisch-römischer Zeit
JSJsup	Supplements to the Journal for the Study of Judaism
JSNT	*Journal for the Study of the New Testament*
JSNTsup	Journal of the Study of the New Testament Supplement Series
JSOTsup	Journal for the Study of the Old Testament: Supplement Series
JSPsup	Journal for the Study of the Pseudepigrapha: Supplement Series
KAT	Kommentar zum Alten Testament
KEKNT	Kritisch-exegetischer Kommentar über das Neue Testament
LBA	La Bible d'Alexandrie
LCL	Loeb Classical Library
LHBOTS	Library of Hebrew Bible/Old Testament Studies
LNTS	Library of New Testament Studies

LSJ	H. G. Liddell, R. Scott, and H. S. Jones, eds. *A Greek-English Lexicon*. 9th edn. Oxford: Oxford University Press, 1996.
JSS	*Journal of Semitic Studies*
JSSsup	Journal of Semitic Studies Supplement
Mikra	J Mulder, ed. *Mikra: Text, Translation, Reading & Interpretation of the Hebrew Bible in Ancient Judaism & Early Christianity*. Reprinted by Grand Rapids: Baker, 2004.
MNTC	The Moffatt New Testament Commentary
MSU	Mitteilungen des Septuaginta-Unternehmens
NCB	New Century Bible
NCBC	New Cambridge Bible Commentary
NICNT	New International Commentary on the New Testament
NIGTC	New International Greek Testament Commentary
NRT	*Nouvelle Revue Théologique*
NTD	Neues Testament Deutsch
NTL	New Testament Library
NTS	*New Testament Studies*
NTsup	Supplements to Novum Testamentum
OBO	Orbis Biblicus et Orientalis
OS	Oudtestamentische Studiën
OTKNT	Ökumenischer Taschenbuchkommentar zum Neuen Testament
OTL	Old Testament Library
OTM	Old Testament Message
OTP	J. H. Charlesworth, eds. *The Old Testament Pseudepigrapha*. 2 vols. Peabody, MA: Hendrickson, 1983.
OTP: MNS	R. Bauckham, J. R. Davila, and A. Panayotov, eds. *Old Testament Pseudepigrapha: More Noncanonical Scriptures*. Vol. 1. Grand Rapids: Eerdmans, 2013.
OTRM	Oxford Theology and Religion Monographs
PBM	Paternoster Biblical Monographs
PT	*Poetics Today*
PTL	*PTL: A Journal for Descriptive Poetics and Theory of Literature*
RB	*Revue Biblique*
RBS	Resources for Biblical Study

RevQ	*Revue de Qumrân*
RNT	Regensburger Neues Testament
SB	Studies in Biblical Literature
SBB	Stuttgarter Biblische Beiträge
SBLDiss	SBL Dissertations
SC	Septuagint Commentary Series
SCS	Septuagint and Cognate Studies
SNTSMS	Society for New Testament Studies
	Monograph Series
SNTU	*Studien zum Neuen Testament und seiner Umwelt*
SP	Sacra Pagina
SPB	Studia Post-Biblica
SRB	Studies in Rewritten Bible
STDJ	Studies on the Texts of the Desert of Judah
Symposium	Society of Biblical Literature Symposium Series
TB	*Tyndale Bulletin*
TCS	Text-Critical Studies
TKZNT	Theologischer Kommentar zum Neuen Testament
TNTC	Tyndale New Testament Commentaries
TOTC	Tyndale Old Testament Commentaries
TSAJ	Texte und Studien zum antiken Judentum
UMSHS	University of Michigan Studies
	Humanistic Series
VCsup	Supplements to Vigiliae Christianae
VT	*Vetus Testamentum*
VTG	Vetus Testamentum Graecum
VTsup	Supplements to Vetus Testamentum
WBC	Word Biblical Commentary
WeBC	Westminster Bible Companion
WUNT	Wissenschaftliche Untersuchungen zum Neuen Testament
ZAW	*Zeitschrift für die alttestamentliche Wissenschaft*
ZNW	*Zeitschrift für die neutestamentliche Wissenschaft und die Kunde der älteren Kirche*

1

THE SCRIBAL APOCALYPSE AND EARLY JEWISH TEXTUAL CULTURE

1.1 Introduction

Textual culture refers to the accepted practices of handling the texts of literary works, including textual production, redaction, reading, oral recitation, exegetical engagement, and transmission, encompassing a network of related sociohistorical features of textual usage in a given period. Situated at the centre of early Jewish textual culture sat the Hebrew Bible (HB), its early versions, and a concerted exegetical engagement with its text, a proclivity shared by the author(s) of the book of Revelation.[1] A controlling and foundational feature of this engagement was the pluriformity of the text of the HB and its versions in the late Second Temple period; pluriformity was both an impetus for and the result of exegetical engagement with scriptural texts.

The book of Revelation, too, was composed within a textual culture in which scriptural texts were pluriform. The procedures by which the Apocalypse was constructed remain elusive, although it is clear that its author[2] constructed it with creative nuance, visionary sensibilities, and great care, a high level of composition masked by its chaos of images and claim to direct visionary revelation. The

---

[1] Martin Hengel, *Judaica, Hellenistica et Christiana* (WUNT 109; Tübingen: Mohr Siebeck, 1999), 1–71; David Andrew Teeter, *Scribal Laws: Exegetical Variation in the Textual Transmission of Biblical Law in the Late Second Temple Period* (FAT 92; Tübingen: Mohr Siebeck, 2014), 199–204, 246–267. Jan Dochhorn, *Schriftgelehrte Prophetie: Der eschatologische Teufelsfall in Apoc Joh 12 und seine Bedeutung für das Verständnis der Johannesoffenbarung* (WUNT 268; Tübingen: Mohr Siebeck, 2010), 255 speaks of Revelation as a 'locked text', only accessible through the identification and understanding of its underlying scriptural traditions: 'Der Text ist verschlüsselt, öffnet sich aber demjenigen, der den vom Autor erwünschten Verstehensvorgang nachvollzieht, welcher über Traditionswissen und über die Identifikation der biblischen Bezugtexte möglich wird.'

[2] The author self-identifies as John. This name and other titles ('the author'; 'the author of Revelation') are employed interchangeably in this study to refer to the

manners in which antecedent scriptural traditions were woven into the fabric of the book of Revelation places its author in league with some Jewish scribes of the late Second Temple period, scribes who were responsible for the concurrent transmission of scriptural works and the production of new literary creations that engage incessantly with Jewish scripture.[3] In a recent important study Jan Dochhorn has described Rev 12 as an example of *schriftgelehrte Prophetie* (scribal prophecy) largely because the chapter's meaning is inaccessible without a detailed knowledge of the scriptural source texts that the author reused.[4] To some extent this observation encompasses the entirety of the book of Revelation, since comprehending John's persistent reuse of and dependence upon the HB and its early Greek versions (OG/ LXX)[5] is essential to understanding this work and its process of composition. In this way, the book of Revelation is the product of an early Jewish scribal culture – a scribal apocalypse.

notional author. I also retain the masculine pronoun, as John is a masculine name. For further discussion, see David Aune, *Revelation 1–5* (WBC 52a; Nashville: Thomas Nelson, 1997), xlvii–lvi; Gerhard Maier, *Die Offenbarung des Johannes: Kapitel 1–11* (HTA; Witten: Brockhaus, 2009), 18–25; Craig R. Koester, *Revelation* (AYB 38A; London: Yale University Press, 2014), 65–69.

[3] I do not primarily use the word 'scribe' – a term that denotes a range of activities and social functions – in this study to refer to professional administrators who produced contracts, etc., although this is certainly an important aspect of the scribal spectrum. While many scribal craftsmen would have created documentary texts and also copied literary works, John is a scribe only insofar as his interpretative engagement with Jewish scriptural texts is similar to the handling and reuse of these texts in other Jewish works of the period. I am *not* arguing in this book that John was a copyist (although he is presented as such in the book), had access to a well-stocked library, or made his living from producing texts. When I describe John as a 'scribe', I refer not to chirographic practices of transcription and the production of copies, but to the broader context of exegetical engagement with Jewish scriptural texts in Early Judaism. See Jonathan D. H. Norton, 'The Question of Scribal Exegesis at Qumran', in *Northern Lights on the Dead Sea Scrolls* (STDJ 80; ed. A. K. Peterson et al.; Leiden: Brill, 2009), 135–154 for a critical discussion on the relationship between exegetical and scribal activity. Norton wishes to distinguish between exegetical and scribal modes, referring to exegetes as 'scribblers' and those who codify these 'scribbles' as scribes, but the two remain overlapping phenomena. Referring to John's exegetical engagement as 'scribal' is appropriate because it is intimately bound to the processes of *literary composition* that characterize Revelation's substance. For the evidence of the administrative function of scribes, see Catherine Hezser, *Jewish Literacy in Roman Palestine* (TSAJ 81; Tübingen: Mohr Siebeck, 2001), 110–168.

[4] Dochhorn, *Prophetie*, 395. I would argue that a detailed knowledge of scriptural intertexts is an important part of reading Jewish prophetic literature generally.

[5] 'OG/LXX' refers to the entirety of the early Greek scriptural tradition including the 'original' Old Greek translations and concurrent Greek revisions of the OG

It is not a simple task to disentangle and isolate antecedent traditions that John reused; they defy simple categorization or description as the studies on John's use of the scriptural traditions in past thirty years have demonstrated. Complex procedures, motivations, rhetorical designs, and textual issues, upon which our author did not explicitly comment (and of which he himself may not have been overtly aware), coalesced to create the Apocalypse. One must reconstruct from the text itself the principles by which the author engaged Jewish scriptural traditions. The book of Revelation is a work that constantly forges connections to antecedent traditions, embedding instances of reuse without explicit marking.[6] John's engagement with these traditions means that he placed weighty demands upon those who contend with his work. In order to understand the Apocalypse, one must struggle with John's reuse of scripture and construct a model that is situated within the textual culture of the late Second Temple period,[7] and which addresses the pluriformity that is constitutive of that culture. What follows in this

towards closer affiliation with a Hebrew *Vorlage*. I adopt OG/LXX as it more accurately represents the chronological features of the OG (the original Old Greek translation of each Hebrew scriptural work) and the LXX (Greek revisions of the OG translations). Similarly '*V*OG' denotes the reconstructed Hebrew *Vorlage* of an OG translation. The abbreviation 'LXX' has, at times, been utilized to refer to the OG translation of the Pentateuch as narrated in the *Letter of Aristeas*, Flavius Josephus' *Jewish Antiquities* (*Ant.* 12.11–118), in Philo (*Mos.* 2.25–44), and in Aristobulus (preserved primarily in Eusebius, *Hist. eccl.* 7.32.14–19, 37; *Praep. Ev,* 8.9.38–10.18a; 9.6.6–8; 13.12.3–8; see C. R. Holladay, *Fragments from Hellenistic Jewish Authors* [vol. 3; Atlanta: SBL, 1995], 128–197), but here it refers to the later revisions of the OG text of each work towards the emerging MT.

[6] Harold Bloom, *The Shadow of a Great Rock: A Literary Appreciation of the King James Bible* (London: Yale University Press, 2011), 293–294 describes Revelation as 'an anxious network of allusions to the Hebrew Bible'.

[7] Other influences also played a role in John's construction of this work and its overtly anti-Roman political ideology, which I do not wish to downplay. Greco-Roman literature, imperial imagery, and material culture also played a central role but are not within the purview of this study. See e.g. Adela Yarbro Collins, *The Combat Myth in the Book of Revelation* (HDR 9; Missoula: Scholars, 1976); Steven J. Friesen, *Imperial Cults and the Apocalypse of John* (Oxford: Oxford University Press, 2001); David Aune, *Apocalypticism, Prophecy and Magic in Early Christianity* (WUNT 199; Tübingen: Mohr Siebeck, 2006), 99–119. See also Jan Willem van Henten's recent article for a rehearsal of the methodological issues associated with examining the relationship between Revelation and Greco-Roman works ('The Intertextual Nexus of Revelation and Greco-Roman Literature', in *Poetik und Intertextualität in der Johannesapokalypse* [WUNT 346; ed. S. Alkier, T. Hieke, and T. Nicklas; Tübingen: Mohr Siebeck, 2015], 395–422).

study is an attempt to provide a description of John's engagement with his scriptural texts in conversation with similar examples located in Jewish works composed between 200 BCE and 200 CE.[8] This description hinges on two related questions. First, how did John, as an ancient reader,[9] encounter and process his diverse scriptural traditions? And, second, what were the social forces that influenced and controlled his scriptural engagement? The results of this discussion are multidimensional. First, this study provides information about John himself and his social setting: the shape of his scriptural traditions, his habits of reading those traditions, his interpretation of scriptural sources, the operations by which he altered his sources, the physical mechanics of text production (the state of John's *Schreibtisch*, if you will), and the various ways in which he presented reused material. I refer to these features collectively as his 'exegetical repertoire', a classification that encompasses unacknowledged or implied features of literary creation, and that provides access to the underlying textual culture to which John belonged. This includes attention to John's own exegetical innovations and his reuse of existing interpretive traditions, particularly as it relates to Jesus tradition. This evidence allows us to begin to paint a portrait of an author of whom we actually know very little. Beyond his self-presentation as Ἰωάννης (Rev 1.1, 4, 9; 22.8), early ecclesiastical traditions and the various apocryphal traditions of his exile to Patmos (which tend to serve particular ideological agendas), John's identity remains mysterious.[10] His movements around the eastern Mediterranean are not as easily traceable as the apostle

---

[8] Second Temple Judaism refers to the period from the construction of the second Temple (ca. 520 BCE) to the end of the century in which the Roman army destroyed the temple (ca. 100 CE). While the temple was destroyed in 70 CE, the textual and literary culture that defines the late Second Temple period did not completely disappear in the immediate aftermath of this catastrophe. While early Judaism refers to a period inclusive of the Second Temple period (ca. 435 BCE– ca. 500 CE), I use this classification here to refer to Jewish literature that does not belong to the Second Temple period, primarily the Targumim (at least in its finalized Babylonian redactions). I retain the collocation 'Second Temple Judaism' because the vast majority of material handled here belongs to this period.

[9] John is a 'reader' in the broadest sense. Not only did he read scripture via textual artefacts, but he also 'read' (i.e. experienced) scripture through aural/oral experience and access to memory of preceding scriptural encounters.

[10] For an evaluation of apocryphal John traditions, see Ian Boxall, *Patmos in the Reception History of the Apocalypse* (OTRM; Oxford: Oxford University Press, 2013). Issues surrounding the authorship of Revelation in the context of the Johannine

Paul's, for example, a comparison that illustrates how little we know about our author. This study excavates data internal to Revelation that allows us to describe facets of John's literary and textual habits and, ultimately, the social reality in which he produced Revelation. Second, the study demonstrates that John read, interpreted, and reused scripture in a manner commensurate with the practices of scriptural reuse operative in Second Temple Judaism. The following analyses suggest that John was keenly aware of both the textual details of his scriptural sources *and* already-extant interpretative traditions pertaining to those sources. Comparing the habits of reading and reuses of scripture preserved in the literature of this period with those witnessed in Revelation demonstrates John's tacit participation in a common textual culture with his Jewish contemporaries (or near-contemporaries as the case may be). Running contrary to the trends of recent research on the composition of Revelation and its author's exegetical proclivities, this participation indicates that John was in fact attuned to the fine details and textual interrelationships inherent in Jewish scripture.

Moreover, I argue that the evidence of John's consciousness of Jewish scripture and traditions of its interpretation present in his appropriation of Zechariah are basic to literary production within his textual culture. The form and functions of John's scriptural reuse are parts of the normal manner in which literature was produced. The book of Revelation is often portrayed as an outlier in the New Testament (NT) canon – it is the sole 'apocalypse' and it blends epistolary form with esoteric visionary material. However, in the context of the larger textual culture of which the NT writings are but a part, features of Revelation – particularly its presentation of reused material – cohere more closely with the norms of its textual culture than do other NT works.[11] This study highlights the close relationship between Revelation and the literature of the Second Temple period in terms of their authors' shared exegetical repertoires.

corpus are intelligently examined in Jörg Frey, 'Das Corpus Johanneum und die Apokalypse des Johannes: Die Johanneslegende, die Problem der johanneischen Verfasserschaft und die Frage der Pseudonymität der Apokalypse', in *Poetik und Intertextualität der Johannesapokalypse* (WUNT 346; ed. S. Alkier, T. Hieke, and T. Nicklas; Tübingen: Mohr Siebeck, 2015), 71–133.

[11] This claim is difficult to quantify as other NT works – Hebrews, Matthew, and Luke-Acts to name a few – reuse scripture using similar principles. Nonetheless, my point remains: the practice of scriptural reuse in Revelation is coherent with modes of reuse in Jewish literature.

Third, this study contributes to the discussion surrounding the reception of John's scriptural engagement by his initial audiences. It is often argued that John's exegetical imagination would not have enriched the experience of his 'original audience', since their literary abilities and sensitivities were too deficient to detect his subtle exegetical tendencies. Because these hearers were unable to reconstruct his process of composition and unexpressed interpretation of scriptural locutions, it would have been wasteful or ill-advised for John to interact so carefully with the substance of his scripture traditions. Therefore, he didn't. The following discussion offers the opportunity to interrogate this position and to examine both the sociohistorical make-up of the early hearers of the Apocalypse and the 'ideal' audience to which John's work might speak most fully in its ancient context. What does a reader of the Apocalypse *need* to know in order to properly understand the substance and message of the work?

Finally, in addition to sociohistorical concerns related to the audience of Revelation, John's use of Zechariah provides insight into the question of his points of access to his scriptural interlocutors. Without minimizing the prevalence of memory and orality as the predominant mediums of transmission in this period, I argue that textual artefacts (i.e. manuscripts or inscribed forms of scriptural works) also played a sizeable role in John's scriptural engagement. Memory is an inherent factor in the process of reuse, but textual artefacts help to cultivate memory and control oral expression. Additionally, the visual experience of reading a manuscript provides layers of interpretative possibilities that do not exist in an aural encounter where traditions of reading are explicit and other purely graphic features are not accessible. This aspect of the study highlights the role that textual artefacts played in the composition of Revelation.[12]

Above all, this study interrogates the reuse of scripture in the book of Revelation in the context of its textual culture. In this way, this book is both historical and textual. Placing Revelation within its

[12] More implicitly, this study also offers an approach for utilizing text-critical data from NT allusions as witnesses to the text of the HB and OG/LXX in Christian antiquity. Obviously, the more overt the presentation of a scriptural reference and the more mimetic its representation of a possible source, the more valuable the material is for this process. The following analyses illustrate the possibilities and limitations of such an approach. See also e.g. B. Kowalski, 'Die Ezechielrezeption in der Offenbarung des Johannes und ihre Bedeutung für die Textkritik', *SNTU* 35 (2010): 51–77.

proper textual context provides a base from which to test its reuse of scripture against works that are native to the broader compositional ethos in which it was constructed. No study that has explored the reuse of scripture in Revelation has engaged with textual culture in this manner.

1.2 Some Definitions and Terminology

The technical nature of this discussion requires a precise set of descriptive terms. NT writers did not provide a native vocabulary that describes their modes of reuse and methods of reading. As such, one must be formulated using categories that are not necessarily native to early Christianity or Second Temple Judaism. The cacophony of competing terms and definitions currently in use in biblical studies increases the chances for misunderstanding and imprecision. In order to be clear with my own language and to avoid potential confusion for readers, it is important that I clarify a number of relevant terms that reappear throughout the study. The terminology draws upon language used in text linguistics, combined with terminology that is common in scholarly discourse relating to the literature of Second Temple Judaism.

To begin, I deploy the term *reference* to generically denote the direct dependence of material from one work upon material from another.[13] A *scriptural reference* refers to an author's reuse of material (locution, wording, theme, syntactic structure, etc.) from a scriptural source. In the case of the reuse of scripture in Revelation, this includes material preserved in influential Jewish works of the period. *References* have three related but independent variables that, together, determine whether a *reference* is a quotation, allusion, or another type of textual relationship: introductory formula, discreetness, and mimesis. First, a reference may or may not have an *introductory formula*. Various formulae, both explicit and implicit, are

---

[13] The term 'reference' is used in a similar way in socio-rhetorical analysis, as a way to denote intertextual dialogue. I use the term only in instances where one work (e.g. Revelation) borrows material from another work (e.g. Zechariah). See Vernon K. Robbins, *Exploring the Texture of Texts: A Guide to Socio-Rhetorical Interpretation* (Valley Forge, PA: Trinity Press, 1996), 40–68 and L. Gregory Bloomquist, 'Methodological Criteria for Apocalyptic Rhetoric: A Suggestion for Expanded Use of Sociorhetorical Analysis', in *Vision and Persuasion: Rhetorical Dimensions of Apocalyptic Discourse* (ed. G. Carey and L. G. Bloomquist; St. Louis: Chalice, 1999), 181–203 (esp. 185–187).

employed in the NT to demarcate or introduce quotations.[14] For the most part, John does not employ explicit introductory formulae (e.g. καθὼς γέγραπται), but he does use *implicit* markers that signal the presence of antecedent material (anaphoric articles, deictic markers, etc.). Second, references have varying levels of discreetness from their surrounding co-texts. The use of an implicit or explicit introductory formula already creates a level of syntactic discreetness between reference and co-text at the front end of the reference. However, if the end of the reference can be delineated from the following co-texts, a higher level of discreetness is present; if the frame of the reference can be clearly distinguished, then it has a high level of discreetness. Third, a reference mimics the wording of (or part of) its source tradition, at least to a degree. The closer the text of a reference follows the wording of its putative source, the higher its mimetic value. These three variables (introductory formula, discreetness [frame], and mimesis) together determine whether a reference is a quotation or an allusion.

A *quotation* refers to the explicit reuse of identifiable antecedent discourse events. For this discussion, these discourse events equate to the formal surface features of the literature of Jewish scripture and Second Temple Judaism. For a locution embedded within Revelation to be considered a quotation of antecedent material, two requirements must be satisfied. First, the locution in question must illustrate a significant level of literal correlation to the wording of a specific source tradition. Literalness is measured by a number of factors including serial fidelity, quantitative representation, lexical consistency, semantic consistency, and morpho-syntactic form.[15] Ancient quotations usually retain both free and literal characteristics. It is important not only to assert that a given reference is literal but also to describe in what sense and by which measurements it is so. Quotation need not consist of an absolute reproduction of source material, although some level of reproduction remains a distinctive feature of quotation.[16] Second, quotations require a high level of discreetness

[14] See Darius Müller, 'Zitatmarkierungen und die Gegenwart der Schrift im Neuen Testament', in *Textual History and the Reception of Scripture in Early Christianity* (SCS 60; ed. J. de Vries and M. Karrer; Atlanta: SBL, 2013), 189–199.

[15] James Barr, *The Typology of Literalism in Ancient Biblical Translations* (MSU 15; Göttingen: Vandenhoeck & Ruprecht, 1979), 294.

[16] Meir Sternberg, 'Proteus in Quotation-Land: Mimesis and Forms of Reported Discourse', *PT* 3 no 2 (1982): 148 states in terms of quotation generally that 'absolute reproductiveness . . . is precluded, or at least actively militated against, by an

from their co-textual environment in the target text. A quotation requires formal autonomy.[17] Meir Sternberg notes that 'representational bond, structural framing, communicative subordination, and perspectival montage or ambiguity' are the four dimensions by which discreetness is measured.[18] In terms of the formal surface features of a text (arrangement of graphic signs on a delivery surface), structural framing is the essential feature that determines the discreetness of a reference. Paratactic and deictic linguistic markers, in contrast to the hypotactic markers of more indirect forms of reference that conflate the reference with other narrative material in the target text, serve as the primary measurements in determining a locution's level of discreetness.[19] The locution need not be introduced by explicit citation markers to be considered discreet from its co-textual environment.

Moreover, Sternberg is concerned to discuss the dialogical relationship between these formal features (the relationship between the quotation and its co-texts) and the representational features (relationship between quoting and quotee text) of a quotation.[20] While these overlapping features are inextricably linked, where the author of Revelation *quotes* Zechariah, the focus of this discussion will primarily address the formal text-linguistic features of a quotation. Occasionally, representational features will figure into the discussion but they are not the primary concern of this study. It is often assumed that, because the author of Revelation did not utilize explicit citation

---

array of communicative factors. Such reproductiveness, therefore, is neither a constitutive feature of direct discourse, that is, one whose absence would entail a shift to another reporting form; nor an obligatory function, whose absence would perforce count as an infringement of a social artistic norm; nor even a primary function, whose absence would launch an interpretive quest for some rhetorical substitute.' Sternberg terms this the 'Proteus Principle'. Moreover, John Whittaker, 'The Value of Indirect Tradition in the Establishment of Greek Philosophical Texts or the Art of Misquotation', in *Editing Greek and Latin Texts: Papers given at the Twenty-Third Annual Conference on Editorial Problems University of Toronto 6–7 November 1987* (ed. J. N. Grant; New York: AMS, 1987), 64 notes that there was a 'persistent inclination of the scholars and writers of the ancient world to introduce into their quotations deliberate alteration'.

[17] Sternberg, 'Proteus', 109.

[18] Ibid.

[19] Ibid., 111.

[20] Sternberg, 'Proteus', 112. Expanding upon this dialectic, Sternberg goes on to suggest, 'each act of quotation serves two masters. One is the original speech or thought that it represents, pulling in the direction of maximal accuracy. The other is the frame that encloses and regulates it, pulling in the direction of maximal efficacy. Reported discourse thus presents a classic case of divided allegiance' (152).

formulae, he does not quote. This assumption is faulty, and others have noted 'implicit' or 'unmarked' quotations in Revelation.[21] *Explicit Allusion* is a form of reported discourse that is less direct than quotation. Like quotation, explicit allusions need not reproduce linguistic material from its source verbatim. However, it must retain a high level of linguistic correspondence to an identifiable source. An explicit allusion must also demonstrate *some* but not necessarily complete discreetness from its surrounding co-texts in the target composition. This discreetness can be a subtle linguistic feature such as a particle (e.g. γάρ), deictic marker (anaphoric article, demonstrative pronoun, etc.), or an indication of direct speech (e.g. λέγων).

Implicit Allusion refers to a scriptural reference that has been represented in the target composition with a minimal level of linguistic correspondence to its source. Some concrete linguistic link must exist, preferably a unique phrase or 'allusive keyword',[22] but an implicit allusion may be embedded into the target composition in a manner where no discreetness exists between locution and co-texts.

It is often assumed that implicit allusions reflect the unconscious action of an author drenched in the language of scripture.[23] While this is a possible explanation, it is by no means definitive. Literary tradents of the Second Temple period fashioned connections between works based on numerous graphic, phonological, literary, textual, ideological, and narrative features implanted in their scriptural works and presented these connections with varying levels of explicitness.[24] The fact that a reference may be more implicit than it needs to have been does not mean that it was created as the result of a sub-cognitive process. The level of explicitness with which antecedent material appears in a target composition only provides information as to how the author wished to present the material. The vast majority of instances of scriptural reuse and interpretation in the

[21] See, for example, S. Moyise, 'The Psalms in the Book of Revelation', in *The Psalms in the New Testament* (ed. S. Moyise and M. J. J. Menken; London: T&T Clark, 2004), 231–246.

[22] This latter phrase is borrowed from Aaron Koller, *Esther in Ancient Jewish Thought* (Cambridge: Cambridge University Press, 2014), 139, who uses the repetition of unique phrases as a license to forge intertextual connections.

[23] See Elisabeth Schüssler Fiorenza, *The Book of Revelation: Justice and Judgment* (Minneapolis: Fortress, 1985), 17–18; G. K. Beale, *John's Use of the Old Testament in Revelation* (JSNTsup 166; Sheffield: Sheffield University Press, 1998), 74.

[24] See W. A. Tooman, 'Between Imitation and Interpretation: Reuse of Scripture and Composition in *Hodayot* (1QHª) 11:6–19', *DSD* 18 (2011): 58–59 who puts forth

Second Temple period were presented implicitly,[25] and one cannot assume that every example of covert reworking is incidental (i.e. not deliberate). The presentation of a reused locution is not necessarily linked with the exegetical or interpretative decisions that underlie the presentation.[26] Ancient authors retained the flexibility to present antecedent material *intentionally*, using various levels of explicitness and discreetness.

Before returning to some other important terms, I must pause and reflect on the stakes of my definitions in the context of broader scholarly discourse. While I use the above nomenclature to describe the types of reported discourse embedded in the book of Revelation, it is not the primary objective of this discussion to categorize *quotations, allusions, echoes*, etc. in the Apocalypse, even though this question has been an important feature of past discourse relating to scriptural reuse in the NT. I utilize these terms in a phenomenological sense, not in a constitutive sense; they are a means to describe and catalogue the formal surface feature differences between mimetically related texts. The stakes involved in the jargon used to categorize these references are, to my mind, very low. I have attempted to adopt nomenclature that stands in a centre ground between terminology used by those who evaluate ancient Jewish literature ('explicit and implicit uses of scripture')[27]

---

three criteria (uniqueness, multiplicity, thematic correspondence) for identifying incidental uses of scripture. See also the earlier important studies of Moshe J. Bernstein, 'The Contribution of the Qumran Discoveries to the History of Early Biblical Interpretation', in *The Idea of Biblical Interpretation: Essays in Honor of James L. Kugel* (ed. H. Najman and J. H. Newman; Leiden: Brill, 2004), 215–238 and Gabriel Barzilai, 'Incidental Biblical Exegesis in the Qumran Scrolls and its Importance for the Study of the Second Temple Period', *DSD* 14 (2007): 1–22 both of whom also address the issue of incidental exegesis in Qumran documents.

[25] See Teeter, *Scribal Laws*, 175.

[26] Ibid., 10–11 n. 16 has crafted a lucid set of criteria for determining deliberate intention in textual change: '1. When there is a clear exegetical or interpretive "pay-off" to a secondary difference, deliberateness is more likely; indeed, this can be seen as a crucial proof. 2. When apparently dissimilar (con)texts are harmonised (deep analogy), this is less likely to be accidental. 3. When a particular pattern or distribution can be discerned, or when one finds other evidence of the application of thought or of a hermeneutic system, it is unlikely to represent accident. 4. When complex or multi-part changes occur.'

[27] For example, Michael Fishbane, 'Use, Authority and Interpretation of Mikra at Qumran', in *Mikra*, 347–348 and George J. Brooke, 'Biblical Interpretation at Qumran', in *The Bible and the Dead Sea Scrolls* (ed. J. H. Charlesworth; vol. 1; Waco: Baylor University Press, 2006), 287–319.

and modern critical discussion of reported discourse (quotation, allusion, echo, influence, etc.).[28] The use of these categories and the nomenclature that I have adopted are inherently anachronistic: ancient authors did not compose with these categories in mind. Yet, because the authors of the NT did not leave their own native vocabulary pertaining to the processes of reuse embedded in their works, these characterizations serve as valuable heuristic devices.

Returning to some important definitions, three collocations that have appeared in many recent studies require discussion: *Textual pluriformity, textual fluidity,* and *variant literary editions. Textual pluriformity* describes the phenomenon of the existence and concurrent circulation of multiple textual exemplars or forms of a given composition, with variant literary arrangements and/or various instantiations of wording, within a single community or textual milieu. The term *textual fluidity* is a subcategory of textual pluriformity, but the two remain distinct. A work that is textually fluid remains adaptable in the process of transmission. Scribes who transmitted fluid texts retained the freedom to alter the wording of their *Vorlagen,* sometimes extensively.[29] To some extent, all hand-copied traditions are fluid, but I refer to the active reworking of texts. A pluriform text is not necessarily fluid (texts circulating in multiple forms may themselves be fixed in their alternative wordings), and a fluid text is not necessarily pluriform (a text may remain adaptable but not exist in multiple distinct forms in any one context). The majority of scriptural work in the Second Temple period and early Judaism existed

---

[28] Of which the most influential in NT studies include John Hollander, *The Figure of Echo: A Mode of Allusion in Milton and After* (London: University of California Press, 1981); Harold Bloom, *The Anxiety of Influence: A Theory of Poetry* (2nd edn; Oxford: Oxford University Press, 1997); Z. Ben-Porat, 'The Poetics of Literary Allusion', *PTL* 1 (1976): 105–28; Julia Kristeva, *Desire in Language: A Semiotic Approach to Literature and Art* (Oxford: Blackwell, 1980); Mikhail Bakhtin, *The Dialogic Imagination: Four Essays* (trans. C. Emerson and M. Holquist; London: University of Texas Press, 1981); Jacques Derrida, *Of Grammatology* (trans. G. C. Spivak; London: The Johns Hopkins University Press, 1998); Gérard Genette, *Narrative Discourse: An Essay in Method* (trans. J. E. Lewin; Ithaca, NY: Cornell University Press, 1980). Numerous other works that have been used in the context of biblical studies could be cited.

[29] This phenomenon is witnessed within the Hebrew Bible itself. See Michael Fishbane, *Biblical Interpretation in Ancient Israel* (Oxford: Oxford University Press, 1985), especially his section on 'Scribal Exegesis' (21–88). For a succinct discussion of the textual fluidity of the Decalogue in antiquity, see Gary D. Martin, *Multiple Originals: New Approaches to Hebrew Bible Textual Criticism* (TCS 7; Atlanta: SBL,

and circulated in both a fluid and pluriform state.[30] A final phrase that needs to be distinguished from textual pluriformity is the collocation *variant literary editions*. Eugene Ulrich defines this phenomenon as 'an intentional reworking of an older form of the book for a specific purpose or according to identifiable editorial principles'.[31] The text of a work that circulated in multiple literary editions was, obviously, at one point fluid. Also if two literary editions of a book circulated simultaneously, that work existed in a textually pluriform state. The primary difference between Ulrich's variant literary editions and textual pluriformity generally is that a text that exists in pluriformity need not have arisen as 'an intentional reworking' of an antecedent form or have been reworked 'according to identifiable editorial principles'. This is a question of transmission, textual growth, and editorial intention, not of concurrent circulation. The burden of proof is much heavier for one who claims that a textual form of a given book is a *variant literary edition* than for one who claims that a book circulated in a single community at a given time in a *textually pluriform* state, because a chain of intentional literary development must be pinpointed to identify a variant literary edition.

Finally, it is important to distinguish between another set of related terms that are often conflated in recent studies. A *work* refers to an overarching literary entity preserved, usually, in numerous copies. The book of Revelation is a work even though its

---

2010), 205–230. In a note appended to James Barr, 'Hebrew עַד, Especially at Job i.18 and Neh. vii.3', in *Bible and Interpretation: The Collected Essays of James Barr* (ed. J. Barton; vol. 3; Oxford: Oxford University Press, 2014), 608–609, Jeremy Hughes, too, notes that prior to the first century CE, the text of the Hebrew Bible was largely fluid.

[30] Teeter, *Scribal Laws*, 246–267 suggests that textual pluriformity and fluidity are attributable to the concurrent existent of multiple scribal models of transmission. 1. A 'facilitating model' is 'characterized by a certain latitude with respect to permitting textual intervention, especially as regards matters of linguistic updating and interpretive changes or expansions' (264); 2. A 'conservative model' that is 'widely represented' and that 'aspired to precise replication of its *Vorlage*, and which appears to have actively avoided the scribal behaviours' of the facilitating model (264). E. Tov, 'The Myth of the Stabilization of the Text of Hebrew Scripture', in *The Text of the Hebrew Bible: From the Rabbis to the Masoretes* (JAJsup 13; ed. E. Martín-Contreras and L. Miralles-Maciá; Göttingen: Vandenhoeck & Ruprecht, 2014), 37–45 argues that the internal stabilization of the text of the proto-MT family of texts was due to intentional controls in copying, while the emergence of this particular family as normative was an accidental development.

[31] Eugene Ulrich, *The Dead Sea Scrolls and the Origins of the Bible* (Cambridge: Eerdmans, 1999), 89.

form and text differs in each manuscript. Zechariah, too, is a work, preserved in multiple languages and in different textual forms.[32] An acceptable level of textual variation exists within a work. A work must be differentiated from a *text*, a term that refers to the graphic representation of ink in the form of graphemes on a writing surface and the semantic implications of a certain arrangement of graphic signs. The text of Zechariah refers to the arrangement of graphemes that constitutes the work; before the advent of the printing press, the text of a work differed in each of its respective copies.[33] Finally, these terms must be distinguished from the words *copy*, *document*, or *manuscript*. In this study, these refer to a physical entity that contains a particular instantiation of a text of a work. The distinction between work, text, and copy is important because they represent different levels of engagement with ancient literature.

In general, this book and its terminological profile are designed to describe the complicated procedures and techniques employed by the authors of these works.[34] I do not wish to impose modern critical theories onto ancient works and the exegetical practices embedded with them. Uncritical reliance upon modern literary criticism can tend towards anachronism, and its use as a substitute for knowledge of ancient practices of reuse continues to be a major area of concern for the discipline, even if these dialogue partners continue to offer fruitful new avenues for thinking about the composition of ancient literature.[35] Ancient Jewish and Christian literature lacks a native

---

[32] I borrow the hierarchy of work, text, document from David C. Parker, *Textual Scholarship and the Making of the New Testament* (Oxford: Oxford University Press, 2012), 10–14, but modify his idea of a work somewhat.

[33] This is true also for sacred works, even in early Christianity. See e.g. J. W. Knust, 'Early Christian Re-Writing and the History of the Pericope Adulterae', *JECS* 14 no 4 (2006): 485–536.

[34] Esp. Robert de Beaugrande and Wolfgang Dressler, *Introduction to Text Linguistics* (New York: Longman, 1981).

[35] For an example of where the employment of these categories has negatively affected an otherwise interesting study, see Jauhiainen's use of Ben-Porat, 'Literary Allusion', (1976) in *The Use*, 29–32. The use of Ben-Porat, John Hollander, Julia Kristeva, Harold Bloom, Mikhail Bakhtin, Jacques Derrida, Gérard Genette, and others in NT studies as lenses to explain the complex and ancient mechanics of reuse is an interesting development. However, mapping these modern theories onto ancient works can hinder the creation of a clear vision of ancient practices of reuse. It seems to me that there are numerous issues with appropriating these theories as a lens

vocabulary to describe various modes of reuse and re-presentation; scribes usually display exegetical dexterity without any explicit meditation on the processes involved. As a result, scholars are forced to create their own extensive vocabulary to describe these phenomena. I employ language borrowed from other disciplines as a vocabulary with which to describe the operative procedures that I have observed in these works.

In addition to text-linguistic terminology, I have adopted in this study vocabulary from Second Temple Jewish studies to describe exegetical procedures embedded in the book of Revelation. Scholars working with Second Temple literature have developed creative ways to describe the reuse of the Jewish scriptural works, based on the variegated ways the scriptural text is handled in these literatures. This reality has not been fully realized in the study of the NT, which has its own long-standing discourse on the 'use of the OT in the NT'.[36] The correlation between NT and Second Temple texts can be drawn, foremost, because of the 'pregnant biblicism' of both literatures.[37] The literature of Second Temple Judaism – of which the NT is a species – is unintelligible without Jewish scripture. As James Kugel has argued

through which to explain the reuse of scripture in ancient Jewish and Christian works. The use of these theories is often accompanied with: 1. only a cursory knowledge of these complex theories, usually in the form of the adoption of jargon; 2. a tendency towards the tacit assumption that ancient authors wrote with unacknowledged suppositions reflected in modern critical theory; 3. misunderstandings of how ancient literatures were composed; 4. little concern for the native literary features of ancient works; 5. little or no justification for why a particular critic was compared to certain authors in nascent Christianity or Judaism. The use of these critics and theories *does* have a place in NT studies, but they ought not be used in place of a working knowledge of ancient literary practices. For a study that deals specifically with Bakhtin, but that highlights what similar literary theorists have and do not have to offer to biblical studies, see Barbara Green, *Mikhail Bakhtin and Biblical Scholarship: An Introduction* (Semeia 38; Atlanta: SBL, 2000). For some perspective on why biblical studies has recently turned to literary-critical approaches, see James Barr, 'Reading the Bible as Literature', in *Bible and Interpretation: The Collected Essays of James Barr* (vol. 1; ed. J. Barton; Oxford: Oxford University Press, 2013), 83–84 and David Brown, *Tradition & Imagination: Revelation & Change* (Oxford: Oxford University Press, 1999), 44–54. While using literary theory to examine reuse and reading the Bible as literature are distinct phenomena, the rise of both approaches is related.

[36] This discourse has recently been described in its own distinctive way by G. K. Beale, *Handbook on the New Testament Use of the Old Testament: Exegesis and Interpretation* (Grand Rapids: Baker, 2012).

[37] William A. Tooman, *Gog of Magog: Reuse of Scripture and Compositional Technique in Ezekiel 38–39* (FAT 2.52; Tübingen: Mohr Siebeck, 2011), 19.

Christianity at its origin was a Jewish sect, and from the beginning it had adopted a number of Jewish assumptions about how to go about interpreting the Bible, as well as a substantial body of Jewish traditions about the meaning of specific biblical passages.[38]

Not only is the NT *like* contemporary Jewish literature, it *is* Jewish literature, at least as it relates to scriptural reuse. Serge Ruzer makes a similar case, arguing that

> if the Second Temple Jewish genesis of nascent Christianity... is taken seriously, it should be expected that its preoccupations with exegesis would reflect, either approvingly or polemically, both exegetical traditions current in rival circles and those of broader circulation. The New Testament 'conversation with Scripture' may thus be seen as bearing witness, at least in some instances, to those broader tendencies.[39]

The literary, exegetical, and textual inclinations and patterns of the Second Temple period do not immediately disappear with the destruction of the temple, nor is there an easily defined parting of the ways. This study contends that the book of Revelation is yet another example of a work that is very much at home in the world of early Jewish literature. A primary goal of this study is to answer a question posed by Ruzer: 'how can the New Testament be used to create a fuller picture of Second Temple Jewish exegesis?'[40] Using the terminological profile employed in Second Temple studies, I argue that the exegetical repertoire preserved in the book of Revelation is an important witness to Jewish exegetical practices of the late Second Temple period.

[38] James L. Kugel, *In Potiphar's House: The Interpretive Life of Biblical Texts* (London: Harvard University Press, 1994), 1; Kugel, *The Bible as it Was* (London: Harvard University Press, 1997), 20. A further example of this phenomenon can be found in the majority of articles in Jean-Sébastian Rey, ed., *The Dead Sea Scrolls and Pauline Literature* (STDJ 102; Leiden: Brill, 2013), particularly in the articles by Rey ('Les manuscrits de la Mer Morte et l'Épître aux Galates: Quelques cas d'interdiscursivité', 17–49 [esp. 35]), Florentino García Martínez ('Galatians 3:10–14 in the Light of Qumran', 51–67), and Lutz Doering ('4QMMT and the Letters of Paul: Selected Aspects of Mutual Illumination', 69–87) where they argue that both Paul and the scribes of the *Yaḥad* drew from a common well of tradition in regard to scriptural interpretation.

[39] Serge Ruzer, *Mapping the New Testament: Early Christian Writings as Witness for Jewish Biblical Exegesis* (JCP 13; Leiden: Brill, 2007), 3–4.

[40] Ibid., 6.

1.3 Design of the Study

With these definitions in mind, my overarching goal is to engage the complexities of the reuse of Jewish scripture in the Second Temple period, including the early Christian works preserved in the NT, and explore the mechanics and motivations by which the text of the HB and its early Greek versions were incorporated into the book of Revelation. Rephrased: this study analyses instance of reuse where there is sufficient textual evidence to suggest that John's formulation of an allusion or quotation is directly dependent upon a particular textual form of an antecedent scriptural tradition that circulated in antiquity. Questions of literary influence or 'intertextuality' in a general sense are not within my purview.[41] The confusion between influence and dependence has created issues in previous studies that examine the reuse of scripture in the NT;[42] I am concerned here only with instances where direct literary dependence can be illustrated based on similarity in wording and other textual features.[43] The reuse of Zechariah in Revelation provides a manageable and defined textual segment that has already been explored in some depth.[44] Also, despite the recent study of Marko Jauhiainen, the reception of Zechariah traditions in early Jewish literature has received a relatively muted level of scholarly attention in comparison to other prophetic works. These facts make this work an ideal test case.

In order to analyse properly the complicated procedures preserved in John's reuse of Zechariah, I cautiously reverse engineered his processes of reuse.[45] However, before this process properly begins, it is necessary to comprehend a pre-eminent feature of the textual culture

---

[41] For a detailed study of the reuse of scripture in Revelation through the lens of intertextual critical theory, see Aune, *Apocalypticism*, 120–149; Gregory Leroy Linton, 'Intertextuality in the Revelation of John' (PhD diss.; Duke University, 1993) where he follows closely Roland Barthes; Steve Moyise, *The Old Testament in the Book of Revelation* (JSNTsup 115; Sheffield: Sheffield Academic Press, 1995), 108–146.

[42] This is noted also by Sverre Bøe, *Gog and Magog: Ezekiel 38–39 as Pre-text for Revelation 19,17–21 and 20,7–10* (WUNT 2.135: Tübingen: Mohr Siebeck, 2001), 13.

[43] See Appendix 1 for examples of Revelation's reuse of Zechariah proposed by other scholars that I have been unable to substantiate on these grounds.

[44] Marko Jauhiainen, *The Use of Zechariah in Revelation* (WUNT 2.199; Tübingen: Mohr Siebeck, 2005).

[45] The language of 'reverse-engineering' is also used fruitfully by Alex P. Jassen, *Scripture and Law in the Dead Sea Scrolls* (Cambridge: Cambridge University Press, 2014), 15 in the context of examining the 'exegetical relationship' between legal texts in the Scrolls and their scriptural base.

in which the book of Revelation was produced (Chapter 2). The most important aspect of Jewish and early Christian textual culture in the first centuries BCE and CE, as it has been handed down to us in the form of scriptural manuscripts and quotations, is a demonstrable *textual pluriformity*. The concurrent circulation of multiple distinct forms (in both Hebrew and Greek) of scriptural works in this period is beyond refutation, and it is a vital preliminary issue in need of detailed consideration. Before one can comment upon *how* the author has reused his texts, the texts of his source traditions must be identified – what was the graphic shape of the surface features of John's scriptural exemplars (regardless of whether he accessed these graphically or through an aural experience)? R. Timothy McLay notes that this issue is often overlooked in NT scholarship:

> one of the weaknesses of some of these studies is that they have not always dealt adequately with the source texts. We can reasonably inquire, 'How can one theorize about *how* exegetical procedures and pesher or midrashic exegesis are used in the NT without first discerning *what* texts the author is citing?'[46]

One cannot say how a source text has been altered in the process of reuse if the form of the work that an author referenced is simply assumed. Engaging with a palpably pluriform textual tradition, and the unacknowledged pressures that this situation exerted on literary composition in this period, is of foundational importance.

Once this issue is sufficiently framed, it is possible to determine, at least in certain cases, which textual form or forms of Zechariah the author of Revelation reused (Chapter 3). This text-critical analysis, comparing the text of Revelation with the surviving forms of Zechariah, is the beginning of the reverse engineering process. We must first determine which form of Zechariah the author referenced before we can properly understand the processes by which he altered the locutions that he embedded in his new composition. Again, this exercise is an essential phase of examining instances of reuse in antiquity.

In the next step in the reverse engineering process I describe and catalogue the various mechanics that John employed in the process of reusing antecedent material (Chapter 4). This area of enquiry is

---

[46] R. Timothy McLay, *The Use of the Septuagint in New Testament Research* (Cambridge: Eerdmans, 2003), 37.

referred to in this study as *techniques of reuse*. Once a specific form of Zechariah has been identified as underlying a particular textual segment within the book of Revelation, the divergence of graphic surface features between texts can be quantified and described. Cataloguing textual differences creates the raw data from which one can extrapolate the operative procedures that account for divergence of surface features between the borrowing and source texts (*strategies of reading*). It is my contention that John's reworking of his source texts often reflects a desire to interpret and explicate the (ambiguous and gapped) text of his sources. This desire is certainly not reflected in every example of allusion in the late Second Temple period or in the book of Revelation. Authors alluded according to diverse motivations, not all of which reflect a desire to interpret or clarify the source tradition.[47] However, the evidence in this chapter suggests that John's reuse of Zechariah is often sensitive to the internal discourse and textual cues of the reused locution's native co-texts, in conversation with other remotely located scriptural traditions. The interpretative choices and textual reshaping that the author executed when reusing Zechariah suggest that he was attentive to the implications of its minute textual details and potential coherence/cohesion issues associated with the surface features of its internal discourse.[48] John's understanding of these features (of either the scriptural text itself or an interpretative tradition associated with it) influenced the wording and function of the pericope in which reused material was embedded, in a tête-à-tête with the other scriptural traditions that John embedded alongside or blended together (*Einschmelzung*) with Zechariah. Closely examining the details of John's reuse of Zechariah aids in understanding the role of reused traditions in Revelation and John's broader communicative or rhetorical aims.

The final step in this project compares these findings with other examples of the reuse of Zechariah in early Jewish works (Chapter 5). This body of comparative literature includes examples of reuse from within the HB itself, in documents discovered at Qumran, the OG/LXX translation, the Targumim, and so-called 'deutero-canonical' literature. These examples provide a control for the phenomena observed in John's reuse that is native to his textual

---

[47] Tooman, 'Between Imitation'; Alexander Samely, *Rabbinic Interpretation of Scripture in the Mishnah* (Oxford: Oxford University Press, 2002) makes this observation regarding explicit quotations in rabbinic literature.

[48] See also Teeter, *Scribal Laws*, 239.

culture. In the final portion of the study, I ask similar questions that have been asked of the author of Revelation in the preceding chapters and compare John's method of reuse to other literati in his textual culture. The discussion concludes with an examination of the significance of the preceding analysis for broader critical questions (Chapter 6) and prospects for future study, including the social mechanics of text production, John's access (or lack thereof) to textual artefacts, his linguistic ability, and the role of reuse in literary composition among others.

1.4 Need for the Study

My approach to this subject is influenced by the many issues that I perceive in previous examinations of John's scriptural reuse. From the late 1980s onward, and sporadically in the century previous,[49] numerous studies on the use of scripture in the book of Revelation appeared. Often, these studies examine the use of particular works within the Apocalypse,[50] and Marko Jauhiainen has recently produced a study that explores the reuse of Zechariah specifically.[51]

---

[49] Eduard Böhl, *Die alttestamentlichen Zitate im Neuen Testament* (Vienna, 1878), 181–182; Adolf Schlatter, *Das alte Testament in der johanneischen Apocalypse* (Gütersloh: Mohn, 1912); Eduard Lohse, 'Die Alttestamentliche Sprache des Sehers Johannes', *ZNW* 52 (1961): 122–126; Albert Vanhoye, 'L'utilisation du livre d'Ézéchiel dans l'Apocalypse', *Biblica* 43 (1962): 436–476. The issue of textual form is also famously discussed in two English language commentaries by H. B. Swete, *The Apocalypse of St John: The Greek Text with Introduction Notes and Indices* (London: Macmillan, 1911) and R. H. Charles, *A Critical and Exegetical Commentary on The Revelation of St. John* (ICC; 2 vols.; Edinburgh: T&T Clark, 1920). For a full historical summary, see Garrick V. Allen, 'Scriptural Allusions in the Book of Revelation and the Contours of Textual Research 1900–2014: Retrospect and Prospects', *CBR* 14 (2016): 319–339.

[50] Bøe, *Gog*; Jan Fekkes, *Isaiah and Prophetic Traditions in the Book of Revelation: Visionary Antecedents and their Development* (JSNTsup 93; Sheffield: Sheffield Academic Press, 1993); G. K. Beale, *The Use of Daniel in Jewish Apocalyptic Literature and in the Revelation of St. John* (New York: University Press of America, 1984); Jean-Pierre Ruiz, *Ezekiel in the Apocalypse: The Transformation of Prophetic Language in Revelation 16,17–19,10* (Frankfurt: Peter Lang, 1989); Beate Kowalski, *Die Rezeption des Propheten Ezechiel in der Offenbarung des Johannes* (SBB 52; Stuttgart: Katholisches Bibelwerk, 2004). See also numerous PhD theses (full citations in bibliography): Trudinger (1963); Ozanne (1964); Ezell (1970); Casey (1981); Vogelgesang (1985); Paulien (1987); Linton (1993); Lo (1999); Hultberg (2001); Rogers (2002); Tsai-Chen (2004).

[51] Jauhiainen, *The Use*. See also Rogers (2002).

Nonetheless, the current study addresses the limitations of previous research, some of which are enumerated in what follows.

1.4.1 Textual Pluriformity

NT scholarship, as a whole, has been slow to wrestle with the implications of a pluriform scriptural tradition.[52] The concurrent circulation of numerous textual forms of Jewish scriptural works in the first century CE necessarily complicates discussions of reuse. Models for managing the surfeit of textual data have developed rapidly since the Judean Desert discoveries and the situation in NT studies is still evolving. Recently, the textual situation has been examined with more sensitivity to the complexity of the data, particularly in certain studies that examine the use of scripture in the Pauline corpus, the Gospels, and the epistle to the Hebrews, due in large part to the density of explicit quotations in these works.[53] These works illustrate the diversity of approaches available for handling a pluriform scriptural tradition and demonstrate that a thoroughgoing method for engaging such a tradition remains a *desideratum*. Although models are continuing to develop in the

---

[52] There were notable exceptions to this trend, even in the mid-twentieth century. See, for example, Krister Stendahl, *The School of St. Matthew and its Use of the Old Testament* (Philadelphia: Fortress, 1968). I am referring to the pluriformity of Jewish scripture here, not the pluriformity of the NT traditions, although this too is an important aspect of examining scriptural reuse. For a clear articulation of this phenomenon see David Parker, *The Living Text of the Gospels* (Cambridge: Cambridge University Press, 1997), esp. 74, 146–147, 172, 182–213.

[53] E.g. Dietrich-Alex Koch, *Die Schrift als Zeuge des Evangeliums: Untersuchungen zur Wendung und zum Verständnis der Schrift bei Paulus* (BZHT 69; Tübingen: Mohr Siebeck, 1986); Christopher D. Stanley, *Paul and the Language of Scripture: Citation Technique in the Pauline Epistles and Contemporary Literature* (SNTSMS 69; Cambridge: Cambridge University Press, 1992), 37–51; M. J. J. Menken in *Old Testament Quotations in the Fourth Gospel: Studies in Textual Form* (CBET 15; Kampen: Kok Pharos, 1996); Menken, *Matthew's Bible: The Old Testament Text of the Evangelist* (BETL 173; Leuven: Peeters, 2004); Florian Wilk, *Die Bedeutung des Jesajabuches für Paulus* (FRLANT 179; Göttingen: Vandenhoeck & Ruprecht, 1998); Radu Gheorghita, *The Role of the Septuagint in Hebrews: An Investigation of its Influence with Special Consideration to the Use of Hab 2:3–4 in Heb 10:37–38* (WUNT 2.160; Tübingen: Mohr Siebeck, 2003); Susan Docherty, *The Use of the Old Testament in Hebrews* (WUNT 2.260; Tübingen: Mohr Siebeck, 2009); Kelli S. O'Brien, *The Use of Scripture in the Markan Passion Narrative* (LNTS 384; London: T&T Clark, 2010); Jonathan D. H. Norton, *Contours in the Text: Textual Variation in the Writings of Paul, Josephus, and the Yahad* (LNTS 430; London: T&T Clark, 2011); Wm. Randolph

examination of scriptural reuse in other NT works, this level of text-critical attention to pluriformity has not been fully incorporated into the discourse surrounding the reuse of scripture in the Apocalypse, largely because the author's presentations of scriptural reuse are not explicit.[54] It is to an appraisal of recent scholarly engagement with textual data in studies on the book of Revelation that we now turn.

1.4.1.1 Monoform Textual Traditions (Hebrew, Greek, Aramaic)

At the outset of the twentieth century, H. B. Swete argued that the language of John's source texts was always Greek and that the influence of Hebrew could only be intuited in his use of some Hebrew names (Rev 9.11; 16.16). He argued that the reuse of scripture in Revelation

> suggests the work of a cunning artist who has formed a design out of the fragments which were at his disposal. But the Apocalyptist's use of his Old Testament materials is artless and natural; it is the work of a memory which is so charged with Old Testament words and thoughts that they arrange themselves in his visions like the changing patterns of a kaleidoscope, without conscious effort on his own part.[55]

Bynum, *The Fourth Gospel and the Scriptures: Illuminating the Form and Meaning of Scriptural Citation in John 19:37* (NTsup 144; Leiden: Brill, 2012); Georg Walser, *Old Testament Quotations in Hebrews: Studies in Their Textual and Contextual Background* (WUNT 2.356: Tübingen: Mohr Siebeck, 2013), among many others.

[54] One of the exceptions here is Bøe, *Gog* who examines all relevant textual traditions. Another exception is Jeffrey Marshall Vogelgesang, 'The Interpretation of Ezekiel in the Book of Revelation' (PhD diss., Harvard University, 1985), 16–23 who offers a balanced appraisal of the textual data but adopts a pragmatic approach in his study based on the complexity of the transmission of Ezekiel: 'The supposition regarding a text-type which provides the most economical and sensible explanation of any given feature of the text of Revelation will be accepted as correct' (23). Alan David Hultberg, 'Messianic Exegesis in the Apocalypse: The Significance of the Old Testament for the Christology of Revelation' (PhD diss., Trinity Evangelical Divinity School, 2001), 45–47 also offers a brief, but intelligent discussion of the textual data.

[55] Swete, *The Apocalypse*, cliv–clv. Swete follows the earlier assessment of Moses Stuart, *A Commentary on the Apocalypse* (Vol. 1; London: Wiley and Putnam, 1845), 231–232 where the inexact nature of quotations suggests, to Stuart, that the author did not actually reference texts when constructing allusions.

He concludes by noting, among other inferences, that John 'availed himself to the Alexandrian version of the Old Testament'.[56] Swete's reconstruction created a model that allowed him to explain textual differences between known forms of the OG/LXX tradition and the allusions embedded in the book of Revelation: the differences are the result of John's (faulty) memory. Although Swete is correct to note that the author did reference Greek traditions, the argument that John utilized *only* Greek sources far exceeds the available evidence.[57]

Standing in stark contrast to Swete is an unpublished PhD thesis by Charles Gordon Ozanne in which he argued that *all* of the nearly 400 allusions that he detected within Revelation derive from 'the original Hebrew and Aramaic of the OT'.[58] This approach is equally problematic. Ozanne's conclusions are based on an approach to the textual data that privileges lexical equivalency over other measures of literalness. He also pays little attention to issues pertaining to exegesis and reuse that exert significant influence on the verbal form of examples of reuse. While it is certain that John was aware of and likely referenced some Hebrew textual forms – as I argue below – it is unwise to assume that this was the case for every one of his allusions.[59] The textual situation in the first century CE is far too complex for a simple solution to this issue.[60]

The text of the HB and its versions became even more complicated upon the discoveries of the manuscripts from the Judean Desert. Inevitably, this new discovery problematized the underlying models of textual transmission and ancient exegesis of even the most erudite textual studies. Studies completed either before the discoveries of the Dead Sea Scrolls themselves or before the new fount of textual data

---

[56] Swete, *The Apocalypse*, clv.

[57] See Vanhoye, 'L'utilisation', 443–444, 460–461; Steve Moyise, 'The Language of the Old Testament in the Apocalypse', *JSNT* 76 (1999): 112–113.

[58] C. G. Ozanne, 'The Influence of the Text and Language of the Old Testament on the Book of Revelation' (PhD diss., University of Manchester, 1964), 2. For Ozanne, 'original OT' = MT. See also Frederick David Mazzaferri, *The Genre of the Book of Revelation from a Source Critical Perspective* (BZNW 54; Berlin: De Gruyter, 1989), 46: 'Rev is replete with OT quotations and allusions because of John's intimate knowledge of the MT.'

[59] This very point was articulated at an early date by D. M. Turpie, *The Old Testament in the New. A Contribution to Biblical Criticism and Interpretation* (Edinburgh: Williams and Norgate, 1868), xv.

[60] Vanhoye, 'L'utilisation', 460–461 made the same point that I am gesturing towards here in 1962, well before the fullness of the textual data from Qumran was understood.

was fully analysed are now, at least to some degree, outmoded. This discovery fundamentally altered scholarly conceptions of the shape and history of the text of the HB and its early Greek versions in antiquity, dispelling numerous paradigms that are no longer viable. The pluriformity witnessed in the Hebrew text of some works is a reality which scholars like Swete or Charles,[61] despite their exegetical erudition and text-critical acumen, could not have conceived based on the uniformity of the medieval evidence for the MT and some secondary evidence from the Samaritan Pentateuch (SP). This situation partially undermines the findings and underlying critical models of this generation of scholarship. Nonetheless, in recent secondary literature, Swete and Charles remain the dominant voices regarding the question of textual form in Revelation.[62] The lasting impact of their erudite works is impressive, but their predominance demonstrates that the discussion of the form of John's scriptures has not come very far since the early twentieth century. The textual data from the Judean Desert has not yet been fully incorporated into scholarly discourse pertaining to the reuse of scripture in Revelation. This study begins to address the pressing need of a fully integrated approach to the complex ancient textual remains preserved in allusions embedded in the book of Revelation, an approach that takes into account the ancient textual data preserved in the scrolls and the early Greek versions. It can no longer be assumed that an author always used the same form of any scriptural work or that the texts these authors accessed fit cleanly in the text families that modern text criticism have constructed.[63]

1.4.1.2 Text and Transmission of Scriptural Works

Some strands of scholarship have simply given insufficient attention to textual questions when discussing reuse. In his monograph on the use of Isaianic traditions in the book of Revelation, Jan Fekkes asserts that

> the present study is relatively unconcerned with the issue of textual sources – that is, John's use of a Hebrew or Greek OT . . . anyone wishing to settle the question in their own

---

[61] Swete, *The Apocalypse* (1911) and Charles, *The Revelation* (1920). Also, Isbon T. Beckwith, *The Apocalypse of John* (New York: Macmillan, 1919).

[62] See the discussion in Moyise, 'Language'.

[63] So Max Wilcox, 'Text Form', in *It is Written: Scripture Citing Scripture* (ed. D. A. Carson and H. G. M. Williamson; Cambridge: Cambridge University 1988), 194.

mind can do so by working though the catena of OT allusions in Revelation 17–18 with a Hebrew and Greek Bible.[64] Fekkes continues: 'text-form is of secondary importance in the study of OT allusions'.[65] These statements betray an essential misunderstanding of the textual milieu in which the book of Revelation was composed. When examining the reuse of a work that circulated in a pluriform state, it is essential to determine, with as much accuracy as the evidence allows, which form an author referenced. This question is particularly fundamental when examining the reuse of Isaiah, a work that is clearly pluriform in its Hebrew traditions and whose Greek tradition does not map easily onto the proto-MT. Regardless of the object of study, the question of textual form is often only addressed in a cursory and unsatisfactory way in recent studies.[66] This study redresses this lacuna by highlighting the question of textual form as a foundational stage of enquiry.

Additionally, studies on the reuse of scripture in the NT are occasionally imprecise in the way they refer to ancient works. This problem is a symptom of the unsatisfactory level of attention to textual issues just noted. Fekkes, for example, asserts that the only possible sources from which John could have drawn are reflected in the 'Hebrew Bible' (*BHS*?) and the 'Greek Bible' (*Rahlfs*?). This presumption is neglectful of the intricacies of the text and transmission of the HB and its early Greek versions.[67] The appeal to scholarly abstractions like the 'Septuagint' and the 'Masoretic Text' as if they reflected ancient sources is a lingering issue for NT studies.[68] Some

---

[64] Fekkes, *Prophetic Traditions*, 16–17.

[65] Ibid., 16 n. 7, following Merrill P. Miller, 'Targum, Midrash and the Use of the Old Testament in the New Testament', *JSJ* 2 (1971): 61.

[66] Moyise, *Old Testament*, 11–12 (Moyise does address this issue more fully in 'Language', 97–113); Ruiz, *Ezekiel*; Beale, *John's Use*, 61–62; Linton, 'Intertextuality'; Jay Smith Casey, 'Exodus Typology in the Book of Revelation' (PhD diss., Southern Baptist Theological Seminary, 1981); Tsai-Chen, 'Zechariah 14'; Robert A. Briggs, *Jewish Temple Imagery in the Book of Revelation* (SB 10; New York: Peter Lang, 1999); Aune, *Revelation* (1997–1998); Pilchan Lee, *The New Jerusalem in the Book of Revelation: A Study of Revelation 21–22 in the Light of its Background in Jewish Tradition* (WUNT 2.129; Tübingen: Mohr Siebeck, 2001), 239–304. Heinrich Kraft, *Die Offenbarung des Johannes* (HZNT 16a; Tübingen: Mohr Siebeck, 1974) is a notable exception.

[67] Again, this is especially true for Isaiah: 1QIsa[a] differs significantly from the proto-MT stream and is certainly still to be considered part of Fekkes's 'Hebrew Bible'.

[68] This problem occurs in G. K. Beale, *The Book of Revelation* (NIGTC; Cambridge: Eerdmans, 1999), 77–78; Stephen S. Smalley, *The Revelation to John: A Commentary on the Greek Text of the Apocalypse* (Downers Grove: IVP, 2005),

notable exceptions exist. Christopher Stanley, for example, emphasizes the importance of a rigorous knowledge of the text of Jewish
scripture in the period in which the NT was written. 'At the very
least', he notes, 'it points up the fallacy of assuming that every divergence from the Masoretic Hebrew text or the printed editions of
the Septuagint reflects a modification introduced into the passage'.[69]
When working with Jewish Greek scriptures particularly, it is necessary to work with specific traditions (OG, καιγε, proto-Hexapla,
Lucianic recension, etc.) or, when valuable, the manuscripts that
comprise these traditions. These revisions and recensions are
abstractions in their own right – and many derive from the second
century CE or later (though they often preserve earlier traditions) –
but they refer to a more limited collection or groups of manuscripts
that share similar textual characteristics.

A similar problem is manifest when scholars equate the HB (the
omnibus of Hebrew language scriptural manuscripts) with *BHS* (a
diplomatic critical edition based on L). This equivalence is most
clearly witnessed in studies that assume that John utilized the MT,
a medieval Jewish text whose formation was the result of a lengthy
process of transmission and paratextual refinement.[70] This supposition is often defined by the inclusion of vocalization and diacritical markings preserved in the Masoretic Hebrew tradition,
or by a tacit assumption that John's reading tradition was identical to that preserved in the MT.[71] It is true that the 'consonantal

8–10; and Lo, 'Ezekiel in Revelation'. See the critiques of Leonard Greenspoon, 'The
Use and Abuse of the Term "LXX" and Related Terminology in Recent Scholarship',
BIOSCS 20 (1987): 21–29; Walser, *Quotations*, 3–5; Gert J. Steyn, 'Which "LXX"
are We Talking about in NT Scholarship?' in *Die Septuaginta: Texte – Kontexte –
Lebenswelten* (WUNT 219; ed. M. Karrer and W. Kraus; Tübingen: Mohr Siebeck,
2008), 697–707; McLay, *Septuagint in New Testament Research*, 1–16; Tooman, *Gog
of Magog*, 16 n. 55.

[69] Stanley, *Language of Scripture*, 47–48.

[70] See M. H. Goshen-Gottstein, 'The Rise of the Tiberian Bible Text', in *Biblical
and Other Studies* (ed. A. Altmann; Cambridge, MA: Harvard University Press,
1963), 79–122. See also Stefan Schorch, 'Rewritten Bible and the Vocalization of
the Biblical Text', in *Rewritten Bible after Fifty Years: Text, Terms, or Techniques?
A Last Dialogue with Geza Vermes* (JSJsup 166; ed. J. Zsengellér; Leiden: Brill, 2014),
137–151.

[71] Ernst Lohmeyer, *Die Offenbarung des Johannes* (HZNT 16; Tübingen: Mohr
Siebeck, 1927 [also in the 1953 edition]); Richard Bauckham, *The Climax of
Prophecy: Studies on the Book of Revelation* (Edinburgh: T&T Clark, 1993), 162–166;
Ruiz, *Ezekiel*; Beale, *Jewish Apocalyptic*; Lee, *New Jerusalem* (2001); Kowalski, *Die
Rezeption*; Bøe, *Gog*; Jauhiainen, *The Use*; Tsai-Chen, 'Zechariah 14', 57; John Andrew

framework'[72] of the MT (= proto-MT) is very ancient; many of the scriptural manuscripts discovered at Qumran, Masada, and elsewhere in the Judean Desert testify to its antiquity. However, the Judean Desert manuscripts witness many examples at variance with the MT.[73] The proto-MT was certainly not the only Hebrew text form for many scriptural works in circulation in the period in which the book of Revelation was composed. Moreover, while implied or oral reading traditions were transmitted with the consonantal Hebrew text in antiquity, the practice of affixing graphic accentuation and vocalization systems to manuscripts reflects a later practice.[74] If John read Hebrew texts, a graphic vocalization system was not affixed to his manuscripts; John read works graphically transmitted only as consonants. And if John experienced Hebrew texts through aural experiences, his understanding of reading traditions was shaped by these encounters. The assumption that he read *the* MT hampers the analysis of techniques of reuse as it limits the semantic, syntactic, and graphic options available in a more ambiguous consonantal text, ambiguities that John may have leveraged to forge textual connections. Assuming that John read the MT restricts the interpretative possibilities and mollifies the inherent gaps of a purely consonantal text. The Tiberian system certainly preserves ancient traditions of reading, but there is no guarantee that John read the Hebrew consonants like the Tiberian Masoretes.

McLean, *The Seventieth Week of Daniel 9:27 as a Literary Key for Understanding the Structure of the Apocalypse of John* (Queenston: Mellen, 1996). Occasionally, the printing of diacritics with Hebrew text is the result of modern editorial practices and not assumptions of ancient textual practices.

[72] I use scare quotes here because, although the framework of the MT (sans diacritical marks that denote emphasis, vowels, etc.) is largely consonantal, some vowels – *matres lectionis* – exist in more or less developed systems in all the works that comprise the proto-MT. While 'consonantal text' is a somewhat imprecise characterization of the proto-MT, it has been retained in this study to refer to the text of MT sans diacritical markings.

[73] See Section 2.3.1.

[74] The Masorah of the MT was not included in manuscripts until the seventh century and a graphic vocalization system (particularly the Tiberian system) is a late practice as well (ca. 500–700 CE). See Emanuel Tov, *Textual Criticism of the Hebrew Bible* (3rd edn; Minneapolis: Fortress, 2012), 24–47. Numerous other vocalization systems were also affixed to Hebrew manuscripts in antiquity beside the Tiberian system. See Paul Kahle, *The Cairo Geniza* (2nd edn; Oxford: Blackwell, 1959), 149–188.

1.4.1.3 Marko Jauhiainen's Approach to Textual Data

In order to ground the abstract objections outlined above in a concrete example, it is instructive to examine closely Marko Jauhiainen's treatment of the use of Zechariah in Revelation. Jauhiainen suggests that John could have made use of eight different 'OT text(s)':

> (1) a Hebrew text as reflected in the MT; (2) a different Hebrew text; (3) a Greek text as reflected in Rahlfs's [*sic*] or the Göttingen Septuagint Project's LXX; (4) a different Greek text [8HevXIIgr]; (5) an Aramaic paraphrase of Hebrew. It is also possible that (6) he had access to a Christian collection or translation of important OT texts; (7) he was alluding to the OT from memory; (8) his sources consist of a combination of two or more of these options.[75]

Although Jauhiainen offers one of the more urbane lists of potential sources in recent studies, problems persist. First, while Rahlfs and the Göttingen critical editions are the modern tools by which scholars usually gain access to the Greek scriptural tradition, they are scholarly fictions, representing a complex collation process and legion editorial judgements pertaining to the manuscript evidence. No Greek text preserved in these editions existed in antiquity, even when the editors stay relatively close to the text of B. These works are indispensable for the study of reuse, but they were not sources for the author of Revelation in this sense. A more accurate designation for (3) is 'Old Greek' or 'OG/LXX'. Second, although L. P. Trudinger argued that John used Aramaic 'proto-Targums' as sources from scriptural references,[76] there is little evidence to suggest that early Christian authors utilized Aramaic sources in this way. It is more likely that, where the allusions in the book of Revelation cohere with readings in Targumim, John and the producers of the Targum drew from a common well of interpretative tradition or responded

---

[75] Jauhiainen, *The Use*, 9–10.

[76] L. P. Trudinger, 'The Text of the Old Testament in the Book of Revelation' (PhD diss., Boston University, 1963), 8–9, 162–163. Trudinger's assertion that references in Revelation are based upon Aramaic sources is reliant on now mostly defunct source-critical approaches to the book of Revelation that posit, at least for parts of the text, an Aramaic original. See also Jon Paulien, *Decoding Revelation's Trumpets: Literary Allusions and the Interpretation of Revelation 8:7–12* (AUSDDS 11; Berrien Springs, MI: Andrews University Press, 1987).

identically to certain textual cues that led to a similar interpretation of a scriptural unit. Apparent dependence on an Aramaic text probably reflects a common tradition of interpretation. Finally, Jauhiainen's options 6–8 are *not* textual sources. Option 8 is simply an observation that the author need not have limited himself to a single textual form even in a single reference. This observation is apt, but represents a confusion of categories – in this case, textual source vs. compositional habits.[77]

Moreover, if an author was working from memory (7), it is the memory of particular textual form, or combinations of forms even if this textual form was encountered aurally, that is recalled. The use of memory may cause divergence from a known form, but that form remains the source of the allusion. The same principle applies to the use of Christian excerptions of numerous works (6). The excerpted texts still derive from a particular form. Their recombination with other texts does not distinguish them from the form of the sources from which they were excerpted. Even though examples of *excerpta* are found in attested in both Greco-Roman and Jewish sources in antiquity,[78] it is difficult to prove that the author of Revelation made use of such *realia*, although some evidence exists that John was aware of antecedent exegetical traditions. Furthermore, the extent to which John drew upon antecedent traditions makes his use of a collection of excerpted texts unlikely. Such a collection, if all his examples of scriptural reuse derived from it and if it took the form of a scroll, wax tablet, or codex, would be nearly as difficult to handle as the works themselves – its physical convenience is minimal in an allusive work like Revelation that lacks a well-defined set of explicit quotations. Jauhiainen's appeal to options 6–8, suggestion of an Aramaic source,[79] and anachronistic presentation of the OG represents a confusion of categories and textual realities that undermine the foundation of his study. This reality is par for the entire field as Jauhiainen himself notes:

> the reasons for this approach are as follows: First, this assumption [referring to John's use of MT and LXX]

---

[77] A parallel example of this confusion is witnessed in E. Earle Ellis, 'Biblical Interpretation in the New Testament Church', in *Mikra*, 691–725. His discussion enmeshes numerous categories including form, method, and reuse in anachronistic and unhelpful ways. See the critique of Tooman, *Gog of Magog*, 15 n. 52.

[78] E.g. Pliny the Younger, *Ep.* 6.20.5; 4Q174–177. See Norton, *Contours*, 34–35.

[79] See Schüssler Fiorenza, *Justice and Judgment*, 16 who notes that the Greek text of Revelation witnesses Hebraisms, not Aramaisms.

appears to be shared by most scholars within the field to which the present study is contributing. By adopting the same assumption, we ensure that some of our results will be comparable to those of earlier studies.[80]

1.4.1.4 Recent Developments

An important exception to the dearth of critical interaction with textual issues is exemplified in recent German language scholarship, particularly in the work of Martin Karrer and Michael Labahn.[81] The work of these scholars is greatly underappreciated in English language research and provides some helpful correctives to the broader conversation surrounding the reuse of scriptural works in the NT. Karrer and Labahn engage fully with the consequences of a textually pluriform scriptural tradition and highlight the relationship between the complex Greek text of the Apocalypse itself[82] and the OG/LXX tradition.[83] A primary research question for Karrer and Labahn is the form of scriptural references preserved in the NT.[84] Textual enquiry dominates the discourse of their work, examinations

---

[80] Jauhiainen, *The Use*, 11.

[81] See also, in the Anglophone world, Brooke, 'Torah', 188–190.

[82] See Martin Karrer, 'Der Text der Johannesapokalypse', in *Die Johannesapokalypse: Kontexte – Konzepte – Rezeption* (WUNT 287; ed. J. Frey, J. A. Kelhoffer, and F. Tóth; Tübingen: Mohr Siebeck, 2012), 43–78.

[83] See especially Martin Karrer, Siegfried Kreuzer, and Marcus Sigismund, eds., *Von der Septuaginta zum Neuen Testament: Textgeschichtliche Erörterungen* (ANTF 43; Berlin: De Gruyter, 2010); Thomas Scott Caulley and Hermann Lichtenberger, eds., *Die Septuaginta und das Frühe Christentum* (WUNT 277; Tübingen: Mohr Siebeck, 2011); Michael Labahn and Martin Karrer, eds., *Die Johannesoffenbarung: Ihr Text und ihre Auslegung* (ABG 38; Leipzig: Evangelische Verlagsanstalt, 2012); Johannes de Vries and Martin Karrer, eds., *Textual History and the Reception of Scripture in Early Christianity* (SCS 60; Atlanta: SBL, 2013).

[84] Martin Karrer, 'Von der Apokalypse zu Ezechiel: Der Ezechieltext der Apokalypse', in *Das Ezechielbuch in der Johannesoffenbarung* (BTS 76; ed. D. Sänger; Neukirchen-Vluyn: Neukirchener, 2004), 84–120; Karrer, 'Ps 22 (MT 23): von der Septuaginta zur Eschatologisierung im frühen Christentum', in *La Septante en Allemagne et en France* (OBO 238; ed. W. Krause and O. Munnich; Göttingen: Vandenhoeck & Ruprecht, 2009), 130–148; Karrer, 'The Angels of the Congregations in Revelation – Textual History and Interpretation', *JECH* 1 no 1 (2011): 57–84; Michael Labahn, 'Ausharren im Leben, um von Baum des Lebens zu Essen und Ewig zu Leben: Zur Textform und Auslegung der Paradiesgeschichte der Genesis in der Apokalypse des Johannes und deren Textgeschichte', in *Florilegium*

that underscore the quantity of central questions related to scriptural reuse with which textual criticism has yet to engage suitably.

Particularly important for this school is the relationship between the parallel transmission of the OG/LXX and NT works in nascent Christianity and the effects of this phenomenon on the theology and message of early Christian works and documents. These are foundational questions. However, the emphasis on the OG/LXX tradition is at times unbalanced and Labahn occasionally downplays instances where it appears that John referenced the proto-MT.[85] The desire to analyse NT allusions as independent witnesses to the OG/LXX, while itself a positive development in NT scholarship, narrows the discussion unnecessarily away from Hebrew text forms.[86] I prefer to view the languages and sources of John's scriptural texts on a gradation, a scale that allows for both the influence of Hebrew and Greek texts from various sources. Nonetheless, Labahn and Karrer provide

Lovaniense: Studies in Septuagint and Textual Criticism in Honour of Florentino García Martínez (BETL 224; ed. H. Ausloos, B. Lemmelijn, and M. Vervenne; Leuven: Peeters, 2008), 291–316; Labahn, '"Geschrieben in diesem Buch": Die "Anspielungen" der Johannesapokalypse im Spannungsfeld zwischen den Referenztexten und der handschriftlichen Überlieferung in den großen Bibelhandschriften', in *Von der Septuaginta zum Neuen Testament: Textgeschichtliche Erörterungen* (ANTF 43; ed. M. Karrer, S. Kreuzer, and M. Sigismund; Berlin: De Gruyter, 2010), 339–383; Labahn, 'Die Macht des Gedächtnisses: Überlegungen zu Möglichkeit und Grenzen des Einflusses hebräischer Texttradition auf die Johannesapokalypse, in ibid., 385–416; Labahn, 'Die Septuaginta und die Johannesapokalypse: Möglichkeiten und Grenzen einer Verhältnisbestimmung im Spiegel von kreativer Intertextualität und Textentwicklung', in *Die Johannesapokalypse: Kontexte – Konzepte – Rezeption* (WUNT 287; ed. J. Frey, J. A. Kelhoffer, and F. Tóth; Tübingen: Mohr Siebeck, 2012), 149–190; Labahn, 'Die Schriftrezeption in den großen Kodizes der Johannesoffenbarung', in *Die Johannesoffenbarung: Ihr Text und ihre Auslegung* (ABG 38; ed. M. Labahn and M. Karrer; Leipzig: Evangelische Verlagsanstalt, 2012), 99–130; Labahn, 'Griechische Textformen in der Schriftrezeption der Johannesoffenbarung? Eine Problemanzeige zu Möglichkeiten und Grenzen ihrer Rekonstruktion anhand von Beispielen aus der Rezeption Ezechielbuches', in *Die Septuaginta – Entstehung, Sprache, Geschichte* (WUNT 286; ed. S. Kreuzer, M. Meiser, and M. Sigismund; Tübingen: Mohr Siebeck, 2012), 529–560; Hermann Lichtenberger, 'Die Schrift in der Offenbarung des Johannes', in *Die Septuaginta und das frühe Christentum* (WUNT 277; ed. T. S. Caulley and H. Lichtenberger; Tübingen: Mohr Siebeck, 2011), 382–390; J. Elschenbroich and J. de Vries, eds., *Worte der Weissagung: Studien zu Septuaginta und Johannesoffenbarung* (ABG 47; Leipzig: Evangelische Verlagsanstalt, 2014).

[85] This is most clearly seen in 'Die Macht', 385–416 and 'Geschrieben', 339–383.

[86] Labahn, 'Griechische Textformen', 536 notes that the Apocalypse is an interesting but difficult field of enquiry as a witness to the text of the Septuagint due to John's style and form of reuse.

a timely corrective for the field that ought to be educative for English language engagement on the reuse of scripture in the Apocalypse.[87] Despite recent positive developments, I am not yet convinced that research on the reuse of scripture in the Apocalypse has properly understood the ramifications of a pluriform textual culture. This study seeks to remedy this situation by underscoring the fundamental textual features of reuse, features that are commensurate with what is known about the textual culture in which the book of Revelation was produced and transmitted. A study that interacts with the complexities of the textual situation behind examples of reuse embedded in Revelation in a cogent manner is essential for the field.

1.4.2 Techniques of Reuse

Another area that requires more attention is *techniques of reuse*. It is customary for scholars to note that the book of Revelation does not retain any explicit citations and that John rarely reproduces longer segments of reused material verbatim.[88] Scriptural references in the book of Revelation always differ in some way from their sources, as was customary in antiquity. However, as the evidence in the following chapters suggests, John's re-presentation of his source material (whether by allusion or quotation) often clarifies gaps or ambiguities embedded in the source's textual substance. In other words, his reworking is exegetically significant. This filling of gaps and explicative reworking signifies that an underlying conceptualization of these sources (interpretation) is preserved within the alterations. The proper methodological starting point for analysing the interpretation of antecedent sources is to catalogue the divergence of formal surface features between source and target text, or to note the textual

---

[87] I should also point to the recent erudite volume of Dochhorn, *Prophetie*, a work that engages John's use of scriptural traditions to some degree. In the midst of displaying a nearly encyclopedic control of all things related to Rev 12, Dochhorn also takes seriously the various textual traditions that may stand behind John's scriptural engagements (e.g. pp. 67–68), including Hebrew as well as various Greek forms. For Dochhorn, these scriptural encounters are fundamental to understanding the composition and meaning of Rev 12.

[88] E.g. Lohse, 'Sprache', 123; Vanhoye, 'L'utilisation', 437; Schüssler Fiorenza, *Justice and Judgment*, 16; Fekkes, *Prophetic Traditions*, 60; Moyise, *Old Testament*, 14; Ian Paul, 'The Use of the Old Testament in Revelation 12', in *The Old Testament in the New Testament: Essays in Honour of J.L. North* (JSNTsup 189; ed. S. Moyise; Sheffield: Sheffield Academic Press, 2000), 256; Paulien, 'Allusions', 4, 53.

connections used to construct allusions (techniques of reuse). This task provides the raw data to determine the textual cues to which the author was responding. The examination of techniques of reuse is often eclipsed by other secondary concerns. Below are some examples of these competing concerns.

1.4.2.1 'Contextual Reuse'

Many critics are keen to argue that NT authors reused their scriptural sources in a way that is sensitive to the native context of the reused locution. G. K. Beale is particularly clear that this interest is an apologetic concern, arguing that John's 'presuppositional lenses' through which he views the OT 'are ultimately traceable also to Christ's own interpretive approach which he probably passed on to his disciples'.[89] This approach allows Beale to draw a definitive distinction between what he perceives to be differences in early Christian and Second Temple Jewish uses of scripture.[90] Moreover, Beale explains away demonstrably non-contextual uses of the HB as instances where the author unconsciously embedded antecedent material into his composition.[91] This approach fails to do justice to the intricacies involved in ancient exegesis and interpretation, as we will see in the main analysis of this study.

A symptom of the assumption of contextual reuse manifests itself in the structure of studies that examine the use of a particular Jewish scriptural work in the NT. Many of these studies commence with an appraisal of how the source tradition ought to be interpreted according to modern standards of exegesis. For example, Jauhiainen offers a 'brief but coherent reading of the book of Zechariah as a whole' in order to 'avoid atomistic exegesis and interpretations that do not do justice to Zechariah' before exploring the use of Zechariah in Revelation.[92] This approach implies that, when faced with the same text, the author of Revelation and the modern critical scholar will respond to the same textual cues in the process of interpretation,

---

[89] Beale, *John's Use*, 45, (see also 67–75).

[90] For more on this, see Beale's comments in an interview with *Christianity Today* in the February 2008 edition.

[91] Beale, *John's Use*, 74.

[92] Jauhiainen, *The Use*, 37. See also Tsai-Chen, 'Zechariah 14', 22–111; Lee, *New Jerusalem*, 6–52; Bøe, *Gog*, 76–89.

and that historical-critical exegesis should act as a control for determining the constitutive features of ancient exegesis. Furthermore, this methodological approach constricts the supposed range of exegetical resources available to the author of Revelation based not on ancient practices of scriptural reuse, but modern modes of biblical interpretation.

Others have argued in the opposite direction, suggesting that John paid minimal attention to the native context of his reused locutions.[93] Moyise, for example, argues that the 'first Christians were not concerned with what the authors of the ancient text had wanted to say', and he suggests that it is an anachronistic concern of modern critics to care about the meaning of source texts.[94] Moyise's argument is well taken, but only to an extent. He is correct that a focus on the 'original context' of reused scriptural segments is prevalent in modern scholarship and that it is problematic to assume that modern habits of reading were operative in antiquity. However, this fact does not necessarily suggest that ancient writers gave no heed to the question of context or the discourse contours (deep structure) of ancient works. The scribes who transmitted, rewrote, and reworked scripture in the Second Temple period played with numerous features of their scriptural sources, including wording, textual rearrangement, narrative framing, and perspective;[95] often these changes are executed based on an awareness of the internal discourse and logic of a given work. Ancient authors did care about what their scriptural works meant, but this creation of meaning differs from the way that modern scholars seek to understand scriptural works.

The debate on the contextual reuse of scripture in the NT is not predicated on the question of ancient habits of reuse or reading, but reflects a dispute about modern hermeneutical presuppositions and the retrojection of these suppositions onto the authors of the NT. The present study, in contrast, determines *how an ancient author understood*

---

[93] See Louis A. Vos, *The Synoptic Traditions in the Apocalypse* (Kampen: Kok, 1965), 21–37 and Moyise, *Old Testament*, 12–13 to some extent; Moyise, 'Does the NT Quote the OT out of Context?' *Anvil* 11 no 2 (1992): 133–143. Beale, *John's Use*, 68–71 lays out the arguments against his own position. Brown, *Tradition*, 131–132 has made this point forcefully in the context of a discussion on the revelatory nature of Christian tradition.

[94] Moyise, *Old Testament*, 12.

[95] See Alexander Samely, in collaboration with Philip Alexander, Rocco Bernasconi, and Robert Hayward, *Profiling Jewish Literature in Antiquity: An Inventory, from Second Texts to the Talmuds* (Oxford: Oxford University Press, 2013), 351.

an antecedent literary work. The goal is not to establish whether ancient authors always incorporated material into a new composition in a manner sensitive to its internal discourse of its source. It is obvious, both from intrinsic possibility and based on numerous examples of contextually and non-contextually sensitive uses of scripture in antiquity, that both options are possible and acceptable for NT writers.[96] It is unlikely that ancient authors would have thought about their scriptural engagements in terms of 'contextual vs. non-contextual'.

The analysis of techniques of reuse provides evidence native to ancient compositional practices that assists in answering the secondary question of 'contextual uses', allowing one to remain neutral to the question of contextual use until all evidence has been gathered. Ancient perceptions of 'contextual fidelity' differed significantly from perceptions embedded in historical-critical exegetical praxis. The discussion of contextual use has become a battleground where arguments over modern hermeneutical and apologetic issues have been reverted back to ancient authors.[97] The following chapters do not directly address this concern. Although it is clear that John was aware of the co-texts of some reused locutions, this reality does not necessarily imply that this was the dominant acceptable mode of reading in this period, nor does it impinge directly on modern apologetic or hermeneutical concerns.

1.4.2.2 Form vs. Function

Another issue that is often conflated with, or emphasized over and above, techniques of reuse is the discussion of the ways in which John 'used' his sources. In this discussion, the *form* (i.e. presentation) of reused material is marginalized in order to focus on the *function* (i.e. purpose or rhetoric) of scriptural reuse.[98] Again, Beale serves as an

---

[96] See Samely, *Rabbinic Interpretation* where he examines, in part, this questions for a restricted collection of Tannaitic literature: the Mishnah. See also comments in Gheorghita, *Role of the Septuagint*, 57–58.

[97] I am thinking of Beale's critique of Moyise's use of 'reader-response theory' in *John's Use*, 41–59. See also the interlinking discussion in Jon Paulien, 'Dreading the Whirlwind: Intertextuality and The Use of the Old Testament in Revelation', *AUSS* 39 (2001): 5–22; G. K. Beale, 'A Response to Jon Paulien on the Use of the Old Testament in Revelation', *AUSS* 39 (2001): 23–34; and S. Moyise, 'Authorial Intention and the Book of Revelation', *AUSS* 39 (2001): 35–40.

[98] This distinction between form and function, and the priority of describing form before function, is clearly articulated by Teeter, *Scribal Laws*, 175–195.

influential example. He offers seven different uses of Jewish scriptural texts in the book of Revelation:

(1) the use of segments of Old Testament scripture as literary proto-types;
(2) thematic use of the Old Testament;
(3) analogical use of the Old Testament;
(4) universalization of the Old Testament;
(5) informal, direct prophetic fulfilment uses of the Old Testament;
(6) informal, indirectly prophetic (typological) fulfilment uses of the Old Testament;
(7) inverted use of the Old Testament.[99]

The uses outlined here reflect a discussion of John's uses of scripture that are a level removed from *techniques of reuse* (form), and they focus exclusively on the *function* of reuse, or fail to recognize the difference. Beale's list categorizes a diverse mixture of motivations for reuse, ideological lenses of interpretation, and presentation of antecedent traditions in the target composition. In order to broach these legitimate but sundry areas of enquiry, the alterations that the author made to his sources (*form*) must first be collected and analysed. Surely, some form of this enterprise stands behind Beale's discussion, but it is left unarticulated. Again, before it is advisable to discuss 'uses' or 'exegetical methods' (*function*) it is necessary to understand *how* the author transformed the textual surface of his source texts (*form*).

1.4.2.3 Identifying Examples of Reuse

Closely related to techniques of reuse are the categories and methods by which examples of reuse are identified. On offer are numerous categorizations: Beale,[100] Fekkes,[101] Moyise,[102] and Bøe[103] present similar categories based on various critical foundations. In contrast to this

---

[99] See Beale, *John's Use*, 75–122.

[100] Beale, *John's Use*, 62–63: Clear Allusion, Probable Allusion, Possible Allusion.

[101] Fekkes, *Prophetic Traditions*, 63–65: Formal Quotation, Informal Quotation, Allusion.

[102] Moyise, *Old Testament*, 118–120 offers four 'forms of imitations': Reproductive, Eclectic, Heuristic, Dialectic.

[103] Bøe, *Gog*, 25–27: Correspondence, Allusion, Quotation or Citation.

trend, Jauhiainen notes that 'criteria for determining OT allusions in Revelation is at least partially misguided and should be laid to rest'.[104] To some extent, Jauhiainen's critique is helpful. 'Scientific' models are useful, but they tend to be rigid and pre-determinative. This type of measurement cannot properly take into account the flexible and creative connections that ancient authors forged within their scriptural source texts. The tenor of the current conversation is problematic because it (often uncritically) relies on a host of literary critical definitions of allusions, particularly that of Israeli literary critic Ziva Ben-Porat,[105] that are not necessarily native to the textual and literary culture of the Second Temple period. The flexible categorizations and textual relationships currently operative in Second Temple studies are more suited for the study of Revelation as this work is, as articulated above, at home in the literary and textual world of this period. The present study does utilize terms like 'quotation' and 'allusion', but I do so in a way that seeks to be universally applicable to literature in general and/or specific to the literary culture in which the book of Revelation was produced (see Section 1.2).

1.5 Conclusion

The analysis of the use of scripture in the book of Revelation continues to garner much scholarly interest. Yet, despite the level of attention paid to this issue in the past thirty years, studies that explore this phenomenon could do more to appreciate the textual and literary complexity of Second Temple Judaism and early Christianity. This study seeks to redress the lacunae articulated above by consciously bringing the focus to the place of Revelation in early Jewish textual culture and describing the ways in which John's composition habits are scribal as it relates to scriptural reuse. Critical issues pertaining to textual culture are routinely addressed in conversations pertaining to inner-biblical exegesis, the reuse of scripture in the Second Temple period, and in other studies that examine the use of scripture in the NT.[106] This study draws the question of the reuse of scripture in the book of Revelation into these wider currents of scholarly discourse,

---

[104] Jauhiainen, *The Use*, 33.

[105] Ben-Porat, 'Literary Allusion' (1976).

[106] See, for example, Fishbane, *Biblical Interpretation*; Matthias Henze, ed., *A Companion to Biblical Interpretation in Early Judaism* (Cambridge: Eerdmans, 2012); Tooman, *Gog of Magog*; Norton, *Contours*; Teeter, *Scribal Laws*.

a discourse that continues to suggest that the models championed by 'OT in the NT' studies require revision. In particular, the tight strictures placed around disciplinary boundaries in previous studies require dissolution. Textual criticism of the Hebrew Bible, Septuagint studies, the textual history of the NT, history of interpretation, composition, exegesis, and reuse are now inextricable in NT studies.[107]

---

[107] See Teeter, *Scribal Laws*, 27: 'Redaction history, text history, exegetical rewriting, and the broader history of interpretation – all prove to be not only contiguous but profoundly interconnected (which is not to say identical) processes. All represent partially overlapping coordinates within the broader exegetical encounter with scripture constitutive of Judaism in the period.' Teeter draws upon the work of Reinhard G. Kratz, *Das Judentum im Zeitalter des zweiten Tempels: kleine Schriften* (FAT 42; 2nd edn; Tübingen: Mohr Siebeck, 2013), 126–156. George J. Brooke has also made the argument in numerous articles that the distinction between higher and lower criticism is now fundamentally artificial. See e.g. *Reading the Dead Sea Scrolls: Essays in Method* (EJL 39; Atlanta: SBL, 2013), 1–17.

2

TEXTUAL PLURIFORMITY IN JEWISH
AND CHRISTIAN ANTIQUITY

The most striking feature of the biblical manuscripts found in the vicinity of Qumran is the diversity of their textual traditions. We refer, not to the multiplicity of individual variant readings within manuscripts nor to the variety of orthographic traditions in which copies of biblical works are inscribed, but to the plurality of distinct text types preserved.[1]

2.1 Introduction

Frank Moore Cross's statement articulates a significant complexity involved in investigating the *Vorlagen* of scriptural references in Jewish and Christian antiquity. The texts of scriptural works were not fixed entities in this period; the wording of a single work remained fluid among its various copies, often creating distinct forms of a given work. Additionally, the physical features of manuscripts (paratexts, segmenting, textual presentation, corrections, repairs, material, clarity of script, etc.) influenced the interpretation of the texts that they carried. Copies that preserve identical texts could be understood very differently by ancient readers in light of their textual presentation. Textual pluriformity is accompanied by and interconnected with a variety of copying practices, scripts, and languages (esp. Hebrew and Greek).

Although I argued in the previous chapter that text-critical concerns are profoundly interconnected with other areas, it is helpful

---

[1] F. M. Cross, 'The Contribution of the Qumrân Discoveries to the Study of the Biblical Text', in *Qumran and the History of the Biblical Text* (ed. F. M. Cross and S. Talmon; London: Harvard University Press, 1975), 278.

here to focus on this issue and its relationship with the material culture of scriptural works before integrating it into the broader discussion of reuse in Revelation. The first issue that requires attention in this chapter is the question of textual form: which form(s) of Zechariah did John reuse? Identifying the form of John's sources is an essential preliminary step that, in turn, permits comment on John's techniques of reuse and habits of reading. This vital step is, however, complicated by the textual pluriformity of the HB and its early Greek versions in the first century CE. The historical sketch that follows suggests that it is probable that John was aware of and familiar with multiple forms of Zechariah, even if he would not necessarily have perceived of these distinctions as discrete forms. Because of this reality, this chapter addresses some foundational background issues: textual pluriformity located in the manuscripts from the Judean Desert, in scriptural references in other NT works, and in the ancient manuscript record of Zechariah specifically. The final section of this chapter examines the various physical features of the ancient scriptural copies that might have influenced John's practices of reading, using the 4QXII manuscripts that contain Zechariah as representative examples. I conclude the chapter by presenting the plausible range of textual forms and possible sources of Zechariah that John may have accessed.

As a whole, this chapter demonstrates that a manifestly pluriform scriptural tradition was a largely unacknowledged reality of the textual culture in which Revelation was composed. The objective is not to describe fully the textual history of Jewish scriptural works, but to recognize that multiple textual exemplars existed and circulated simultaneously in a single milieu, sometimes in ways that defy straightforward text-critical categorization, and that it was plausible that John had access to a selection of these forms through various points of access. This aspect of scriptural reuse in Revelation has been underappreciated in recent studies, and I hope to draw attention to it. However, one must remember that textual pluriformity is but one aspect of what defines early Jewish textual culture, albeit an important one.

2.2 Textual Pluriformity Before Qumran

Let us begin by briefly tracing the major contours of the scholarly conversation as it relates to textual pluriformity before the discoveries in the Judean Desert. Armin Lange notes that even the earliest critical models of how the MT became the *textus receptus* reflected the perspective that, prior to the destruction of the temple in 70 CE, the proto-MT was not the only textual form in existence.[2] In the late eighteenth century, Ernst Friedrich Karl Rosenmüller suggested that the MT became the prevalent text as the 'result of a conscious textual revision of earlier textual traditions'.[3] And Wilhelm Gesenius argued that the shared variants of the SP and OG/LXX reflected the many 'vulgar' texts in circulation before the destruction of the temple.[4] For the majority of this period, the pluriformity of the HB pre-70 CE was a negative reality. Pluriformity was acknowledged, but the value of the OG/LXX and, especially, the SP were considered minimal compared to the voluminous and consistent medieval evidence for the MT.

Paul Kahle's[5] engagement with nineteenth-century giant P. de Lagarde[6] regarding *Urtexte* and 'vulgar' texts also acknowledged textual pluriformity, although, again, both scholars privileged the MT over other textual forms.[7] Lagarde viewed non-MT textual forms

---

[2] Armin Lange, '"They Confirmed the Reading" (*y. Ta'an* 4.68a): The Textual Standardization of the Jewish Scriptures', in *From Qumran to Aleppo: A Discussion with Emanuel Tov about the Textual History of Jewish Scriptures in Honor of his 65th Birthday* (FRLANT 230; ed. A. Lange, M. Weigold, and J. Zsengellér; Göttingen: Vandenhoeck & Ruprecht, 2009), 31.

[3] Ibid. See E. F. C. Rosenmüller, *Handbuch für die Literatur der biblischen Kritik und Exegese* (vol. 1; Göttingen: Vandenhoeck & Ruprecht, 1797).

[4] W. Gesenius, *De Pentateuchi Samaritani origine, indole, et auctoritate commentatio philoligo-critica* (Halle: Rengersche Buchhandlung, 1815). See Lange, 'Confirmed', 31.

[5] See Kahle, *Cairo Geniza* (1959).

[6] See Paul de Lagarde, *Anmerkungen zur griechischen Übersetzung der Proverbien* (Leipzig: Brockhaus, 1863) for example.

[7] Z. Frankel, *Ueber den Einfluss der palästinischen Exegese auf die alexandrinische Hermeneutik* (Leipzig: Verlag von Joh. Ambr. Barth, 1851) and his student, S. Kohn, *De Pentateucho Samaritano – Ejusque cum Versionibus Antiquis Nexu* (Leipzig: G. Kreysing, 1865), 27–42 continued the conversation, disagreeing with Gesenius that the presence of the SP and OG/LXX suggested multiple ancient Hebrew textual forms. For Frankel and Kohn, these versions were late and shoddy corruptions of the *textus receptus* (MT). In contrast to Frankel and Kohn, A. Geiger, *Urschrift in Übersetzungen der Bibel in ihrer Abhängigkeit von der inneren Entwicklung des Judentums. Zweite Auflage mit einer Einführung von Prof. Dr. Paul Kahle und einem Anhang enthaltend: Nachträge zur Urschrift, Verzeichnis der Bibelstellen und Bibliographie zusammengestellt und bearbeitet von Dr. Nachum Czortkowski* (2nd edn; Frankfurt am Main: Verlag Madda, 1928 [1st edn; Breslau: Julius Hainauer, 1857]) suggests that multiple Hebrew forms coexisted in Jewish communities in the Second Temple period. The short, but influential article of Saul Liebermann ('The

as variant from the 'original' proto-MT, and Kahle, in line with Gesenius, suggested that non-MT forms were popular *Vulgärtextes*. Following from the discussion of the eighteenth and nineteenth centuries, the twentieth century witnessed a prolonged discussion regarding how and when the 'standard' form of the HB became the proto-MT.[8] Assumed in these discussions is that at one point the (proto-) MT was *not* the only existing Hebrew textual form.

Even without the data furnished by the Judean Desert finds of the twentieth century, the contours of scholarly discourse clearly accepted that multiple forms of Hebrew scripture existed in antiquity. This observation applied primarily to the three known text types of the Torah – MT, OG/LXX, and the SP.[9] Nonetheless, the SP was often derided as a sectarian expansionistic edition of the MT based on, according to Ulrich, religious prejudice against the Samaritans.[10] Likewise, the importance of the OG/LXX was frequently downplayed as a secondary witness because the major differences it preserved in relation to MT were considered 'corruptions or deliberate changes from the inspired text. [The OG/LXX] was charged with being a poor translation or a loose paraphrase' even though the manuscript evidence for the OG/LXX long pre-dated that of the medieval MT.[11] Nevertheless, preceding the discoveries at Qumran, scholars accepted the reality of textual pluriformity in early Judaism because they were faced with varying textual witnesses adopted by different communities following the turbulent era of 70–135 CE.

Text of Scripture in the Early Rabbinic Period', in *Hellenism in Jewish Palestine* [New York: Jewish Theological Seminary of America, 1950], 20–27) also indicated that textual variation existed in the Second Temple period. However, his approach suggested that the ideal scriptural copies were housed and managed in the temple, while *vulgata* circulated popularly. The idea that the temple actually housed conservatively copied exemplars is tentative at best. See the evaluation of these positions in Teeter, *Scribal Laws*, 212–215.

[8] Lange, 'Confirmed', 33–45. For more the on the issues surrounding the idea of a 'standard text', see Teeter, *Scribal Laws*, 246–254.

[9] See Ulrich, *The Dead Sea Scrolls*, 101; James VanderKam and Peter Flint, *The Meaning of the Dead Sea Scrolls: Their Significance for Understanding the Bible, Judaism, Jesus, and Christianity* (New York: HarperCollins, 2002), 91–92; R. T. Anderson and T. Giles, *The Samaritan Pentateuch: An Introduction to Its Origin, History, and Significance for Biblical Studies* (RBS 72; Atlanta: SBL, 2012) for an introduction to all issues related to the (pre) SP.

[10] Ulrich, *The Dead Sea Scrolls*, 101.

[11] Ibid.

Again, during the pre-Scrolls epoch of scholarship, pluriformity was largely viewed negatively. Hans Debel states that

> even if MT, the Samaritan Pentateuch . . . and the Hebrew *Vorlage* of LXX were considered the three 'pillars' of the biblical text, the divergences of the latter two vis-á-vis the former were often discarded as the products of, respectively, the sectarian traits of the Samaritan community and the free approach of the Greek translators.[12]

Non-MT text families were regarded as secondary, sectarian, or (in the case of the Greek versions) poor translations. The MT was the 'inspired' or 'original' text and was the textual witness that most closely reflected the possible *Urtext* in the mind of most scholars.[13] This perspective continues to hold sway in some sectors of popular perception. However, the finds of Qumran have forced a complete reconsideration of the textual evidence.[14]

---

[12] Hans Debel, 'Greek "Variant Literary Editions" to the Hebrew Bible?', *JSJ* 42 (2010): 165. Likewise, Werner Kelber, 'The History of the Closure of Biblical Texts', in *The Interface of Orality and Writing: Speaking, Seeing, Writing in the Shaping of New Genres* (WUNT 260; ed. A. Weissenrieder and R. B. Coote; Tübingen: Mohr Siebeck, 2010), 75–76 critiques Millar Burrows's initial handling of the textual character of 1QIsaᵃ and notes that certain text-critical and theological paradigms operative in certain sectors of scholarship in the 1950s led to an initial negative reception of textual data that did not cohere to the MT.

[13] Norton, *Contours*, 6 notes that this same attitude towards the MT and other textual forms of the HB by Emil Kautzch (1869), Hans Vollmer (1895), and Whiston (1772) and that this perspective illustrates that these scholars' 'understanding of the "biblical" text in the first century is commensurate with the text-critical assumptions and concerns of Vollmer's day'. Jassen, *Scripture and Law*, 43–44 notes that models of canon formation dominated the discussion of textual issues in this period. Textual variation was viewed negatively in light of the supposed linear development of canon.

[14] For a similar survey, see Emanuel Tov, 'The History and Significance of a Standard Text of the Hebrew Bible', in *HB/OT*, 50–54; Shemaryahu Talmon, 'Textual Criticism: The Ancient Versions', in *Text in Context: Essays by Members of the Society for Old Testament Study* (ed. A. D. H. Mayes; Oxford: Oxford University Press, 2000), 143–150; Arie van der Kooij, 'The Textual Criticism of the Hebrew Bible Before and After the Qumran Discoveries', in *The Bible as Book: The Hebrew Bible and the Judean Desert Discoveries* (ed. E. D. Herbert and E. Tov; London: British Library, 2002), 167–169 and Debel, 'Variant Literary Editions', 161–165; and the very accessible Timothy Michael Law, *When God Spoke Greek: The Septuagint and the Making of the Christian Bible* (Oxford: Oxford University Press, 2013), 19–32.

2.3 Textual Pluriformity Witnessed at Qumran

Although pluriformity was acknowledged before the finds at Qumran, the MT was considered the most reliable witness to the text of the HB. Adam van der Woude's comment is telling:

> Thus before 1947, the year in which the Dead Sea scrolls were discovered, we could console ourselves with the thought that the original text of the Old Testament had come down virtually unchanged through the centuries.[15]

This notion was drastically altered by the discovery of the scrolls in the Judean Desert. Ulrich states the case bluntly:

> After reviewing the parade of biblical manuscripts from Qumran and the major variants in the MT, SP, and OG that can be seen and appreciated in clearer focus due to the Qumran scrolls, what lessons do they offer? The first headline that immediately flashes is 'textual pluriformity.'[16]

Likewise, Emanuel Tov has argued that Qumran has 'taught us no longer to posit the MT at the center of our textual thinking'.[17] Ulrich, Tov, and others have arrived at this conclusion based on the variety of textual forms of scriptural works found at Qumran, the multiple *Vorlagen* of 'non-biblical'[18] compositions at Qumran, and the variety

---

[15] Adam S. van der Woude, 'Pluriformity and Uniformity: Reflections on the Transmission of the Text of the Old Testament', in *Sacred History and Sacred Texts in Judaism* (CBET 5; ed. J. N. Bremmer and F. García Martínez; Kampen: Kok Pharos, 1992), 152–153. See also the summaries of Eugene Ulrich, 'The Dead Sea Scrolls and the Hebrew Scriptural Texts', in *The Bible and the Dead Sea Scrolls* (vol. 1; ed. J. H. Charlesworth; Waco: Baylor University Press, 2006), 77–79 and Teeter, *Scribal Laws*, 218–267.

[16] Eugene Ulrich, 'The Jewish Scriptures: Texts, Versions and Canons', in *The Eerdmans Dictionary of Early Judaism* (ed. J. J. Collins and D. C. Harlow; Grand Rapids: Eerdmans, 2010), 110.

[17] Emanuel Tov, 'Hebrew Biblical Manuscripts from the Judaean Desert: Their Contribution to Textual Criticism', *JJS* 38 (1988): 7. This sentiment is echoed by E. Ulrich, 'Light from 1QIsaᵃ on the Translation Technique of the Old Greek Translator of Isaiah', in *Scripture in Transition: Essays on Septuagint, Hebrew Bible, and Dead Sea Scrolls on Honour of Raija Sollamo* (JSJsup 126; A. Voitila and J. Jokiranta, ed.; Leiden: Brill, 2008), 194.

[18] The term 'biblical' in this discussion refers to texts that eventually became part of the later rabbinic canon (Tanak). The use of this term is anachronistic, but it remains a tool to identify a specific category of texts. I make no judgements as to whether these texts were considered scriptural by the community that preserved them. Many of the 'non-biblical' works were considered scriptural in this period. See Florentino

of textual forms witnessed in the explicit and implicit references to scripture in the non-biblical documents. It is to a brief sampling of this data that we now turn.

2.3.1 Pluriform Scriptural Texts

The scriptural texts uncovered in the Judean Desert reflect a multiplicity of textual forms. 'It is safe to say,' says Tov, 'that [the Qumran community] paid no special attention to textual differences' and that the 'traditional Jewish text, MT, is *not* the Bible but only one of several text forms and/or representatives'.[19] These assertions are confirmed when the scriptural manuscripts are analysed.

García Martínez, 'Rethinking the Bible: Sixty Years of Dead Sea Scrolls Research and Beyond', in *Authoritative Scriptures in Ancient Judaism* (JSJsup 141; ed. M. Popović; Leiden: Brill, 2010), 19–24 and the terminological discussion in Peter W. Flint, 'The Shape of the "Bible" at Qumran', in *The Judaism of Qumran: A Systematic Reading of the Dead Sea Scrolls* (HdO 57.5.2; ed. A. J. Avery-Peck, J. Neusner, and B. Chilton; Leiden: Brill, 2001), 45–58. For an articulate discussion of the problem of interrelating textual standardization, scripturalization, and canon, see Teeter, *Scribal Laws*, 252–254.

[19] Emanuel Tov, 'The Biblical Text from the Judean Desert – An Overview and Analysis of the Published Texts', in *The Bible as Book: The Hebrew Bible and the Judean Desert Discoveries* (ed. E. D. Herbert and E. Tov; London: British Library, 2002), 156 and Tov, 'The Many Forms of Hebrew Scripture: Reflections in Light of the LXX and 4QReworked Pentateuch', in *From Qumran to Aleppo: A Discussion with Emanuel Tov about the Textual History of Jewish Scriptures in Honor of his 65th Birthday* (FRLANT 230; ed. A. Lange et al.; Göttingen: Vandenhoeck & Ruprecht, 2009), 12. I would alter Tov's choice of words somewhat, and suggest that the level of variation witnessed in the scriptural scrolls suggests that the community, and Judaism more broadly, *valued* textual variation. Nonetheless, Tov is correct that scriptural works were not confined to a single textual form. Not all scholars would describe textual pluriformity in this way, but the vast majority of scholars agree that, in the Second Temple period (up to 70 CE and beyond), most scriptural texts existed in a pluriform state. Many scholars focused on the Dead Sea Scrolls and the shape of the HB in the late Second Temple period explicitly acknowledge the pluriformity of the scriptural text. See (among a plethora of others) F. M. Cross, 'The Biblical Scrolls from Qumran and the Canonical Text', in *The Bible and the Dead Sea Scrolls* (vol. 1; ed. J. H. Charlesworth; Waco: Baylor University Press, 2006), 69; Cross, 'Contribution', 278; Shemaryahu Talmon, 'The Old Testament Text', in *Qumran and the History of the Biblical Text* (ed. S. Talmon and F. M. Cross; London: Harvard University Press, 1975), 26–27; Talmon, 'Aspects of the Textual Transmission of the Bible in Light of Qumran Manuscripts', in ibid., 227; Talmon, 'The Transmission History of the Text of the Hebrew Bible in the Light of Biblical Manuscripts from Qumran and Other Sites in the Judean Desert', in *The Dead Sea Scrolls Fifty Years After Their Discovery* (ed. L. Schiffman, E. Tov, and J. VanderKam; Jerusalem: Israel Exploration Society, 2000), 47; D. Barthélemy, 'Histoire du Texte Hébraïque de l'Ancien Testament', in *Études*

D'Histoire du Texte de L'Ancient Testament (OBO 21; Göttingen: Vandenhoeck & Ruprecht, 1978), 341; Eugene Ulrich, 'Pluriformity in the Biblical Text, Text Groups, and Questions of Canon', in *The Madrid Qumran Congress* (STDJ 11; ed. J. Trebolle Barrera and L.

Vegas Montaner; Leiden: Brill, 1992), 24; Ulrich, 'The Absence of "Sectarian Variants" in the Jewish Scriptural Scrolls Found at Qumran', in *The Bible as Book: The Hebrew Bible and the Judean Desert Discoveries* (ed. E. D. Herbert and E.

Tov; London: British Library, 2002), 180; Ulrich, 'The Evolutionary Production and Transmission of the Scriptural Books', in *Changes in Scripture: Rewriting and Interpreting Authoritative Traditions in the Second Temple Period* (BZAW 419; ed. H. von Weissenberg et al.; Berlin: De Gruyter, 2011), 49; P. S. Alexander, 'The Bible in Qumran and Early Judaism', in *Text in Context: Essays by Members of the Society for Old Testament Study* (ed. A. D. H. Mays; Oxford: Oxford University Press, 2000), 41; George J. Brooke, 'The Rewritten Law, Prophets and Psalms: Issues for Understanding the Text of the Bible', in *The Bible as Book: The Hebrew Bible and the Judean Desert Discoveries* (ed. E. D. Herbert and E. Tov; London: British Library, 2002), 36; Brooke, 'New Perspectives on the Bible and its Interpretation in the Dead Sea Scrolls', in *The Dynamics of Language and Exegesis at Qumran* (FAT 2.35; ed. D. Dimant and R. G. Kratz; Tübingen: Mohr Siebeck, 2009), 21; Armin Lange, 'The Status of the Biblical Texts in the Qumran Corpus and the Canonical Process', in *The Bible as Book: The Hebrew Bible and the Judean Desert Discoveries* (ed. E. D. Herbert and E. Tov; London: British Library, 2002), 27; Lange, 'From Literature to Scripture: The Unity and Plurality of the Hebrew Scriptures in Light of the Qumran Library', in *One Scripture or Many? Canon from Biblical, Theological, and Philosophical Perspectives* (ed. C. Helmer and C. Landmesser; Oxford: Oxford University Press, 2004), 55; Lange, 'The Textual Plurality of Jewish Scriptures in the Second Temple Period in Light of the Dead Sea Scrolls', in *Qumran and the Bible: Studying Jewish and Christian Scriptures in Light of the Dead Sea Scrolls* (CBET 57; ed. N. Dávid and A. Lange; Leuven: Peeters, 2010), 43–96; Sidnie White Crawford, 'Reading Deuteronomy in the Second Temple Period', in *Reading the Present in the Qumran Library: The Perception of the Contemporary by Means of Scriptural Interpretations* (Symposium 30; ed. K. De Troyer and A. Lange; Atlanta: SBL, 2005), 128; Hans Debel, 'Rewritten Bible, Variant Literary Editions and Original Text(s): Exploring the Implications of a Pluriform Outlook on the Scriptural Tradition', in *Changes in Scripture: Rewriting and Interpreting Authoritative Traditions in the Second Temple Period* (BZAW 419; ed. H. von Weissenberg et al.; Berlin: De Gruyter, 2011), 67; David J. A. Clines, 'What Remains of the Hebrew Bible? The Accuracy of the Text of the Hebrew Bible in Light of the Qumran Samuel (4QSam[a])', in *Studies on the Text and Versions of the Hebrew Bible in Honour of Robert Gordon* (VTsup 149; ed. G. Kahn and D. Lipton; Leiden: Brill, 2012), 219; Charlotte Hempel, 'The Social Matrix that Shaped the Hebrew Bible and Gave us the Dead Sea Scrolls', in ibid., 222. Additionally, scholars who examine inner-biblical exegesis have also grappled with this reality. See e.g. Yair Zakovitch, 'Inner-Biblical Interpretation', in *CBIEJ*, 35. Septuagintalists generally acknowledge the pluriformity of scriptural texts. See e.g. Natalio Fernández Marcos, *The Septuagint in Context: Introduction to the Greek Version of the Bible* (trans. W. G. E. Watson; Leiden: Brill, 2001), 248–249; James A. Sanders, 'Origen and the First Christian Testament', in *Studies in the Hebrew Bible, Qumran, and the Septuagint Presented to Eugene Ulrich* (ed. P. Flint, E. Tov, and J. VanderKam; Leiden: Brill, 2006), 134–136; Jong-Hoon Kim, 'Zu den Textformen der neutestamentlichen Zitate aus dem Zwölfprophetenbuch', in *Der Antiochenische Text der Septuaginta in seiner Bezeugung und seiner Bedeutung* (DSI 4; ed. S. Kreuzer and

Every one of the twenty-three scriptural texts found outside of Qumran (at Masada, Wadi Sdeir, Nahal Se'elim, Nahal Hever, and Wadi Murabba'at), with the exception of 8HevXIIgr,[20] reflect the consonantal proto-MT[21] and derive from the post-70 CE era.[22] The unified textual alignment of these documents stands in stark contrast to the evidence from eleven caves near Qumran.

First, many of the excerpted texts from Qumran reflect a number of different Hebrew textual forms. There is a mixing of proto-MT, *V*OG/ LXX, and pre-SP readings, especially among *tefillin*.[23] Additionally, a quotation of Exod 20.18 in 4QTestimonia (4Q175) is more closely related to the readings located in SP and 4QRP[a] than the proto-MT.[24] In fact, apart from scattered *tefillin* and *mezuzot*, no excerpted scriptural texts reflect readings associated with the proto-MT.[25] The evidence suggests that there were multiple textual forms that served as the source for these excerpted manuscripts.

Second, among the 'regular' scriptural texts, there is a staggering variety in textual form. Tov's statistical analysis is instructive. Of the Torah manuscripts long enough to warrant analysis, 52% reflect the proto-MT ('or are equally close to the MT and SP'), 37%

M. Sigismund; Göttingen: Vandenhoeck & Ruprecht, 2013), 163–165. A similar acknowledgement to the pluriformity of work in the HB can also be found in examinations of the use of scripture in early Christianity. See e.g. G. K. Beale, 'A Reconsideration of the Text of Daniel in the Apocalypse', *Biblica* 67 (1986): 539–543; Edmon L. Gallagher, *Hebrew Scripture in Patristic Biblical Theory: Canon, Language, Text* (VCsup 114; Leiden: Brill, 2012), 10–11.

[20] See Section 2.6.1.

[21] Tov, 'Biblical Texts', 146; Tov, *Textual Criticism*, 97.

[22] The Masada text originated before 73/74 CE and Nahal Hever and Murabba'at texts ca. 135 CE.

[23] Tov, 'Biblical Texts', 149. George Brooke, 'Deuteronomy 5–6 in the Phylacteries From Qumran Cave 4', in *Emanuel: Studies in Hebrew Bible, Septuagint and the Dead Sea Scrolls in Honor of Emanuel Tov* (VTsup 94; ed. S. M. Paul et al.; Leiden: Brill, 2003), 61 argues that 4QPhyl B 10 harmonizes Deut 5.22 with Deut 4.11–13. This harmonization is present in 4QPhyl J 25, SP, and OG/LXX. According to Brooke, all readings in the phylacteries that differ from proto-MT are evinced in other witnesses (70). Tov, *Textual Criticism*, 109 also notes the line between 'excerpted text' and 'scriptural text' is somewhat manufactured.

[24] See Ulrich, 'Absence', 188. Peter Flint, 'Scriptures in the Dead Sea Scrolls: The Evidence from Qumran', in *Emanuel: Studies in Hebrew Bible, Septuagint and Dead Sea Scrolls in Honor of Emanuel Tov* (VTsup 94; ed. S. M. Paul et al.; Leiden: Brill, 2003), 301 classifies 4QTestimonia itself as a scriptural text.

[25] Tov, 'Biblical Texts', 150. For further information on excerpted texts, see Tov, *Hebrew Bible, Greek Bible and Qumran: Collected Essays* (TSAJ 121; Tübingen: Mohr Siebeck, 1999), 27–41; Tov, 'Scriptures: Texts', in *EDSS* 2.835.

are non-aligned,[26] 6.5% pre-SP, and 4.5% *V*OG/LXX.[27] The statistics are similar for the remainder of the scriptural texts: 44% reflect proto-MT ('or equally close to MT and LXX'), 53% are non-aligned, and 3% reflect *V*OG/LXX.[28] The high percentage of non-aligned textual forms, mixed manuscripts that were unattested in the medieval manuscript evidence and unknown before the Qumran finds, greatly complicates the relatively straightforward picture of distinct text families, indicating instead a fluid textual tradition. As Debel notes, it suggests that 'Qumran blatantly contradicts such a tripartite division' of text families and that the textual character of the HB in the first century is more complex than once imagined.[29]

A good example of pluriformity in the Qumran scrolls is illustrated in the relationship of 1QIsa[a] and 1QIsa[b].[30] Martin Abegg's statistical analysis of 1QIsa[a] demonstrates that, even when orthographic and morphological differences are excluded, in columns X (9.9%), XX (12.5%), and XXXV (18.5%) a significant percentage of the words differ from the MT.[31] Alternatively, 1QIsa[b] merely differs from the

---

[26] Non-aligned is a term used to describe a text form which does not neatly fit into the three main textual families known for the Torah before Qumran. These texts often reflect a mixture of proto-MT, pre-SP, and/or *V*OG/LXX readings.

[27] Tov, 'Biblical Texts', 153. It must be stated that the statistics differ from scholar to scholar and that continued reflection on these manuscripts is bound to change that data. In this way, it is necessary to heed the warning in Lange, 'From Literature', 75: 'Due, however, to the elements of chance involved in the preservation of textual tradition of the analysed texts, caution must be exercised when interpreting the statistics of textual foci.'

[28] Tov, 'Biblical Texts', 153. See Tov, *Textual Criticism*, 107–110 for an updated statistical analysis textual character of Qumran scrolls. This data is not included in the body of the text here because Tov's updated numbers are slightly skewed due to his exclusion of texts that he deems to have been manufactured using 'Qumran Scribal Practice'.

[29] Debel, 'Variant Literary Editions', 170. See also Ulrich, 'Dead Sea Scrolls', 93 and Jassen, *Scripture and Law*, 44–50.

[30] There are many equally compelling examples that come to mind, Jeremiah, the Torah, Daniel, and Psalms being the most obvious. See Michael Segal, 'Between Bible and Rewritten Bible', in *Biblical Interpretation at Qumran* (ed. M. Henze; Cambridge: Eerdmans, 2005), 13–17 for a brief summation of the scholarly discussion surrounding the text forms of Jeremiah and the Torah. See also Loren T. Stuckenbruck, 'The Formation and Re-Formation of Daniel in the Dead Sea Scrolls', in *The Bible and the Dead Sea Scrolls* (vol. 1; ed. J. H. Charlesworth; Waco: Baylor University Press, 2006), 101–130 for information on Daniel at Qumran, and Peter W. Flint, 'Psalms and Psalters in the Dead Sea Scrolls', in *The Bible and the Dead Sea Scrolls* (vol. 1; ed. J. C. Charlesworth; Waco: Baylor University Press, 2006), 233–272 for further information on the state of the Psalter at Qumran.

[31] Martin G. Abegg, '1QIsa[a] and 1QIsa[b]: A Rematch', in *The Bible as Book: The Hebrew Bible and the Judean Desert Discoveries* (ed. E.D. Herbert and E. Tov; London: British Library, 2002), 222.

MT in 4.3% of its readings. In accordance with Abegg's data, Tov classifies 1QIsa[b] as proto-MT and 1QIsa[a] as non-aligned.[32] While statistical evaluation of textual variants is not a conclusive tool, it does suggest that various forms of a scriptural work (Isaiah) existed side by side in a single ancient community, documents preserved alongside one another in a single cave.

2.3.2 Pesharim and 'Rewritten Bible'

Another component of textual pluriformity is the variety of the *Vorlagen* witnessed in the scriptural lemmata of the *pesharim* and reworked material in the rewritten scriptural texts.[33] There is much debate regarding which texts belong in these categories, and if the latter category should exist at all. Nonetheless, the texts that are commonly subsumed under these headings reflect readings that agree with multiple *Vorlagen* – the texts of these documents exhibit characteristics of several base textual traditions.[34] Moshe Bernstein argues that the *Vorlage* of the scriptural lemmata of *Habakkuk Pesher* (1QpHab) 'appears to be at variance from time to time with the Masoretic Text ... some of these variants are of a fairly insignificant nature, but others are more important and at times agree with other ancient textual traditions of Habakkuk'.[35] Timothy Lim confirms Bernstein's

---

[32] Tov, 'Biblical Texts', 154, 156.

[33] See Teeter, *Scribal Laws*, 186–187 for comment on the problematic distinction between textual and exegetical issues in the *pesharim*.

[34] Geza Vermes, *Scripture and Tradition in Judaism: Haggadic Studies* (SPB 4; Leiden: Brill, 1961), 95 coined the term 'rewritten bible' and suggested that the Palestinian Targumim, Josephus' *Jewish Antiquities*, Pseudo-Philo's *Liber Antiquitatum Biblicarum*, *Jubilees*, and the *Genesis Apocryphon* fit into this category. However, Segal, 'Between', 12 suggests that rewriting is a common trait of Second Temple compositions and expands the list further to include large portions of the biblical corpus including Chronicles, Deuteronomy, and Jeremiah among others. Kristin De Troyer, *Rewriting the Sacred Text: What the Old Greek Tells Us about the Literary Growth of the Bible* (TCS 4; Leiden: Brill, 2004) argues that the OG of Esther, Joshua, and 1 Esdras represent rewritten editions of texts. For the purposes of this discussion, it is necessary to limit our discussion to the Qumran rewritten texts. See George J. Brooke, 'Rewritten Bible', in *EDSS* 2.777–780 for a full account of texts that traditionally belong to this category. For an overview on which texts constitute the category '*pesharim*', see Shani L. Berrin, 'Pesharim', in *EDSS* 2.644–647; George J. Brooke, 'Thematic Commentaries on Prophetic Scripture', in *Biblical Interpretation at Qumran* (ed. M. Henze; Cambridge: Eerdmans, 2005), 134–157.

[35] Moshe Bernstein, 'Pesher Habakkuk', in *EDSS* 2.647. Because this is the least fragmentary *pesharim*, it more easily submits to *Vorlagen* analysis than the other

conclusion, arguing that *Habakkuk Pesher*'s source text was 'eclectic'.[36] He concludes that the lemmata of the pesher never existed as an independent unit but that they were constructed from a number of different textual forms.[37] Jonathan Norton provides an excellent example of this phenomenon in his evaluation of 1QpHab 11.8–11 (cf. Hab 2.16), a text first examined by William H. Brownlee.[38]

1QpHab 11.8–11	שבעתה קלון מבוד שתה גם אתה <u>והרעל</u> תסוב עליכה כוס ימין ⟨יהוה⟩ וקיקלון על כבודכה פשר על הכוהן אשר גבר קלונו מכבודו כיא לוא מל את <u>עורלת</u> לבו
	You were more satisfied with dishonour than glory, drink you too, and *stagger*. The cup of YHWH's right hand will turn against you and disgrace will come upon your glory. Its interpretation concerns the priest whose disgrace was greater than his glory, for he *did not circumcise* the foreskin of his heart.
Hab 2.16[pM]	שבעת קלון מכבוד שתה גם־אתה <u>והערל</u>
	You were more satisfied with dishonour than glory, drink you too, and be *uncircumcised*.
Hab 2.16[OG]	πλησμονὴν ἀτιμίας ἐκ δόξης πίε καὶ σὺ καὶ <u>διασαλεύθητι καὶ σείσθητι</u>
	Drink, you too, an abundance of dishonour from glory, and *shake and tremble*.

The scribe who composed this text included both variant readings found in OG *and* proto-MT Habakkuk. Hab 2.16[OG] reads διασαλεύθητι

fragmentary *pesharim* – 4Q166–167 (Hosea), 4Q161–165, 3Q4 (Isaiah), 4Q169 (Nahum), 1Q16, 4Q171, 4Q173 (Psalms), 1Q15 (Zephaniah), and possibly 4Q168 (Micah).

[36] This description is correct inasmuch as it 'eclectic' relates to modern conceptions of textual families. Timothy Lim, 'Biblical Quotations in the Pesharim and the Text of the Bible', in *The Bible as Book: The Hebrew Bible and the Judean Desert Discoveries* (ed. E. D. Herbert and E. Tov; London: British Library, 2002), 76.

[37] Tov, 'Biblical Text', 147–148 suggests, against Bernstein and Lim, that the *Vorlage* of 1QpHab is the MT. However, he does acknowledge significant textual variation in lemmatic sections, but he does not comment on them further.

[38] Brownlee, 'Biblical Interpretation among the Sectaries of the Dead Sea Scrolls', *The Biblical Archaeologist* 14 (1951): 54–76 (esp. 68–69); Norton, *Contours*, 82–84. P. S. Alexander, 'Why no Textual Criticism in Rabbinic Midrash? Reflections on the Textual Culture of the Rabbis', in *Jewish Ways of Reading the Bible* (JSSsup 11; ed. G. J. Brooke; Oxford: Oxford University Press, 2000), 181 argues that this type of procedure suggests that the scribes who produced 1QpHab accepted multiple textual variants are equally inspired.

καὶ σείσθητι ('shake and tremble'), reflecting the reading of the lemma והרעל ('stagger') of the interpretative unit (1QpHab 11.9). In the interpretation of this lemma (1QpHab 11.13), the scribe of this work included the phrase כיא לוא מל את עורלת לבו ('for he did not circumcise [ערל] the foreskin of his heart'), which echoes the proto-MT's reading והערל ('he circumcised'). The readings of *both* the OG and proto-MT traditions are preserved in this unit: one in the lemma (והרעל), the other in its interpretation (עורלת). Norton suggests that this exegesis arises out the multiple 'sense contours' present in this semantic unit based on their graphic similarity.[39] The scribe who composed 1QpHab used metathesis as a way to interpret a potential semantic and textual problem in the lemma, exploiting readings that are also witnessed in different textual forms of Habakkuk. This, in turn, may suggest that multiple forms of the text of Habakkuk (and most likely the Minor Prophets) were available to and used by this exegete, or at least that multiple exemplars with variant arrangements of wording circulated concurrently in a single textual culture.

The text of the rewritten scriptural works, too, suggests that the scriptural *Vorlagen* of these compositions differed. For example, as many have noted,[40] 4QReworkedPentateuch (4QRP)[41] reflects textual forms that are very close to the pre-SP family and often divergent from the proto-MT family and *V*OG/ LXX. VanderKam also notes that the *Vorlage* of the Temple Scroll[42] often agrees with pre-SP and *V*OG/LXX against the proto-MT.[43] Magnus Riska has identified specific redeployments of

---

[39] Norton, *Contours*, 82. Norton also concludes that this type of exegetical activity is present in other Qumran documents (CD^A סוכת/סכות; 4Q252 שלו/שלה and דגלים/רגלים). He argues that the 'distinct sense contours they produce echo known textual traditions, showing that they are working with known alternatives' (103). See, previously, Brownlee, 'Biblical Interpretation', 60–62, esp. hermeneutical principles 9–10: 'Sometimes the prophet veiled his message by writing one word instead of another, the interpreter being able to recover the prophet's meaning by a *rearrangement of the letters in a word*, or by 10. *The substitution of similar letters*.'

[40] Sidnie White Crawford, 'Reworked Pentateuch', in *EDSS* 2.775; Brooke, 'Rewritten', 36; James VanderKam, 'The Wording of Biblical Citations in Some Rewritten Scriptural Works', in *The Bible as Book: The Hebrew Bible and the Judean Desert Discoveries* (ed. E. D. Herbert and E. Tov; London: British Library, 2002), 45; Tov, DJD XIII, 196.

[41] 4Q158, 4Q364–367.

[42] 11Q19–20, 4Q524, 4Q365a, 11Q21.

[43] VanderKam, 'Wording', 47. Sidnie White Crawford, *The Temple Scroll and Related Texts* (Sheffield: Sheffield Academic Press, 2000), 21–22 also acknowledges textual variation in the *Vorlage* of the Temple Scroll.

scriptural text in the first twelve columns of the Temple Scroll that tend to be closer to *V*OG/LXX than proto-MT or pre-SP.[44] These competing observations suggest that the composer of this scroll used different text forms to rewrite large swathes of the Torah, indicating that the text of the Torah (arrangement of graphemes) was variable and authoritative in its different available wordings.[45] This small overview of works suggests that textual pluriformity was not just a reality reflected in manuscript evidence, but in the attitudes of those using scripture to craft new compositions, compositions that may themselves have been considered scriptural by the communities that created them.[46]

2.3.3 Scriptural References

In light of the previous evidence, it is unsurprising that the wording of instances of scriptural reuse in non-scriptural works at Qumran

[44] Magnus Riska, 'The Temple Scroll – Is it More or Less Biblical?' in *Scripture in Transition: Essays on Septuagint, Hebrew Bible, and Dead Sea Scrolls in Honour of Raija Sollamo* (ed. A. Voitila and J. Jokiranta; Leiden: Brill, 2008), 607–608.

[45] This text largely rewrites and harmonizes legal material from the Torah with Deut 12–23. See Florentino García Martínez, 'Temple Scroll', in *EDSS* 2.927–933 for more information.

[46] For discussion on the authoritative nature of the Rewritten Scriptural texts, see Michael Segal, '4QReworked Pentateuch or 4QPentateuch?', in *The Dead Sea Scrolls Fifty Years After Their Discovery* (ed. L. H. Schiffman, E. Tov, and J. VanderKam; Jerusalem: Israel Exploration Society, 2000), 391–399; David M. Carr, *Writing on the Tablet of the Heart: Origins of Scripture and Literature* (Oxford: Oxford University Press, 2005), 34–46, 228–238; Anders Klostergaard Petersen, 'Rewritten Bible as a Borderline Phenomenon – Genre, Textual Strategy, or Canonical Anachronism', in *Flores Florentino: Dead Sea Scrolls and Other Early Jewish Studies in Honour of Florentino García Martínez* (JSJsup 122; ed. A. Hilhorst et al.; Leiden: Brill, 2007), 285–306; Sidnie White Crawford, *Rewriting Scripture in Second Temple Times* (Cambridge: Eerdmans, 2008) 56–57; Debel, 'Rewritten', 76–85; E. Tov, 'From 4QReworked Pentateuch to 4QPentateuch (?)', in *Authoritative Scriptures in Ancient Judaism* (JSJsup141; ed. M. Popović; Leiden: Brill, 2010), 73–91 wherein he sets forth specific criteria for judging the authoritative nature of a specific scriptural manuscript (cf. esp. 87–90). There is a growing consensus among scholars that 4QRP, Jubilees, and the Enochic traditions (among others) were considered to be scriptural by the Qumran community. Armin Lange, 'The Parabiblical Literature of the Qumran Library and the Canonical History of the Hebrew Bible', in *Emanuel: Studies in Hebrew Bible, Septuagint and Dead Sea Scrolls* (VTsup 94; ed. S. M. Paul et al.; Leiden: Brill, 2003), 305 suggests that the 'parabiblical' literature (including rewritten Bible) from Qumran should be considered to be 'a form of scriptural revelation, comparable to the phenomenon of literary prophecy'. For a coherent methodology on the classification of Qumran texts as scriptural, including a list of scriptural texts (most of which never became 'biblical') from Qumran, see Flint, 'Scriptures', 293–304. Michael A. Knibb, 'Reflections on the Status of the Early Enochic Writings', in *Authoritative Scriptures in Ancient Judaism* (JSJsup 141; ed.

reflects multiple text forms;[47] often, this occurs *within* a single composition.[48] An example of this phenomenon can be found in the aforementioned 4QTestimonia (4Q175).[49] Ulrich has identified scriptural citations to different textual forms of the HB in this composition.[50] For example, the reference to Exod 20.18 (line 1) is a short, but near verbatim quotation of pre-SP, differing from its instantiation in the proto-MT. In contrast, the lengthy composite of Deut 5.28–29 and 18.18–19 (lines 1–8) follows the wording of the proto-MT family. This variation *within a single composition* is a telling signpost signalling that multiple textual forms existed side by side in the Second Temple period within a single community.

Likewise, scholars have observed textual variations in the scriptural references in the Damascus Document (CD). Solomon Schechter, its first commentator, notes that

> altogether, the quotations from the Scriptures are seldom correctly given, so that sometimes the source is hardly recognizable . . . As a rule these deviations from the Massoretic text are mere textual corruptions of a careless scribe and not to be explained by the variae lectiones suggested by any known version, or quotation by any ancient authority.[51]

M. Popović; Leiden: Brill, 2010), 143–154 offers a concise discussion of the authoritative status of early Enochic writings arguing that nearly all the evidence from Qumran suggests that *1 Enoch* was viewed as authoritative.

[47] This observation is confirmed by Russell Fuller, 'Some Thoughts on How the Dead Sea Scrolls Have Changed Our Understanding of the Text of the Hebrew Bible and Its History and the Practice of Textual Criticism', in *The Hebrew Bible in Light of the Dead Sea Scrolls* (FRLANT 239; ed. N. Dávid et al.; Göttingen: Vandenhoeck & Ruprecht, 2012), 24: 'the citations [of scriptural texts in the non-biblical texts at Qumran] reveal a similar fluidity to the form of the biblical text to that which is revealed by the biblical scrolls'.

[48] Segal, 'Between', 18–19 argues that it is even difficult to determine the *Vorlage* of a 'biblical' text – 1–2 Chronicles – suggesting that it sometimes agrees with MT, LXX, and 4QSamᵃ. Examples of this phenomenon have also been identified is in the *Lives of the Prophets*. D. R. A. Hare, 'The Lives of the Prophets: A New Translation and Introduction', in *OTP*, 381 notes that 'sometimes the document reflects dependence upon the Hebrew text of the Bible, at other points it clearly evidences familiarity with a Greek translation.' From an early stage, Preben Wernberg-Møller, 'The Contribution of the Hodayot to Biblical Textual Criticism', *Text* 4 (1964): 134 found that the Hodayot from Qumran sometimes reused scriptural texts that do not correlate to the proto-MT.

[49] See DJD V, 57–60.

[50] Ulrich, 'Absence', 188.

[51] S. Schechter, *Documents of Jewish Sectaries: Fragments of a Zadokite Work Edited from Hebrew Manuscripts in the Cairo Geniza Collection now in the Possession*

Although Schechter correctly recognized that scriptural references in CD differed from the MT, his attribution of these changes to inept scribes was based entirely on his conception of the MT as *the* authoritative scriptural text. J. de Waard offers another way forward. He too recognizes that quotations in CD and 4QD do not always agree with MT: seven of the thirty-four Torah quotations, eighteen of the forty-five prophetic quotations, and five of the seventeen quotations of the Ketuvim do not reflect the MT.[52] He does not attribute the textual variation of references to the work of amateur scribes, but finds parallels with other text forms. For example, the quotation of Lev 19.18 in CD 4.20 is nearly identical to manuscripts in the (*V*)OG/LXX family of texts, differing from readings in the proto-MT family.[53]

This small sample of scriptural manuscripts, representing works that rely heavily on scriptural base texts, and works that cite scripture suggests that multiple textual forms circulated simultaneously within a single community. Scribal error cannot fully account for the variety of textual forms preserved in the documents from the Judean Desert. At Qumran there was not *a text* of scripture, but many differing textual *forms* of a given work.[54]

2.4 Pluriformity in Judaism at Large?

The manuscripts recovered from the caves at Qumran clearly evidence the existence of textual pluriformity within a single community. However, the question remains as to the textual situation in late Second Temple Judaism more generally. Do the scrolls reflect the form of

---

of the University Library, Cambridge (vol. 1; Cambridge: Cambridge University Press, 1910), xi–xii.

[52] J. de Waard, *A Comparative Study of the Old Testament Text in the Dead Sea Scrolls and in the New Testament* (STJD 4; Leiden: Brill, 1975), 30.

[53] Ibid., 34. For further discussion of the source text of quotations in CD and 4QD see Geza Vermes, 'Biblical Proof-Texts in Qumran Literature', *JSS* 34 no 2 (1989): 493–508; Eibert Tigchelaar, 'The Cave 4 Damascus Document Manuscripts and the Text of the Hebrew Bible', in *The Bible as Book: The Hebrew Bible and the Judean Desert Discoveries* (ed. E. D. Herbert and E. Tov; London: British Library, 2002), 93–111.

[54] John C. Trever, *The Untold Story of Qumran* (Westwood, NJ: Revell, 1965), 157 states this seemingly ironic fact, at an early stage in Qumran research, bluntly: 'One thing is clear: there was no fixed textual tradition at Qumran, despite [I would argue *because of*] the sect's zealous devotion to Scripture.'

the HB as a whole in this period? Or, do they represent an anomalous or aberrant collection of overtly sectarian literature as some have suggested?[55] Is the data from Qumran representative of the broader Jewish textual culture of the period?

The evidence strongly suggests that these manuscripts represent the textual reality for the entirety of Palestinian Second Temple Judaism and nascent Christianity.[56] First, as previously noted (Section 2.3.1), the proto-MT was not the fixed *textus receptus* in the late Second Temple period, but simply one Hebrew form among many. The manuscript evidence within the proto-MT family from the Judean Desert outside Qumran does not evince text fixity to the level of morphology and *plene* spellings, and individual variant readings exist within this textual family.[57] Also, there is no evidence that the textual form for each book that eventually comprised the MT were located in a 'unified, identifiable collection of texts'.[58] The MT itself is an aggregate, a heterogeneous collection of forms of works that, once collected, share no underlying set of editorial principles. Moreover, according to Ulrich

---

[55] See e.g. E. Y. Kutscher, *The Language and Linguistic Background of the Isaiah Scroll (1QIsa^a)* (STDJ 6; Leiden: Brill, 1974, 77–89. Carr, *Writing*, 272 also notes that the 'marginalized' group at Qumran handled its text differently than other groups, accounting for a higher level of textual fluidity. J. J. Collins, *The Scepter and the Star: Messianism and the Dead Sea Scrolls* (2nd edn; Cambridge: Eerdmans, 2010), 6 refutes the idea that the textual situation at Qumran differed significantly from a broader Palestinian textual culture.

[56] Kelber, 'The History', 77 goes so far as to say, 'textual pluriformity was a *way of life* at a time when both Christianity and rabbinic Judaism were in their formative stages' (emphasis added). See also Jörg Frey, 'Paul's View of the Spirit in the Light of Qumran', in *The Dead Sea Scrolls and Pauline Literature* (STDJ 102; ed. J.-S. Rey; Leiden: Brill, 2014), 240; Teeter, *Scribal Laws*, 256–257.

[57] Ian Young, 'The Stabilization of the Biblical Text in the Light of Qumran and Masada: A Challenge for Conventional Qumran Chronology?', *DSD* 9 no 3 (2002): 370–379 is correct to note that, based on the limited quantity and poor quality of manuscripts from Masada, it is conceivable that there once existed other text forms at the site and that these texts sometimes witness readings not found in any other manuscript. Also, Ulrich, 'Pluriformity', 29 suggests that the prevalence of proto-MT texts at Masada and Nahal Hever is 'not due to the "victory" of the MT but to an "accident of survival"'. Tov, *Textual Criticism*, 179 suggests that the prevalence of the proto-MT at non-Qumran Judean Desert sites is due to 'socio-religious' considerations. However, this perspective is based more on his broad understanding of how the biblical text, as a whole, developed and not on actual textual observations.

[58] Ulrich, 'Absence', 180.

everything we know about the biblical text prior to the end of the first century C.E. – for example, the Samaritan Pentateuch, the Septuagint, Philo, Josephus, the New Testament, Rabbinic quotations, as well as in [the proto-MT] – indicates that the text was pluriform.[59] The text of most scriptural works that eventually comprised the MT was one of multiple forms of those works in circulation in the first century. There is nothing particularly sectarian about the pluriformity of the scriptural texts at Qumran – the evidence extends beyond the community into every corpus of early Jewish literature, including the NT.

Second, although many of the works discovered at Qumran are sectarian, *the textual characteristics* of the scriptural manuscripts do not indicate that the copies of scriptural works found in the eleven caves were sectarian. Despite the reality that some conflict likely existed between the Qumran community and the Jerusalem hierarchy during various periods, their differences did not extend to the wording or shape of the scriptural text.[60] According to Ulrich, 'no variants emerged to indicate that any group – whether Pharisaic, Sadducean, Samaritan, Essene, Christian, or other – had tampered with Scripture in order to bolster their particular beliefs'.[61] There is no evidence for sectarian adoption of particular textual forms of scriptural works in the material from the Judean Desert. In addition to the lack of sectarian characteristics of the scriptural text at Qumran, the contents of the scrolls point to a group that was not unengaged with the textual and literary realities

---

[59] Ulrich, *Dead Sea Scrolls,* 9. For a recent detailed analysis of many of these sources see Norton, *Contours.* Note also that as early as 1930 H. St. J. Thackeray in the introduction (xii) to Josephus, *Ant.* 1–3 (LCL) suggests that Josephus 'has employed at least two forms of Biblical text, one Semitic – whether the original Hebrew or Aramaic, for there are indications in places that he is dependent on an early Targum – the other Greek'. And even before Thackeray, Adam Mez, *Die Bibel des Josephus: untersucht für Buch V–VII der Archäologie* (Basel: Jaeger & Kober, 1895), 1–4, 79–84 made similar observations regarding Josephus' use of multiple textual forms of the Hebrew Bible. Josephus himself (*Ant.* 1.5) claims to have translated his *Antiquities* from 'the Hebrew records' (τῶν Ἑβραϊκῶν μεθηρμηνευμένη γραμμάτων), which he goes on to refer to as 'sacred' or 'holy' (*Ant.* 1.13, 2.347, 3.81).

[60] According to Tov, 'Biblical Texts', 155, 52 per cent of Torah manuscripts from Qumran are proto-MT and 44 per cent of other texts are in the proto-MT family.

[61] Ulrich, 'Absence', 191. This is true except for the Mount Gerizim/Ebal redaction in Deut 27 – the only true sectarian variant Ulrich identified. See also Brooke, 'Deuteronomy 5–6', 58 and Stefan Schorch, 'What Kind of Authority? The Authority

of Judaism at large. While the community produced its own distinctive compositions, it also retained nearly all the texts that became biblical[62] and other texts that circulated widely in Second Temple Judaism, including Tobit,[63] Enochic literature,[64] and Jubilees.[65] The most certain evidence for the nature of the community is reflected in their 'library', a collection of works that only seems to be 'sectarian' in the sense that they produced their own distinctive works.[66] The texts of the scriptural manuscripts bear no marks of sectarian influence, and the contents of the 'library' indicate that the community was engaged in broader literary currents.[67]

Furthermore, as Tov notes, not all manuscripts of works that later became biblical were manufactured at Qumran. Thirty-one scrolls pre-date the settlement of the community and were likely manufactured elsewhere.[68] And if Tov's Qumran Scribal Practice theory is valid,[69] only 21 per cent of scriptural manuscripts were

---

of the Torah during the Hellenistic and Roman Periods', in *Scriptural Authority in Early Judaism and Ancient Christianity* (DCLS 16; ed. I. Kalimi, T. Nicklas, and G. G. Xeravits; Berlin: De Gruyter, 2013), 1–15.

[62] Famously with the exception of Esther and (possibly) Nehemiah. A. Schofield, 'Between Center and Periphery: The *Yahad* in Context', *DSD* 16 (2009): 337 confirms that the *Yaḥad* 'were not unaware of or unengaged with other literary traditions of their day'.

[63] 4Q196–200.

[64] 1Q23–24; 2Q26; 4Q201–212; 4Q247; 4Q530–533; 6Q8.

[65] 1Q17–18; 2Q19–20; 4Q176a; 4Q216–227; 4Q482; 11Q12. See DJD XXXIX; Tov, *Textual Criticism*, 96 n. 161.

[66] When it comes to Qumran the term 'library' is fraught, although I pass over the controversy for this discussion. See the collection of essays in Sidnie White Crawford and Cecilia Wassen, eds., *The Dead Sea Scrolls at Qumran and the Concept of a Library* (STDJ 116; Leiden: Brill, 2016).

[67] George Brooke, '2 Corinthians 6:14–7:1 Again: A Change in Perspective', in *The Dead Sea Scrolls and Pauline Literature* (STDJ 102; ed. J.-S. Rey; Leiden: Brill, 2014), 16 notes that '2 Cor 6:14–7:1 helps us to see that the Qumran texts themselves, though often with a particular perspective, belong to and were part of a geographically widespread set of Jewish ideas.'

[68] Emanuel Tov, 'Some Thoughts about the Diffusion of Biblical Manuscripts in Antiquity', in *The Dead Sea Scrolls: Transmission of Traditions and Production of Texts* (STDJ 92; ed. N. Hilton et al.; Leiden: Brill, 2010), 153. See also, previously, Ulrich, 'The Dead Sea Scrolls', 98 who arrives at a similar conclusion.

[69] See Emanuel Tov, *Scribal Practices and Approaches Reflected in the Texts Found in the Judean Desert* (STDJ 54; Leiden: Brill, 2004) and Eibert Tigchelaar, 'Assessing Emanuel Tov's "Qumran Scribal Practice"', in *The Dead Sea Scrolls: Transmission of Tradition and Production of Texts* (STDJ 92; Leiden: Brill, 2010), 173–205.

copied at Qumran,[70] indicating that many of them that are not related to the proto-MT family originated outside the community. Ulrich affirms this conclusion, noting that the scrolls were *found* at Qumran, not *composed* there, and that not all copies of texts were manufactured on site.[71] This observation necessitates that textual pluriformity was a reality beyond the confines of the *Yaḥad* in late Second Temple period. Again, Ulrich synthesizes the reach and significance of this evidence bluntly:

> Some speak and write as though Qumran were an isolated side-show, a curious 'sect' . . . that is highly interesting but ultimately irrelevant. Thus, the biblical texts found there may be interesting, but they do not really reflect the real Bible.[72]

He argues against this perspective by commenting that

> the scriptural scrolls from Qumran are not 'sectarian' but present the scriptures of general Judaism. They are the oldest, most valuable, and most authentic evidence for the shape of the Scriptures as they circulated in Palestine at the time of the origins of Rabbinic Judaism and Christianity.[73]

The reality that must be grappled with is that 'at Qumran, a single locality, we have a wide variety of quite diverse texts and text types in what was a rather strong-minded and single-minded group.'[74] Confirming Ulrich's perspective, Tov notes, 'the fact that these different texts were found in the same caves reflects a textual plurality at Qumran *and in the country as a whole* between the 3rd century BCE and the 1st century CE.'[75]

---

[70] Tov, 'Biblical Texts', 154.

[71] Ulrich, 'The Scrolls', 35.

[72] Ulrich, 'Qumran', 52. James A. Sanders, 'The Dead Sea Scrolls and Biblical Studies', in *Sha'arei Talmon: Studies in the Bible, Qumran, and the Ancient Near East Presented to Shemaryahu Talmon* (ed. M. Fishbane and E. Tov; Winona Lake, IN: Eisenbrauns, 1992), 323 correctly acknowledges the Scrolls represent a 'remarkable store of information about the inner thinking of a Jewish denomination in existence when Christianity was born'.

[73] Ulrich, 'Evolutionary', 49; Ulrich, 'Qumran', 52.

[74] Ulrich, *Dead Sea Scrolls*, 83. Ulrich demonstrates this point further in his discussion on the palaeo-Hebrew manuscripts found in Cave 4 (147).

[75] Tov, *Textual Criticism*, 110 (emphasis added).

The scrolls from the Judean Desert also reflect late Second Temple and early Jewish textual culture in that they share common habits of reuse.[76] Norton makes a convincing case that 'the exegetical techniques in Sectarian compositions, including exegetical use of textual plurality, belong to this common exegetical heritage.'[77] He distinguishes between professional scribes (represented by Qumran covenanters) and 'literate non-scribal exegetes' (Paul and Flavius Josephus), but suggests that exegetical techniques employed by these writers (or group of writers) 'were widely current in ancient Judaism'.[78] Norton's insight is not revolutionary here – George Brooke, for example, arrived at a similar conclusion earlier, arguing that 'the Qumran scribes were not acting independently of contemporary Judaism'[79] – but his presentation of the findings in this manner clearly emphasizes the importance of this point for understanding the reuse of scriptural traditions in the NT. The exegetical techniques witnessed in the scrolls are part of a larger ambient textual culture of which the NT is also a part.

The observations of Ulrich, Brooke, and Norton suggest two vital conclusions that bear upon John's reuse of Zechariah in the book of Revelation. First, the pluriformity exhibited in the scriptural texts at Qumran genuinely reflected the textual culture of early Judaism. Thus, it is plausible that John was aware of and had access to multiple forms of the text of Zechariah. This fact necessitates that any investigation of reuse in Revelation begin with identifying the *Vorlage(n)* of scriptural references before discussing John's habits of reading.

Second, the textual pluriformity exhibited in the scriptural manuscripts from Qumran establishes the plausibility that John *intentionally* referenced multiple text forms. The existence of Qumran compositions that reference varying textual forms suggests that it is indeed conceivable that John used scripture in a similar fashion. Based on the similar nature of the exegetical techniques employed by Josephus, the Qumran covenanters, and Paul, which includes the exegetical use of textual pluriformity, one expects that John's use of scripture was concordant with his common textual milieu. The exegetical use of textual pluriformity was common across a wide swathe of Judaism in the first century. The comparative evidence indicates

---

[76] This topic is discussed more fully in Chapter 5.

[77] Norton, *Contours*, 108.

[78] Ibid., 110.

[79] George J. Brooke, *Exegesis at Qumran: 4QFlorilegium in its Jewish Context* (JSOTsup 29; Sheffield: SBL, 1985), 5.

both that John had access to pluriform textual traditions and that he possessed the requisite exegetical repertoire to exploit the interpretative possibilities latent in this tradition.

2.5 Textual Pluriformity in the New Testament

The notion that NT authors referenced pluriform scriptural traditions is not ground-breaking, and many scholars have acknowledged the effect that textual pluriformity has wrought in the investigation of scriptural references in the NT.[80] Below, I explore three examples of other early Christian works, apart from Revelation, that quote portions of Jewish scripture. I focus on examples that clearly demonstrate that

[80] Swete, *The Apocalypse*, cliv–clv; Kenneth J. Thomas, 'Torah Citations in the Synoptics', *NTS* 1 (1977): 85–96; Menken, *Fourth Gospel*; Menken, 'The Quotation From Jeremiah 31(38).15 in Matthew 2.18: A Study of Matthew's Scriptural Text', in *The Old Testament in the New Testament: Essays in Honour of J. L. North* (JSNTsup 189; ed. S. Moyise; Sheffield: Sheffield Academic Press, 2000), 106–110; Menken, 'The Minor Prophets in John's Gospel', in *The Minor Prophets in the New Testament* (LNTS 377; ed. M. J. J. Menken and S. Moyise; London: T&T Clark, 2009), 82–83; Timothy Lim, *Holy Scripture in the Qumran Commentaries and Pauline Letters* (Oxford: Clarendon, 1997), 158–160; Lim, 'The Qumran Scrolls, Multilingualism, and Biblical Interpretation', in *Religion in the Dead Sea Scrolls* (ed. J. J. Collins and R. A. Kugler; Cambridge: Eerdmans, 2000), 57; R. Timothy McLay, 'Biblical Texts and the Scriptures for the New Testament Church', in *Hearing the Old Testament in the New Testament* (ed. S. E. Porter; Cambridge: Eerdmans, 2006), 55; Karen H. Jobes, 'The Septuagint Textual Tradition in 1 Peter', in *Septuagint Research: Issues and Challenges in the Study of the Greek Jewish Scriptures* (SCS 53; ed. W. Kraus and R. G. Wooden; Leiden: Brill, 2006), 311–333; Martin Karrer, 'The Epistle to the Hebrews and the Septuagint', in ibid., 335–353; Dieter Böhler, 'Abraham und Seine Kinder im Johannesprolog. Zur Vielgestaltigkeit des Alttestamentlichen Textes bei Johannes', in *L'ecrit et l'esprit: Etudes d'histoire du texte et de théologie biblique en hommage à Adrian Schenker* (OBO 214; ed. D. Böhler, I. Himbaza, and P. Hugo; Göttingen: Vandenhoeck & Ruprecht, 2005), 17; Charlene McAfee Moss, *The Zechariah Tradition and the Gospel of Matthew* (BZNW 156; Berlin: De Gruyter, 2008), 5–7; Christopher R. Bruno, 'The Deliverer From Zion: The Source(s) and Function of Paul's Citation in Romans 11:26–27', *TB* 59 no 1 (2008): 119–134; Susan Docherty, 'The Text Form of the OT Citations in Hebrews Chapter 1 and the Implications for the Study of the Septuagint', *NTS* 55 no 3 (2009): 364–365; Huub van de Sandt, 'The Minor Prophets in Luke-Acts', in *The Minor Prophets in the New Testament* (ed. M. J. J. Menken and S. Moyise; London: T&T Clark, 2009), 57–58; Radu Gheorghita, 'The Minor Prophets in Hebrews', in *The Minor Prophets in the New Testament* (LNTS 377; ed. M. J. J. Menken and S. Moyise; London: T&T Clark, 2009), 117–120; Bynum, *Fourth Gospel*, 1–5; Ronald H. van der Bergh, 'Differences Between the MT and LXX Contexts of Old Testaments Quotation in the New Testament: Isaiah 45:18–25 as a Case Study', in *Septuagint and Reception* (VTsup127; ed. J. Cook; Leiden: Brill, 2009), 159–176; Matthew S. Harmon, *She Must and Shall Go Free: Paul's Isaianic Gospel in Galatians* (BZNW 169; Berlin: De Gruyter, 2010); Steve Moyise, 'Matthew's Bible in the Infancy Narrative', in *The Scriptures of Israel*

multiple forms of a single scriptural work were quoted within a particular NT work. These examples establish that early Christians, too, tacitly participated in an ambient textual culture with early Judaism, pointing to the reality of the presence of wordings that follow the witness of differing textual forms embedded within a single work. Even if the authors of the following works did not quote directly from scriptural manuscripts, but borrowed these quotations from early exegetical traditions, it still demonstrates that various exegetical traditions were encoded to correspond to particular forms of Jewish scripture. In other words, if these quotations are drawn from other circulating traditions, their adherence to the wording of distinct forms suggests a pluriform and complex textual culture as the setting of early Christian literary production. These examples are far from exhaustive, but suggest that John may have referenced multiple forms of Zechariah in Revelation.

2.5.1 The Psalter in the Gospel of John

In John 2.17 and 13.18, the evangelist quotes Ps 69(68).10a and 41(40).10b respectively. The text of these quotations suggests that the evangelist quoted different forms of the Psalter. I commence by examining the textual form of Ps 69(68).10a in John 2.17, a quotation that likely preserves a Greek form of the Psalm.

John 2.17	ἐμνήσθησαν οἱ μαθηταὶ αὐτοῦ ὅτι γεγραμμένον ἐστίν ὁ ζῆλος τοῦ οἴκου σου καταφάγεταί με
	His disciples remembered that it is written: 'The zeal of your house will consume me.'
Ps 68.10a^OG	ὅτι ὁ ζῆλος τοῦ οἴκου σου κατέφαγέν με
	For the zeal of your house consumed me.
Ps 69.10^pM	כי־קנאת ביתך[81] אכלתני
	For zeal of your house consumed me.

---

in Jewish and Christian Tradition: Essays in Honour of Maarten J. J. Menken (NTsup 148; Leiden: Brill, 2013), 12 suggests that the quotation in in 'Matt 2:18 appears to be an eclectic mix' of textual traditions of Jer 31.15 (38.15); Labahn, 'Ausharren im Leben', 291–316; Labahn, 'Die Septuaginta und die Johannesapokalypse', 162–188; Walser, *Quotations*, 187–188; Law, *When God Spoke Greek*, 84–116. For exceptions, see Hans Hübner, 'New Testament Interpretation of the Old Testament', in *HB/OT*, 338–339, 372.

[81] The editors of 4QPs^a III 19 ii-20 reconstructed this word as ביתכה. See Eugene Ulrich, ed., *The Biblical Qumran Scrolls: Transcriptions and Textual Variants* (VTsup 134; Leiden: Brill, 2010), 648.

There is no evidence to suggest that the *Vorlage* of the OG disagrees with the proto-MT at this point in the psalm. Every element of Ps 69(68).10a[PM] is reflected in the OG translation in the proper word order. Maarten J. J. Menken confirms this observation, stating that the OG/LXX translation is 'an adequate translation from the Hebrew words כי־קנאת ביתך אכלתני'.[82] The quotation in John 2.17 also adequately reflects the locution from the proto-MT. However, the quotation is a nearly verbatim representation of Ps 69(68).10a[OG].

The two Greek phrases are identical (syntactically, morphologically, semantically, and in terms of word order) except for the tense and voice of the verb: καταφάγεται (future middle) in John 2.17 κατέφαγέν (aorist active) in the psalm.

The difference between the verb in John 2.17 and Ps 69(68).10a[OG] does not disqualify the OG as the source for the quotation for two reasons. First, both texts preserve the same root lexeme (κατεσθίω), albeit with a minor morphosyntactic difference. Second, some witnesses to the OG tradition preserve a variant in Ps 69(68).10a[OG] that corresponds identically with John 2.17: καταφάγεταί instead of κατέφαγέν (B א).

Menken suggests that the variant reading in the Greek Psalm tradition is a later adaptation of the Greek text made to correspond to the quotation in John 2.17. This reconstruction of the textual history of the psalm is possible; however it does not detract from the argument that the evangelist quoted the OG instead of the proto-MT. First, a quotation need not exactly reproduce every element of its source text verbatim. Exact quotations are the exception in Second Temple literature and the NT, not the rule.[83] Wm. Randolph Bynum argues that John's slight alteration of a source text – which he argues is the OG in this case – 'demonstrates that John is at home in the biblical textual context of the era'.[84] Second, as Menken points out, if the evangelist translated from the proto-MT, there were two possible points for alternative translation.[85] First, בית could have been

[82] Menken, *Old Testament Quotations*, 38.

[83] Crawford Toy, *Judaism and Christianity: A Sketch of Thought From the Old Testament to New Testament* (Boston: Little, Brown, and Company, 1892), 136 observed this phenomenon noting that 'on account of the absence of historical-exegetical feeling, the greatest liberty was assumed in the interpretation and application of Scriptural passages'. This observation retains its veracity in terms verbal identify of references in target texts to their given source text.

[84] Bynum, *The Fourth Gospel*, 126.

[85] Menken, *Old Testament Quotations*, 39.

translated by οἰκία,[86] a word that the evangelist used five times,[87] and אכל could have been translated with multiple Greek words. For example, the word could be translated by a form of φάγω without a prefix.[88] The OG/LXX translators made use of twenty-seven different translation options for the verbal form of אכ"ל in the *qal* binyan alone.[89] The preceding observations and the striking verbal similarity between John 2.17 and Ps 69(68).10a[OG] suggest that the evangelist referenced the OG text of Ps 69(68).10a in constructing this quotation.

A second example of an explicit quotation of the Psalter occurs in John 13.18 where the evangelist cites Ps 41(40).10b.[90] In contrast to the preceding example, the following evidence suggests that the text of the evangelist's quotation is closer to the proto-MT tradition than a Greek tradition.

John 13.18	ἵνα ἡ γραφὴ πληρωθῇ· ὁ τρώγων μου[91] τὸν ἄρτον ἐπῆρεν ἐπ᾽ ἐμὲ τὴν πτέρναν αὐτοῦ
	In order that the scripture might be fulfilled: 'The one eating my bread raised up his heel against me.'
Ps 40.10b[OG]	ὁ ἐσθίων ἄρτους μου, ἐμεγάλυνεν ἐπ᾽ ἐμὲ πτερνισμόν
	The one eating my bread, made great deception against me.[92]
Ps 41.10b[pM]	אוכל לחמי הגדיל עלי עקב
	The one eating my bread brought up a heel against me.

---

[86] Instead of οἴκου.

[87] John 4.53; 8.35; 11.31; 12.3; 14.2.

[88] Menken, *Old Testament Quotations*, 39.

[89] See HRCS (Hebrew index), 225.

[90] 41.9b in English Bibles. Andreas J. Köstenberger, *John* (BECNT; Grand Rapids: Baker, 2004), 411; Andrew T. Lincoln, *The Gospel According to Saint John* (BNTC; London: Continuum, 2005), 373; Ulrich Rüsen-Weinhold, *Der Septuagintapsalter im Neuen Testament: Eine textgeschichtliche Untersuchung* (Neukirchen-Vluyn: Neukirchener, 2004), 297–302; and J. Ramsey Michaels, *The Gospel of John* (NICNT; Cambridge: Eerdmans, 2010), 740 confirm that Ps 41(40).10b is the correct referent of the quotation in John 13.18.

[91] A variant is witnessed in some manuscripts here: μετ᾽ ἐμοῦ. Although this reading is present in a number of manuscripts, Bruce M. Metzger, *A Textual Commentary on the Greek New Testament* (London: UBS, 1975), 240 suggests that the phrase is an assimilation with Mark 14.18. The doubt of this variant is also confirmed by Menken, *Old Testament Quotations*, 123.

[92] NETS, 567 translates the second clause as '[he] magnified trickery against me'.

As in the previous example, the *V*OG/LXX of Ps 41(40).10b is the same as the consonantal text of the proto-MT at this point in the psalm. The verb ἐμεγάλυνεν reflects faithfully הגדיל and the rest of the OG/LXX is replete with examples where forms of ἐμεγάλυνεν translated the *hiphil* of גד"ל.[93] Also, although πτερνισμόν is rarely employed in the OG/LXX,[94] it does translate עק"ב on occasion in its adjectival form, which carries the meaning of 'deceitful, sly'.[95] Despite the rarity of the translation, the OG/LXX translator represented every element of his *Vorlage*, insofar as the text of this *Vorlage* corresponded to the proto-MT, with serial fidelity.

Unlike the previous example, however, the quotation in John 13.18 differs significantly from the OG translation.[96] First, John 13.18 does not witness ἐσθίων but a synonymous participle: τρώγων. Second, in agreement with the proto-MT the quotation reads ἄρτον (singular) instead of the OG/LXX plural reading (ἄρτους). Third, the texts differ in their translation of הגדיל. Menken notes that the OG translation is a 'literal' translation as ἐμεγάλυνεν means 'he made great'.[97] The Johannine translation in 13.18 (ἐπῆρεν), although different than the OG, is a well-attested translation of גד"ל as it can mean 'to raise' and 'to lift'.[98] Fourth, although the translations are graphically similar, John 13.18 translates עקב as πτέρναν ('heel') while Ps 41(40).10b^OG/LXX represents it with the less common noun πτερνισμόν ('deceitful, sly, supplanter'). The translation of πτέρναν for עקב in John 13.18 is a common translation equivalent in the OG/LXX.[99] Fifth, John 13.18 witnesses the addition of the third-person possessive pronoun αὐτοῦ. This pronoun is absent in both the OG and proto-MT. Sixth, and finally, John 13.18 and Ps 41(40).10b^OG differ in serial arrangement. The pronoun modifying ἄρτον (or ἄρτους) precedes the noun it modifies in

93 See HRCS, 902. In the Psalter alone analogous translations occur at 126(125).2, 3; 138(137).2.

94 See HRCS, 1237. The only other occurrence of this word in the OG/LXX occurs in 2 Kgs 10.19. See also LSJ, 1546 which notes that the noun πτερνισμόν can mean 'supplanter' or 'craft'.

95 See Jer 17.9 and Ben Sira 36.25.

96 Menken, *Old Testament Quotations*, 124 n.10 notes that Aquila and Theodotion also differ significantly from the Johannine text.

97 Ibid., 124.

98 *HALOT*, 179.

99 See HRCS, 1237. The Johannine translation is paralleled eight times (Gen 3.15; 25.26; 49.17; Judg 5.22; Ps 49(48).5; 56(55).6, Cant 1.8; Jer 13.22) while the translation in Ps 41(40).10b^OG is paralleled (inexactly) only in 2 Kgs 10.19.

John and follows the noun in the OG. Menken attributes the difference to 'Johannine style',[100] and this possible stylistic change illustrates further the dissonance between John 13.18 and Ps 41(40).10b[OG]. This volume of evidence suggests that the evangelist did *not* quote the OG in this instance. However, the question of its source remains. The evidence, instead, directs us towards a different conclusion: the evangelist independently translated Ps 41(40).10b[PM]. The only semantic element in the quotation in John 13.18 that cannot be a representation of the proto-MT is the addition of the possessive pronoun αὐτοῦ. Nonetheless, the text of John 13.18 is an equally plausible translation of the proto-MT in comparison to the OG. For example, πτέρναν is a much more common translation of עקב than πτερνισμόν and the use of the singular ἄρτον reflects the reading tradition of the MT (לחמי). The OG reading (ἄρτους) translates לחמי as a plural – an equally valid rendering in the consonantal text. Another possible issue with the translation in John 13.18 is the verb ἐπῆρεν for הגדיל. There are no parallel examples where a form of ἐπῆρεν translates גד"ל or a graphically similar word in the OG/LXX. However, the semantics of the translation match with the sense of 'lifting up' that the *hiphil* of גד"ל can represent. Finally, the OG/LXX tradition of Ps 41(40).10b *never* agrees with John 13.18 in its rendering of הגדיל.[101]

The textual data suggest that the quotation in John 13.18 is the evangelist's own translation of Ps 41(40).10b[PM].[102] His source is certainly not the OG, and the close relationship between the quotation and the proto-MT suggest a direct relationship. Menken agrees stating that 'the peculiar rendering of Ps 41:10 in John 13:18 is best explained as the evangelist's own translation from Hebrew'.[103]

This brief analysis of Psalter quotations in John demonstrates that the evangelist explicitly quoted the same scriptural book in

---

[100] Menken, *Old Testament Quotations*, 123.

[101] Aquila, Symmachus, and Theodotion do alter the OG, but none of these revisions bring the wording into agreement in John 13.18 (ἐπῆρεν). Each preserves κατεμεγαλύνθη.

[102] It is theoretically possible that the Evangelist referenced a no-longer-extant Greek form, but this argument is difficult to qualify.

[103] Menken, *Old Testament Quotations*, 138. Menken also suggests that the Hebrew translation is made under the influence of proto-MT 2 Sam 12.28 or a 'corrected Greek version'. If this is the case, it does not detract from the fact that John used the proto-MT of Ps 41(40).10b to construct this quotation.

two distinct forms within a single composition. In John 2.17, Ps 69(68).10a[OG] was quoted nearly verbatim and, in John 13.18, the author translated Ps 41(40).10b[PM]. The author of John had access to and referenced multiple textual forms of the Psalter. These quotations signify that multiple textual forms of the Psalter not only existed and circulated at the time of the composition of the Gospel of John, but that they were known and used by its author(s).

2.5.2 The Epistle to the Romans and Isaiah

Another example of textual pluriformity in NT quotations is found in Paul's use of Isaiah in Rom 9. I examine two quotations to determine their *Vorlage(n)*,[104] the first of which is the use of Isa 8.14 and 28.16 in Rom 9.33.

Rom 9.33	καθὼς γέγραπται· ἰδοὺ τίθημι ἐν Σιὼν λίθον προσκόμματος καὶ πέτραν σκανδάλου, καὶ ὁ πιστεύων ἐπ᾽ αὐτῷ οὐ καταισχυνθήσεται
	As it is written, 'Behold I am placing in Zion a stone of stumbling and a rock of temptation and the one who believes on him will not be put to shame.'
Isa 8.14[OG105]	καὶ ἐὰν ἐπ᾽ αὐτῷ πεποιθὼς ᾖς, ἔσται σοι εἰς ἁγίασμα, καὶ οὐχ ὡς λίθου προσκόμματι συναντήσεσθε αὐτῷ οὐδὲ ὡς πέτρας πτώματι, ὁ δὲ οἶκος Ιακωβ ἐν παγίδι, καὶ ἐν κοιλάσματι ἐγκαθήμενοι ἐν Ιερουσαλημ.
	And if you trust in him, he will be to you a sanctuary and you will not meet him as a stumbling stone nor as a falling rock. But the house of Jacob is dwelling in a snare and in a hollow in Jerusalem.
Isa 8.14[PM106]	והיה למקדש ולאבן נגף ולצור מכשול לשני בתי ישראל לפח ולמוקש ליושב ירושלם
	He will be a sanctuary and a stone of offence and a rock of stumbling to both houses of Israel, a trap and a snare to those dwelling in Jerusalem.

---

[104] For a full view of the current issues pertaining to the interpretation of Rom 9–11, see F. Wilk and J. R. Wagner, eds., *Gospel and Election: Explorations in the Interpretation of Romans 9–11* (WUNT 257; Tübingen: Mohr Siebeck, 2010).

[105] The OG/LXX text of Isaiah is taken from Joseph Ziegler, *Isaias* (VTG 14; Göttingen: Vandenhoeck & Ruprecht, 1939).

[106] Norton, *Contours*, 143 notes that the proto-MT reading or 'stream' in this instance is witnessed by 1QIsaᵃ, α, θ, and σ.

Isa 28.16^OG

διὰ τοῦτο οὕτως λέγει κύριος Ἰδοὺ ἐγὼ ἐμβαλῶ εἰς τὰ θεμέλια Σιων λίθον πολυτελῆ ἐκλεκτὸν ἀκρογωνιαῖον ἔντιμον εἰς τὰ θεμέλια αὐτῆς, καὶ ὁ πιστεύων ἐπ' αὐτῷ οὐ μὴ καταισχυνθῇ.

Therefore, because of this, the Lord says, 'behold I set in the foundation of Zion a costly, chosen, honoured cornerstone in its foundation and *the one who believes on him was never put to shame.'*

Isa 28.16^PM

לכן כה אמר אדני יהוה הנני יסד בציון אבן אבן בחן פנת יקרת מוסד
מוסד המאמין לא יחיש

Therefore, thus says my lord YHWH, 'behold, I am setting in Zion a tested and costly foundation corner stone, a sure foundation. *The one who believes will not come quickly.'*

Paul's quotation in Rom 9.33 is a conflation of Isa 8.14 and 28.16,[107] a connection forged upon the shared vocabulary of both locutions.[108] The first clause of the quotation (ἰδοὺ τίθημι ἐν Σιὼν λίθον προσκόμματος καὶ πέτραν σκανδάλου) derives largely from Isa 8.14 with the exception of the substitution of Σιών/ציון for ἁγίασμα/למקדש. The grammatical structures of proto-MT and OG Isa 8.14 differ quite substantially in the protasis of the quotation. The proto-MT 'expresses a striking idea: God can be both a sanctuary and a stumbling stone to Israel'.[109] This idea is significantly softened by the OG translator through the augmentation of the locution into a conditional clause: '*if you trust* in him, he will be to you a sanctuary and you will *not* meet him as a stumbling stone nor as a falling rock'. For the translator, God will be either a sanctuary or a stumbling stone, but not both.

---

[107] This fact is confirmed by Joseph A. Fitzmyer, *Romans* (AB 33; London: Doubleday, 1993), 579 who notes that this conflation 'disregards the context of the original and makes the OT say almost the opposite of what it actually does say. Paul thus accommodates Isaiah's meaning to his own literary purpose.' Other scholars confirm this view as well, including Robert Jewett, *Romans* (Hermeneia; Minneapolis: Fortress, 2007), 613 (although he does leave open the fact the Paul may be citing an unknown Greek text); James D. G. Dunn, *Romans 9–16* (WBC 38b; Dallas: Word, 1988), 583–585; Douglas J. Moo, *The Epistle to the Romans* (NICNT; Cambridge: Eerdmans, 1996), 629–630.

[108] Both verses refer to 'stones', λίθος/אבן, and a 'sacred place', ἁγίασμα/למקדש, or 'Zion', Σιών/ציון.

[109] Norton, *Contours*, 143.

The logic of the conflation in Rom 9.33 suggests that the inclusion of Isa 28.16 offers a solution to the problem of God being both a stumbling stone and a sanctuary – 'the one who believes on him will not be put to shame'. Norton notes that this theological tension 'resonates curiously closely with Paul's anxieties about the fate of Israel in Romans'.[110] Isa 28.16 refers to a costly foundational cornerstone in contrast to the stumbling stone in Isa 9.33, and, by conflating these locutions, Paul implicitly affirms the semantic sense of the proto-MT – God is both stone and sanctuary – but he presents an alternative to stumbling stone. Instead of a stumbling stone, God can be a cornerstone to 'the one who believes on him' (ὁ πιστεύων ἐπ' αὐτῷ). The conditional nature of God acting as *either* stumbling stone *or* sanctuary is already present in Isa 8.14[OG] (καὶ ἐὰν ἐπ' αὐτῷ πεποιθώς) and, if Paul were referencing this text form, there would have been no reason for him to include his own conditional nuance by conflating the locution with Isa 28.16. The close verbal correspondences between Isa 8.16[PM] and Rom 9.33, along with their semantic similarity, suggest that Paul used a text situated within the semantics of the proto-MT tradition to craft this citation. Norton agrees: 'while the majority of Paul's Isaiah citations broadly reflecting the OG-form are supportive, the form of Isa 8.14[PM] Paul cites semantically structures his thought, and *only* this form is useful.'[111]

The source of the second clause of the citation (καὶ ὁ πιστεύων ἐπ' αὐτῷ οὐ καταισχυνθήσεται) is less complicated to identify. The OG translates the final negated verb of Isa 28.16, 'it will not come quickly' (לֹא יָחִישׁ), as οὐ μὴ καταισχυνθῇ ('he was never put to shame'). There are no other examples of any form of καταισχύνειν translating וחיש, and Hatch and Redpath mark this translation with an obelus because these words share no semantic value.[112] Although Paul modifies the locution from the source text by omitting μή and changing the morphological value of καταισχυνθῇ (aorist passive subjunctive) to καταισχυνθήσεται (future passive indicative), it is unlikely that he would have translated יָחישׁ as καταισχυνθήσεται independently of the OG. The second clause of Paul's quotation derives from a Greek textual form.

[110] Ibid., 144.
[111] Ibid., 145.
[112] HRCS, 731–732.

In Rom 9.33, Paul exploited textual pluriformity to his exegetical advantage within the confines of a single quotation. Paul appears to be aware of at least two forms of Isaiah, referencing a form of Isaiah^{PM} and Isaiah^{OG} in a single quotation. As noted above, the majority of Paul's quotations reflect the OG/LXX tradition, but examples like this one caution against drawing blanket conclusions on this point. Nonetheless, a final example of the use of Isaiah in Rom 9 demonstrates conclusively that Paul also quoted the OG/LXX tradition (as is his normal practice). While the previous example demonstrates that Paul was aware of and utilized textual pluriformity within a single verse, the following example broadens the analysis further by examining Paul's citation in Rom 9.29, the citation that immediately precedes Rom 9.33.

Rom 9.29   καὶ καθὼς προείρηκεν Ἠσαΐας· εἰ μὴ κύριος σαβαώθ
ἐγκατέλιπεν ἡμῖν σπέρμα, ὡς Σόδομα ἂν ἐγενήθημεν καὶ ὡς
Γόμορρα ἂν ὡμοιώθημεν

And just as Isaiah previously said, 'unless the Lord Sabaoth left
to us a seed, we had become like Sodom and we were made
like Gomorrah.'

Isa 1.9^{OG} καὶ εἰ μὴ κύριος σαβαωθ ἐγκατέλιπεν ἡμῖν σπέρμα, ὡς
Σοδομα ἂν ἐγενήθημεν καὶ ὡς Γομορρα ἂν ὡμοιώθημεν.

And unless the Lord Sabaoth left to us a seed, we had become
like Sodom and we were made like Gomorrah.

Isa 1.9^{PM} לולי יהוה צבאות הותיר לנו שריד כמעט כסדם היינו לעמרה דמינו

If it were not for YHWH Sabaoth leaving to us a small
remainder, we were as Sodom, we resembled Gomorrah.

The wording of the *Vorlage* of Isa 1.9^{OG} is very similar to proto-MT.[113] Both forms are semantically and syntactically identical with the exception of σπέρμα ('seed'), representing the phrase שריד כמעט ('a little remainder').[114] This translation is unique as σπέρμα is almost always a translation of a form of זרע and never a translation

---

[113] 1QIsa^a is identical to the proto-MT in this locution, only with fuller orthography. See Ulrich, *Biblical*, 331. Fitzmyer, *Romans*, 575 argues the proto-MT is the *Vorlage* of OG/LXX here. Hans Hübner, *Gottes Ich und Israel: Zum Schriftgebrauch des Paulus in Römer 9–11* (FRLANT 136; Göttingen: Vandenhoeck & Ruprecht, 1984), 58 offers an opposing position on textual form, asserting that Paul cites Isa 1.9^{LXX}, and noting that the Greek tradition is 'unterschiedlich gegenüber MT'.
[114] See BDB, 590.

of any phrase including שריד and/or כמעט.[115] However, the translator's use of σπέρμα does not defy logic. This is a probable example of an explicative translation: the translator clarified the identity of the 'little remainder'. They are a 'seed'.[116] Gottfried Quell suggests that this is an example of a 'very free' translation in light of the proto-MT that highlights Israel's covenantal unfaithfulness.[117] He is correct insofar as he recognizes that the OG moves beyond its *Vorlage* in specifying the identity of this group, and that this interpretation creates a semantic difference between sources. Regardless of the translator's ideology, the proto-MT (= 1QIsaᵃ in this locution) is the *V*OG of Isa 1.9.

It is precisely this difference between traditions that sheds light on the *Vorlage* of the citation in Rom 9.29. Although Isa 1.9ᴾᴹ and Rom 9.29 are similar syntactically and semantically, Rom 9.29 witnesses the OG's interpretative translation σπέρμα. In addition to reflecting this specific reading, Rom 9.29 is a *verbatim citation* of Isa 1.9ᴼᴳ by every text-linguist measure.[118] Paul is clearly familiar with the wording of Isa 1.9ᴼᴳ.

Paul's citation in Rom 9.29 demonstrates that he is familiar with Isaiahᴼᴳ as he cites the Greek text verbatim, introducing it with the introductory formula καὶ καθὼς προείρηκεν Ἡσαΐας. However, four verses later, Paul's citation of Isa 8.14 and 28.16 suggests that he also knows the specific semantic sense that is reflected in *only* Isa 8.16ᴾᴹ. Furthermore, the reference to the proto-MT is conflated with a reference to Isa 28.16ᴼᴳ. Paul seems to demonstrate an awareness of multiple textual forms of the book of Isaiah, or at least various semantic contours that the various forms of the text embody. Before moving on to explore the textual tradition of Zechariah specifically, it is helpful to examine one further example of textual variation within NT quotations.

---

[115] See HRCS 1282–1283. HRCS marks σπέρμα in Isa 1.9 with an obelus suggesting that the word is a paraphrase of its translational equivalent – שריד כמעט. Interestingly, α witnesses λεῖμμα, a translation which is faithful to the proto-MT and lacking any interpretation of the source text.

[116] This identification corresponds to the employment of זרע in the HB, a term that carries covenantal connotations. See H. D. Preuss, 'זרע', in *Theological Dictionary of the Old Testament* (vol. 4; ed. G. J. Botterweck and H. Ringgren; trans. D. E. Green; Grand Rapids: Eerdmans, 1980), 154.

[117] Gottfried Quell, 'σπέρμα', in *Theological Dictionary of the New Testament* (vol. 7; ed. G. Friedrich; trans. G. W. Bromiley; Grand Rapids: Eerdmans, 1971), 540.

[118] See also J. Ross Wagner, 'Isaiah in Romans and Galatians', in *Isaiah in the New Testament* (ed. S. Moyise and M. J. J. Menken; London: T&T Clark, 2005), 110–111; Beate Kowalski, 'Zur Funktion der Schriftzitate in Röm 9,19–20', in *The Letter to the Romans* (BETL 226; ed. U. Schnelle; Leuven: Peeters, 2009), 729.

2.5.3 Mark's Use of Isaiah

Mark's use of scripture, and Isaiah in particular, is extensive.[119] Within his many scriptural references, there is evidence that Mark quoted from and referenced different textual forms. First, I analyse the textual form of Isa 29.13 preserved in Mark 7.6–7.

Mark 7.6–7[120] οὗτος ὁ λαὸς τοῖς χείλεσίν με τιμᾷ, ἡ δὲ καρδία αὐτῶν
πόρρω ἀπέχει ἀπ᾽ ἐμοῦ· μάτην δὲ σέβονταί με
διδάσκοντες διδασκαλίας ἐντάλματα ἀνθρώπων

'This people honour me with lips but their heart is far off from me and they worship me in futility, teaching instructions and commandments of men.'

Isa 29.13^OG Καὶ εἶπε κύριος Ἐγγίζει μοι ὁ λαὸς οὗτος τοῖς χείλεσιν
αὐτῶν τιμῶσί με, ἡ δὲ καρδία αὐτῶν πόρρω ἀπέχει
ἀπ᾽ ἐμοῦ, μάτην δὲ σέβονταί με διδάσκοντες ἐντάλματα
ἀνθρώπων καὶ διδασκαλίας

And (the) Lord said, 'This people draw near to me, with their lips they honour me, but their heart (is) far off from me, and they worship me in futility, teaching commandments of men and instruction.'

Isa 29.13^PM ויאמר אדני יען כי נגש העם הזה בפיו ובשפתיו כבדוני ולבו רחק ממני
ותהי יראתם אתי מצות אנשים מלמדה

And my Lord said that, 'this people drew near with their mouth and with their lip they glorified me. But their heart was far from me and their worship of me (is like) the trained command of men.'

The *Vorlage* of Isa 29.13^OG is quite similar to proto-MT. However, significant quantitative differences between the texts are present that cannot be accounted for in terms of translation technique. First, the word בפיו ('with his mouth') is absent in the translation. Second, the dative pronoun μοι does not have an equivalent in proto-MT. If the pronoun was in the genitive (μου) and modified κύριος, then the use of the pronoun would cohere with proto-MT. Third, the translator included the word μάτην ('futile'), an equivalent for which is not present in proto-MT. However, the word וַתְּהִי, a third-person feminine singular form of היה as read by the Masoretes, is graphically similar

---

[119] See O'Brien, *Use of Scripture*, 203–289.

[120] M. Eugene Boring, *Mark: A Commentary* (NTL; London: WJK, 2006), 200 and Robert H. Stein, *Mark* (BECNT; Grand Rapids: Baker, 2008), 341 confirm this reference.

to וּתֹהוּ ('formless, confusion').[121] While תהו was translated four times as μάταιος ('vain, empty') within Isaiah,[122] there are no extant examples of μάτην translating תהו. It is possible that the OG translator read תהו for תהי and made a unique translation of it. Either way, this rendering is unique among our remaining evidence. This fact, along with the absence of an equivalent for בפיו and the confusion in personal pronoun, suggest that, while the *Vorlage* of this locution was similar to the proto-MT, it may have differed in detail.[123]

Which textual form, then, did the evangelist quote in Mark 7.6–7? In this case, the source text is undeniably the OG.[124] Despite minor differentiation in word order, large portions of this quotation match verbatim to the OG family. The only quantitative differences between these two texts are the evangelist's omissions of the first instance of αὐτῶν and καί in the final clause. Also, Mark 7.6–7 agrees with OG where it differs with proto-MT. The evangelist did not include an equivalent of בפיו and μάτην is included in the Gospel text. It is unlikely that the evangelist would have made an identical unique translation as the OG translator – specifically the unique renderings of μάτην. The unlikeliness of this is even more pronounced when the possibility that the OG translator misread a word in his *Vorlage* is considered, especially since there is no evidence for this reading in any Hebrew witnesses.[125] Mark's transmission of the OG's confusion (or exploitation) of *yod* and *waw* similarity, and the citation's nearly verbatim correlation to Isa

---

[121] BDB, 1067.

[122] Isa 44.9; 45.19; 49.4; 59.4.

[123] Ronald L. Troxel, *LXX-Isaiah as Translation and Interpretation: The Strategies of the Translator of the Septuagint of Isaiah* (JSJsup 124; Leiden: Brill, 2008), 73–85 states that 'reconstructing a translators *Übersetzungsweise* would be a simple matter if the translation were consistently transparent to the MT, but that is seldom the case and is certainly not true for LXX-Isaiah' (74). Also, he concludes 'that LXX-Isaiah both contains interpretive elements and attests variants [from proto-MT]' (75). Rikki E. Watts, *Isaiah's New Exodus and Mark* (WUNT 2.88; Tübingen: Mohr Siebeck, 1997), 213 argues that the awkward construction ותהי יראתם suggests that the proto-MT of this locution may witness a secondary, although ancient, reading in comparison to the OG.

[124] Watts, *New Exodus*, 211 and Morna D. Hooker, 'Isaiah in Mark's Gospel' in *Isaiah in the New Testament* (ed. S. Moyise and M. J. J. Menken; London: T&T Clark, 2005), 39 confirm that the *Vorlage* for this quotation is Isaiah[OG].

[125] The only Judean Desert manuscript that witnesses Isa 29.13 is 1QIsaᵃ which reads ותהיה – a third person feminine singular *waw* consecutive imperfect verb with the plene spelling.

29.13^{OG} strongly suggest that this textual form was the source for the quotation. Kelli O'Brien concurs: 'Mark may have quoted directly from his Greek MS.'[126] The author of Mark used the OG family of texts to craft this citation. A second example, however, indicates that Mark also quoted from the semantic streams represented by the Hebrew textual traditions of Isaiah.

Mark 13.25   καὶ οἱ ἀστέρες ἔσονται ἐκ τοῦ οὐρανοῦ πίπτοντες, καὶ αἱ
δυνάμεις αἱ ἐν τοῖς οὐρανοῖς σαλευθήσονται

And the stars will fall from heaven and the armies in the heavens will be shaken.

Isa 34.4^{OG} καὶ ἑλιγήσεται ὁ οὐρανὸς ὡς βιβλίον, καὶ πάντα τὰ ἄστρα
πεσεῖται ὡς φύλλα ἐξ ἀμπέλου καὶ ὡς πίπτει φύλλα
ἀπὸ συκῆς

And the heavens will roll up as a scroll and all the *stars will fall* as a leaf from the vine and as a leaf fell from a fig.

Isa 34.4^{pM} ונמקו כל־צבא השמים ונגלו כספר השמים וכל־צבאם יבול כנבל עלה מגפן
וכנבלת מתאנה

And all the heavenly bodies will moulder and the heavens will roll up like a scroll and all creation will wither as a withering leaf of the vine and a withering fig.

1QIsa^a 34.4[127]   והעמקים יתבקעו וכול צבא השמים יפולו ונגלו כספר השמים וכול צבאם
יבול כנובל עלה מגופן וכנובלת מן תאנה

And the valleys will be cleft and all the heavenly bodies *will fall* and the heavens will roll up like a scroll and all creation will wither as a withering leaf of the vine and as one that withers from a fig.

The quotation in Mark 13.25 does not correspond exactly with any known form of Isa 34.4 but obvious verbal parallels are present.[128] The textual forms of Isa 34.4 differ significantly from one another, and each presents unique readings. First, it is clear that the *V*OG is not proto-MT. The OG does not witness the first clause in proto-MT (ונמקו כל־צמא השמים). Also, the translation of τὰ ἄστρα for צבאם is rare, occurring only one other time in the OG/LXX tradition.[129] This

---

[126] O'Brien, *Use of Scripture*, 205.

[127] Text from John C. Trever, 'The Isaiah Scroll', in *The Dead Sea Scrolls of St. Mark's Monastery: The Isaiah Manuscript and Habakkuk Commentary* (vol. 1; ed. M. Burrows and J. C. Trever; New Haven, CT: American Schools of Oriental Research, 1950) and Ulrich, *Biblical Qumran Scrolls*, 396.

[128] Boring, *Mark*, 372, 406; Stein, *Mark*, 612; C. S. Mann, *Mark* (AB 27; Garden City, NY: Doubleday, 1986), 531 confirm that Mark 13.25 does draw material from Isa 34.4.

[129] Cf. Isa 45.12.

translation is not semantically impossible, but specifies particular celestial bodies instead of heavenly bodies in general. Finally, there is semantic incongruity in equating πεσεῖται with יבול. There is no other example of a form of πίπτω translating נב"ל. It is possible that the translator confused נבל ('to wither') with נפל ('to fall'), but it is more likely that the translator used a different *Vorlage* for his rendering of this locution – especially considering that נפל is witnessed in 1QIsaᵃ.

Although the OG and 1QIsaᵃ share this specific reading, it is unlikely that 1QIsaᵃ as it stands represents the *V*OG. First, 1QIsaᵃ is quantitatively longer that proto-MT and witnesses the locution והעמקים יתבקעו ('and the valleys will be cleft') at the beginning of the verse. If 1QIsaᵃ is the *V*OG, the translation is quantitatively divergent from the source text – even more so than if its *Vorlage* was proto-MT. Also, although both texts describe the 'stars' or 'heavenly bodies' *falling*, the corresponding verbs are found at different places in the locution. In relation to proto-MT, 1QIsaᵃ includes יפולו in the midst of השמים and ונגל. The retroverted *V*OG reads יפול where 1QIsaᵃ reads יבול in agreement with proto-MT.

The textual history of Isa 34.4 is complex. Nevertheless, the question remains: which text form did the author of Mark use to craft this reference?[130] The reference in Mark does not correspond exactly to any known text form, indicating that the author of Mark altered the source locution in the process of incorporating it into his own composition. Despite this complication, the evidence intimates that the Markan evangelist reused material from multiple textual forms.[131] First, the presence of the phrase οἱ ἀστέρες (Mark 13.25) points to the conclusion that the evangelist referenced the OG in this instance. As previously mentioned, the only two times that any form of ἀστήρ translates צבא occur in Isa 34.4 and 45.12, signifying either that the author of Mark translated צבא exactly the same as the translator of Isaiah^OG or that the evangelist was aware of the Greek text. Based on the evidence of his previous awareness of the OG tradition, it is likely that the inclusion of οἱ

---

[130] Regarding the Synoptic problem, it must be noted that the apodosis of this locution in Mark is not unique. It is of the triple tradition as it is witnessed in both Luke 21.26 and Matt 24.29, although not verbatim. Matthew also references the stars falling from heaven. In all likelihood, both Matthew and Luke reused Markan material.

[131] These particular readings may have been inscribed on a single exemplar, but they represent different textual forms insofar as the traditions have been transmitted to us.

ἀστέρες is evidence of the author's reliance upon OG. However, his description of the heavenly host in the apodosis as αἱ δυνάμεις suggests that the evangelist is also aware of a Hebrew tradition, most likely a tradition similar to 1QIsaᵃ because it includes the verb יפולו in reference to the heavenly bodies (in contrast to the proto-MT stream). The phrase αἱ δυνάμεις αἱ ἐν τοῖς οὐρανοῖς ('the heavenly armies') is closely related to the phrase צמא השמים ('heavenly bodies/armies') – δυνάμεις is the prevalent translation of צמא in the OG/LXX tradition.[132] The idea of heavenly armies or powers is notably absent in the OG as ὁ οὐρανός and τὰ ἄστρα are the translations of צמא השמים and צבאם. The reference to heavenly powers or armies in the Mark 13.25 suggests that the author cited a Hebrew text similar to 1QIsaᵃ.

In sum, the preceding information supports the conclusion that the author of Mark quoted different textual forms of Isaiah in the process of composing this quotation. In 7.6–7 he explicitly cites Isa 29.13ᴼᴳ, matching the source text almost word for word. In contrast, his quotation in 13.25 differs from all extant text forms, but the textual data intimates that he drew from *both* the OG and a Hebrew text – probably a text similar to 1QIsaᵃ. Even if the *Vorlage* of the reference in Mark 13.25 cannot be identified with certainty, it is clear that Isaiahᴼᴳ is not the sole textual source of the reference. The author of Mark was aware of multiple textual traditions of Isaiah.

The textual evidence from Qumran implies that the text of Jewish scripture in the late Second Temple period circulated concurrently in multiple forms. The preceding examples indicate that multiple early Christian authors were aware of and referenced different textual forms of the same book within a single composition, or at least that they were aware of the various semantic contours that different text families preserve. Early Christian writers encoded various Jewish scriptural traditions in diverse forms in their own works. This evidence suggests that a similar pattern of scriptural referencing might also be operative in the use of Zechariah in the book of Revelation. The first step to determine whether John used multiple forms of Zechariah is to examine the ancient manuscript evidence of the Book of the Twelve.

---

[132] HRCS, 350–352.

2.6 Textual Pluriformity, Material Culture, and Zechariah

2.6.1 The Book of the Twelve

Thus far, I have argued that many scriptural works existed in a pluriform state in the first century and that ancient authors referenced multiple forms of the same book within single compositions. I now want to narrow the area of enquiry to the ancient evidence of Zechariah. What does the remaining manuscript evidence of Zechariah suggest about the possibility that it circulated in differing textual forms, and what conclusions can be drawn about possible sources for John's scriptural references to Zechariah?

In antiquity Zechariah was not transmitted as an independent work, but as part of the corpus of the Twelve; or, at least, it was transmitted along with other prophetic works that came to be associated with the Book of the Twelve.[133] The ancient manuscript evidence of the Twelve is fragmentary and Zechariah is not extant in each 4QXII manuscript. However, the evidence suggests that the Twelve circulated as a single, although not static, literary unit in antiquity.[134] The realities of transmission expand our search, first, to the entirety of the ancient textual evidence of the Twelve. A complete table of manuscript evidence for the Book of the Twelve found in the Judean Desert follows.[135]

---

[133] Armin Lange, *Handbuch der Textfunde vom Toten Meer* (vol. 1; Tübingen: Mohr Siebeck, 2009), 335 argues that every copy of the Twelve at Qumran once contained the entirety of the corpus (with the possible exception of 5QXII [Amos]).

[134] Barry Alan Jones, *The Formation of the Book of the Twelve: A Study on Text and Canon* (SBLDiss 149; Atlanta: Scholars, 1995), 2. See also Clay Alan Ham, 'The Minor Prophets in Matthew's Gospel', in *The Minor Prophets in the New Testament* (LNTS 377; ed. M. J. J. Menken and S. Moyise; London: T&T Clark, 2009), 39. Russell Fuller, 'Textual Traditions in the Book of Hosea and the Minor Prophets', in *The Madrid Qumran Congress: Proceedings of the International Congress on the Dead Sea Scrolls Madrid 18–21 March, 1991* (STDJ 11; ed. J. Trebolle Barrera and L. Vegas Montaner; Leiden: Brill, 1992), 247 suggests that each of the 4QXII manuscripts likely contained complete copies of the Minor Prophets.

[135] The 'Textual Affiliation' column is based on the data in Russell E. Fuller, 'The Biblical Prophetic Manuscript from the Judaean Desert', in *Prophecy after the Prophets? The Contribution of the Dead Sea Scrolls to the Understanding of Biblical and Extra-Biblical Prophecy* (CBET 52; ed. K. De Troyer and A. Lange; Leuven: Peeters, 2009), 4–5. See also the chart in Takamitsu Muraoka, 'Introduction aux Douze Petits Prophètes', in *Les Douze Prophètes: Osée* (LBA 23.1; ed. E. Bons, J. Joosten, and S. Kessler; Paris: Éditions du Cerf, 2002), iv. In this article and in 'Textual Traditions', 253 (esp. n. 18), Fuller emphasizes the numerous Hebrew textual traditions of the Minor Prophets at Qumran. He is correct, based on extant evidence, that readings in

Table 2.1 *Manuscript evidence for the Book of the Twelve from the Judean Desert*

Manuscript	Books Preserved	Textual Affiliation
4QXII[a]	Zechariah, Malachi, Jonah	Non-aligned
4QXII[b]	Zephaniah, Haggai	Proto-MT
4QXII[c1]	Hosea, Joel, Amos, Zephaniah, Malachi	Non-aligned
4QXII[d]	Hosea 1.6–2.5	Possibly non-aligned/ proto-MT[2]
4QXII[e]	Haggai, Zechariah	Close to *V*OG/LXX
4QXII[f]	Jonah 1.6–8, 10–16; Micah 5.1–2	Possibly proto-MT
4QXII[g]	Hosea, Joel, Amos, Obadiah, Jonah, Micah, Nahum, Habakkuk, Zephaniah, Zechariah	Non-aligned
5QXII (5Q4)[3]	Amos	Too fragmentary to classify
MurXII[4]	Joel, Amos, Obadiah, Jonah, Micah, Nahum, Habakkuk, Zephaniah, Haggai, Zechariah	Proto-MT
8HevXIIgr[5]	Jonah, Micah, Nahum, Habakkuk, Zephaniah, Zechariah	Non-aligned (recension of OG)

[1] For helpful insights into some of the scribal habits exhibited in these manuscripts, specifically in 4QXII[c], see Hanne von Weissenberg, 'Changing Scripture? Scribal Corrections in MS 4QXII[c]', in *Changes in Scripture: Rewriting and Interpreting Authoritative Traditions in the Second Temple Period* (BZAW 419; ed. H. von Weissenberg et al.; Berlin: De Gruyter, 2011), 247–271.

[2] Heinz-Josef Fabry, 'The Reception of Nahum and Habakkuk in the Septuagint and Qumran', in *Emanuel: Studies in the Hebrew Bible, Septuagint and Dead Sea Scrolls in Honor of Emanuel Tov* (VTsup 94; ed. S. M. Paul et al.; Leiden: Brill, 2003) notes that this manuscript is close to proto-MT.

[3] See DJD III, plate XXXVI; Lange, *Handbuch*, 342–343.

[4] See DJD II, lvi–lxxiii. The variations between Mur88 and MT have been catalogued in Russell Fuller, 'The Form and Formation of the Book of the Twelve: The Evidence from the Judean Desert', in *Forming Prophetic Literature: Essays on Isaiah and the Twelve in Honor of John D. W. Watts* (JSOTsup 235; ed. J. W. Watts and P. R. House; Sheffield: Sheffield Academic Press, 1996), 88–89 n. 5.

[5] See DJD VIII. Additionally, it has been argued by some that 7Q5 is fragment that preserves Zech 7.3c–5 (see M. V. Spottorno, 'Can Methodological Limits be set in the Debate on the Identification of 7Q5', *DSD* 6 [1999]: 66–77], although others have noted that the text might be a Greek version of *1 En.* 15.9 or even Mark 6.52–53! (see J. O'Callaghan, '¿Papiros neotestamentarios en la cueva 7 de Qumran?' *Biblica* 53 [1972]: 91–100). Even if this material is considered to contain material from Zechariah, its fragmentary state offers little value to this discussion.

Russell Fuller suggests that the very fragmentary nature of the vast majority of these manuscripts requires caution when attempting to assign textual affiliation to the manuscripts.[136] This caution is certainly valid. Nonetheless, the textual evidence suggests that 'there is textual diversity and there is no unambiguous evidence that any one type of text was favored over another.'[137] According to Fuller, among the manuscripts found in the Judean Desert at least four textual forms are discernible: 1. proto-MT family (MurXII[138]; 4QXII[b, f]); 2. The *Vorlage* of OG[139] (4QXII[e] [= proto-MT?]); 3. The earliest known recension of OG (8HevXIIgr); 4. Various non-aligned

---

the 4QXII manuscripts do at times underlie readings known only from the OG/LXX translation or are independent of proto-MT and OG/LXX. However, based on the extant evidence alone it is difficult to discern clearly divergent textual traditions, only a collection of variants that move in multiple directions of textual affiliation. See DJD XV, 221–318. I have not included the small 4QMicah fragment in this list (cf. R. Fuller, '4QMicah: A Small Fragment of a Manuscript of the Minor Prophets from Qumran, Cave IV', *RevQ* 16 [1993]: 193–202).

[136]   Russell Fuller, 'Minor Prophets', in *EDSS* 1.555.

[137]   Ibid.

[138]   Regarding MurXII and its relation to the proto-MT family, Dominique Barthélemy, *Critique Textuelle de l'Ancien Testament: Ézéchiel, Daniel et les 12 Prophètes* (vol. 3; Göttingen: Vandenhoeck & Ruprecht, 1992), states that 'Notons d'emblée que, *sur 3605 mots plus ou moins identifiables, on ne relève que 42 variantes* par rapport au [MT] tel que l'édite BH3. *Cette proportion ne dépasse pas la proportion de variantes qu'offrent certains témoins du [MT] . . . Aucune de ces variantes ne dépasse en importance celle qui distinguent des mss médiévaux de [MT]'* (the emphasis belongs to Barthélemy). See also Young, 'Stabilization', 373 who notes that MurXII varies from L once every 222 words, while 4QXII[f], which is clearly part of the proto-MT family, differs on average every 41 words from L.

[139]   See Russell Fuller, 'The Minor Prophets Manuscripts from Qumran, Cave IV' (PhD Diss., Harvard University, 1988), 140. However, George J. Brooke, 'The Twelve Minor Prophets and the Dead Sea Scrolls', in *Congress Volume Leiden 2004* (VTsup 109; ed. A. Lemaire; Leiden: Brill, 2006), 24 prefers to classify this manuscript as non-aligned. Also, as some have argued, the *Vorlage* of Zechariah[OG] likely shared many textual characteristics with Zechariah[PM] (see C. Dogniez, 'La reconstruction du Temple selon la Septante de *Zacharie*', in *Congress Volume Leiden 2004* [VTsup 109; ed. A. Lemaire; Leiden: Brill, 2006], 52). As the analyses from Chapter 3 suggest, where the author of Revelation references Zechariah, the proto-MT is close to, if not synonymous with, the *V*OG. Jan Joosten, 'A Septuagintal Translation Technique in the Minor Prophets: The Elimination of Verbal Repetitions' in *Interpreting Translation: Studies on the LXX and Ezekiel in Honour of Johan Lust* (BETL 192; ed. F. García Martínez and M. Vervenne; Leuven: Peters, 2005), 217 suggests that the 'best way to characterize the approach of the translator [of the Twelve] is to say that it is creatively faithful' and he suggests that the *Vorlage* of the translation is the proto-MT. Muraoka, 'Introduction', ix–x indicates that the translation of the entirety of the Twelve (including Zechariah) was undertaken by a single translator. This view is confirmed by Arie van der Kooij, 'The Septuagint to

texts (4QXII[a, c, d, g]).[140] Barry Alan Jones highlights 4QXII[a] specifically as an example of a 'variant literary edition', although the term 'variant' might not be appropriate since it is the oldest manuscript of the Book of the Twelve (150–100 BCE).[141] Some issues remain, however, with Fuller's analysis. First, the distinction between the proto-MT and *V*OG category is somewhat artificial. There is wide agreement that the *V*OG of Zechariah is *very close* to (if not identical with) the consonantal framework of the MT, which makes the category distinction less decisive. Arie van der Kooij argues that differences between the proto-MT and OG of the Twelve can be explained as interpretations by the OG translator; he assumes a proto-MT *Vorlage*.[142] James Palmer finds that 'the LXX rarely witness to a text other than that of the MT' and 'more frequently than not, the divergences between MT and LXX are differences of understanding'.[143] To complete the sense of consensus, Jan Joosten notes that 'the *Vorlage* of the translator [of the Twelve] corresponds broadly to the Massoretic Text, at least in quantitative terms.'[144] Based on the evidence currently

Zechariah as Witness to an Early Interpretation of the Book', in *The Book of Zechariah and its Influence* (ed. Christopher Tuckett; Hampshire, UK: Ashgate, 2003), 53–64; James K. Palmer, '"Not made with Tracing Paper": Studies in the Septuagint of Zechariah', *TB* 57 no 2 (2006): 320; Thomas Pola, 'The Greek Text of Zechariah: A Document From Maccabean Jerusalem?' in *Tradition in Transition: Haggai and Zechariah 1–8 in the Trajectory of Hebrew Theology* (LHBOTS 475; ed. M. Boda and M. Floyd; London: T&T Clark, 2008), 291–300; Pola, 'Sach 9,9–17[LXX] – Indiz für die Entstehung des griechischen Dodekaprophetons im makkabäischen Jerusalem', in *La Septante en Allemagne et en France: Textes de la Septante à Traduction Double ou à Traduction très Littérale* (OBO 238; ed. W. Kraus and O. Munnich; Göttingen: Vandenhoeck & Ruprecht, 2009), 238–251.

[140] Brooke, 'The Twelve', 32 suggests 4QXII[c] is very close to the *V*OG.

[141] Jones, *Formation*, 7. See also Fuller, 'Minor Prophets', 555. Ulrich, 'Qumran', 55 also acknowledges textual variation in the manuscript evidence of the Twelve from Cave 4. Fabry, 'Reception', 246 suggests that 4QXII[a] 'predates a formation of the Masoretic text and signifies a stage in which the twelve minor prophets were not yet textually finalized'.

[142] van der Kooij, 'Septuagint', 53–64.

[143] Palmer, 'Tracing Paper', 294; Pola, 'Sach 9,9–17[LXX]', 238–251; Myrto Theocharous, *Lexical Dependence and Intertextual Allusion in the Septuagint of the Twelve Prophets: Studies in Hosea, Amos and Micah* (LHBOTS 570; London: T&T Clark, 2012), 9; G. E. Howard, 'To the Reader of the Twelve Prophets', in *NETS*, 777. Tov, *Textual Criticism*, 126–139. This is true with the exception of Hosea. See A. A. Macintosh, *Hosea* (ICC; Edinburgh: T&T Clark, 1997), lxxiv–lxxix.

[144] Jan Joosten, *Collected Essays on the Septuagint* (FAT 83; Tübingen: Mohr Siebeck, 2012), 21.

available, it is all but certain that the *Vorlage* of Zechariah[OG] is similar to the proto-MT. With reference to 4QXII[e] specifically, while this manuscript preserves readings that agree with OG against proto-MT,[145] many of the parallels with OG rely on textual reconstruction of questionably legible letters or are based on minor morphological differences. In my estimation 4QXII[e] belongs in the proto-MT family, against Fuller's argument that it is part of the *V*OG family, especially in light of the fact that the labels proto-MT and *V*OG describe highly similar textual traditions.[146]

Second, Fuller's assignment of manuscripts to a 'non-aligned' category raises similar questions. 4QXII[a, c, d, g] differ from proto-MT family of texts in numerous places. These differences are largely due to issues of orthography, metathesis, *waw* elision, sibilant interchange, and a variety of (mostly) minor morphosyntactic structures. Many of these variants rely, at least partially, on editorial reconstructions. While one must acknowledge some variation, larger scale textual differences (e.g. large pluses, minuses, or rearrangements vis-à-vis the proto-MT) are not witnessed (although small quantitative differences do occasionally occur in this manuscript group).[147] Despite these small-scale differences, it is difficult to see how this group differs significantly from proto-MT or what criteria might determine, in this sense, an alternative textual form. In my estimation, these manuscripts are exemplars of the proto-MT in a highly fluid copying environment. They largely reflect the proto-MT but retain small-scale[148] textual differences that evidence malleability in transmission, copying, presentation, and reading. Elements of the Hebrew text of the Twelve demonstrate a subtle desire to facilitate understanding, creating a level of fluidity in the wording of manuscripts. Nevertheless, the variations in wording preserved in the 4QXII manuscripts do not provide decisive evidence of pluriformity within the Hebrew manuscripts of the Book of the Twelve. The evidence from the 4QXII manuscripts (along with MurXII) presents a fluid text of the Twelve, but also suggests that one overarching Hebrew textual form of the Twelve (proto-MT) existed in this period.[149]

---

[145] E.g. ומשיתי = ψηλαφήσω vs. ומשתי (proto-MT) in Zech 3.9.

[146] So Lange, *Handbuch*, 339.

[147] See Hos 12.10(9) in 4QXII[g] for example.

[148] By 'small-scale' I refer to quantitatively small differences, in reference to the number of grapheme on a page.

[149] Jong-Hoon Kim, 'Die hebräischen Textformen der hellenistische-frühjüdischen Zeit: Ausgehend vom Habakuk-Text der griechischen Zwölfprophetenrolle aus Nahal Hever (8HevXIIgr)', in *Text – Textgeschichte – Textwirkung: Festschrift zum 65.*

Regardless of how these manuscripts are classified, it is clear that the textual variation of the Twelve moves in two directions, internal and external to the proto-MT family: 1. Internally, the proto-MT family remained fluid in this period. The wording of MurXII and the probable proto-MT (or 'MT-like' texts = Fuller's 'non-aligned') texts from Qumran (4QXII $^{a-g}$) do not agree completely in all points of detail.[150] 2. External to the proto-MT family, the textual characteristics of 8HevXIIgr (see below) indicate that the Greek text of the Twelve was pluriform in this period. Both OG and early Greek revisions towards a particular Hebrew form circulated during the end of the first century BCE. The ancient manuscripts of the Twelve strongly suggest that the Hebrew text of the Twelve was fluid, although related to the proto-MT, and that multiple Greek forms of the Twelve circulated concomitantly in the late Second Temple period. The Greek forms of the Twelve revolve around the features of the proto-MT, as the *V*OG was likely stood within the (fluid) proto-MT tradition and the revising traditions (exemplified most clearly by the text of 8HevXIIgr) altered the existing OG tradition towards a more literal adherence to the wording of the proto-MT. In this way, the proto-MT tradition is the anchor of the textual history of the Twelve, although a decided level of variation (in Hebrew and Greek) existed in the late Second Temple period.

Despite the shared reliance on the text of the proto-MT, the Twelve were pluriform within the Greek tradition as I have noted. This reality is best illustrated by examining two pre-Hexaplaric manuscripts and

---

Geburtstag von Sigfried Kreuzer (Alter Orient und Altes Testament 419; ed. T. Wagner, J. M. Robker, and F. Ueberschaer; Münster: Ugarit Verlag, 2014), 347–357 argues that the Hebrew textual tradition of Habakkuk was not 'standardized' (*vereinheitlich*) in the first century BCE, a point that I would agree with. Although his assertion that this fluidity of wording indicates the presences of distinct Hebrew *Textformen* is questionable.

[150] No two manuscripts that comprise the MT-family (from antiquity and the Middle Ages) are exactly alike. For information on the development of the (proto-) MT, see Tov, 'The Dead Sea Scrolls and the Textual History of the Masoretic Bible', in *The Hebrew Bible in Light of the Dead Sea Scrolls* (FRLANT 239; ed. N. Dávid et al.; Göttingen: Vandenhoeck & Ruprecht, 2012), 41–53 where he suggests a theory regarding the four-stage development of the (proto-) MT family. Beyond internal textual development, the textual characteristics of the works that constitute the Twelve are an aggregate that differ according to book. See Teeter, *Scribal Laws*, 264 and John Van Seters, 'Did the *Sopherim* Create a Standard Edition of the Hebrew Scriptures?' in *The Text of the Hebrew Bible: From the Rabbis to the Masoretes* (JAJsup 13; ed. E. Martín-Contreras and L. Miralles-Maciá; Göttingen: Vandenhoeck & Ruprecht, 2014), 47–61 (esp. 58–61).

the OG translation: 8HevXIIgr[151] and the Washington Manuscript of the Minor Prophets (W),[152] in addition to Zeigler's reconstructed OG text.[153] Traditionally, 8HevXIIgr has been viewed as a 'nouvelle recension du texte grec'.[154] This manuscript is undeniably pre-Hexaplaric and its date has gradually moved earlier as it has spent more time in the hands of scholars. Barthélemy dated the manuscript to between 70 and 135 CE arguing that it represented 'très vraisemblablement, dans ce qu'elles ont d'original, une recension rabbinique de la Septante qui avait cours entre 70 et 135'.[155] He based this conclusion largely on its close correspondence to Justin Martyr's quotations of the Twelve in *Dialogue with Trypho* and the supposed superiority of the proto-MT in this period. Paul Kahle, following the palaeographic analysis of C. H. Roberts, opined that the manuscript was produced between 50 BCE and 50 CE.[156] Peter Parsons narrowed Kahle's suggestion even further, tentatively arguing that none of the palaeographic features of the manuscript require a first century CE date while many suggest that it was composed in the first century BCE.[157]

---

[151] Also known as 8Hev1 and Rahlfs 943.

[152] I follow Rahlfs designation. The manuscript is also known as Washington MS V, Kenyon X, van Haelst 284. For a detailed introduction to the Freer Collection see Kent D. Clarke, 'Paleography and Philanthropy: Charles Lang Freer and His Acquisition of the "Freer Biblical Manuscripts", in *The Freer Biblical Manuscripts: Fresh Studies of an American Treasure Trove* (TCS 6; ed. L. W. Hurtado; Leiden: Brill, 2006), 17–73.

[153] The reconstructed OG text is represented throughout this discussion by Joseph Ziegler, ed., *Duodecim Prophetae* (VTG 13; Göttingen: Vandenhoeck & Ruprecht, 1943).

[154] Dominique Barthélemy, 'Redécouverte d'un chaînon manquant de l'histoire de la Septante', *RB* 60 no 1 (1953): 20. For the provenance of this manuscript see Y. Aharoni, 'Expedition B – The Cave of Horror', *IEJ* 12 no 3/4 (1961): 186–199 and B. Lifshitz, 'The Greek Documents from the Cave of Horror', *IEJ* 12 no 3/4 (1961): 201–207. Julio Trebolle, 'A "Canon Within a Canon": Two Series of Old Testament Books Differently Transmitted, Interpreted and Authorized', *RevQ* 75 no 19 (2000): 384 notes that this manuscript was of special importance to zealots at Nahal Hever as they 'destroyed by fire all their documents except a well-used copy of this book (8HevXIIgr) that they buried with their dead in the innermost parts of the Cave of Horror'. See also Brook W. R. Pearson, 'The Book of the Twelve, Aqiba's Messianic Interpretations, and the Refuge Caves of the Second Jewish War', in *The Scrolls and the Scriptures: Qumran Fifty Years After* (JSPsup 26; ed. S. E. Porter and C. A. Evans; Sheffield: Sheffield Academic Press, 1997), 221–239.

[155] Barthélemy, 'Redécouverte', 21.

[156] Kahle, *Cairo Geniza*, 226.

[157] Peter J. Parsons, 'Scripts and Their Dates', in *The Greek Minor Prophets Scroll from Nahal Hever (8 Hev XIIgr)* (DJD VIII, 25–26).

Both Barthélemy and Tov agree that this is not a new translation of a Hebrew text from the proto-MT family, but was made to revise the OG translation towards the proto-MT.[158] Based on his impressive amount of textual data, Tov concludes that the text of this manuscript strives for a close adherence to the proto-MT, correcting some instances where the OG tradition erred in sufficiently representing the features of this tradition. 8HevXIIgr does agree with proto-MT against OG on fifty-nine occasions, but it also agrees with OG against consonantal MT in fourteen readings,[159] signifying that it represents a partial revision towards the text of the proto-MT. It is also likely that its tradition enjoyed wide circulation in antiquity. Tov notes the many similarities between 8HevXIIgr and Hexaplaric evidence, W, and the text quoted by Justin.[160] The recognition of this text's seemingly widespread influence led Barthélemy to suggest that 8HevXIIgr is perhaps an early version of the Aquilanic recension and to posit the existence of a systematic revision of much of the biblical text[161] of which 8HevXIIgr is the best example: the καιγε recension.[162] While the extent of the circulation of this tradition is tentative, the

---

[158] See DJD VIII, 103. The view that 8HevXIIgr is not an independent translation of a Hebrew *Vorlage* but a revision of OG is still the scholarly consensus, although Fuller, 'Minor Prophets', 555 raises valid issues with the conclusion. He notes that this manuscript does not perfectly correlate to the MT or any known proto-MT manuscript and that to suggest that this a revision towards the proto-MT assumes that the MT is the privileged, authoritative Hebrew text. There is no evidence for this perspective in the first century CE, let alone the first century BCE. However, some scholars (James A. Sanders, 'The Impact of the Judean Desert Scrolls on Issues of Text and Canon of the Hebrew Bible', in *The Bible and the Dead Sea Scrolls* [vol. 1; ed. J. H. Charlesworth; Waco: Baylor University Press, 2006], 31 and Cross, 'Biblical Scrolls', 70 [esp. n. 9] for example) argue that 8HevXIIgr is the earliest evidence of the standardization of the MT. Nonetheless, the fact that a first-century (probably BCE) Greek manuscript that stands between proto-MT and OG exists is rather strong evidence for textual pluriformity.

[159] DJD VIII, 145–146.

[160] Ibid., 158.

[161] This includes much of the Deuteronomic History, Ruth, Lamentations, Daniel, Job, Jeremiah, and perhaps Psalms. See Karen H. Jobes and Moisés Silva, *Invitation to the Septuagint* (Grand Rapids: Baker, 2000), 171–172.

[162] He called this revision καιγε because of the stereotypical translation of the Hebrew particle גם. In *Les Devanciers D'Aquila* (VTsup 10; Leiden: Brill, 1963), 31 Barthélemy suggests that 'Si l'on remarque d'autre part qu'il existe toute une série de livres de la Bible grecque où les traducteurs ou recenseurs se son également appliqués à distinguer גם par καιγε, sans pourtant se préoccuper de traduire la particule d'accusatif.' For further developments on research in relation to the καιγε recension, see Fernández Marcos, *The Septuagint,* 142–154. Sidney Jellicoe, *The Septuagint and Modern Study*

assertion that this manuscript represents a textual form that differs from OG is obvious. The tradition preserved in 8HevXIIgr is another textual form to which John may have had access when composing Revelation.[163] Another pre-Hexaplaric example of a different Greek textual form of the Twelve is found in W. Its editors argue that this early papyrus dates to the mid-to-late third century CE.[164] This manuscript post-dates the composition of the book of Revelation, but it is instructive for understanding the nature of the Greek scriptural text in antiquity and it likely reflects earlier textual traditions. Also, 'in so old a manu-script as this papyrus one may safely assume freedom from the influ-ence of Origen as well as from later editions'.[165]

In terms of the textual character, Sanders and Schmidt suggest that W was deeply influenced by 'the original Hebrew',[166] and that is it quite unique from the uncials[167] and the minuscule manuscripts from the Göttingen apparatus. Of the variants in W, in compari-son to the uncials and later versions, almost 22 per cent of variant readings were unique to W.[168] Sanders and Schmidt attribute this high level of unique readings to a subtle revising of the 'regular Septuagint' towards the 'original Hebrew'. This process of revision is not surprising because 'the pre-Origen text of the Septuagint had had centuries of life and development'.[169] In reference to Jonah in W, Kristin De Troyer concludes that 'the Freer Minor Prophets Codex

---

(Oxford: Clarendon, 1968), 92 closely ties the later Theodontic recension to the καιγε group – 'a group whose work was brought to its climax in the version of Aquila'.

[163] Sigfried Kreuzer, 'Ursprüngliche Septuaginta (Old Greek) und hebraisier-ende Bearbeitung: Die Entwicklung der Septuaginta in ihrer Bedeutung für die Zitate und Anspielungen im Neuen Testament, untersucht anhand der Zitate aus dem Dodekaphropheton', in *Worte der Weissagung: Studien zu Septuaginta und Johannesoffenbarung* (ABG 47; ed. J. Elschenbroich and J. de Vries; Leipzig: Evangelische Verlagsanstalt, 2014), 21 notes 8HevXIIgr is evidence for multi-ple Greek textual forms, which NT authors may have reused.

[164] Henry A. Sanders and Carl Schmidt, *The Minor Prophets in the Freer Collection and the Berlin Fragment of Genesis* (UMSHS XXI; London: Macmillan, 1928), 12. This date is confirmed by Malcolm Choat, 'The Unidentified Text in the Freer Minor Prophets Codex', in *The Freer Biblical Manuscripts: Fresh Studies of an American Treasure Trove* (TCS 6; ed. L. W. Hurtado; Leiden: Brill, 2006), 93.

[165] Sanders and Schmidt, *Minor Prophets*, 25.

[166] By which they certainly mean MT.

[167] A B Q א.

[168] Ibid, 29–30.

[169] Ibid., 38.

offers us a peek at the actual writing *and rewriting* of the Old Greek (OG) text'.[170] W is related to traditions preserved in 8HevXIIgr, but also retains features that suggest it is a further development of the reworking of the Greek tradition.[171]

W stands in a chain of tradition that is parallel but not identical to 8HevXIIgr. 8HevXIIgr, in turn, stands between the OG and proto-MT traditions. Although it is unlikely that John had access to the text of Zechariah witnessed in W, this manuscript is important for this discussion because it illustrates that the Greek text of the Twelve was not fixed or monoform, even into the third century CE. Its many disagreements with OG, 8HevXIIgr, the uncials, and minuscule evidence testifies to the pluriformity and fluidity in the Greek textual traditions of the Twelve. In order to identify properly John's *Vorlage(n)*, we must contend with a pluriform Greek tradition and a fluid Hebrew tradition exemplified by the proto-MT family.

Based on the preceding evidence, the textual situation of the Book of the Twelve in the first century is identical to the textual situation of the rest of the HB and its early Greek versions: it is both pluriform and fluid.[172] Numerous exemplars of the Twelve, in Hebrew and Greek, circulated concurrently in the late Second Temple period. This evidence is crucial for determining the textual options to which the authors of the NT had access, a task that is the foundation for understanding his broader textual culture and the social realities that underlie their habits of text production and uses of scripture.

2.6.2 Zechariah Among the Twelve

In light of this data, it is essential to briefly describe the ancient textual evidence of Zechariah specifically, since each work included in the Twelve also has its own unique textual history. The manuscript evidence from the Judean Desert is as follows.

---

[170] Kristin De Troyer, 'The Freer Twelve Minor Prophets Codex – A Case Study: The Old Greek Text of Jonah, Its Revisions, and Its Corrections', in *The Freer Biblical Manuscripts: Fresh Studies of an American Treasure Trove* (TCS 6; ed. L. W. Hurtado; Leiden: Brill, 2006), 78 (emphasis added).

[171] See ibid. and Bynum, *The Fourth Gospel*, 98.

[172] For a full introduction to the textual witnesses of the Twelve, see *BHQ*, 5–10*.

Table 2.2 *Manuscript evidence for Zechariah from the Judean Desert*

Text	Manuscript
1.1–4, 12–14	8HevXIIgr
1.1–4	MurXII
1.4–6, 9–10, 13–14	4QXII^e
2.2–4, 7–9, 11–12, 16–17 (=OG 1.19–21;	8HevXII gr
2.3–5, 7–8, 12–13)	
2.10–14	4QXII^e
3.1–2, 4–7	8HevXIIgr
3.2–10	4QXII^e
4.1–4	4QXII^e
5.8–11	4QXII^e
6.1–5	4QXII^e
8.2–4, 6–7	4QXII^e
8.19–21, 23–9.5	8HevXIIgr
10.11–11.2, 12.1–3	4QXII^g
12.7–12	4QXII^e
14.8	4QXII^a

The fragmentary remnants of Zech 1.1–4 witnessed in MurXII (50–100 CE) do not differ from the consonantal MT.[173] The text of MurXII will not be referenced individually due to its fragmentary nature and close affiliation with proto-MT. Similarly, the fragmentary preservation of Zech 14.8 in 4QXII^a does not differ in wording from the proto-MT in this instance.

The text of 4QXII^e as a witness to Zechariah is much more interesting. It is one of the oldest copies of the Book of the Twelve (ca. 75 BCE),[174] and its wording sometimes reflects reconstructed formulations of the *V*OG (= proto-MT; see Section 2.6.1).[175] An analysis of the textual data of 4QXII^e itself will take place when the author of Revelation references a text that is witnessed in this manuscript. 4QXII^g, while only preserving parts of fourteen words of Zechariah, does preserve an interesting variant in 10.12, reading יתה[ללו (for יתהלכו), agreeing with the reading preserved in the OG/LXX tradition (κατακαυχήσονται). This reading provides further evidence that the OG/LXX tradition of the Twelve often reflects particular Hebrew readings, even if those readings are not found in the MT. However, I hesitate to identify this manuscript more explicitly with *V*OG as a

---

[173] See Beate Ego et al., eds., *Minor Prophets* (BQ 3b; Leiden: Brill, 2005); Tov, *Textual Criticism*, 29.

[174] Fuller, 'Minor Prophets', 555.

[175] For a summary of the conversation on the textual character of this manuscript, see Lange, *Handbuch*, 339.

distinct form from the proto-MT because their overarching agreements are greater than the sum of the difference of a single grapheme.

As mentioned above, 8HevXIIgr (50 BCE–50 CE) is a Greek manuscript whose text differs in significant ways from the OG, conforming more closely to the proto-MT in its text, division of sense units, and order of Twelve. This manuscript is an important witness to the Greek tradition and I have reconstructed the textual segments referenced by the author of Revelation based on the textual data available in DJD VIII, the Hebrew-Greek Index prepared by Dries de Crom et al., and broader trends in the revising Greek scriptural tradition with special attention to Hexaplaric readings.[176] The (reconstructed) text of this manuscript is referenced where it is relevant to the analyses in the following chapters. The text of W is also referenced when it differs from the OG or 8HevXIIgr.

Beyond the textual characteristics of the Judean Desert forms of Zechariah, the physiognomies of these manuscripts provide evidence for their use and importance in this period, providing insight into the possible mediums by which the author of Revelation may have interfaced with Zechariah and the texts of scriptural works more generally. Textual culture extended beyond the wording of manuscripts to the artefacts themselves and the presentation of their texts (material culture). In the process of examining John's scriptural interpretation and practices of handling antecedent texts, it is important to bear in mind the physical reality of the textual encounter, especially if the source for this encounter is a scriptural manuscript (or a memory thereof) as opposed to a circulating exegetical tradition or a quotation purely from memory. Variable palaeographic practices are recorded in the 4QXII manuscripts, and different representations of graphemes may have stimulated different interpretative actions, based on the different textual connections that the shapes of graphemes may have engendered. Likewise, orthographic practices, particularly in copies where the use of *matres* is sparse, allow morphological ambiguity to seep into the text, providing multiple possibilities for applying particular reading traditions to a locution. Of the manuscripts that preserve Zechariah, the following features are illuminating for

---

[176] See Appendix 2. Dries de Crom, Elke Verbeke, and Reinhart Ceulemans, 'A Hebrew–Greek Index to 8HevXIIgr' *RevQ* 95 no 3 (May 2010): 331–349. E. Peuch's publication of a Greek fragment of Zech 4.8–10 will also be noted where relevant ('Les fragments non identifiés de 8KhXIIgr et le manuscrit grec des Douze Petites Prophètes', *RB* 98 [1991]: 161–169 and Peuch, 'Notes en marge de 8KhXIIgr', *RevQ* 15 [1991–1992]: 583–593).

ancient processes of reading, features that aid in building a more comprehensive portrait of ancient scriptural encounters that eventually culminated in instances of reuse that partially constituted acts of early Christian literary production.

Although 4QXII[a] witnesses only a portion of Zech 14.8 (in addition to sections of Malachi and Jonah), it is the oldest Hebrew manuscript of the Twelve (ca. 150–125 BCE) and, interestingly, seems to include Jonah at the end (or at least near the end) of the manuscript.[177] This reality could indicate the presence of an additional literary edition of the Twelve, presenting a different order to the smaller units of the work as witnessed in the MT (=8HevXIIgr) and the OG tradition. It may not be textually anomalous, but the arrangement of its constituent parts suggests the presence of varying editions or interpretative traditions pertaining to the Twelve as a unit. The varying order of books potentially alters the broader literary context in which Zechariah was encountered, perhaps shaping ancient interpretive engagement. If evidence exists that John read the Twelve as a work, and not merely as individual works transmitted as a corpus, then the arrangement of the Twelve would need to be revisited. At the very least, one should keep in mind that the serial arrangement of the Twelve (particularly Jonah, it appears) remained fluid in this period.

4QXII[e], the primary witness to the Hebrew text of Zechariah in the scrolls, is interesting not only for its text, but for its palaeographic features and collection of corrections (cf. Zech 2.12; 3.5; 5.9 and an unidentified fragment).[178] Corrections, both *prima manu* and later interventions, like those preserved in this exemplar,[179] were a reality of the textual encounter. Although the quantity and style of corrections differed from manuscript to manuscript, these created a level of semantic ambiguity as they usually generated access to the meaning of both layers of traditions: the original reading and the correction.[180] We should not imagine ancient authors engaging pristine

---

[177] Brooke, 'The Twelve', 21–22; DJD XV, 221–222; Lange, *Handbuch*, 336–337.

[178] See Lange, *Handbuch*, 339.

[179] 4QXII[g] also witnesses corrections at Hos 2.5; 10.8; 12.3, 8; Joel 2.6; Amos 1.14; 2.2; Obad 4. See DJD XV, 275. See also von Weissenberg's analysis of scribal habits in 4QXII[c] which does not preserved Zechariah ('Changing Scripture?', 253–269).

[180] E.g. see the unidentified fragment in 21 2 of 4QXII[e], which reads אדני, preserving both the original pronoun 'I' and the corrected 'Adonai' through supralinear insertion.

copies or immaculate traditions, but copies that were physically and textually imperfect and semantically ambiguous, due to the lack of diacritical vocalization marks and other readerly helps (accents, paratexts, readings traditions, cantillation marks, etc.) and variations in deployment of *matres lectionis* and word divisions. Copies were not necessarily designed to be 'reader-friendly', a reality that increased the level of ambiguity already present in sometimes-gapped works.

4QXII[g], containing sections of Zech 10–12 (among other portions of the Twelve),[181] also provides information about the interface with the *realia* of reading in antiquity, particularly as it relates to textual segmenting. While the fragments of this manuscript are in need of further attention (despite their lengthy treatment in DJD),[182] the way in which the textual segments in the manuscript were divided provides a general lesson for encountering texts in antiquity. The scribe of this manuscript used different methods to establish paragraph divisions, including the deployment of blank lines and indentations. A variety of textual divisions and segmenting were on offer in this period and the various means of signalling paragraph divisions and sense contours (often deployed inconsistently) could have given rise to differing approaches to a text.[183] It is possible that the perception of sense contours in ancient texts differed for someone like John, who had no recourse to standardized critical editions. This reality should be kept in mind when attempting to delineate the boundaries or purview of John's scriptural encounters.[184]

Finally, some of the features of 8HevXIIgr provide further evidence for the *realia* of scriptural engagement. Among other features,[185] this manuscript represents the divine name as the Tetragrammaton in palaeo-Hebrew script.[186] This phenomenon points up the fact,

---

[181] See Lange, *Handbuch*, 341.

[182] DJD XV, 271–272; Brooke, 'The Twelve', 25.

[183] It is interesting to note that 8HevXIIgr's division into sense unit corresponds closely to the system later encoded in the MT. See DJD VIII, 9–12.

[184] The boundaries of John's reading habits, as preserved in concrete examples of reuse, might be further restrained or controlled by existing exegetical traditions attached to a particular text or texts, or the segmenting or aural remembrances.

[185] For a full description of its physical traits see DJD VIII, 1–26 and Lange, *Handbuch*, 343–345.

[186] Cf. P.Oxy. 656 (Rahlfs 905) as well as P.Oxy. 1007 and 3522 as further examples of this phenomenon. This also occurs in some Hebrew manuscripts, e.g. 4Q171 (4QpPs[a]) and 1QpHab. Cf. Patrick W. Skehan, 'The Divine Name at Qumran, in the Masada Scroll, and in the Septuagint', *BIOSCS* 13 (1980): 14–44.

among other considerations, that even if John accessed Zechariah through the medium of a Greek tradition, the Hebrew tradition was not necessarily conceptually absent within the encounter. This inbuilt bilingualism (or, at least, graphic presentation of signs from different language groups, one of which is encoded in an archaic script) functions as a reminder of the Greek tradition's underlying attachment to the Hebrew tradition. If John used a Greek tradition, particularly one revised towards the proto-MT like the text of 8HevXIIgr that contained some explicit Hebrew elements, he likely did so with the supposition that its message faithfully represented the deep structure (if not the surface features) of a Hebrew text – that it represented the meaning of the work as a polyglossic whole. This is true also if John encountered Greek texts through the medium of a pre-existing exegetical tradition (e.g. Section 3.2.1).

8HevXIIgr also witnesses a change in scribal hands in the vicinity of Zech 8.[187] This transcriptional reality suggests that readers of a single scroll were occasionally forced to decode the palaeography, scribal marks, and paratextual features of two different scribes (or more), even within the confines of a single work. The change of hands inserts an additional layer of ambiguity in this scroll since hand A left little or no spaces between words, while B's word divisions were much more clear. Also, the scroll may have consisted of a damaged copy that was repaired and finished by the second hand,[188] providing another potential obstacle to the facilitation of reading by physical copies: damage brought about by wear and tear or other inauspicious circumstances.

The physical presentation of a Twelve in antiquity differed from manuscript to manuscript and it is possible that a reader of the Twelve, like John, may have experienced the wording of Zechariah in different arrangements and styles, languages, and mediums (scriptural manuscript, aural experiences, exegetical tradition). Some of these features (e.g. Hebrew orthography) are especially relevant only if John had access to Hebrew manuscripts, although most features (e.g. segmenting, lack of diacritical reading aids, differences in word division, presence of corrections) were a reality of ancient textual encounters across languages. These features are also by extension

---

[187] See DJD VIII, 12–14.
[188] See Lange, *Handbuch*, 343–344.

features of textual *production*, as distinct from textual copying.
A conception of the social and scribal realities that underlie John's composition of Revelation must take into account the physical features of his textual culture, including the materials of writing, access to manuscripts of differing textual character, his presentation of the text (or the exegetical processing of visionary experiences) in a physical form, and the realities of revision or editing at an early stage in the process of composition.

These features are especially important in the context of this discussion insofar as they relate to the practices of scriptural reuse, especially John's access of various textual forms preserved in different mediums, the physical reality of reading manuscripts (in combination with the dominant oral environment of the period), and the question of his detailed and thorough attention to the details of particular textual traditions. In other words, the medium of scriptural transmission impacted the way that the textual tradition was understood by those who read and reused texts. The evidence from Judean Desert intimates that the question of access and recourse to material from known traditions (through both artefactual and oral avenues) is not an unlikely reality for John.

It is also helpful here to briefly note that the image of John immediately transcribing his visionary experiences alone in a cave on Patmos does not square with the care and intentionality embedded in the complex literary work that is Revelation.[189] Its careful structure and correlation of its segments suggests a controlled environment of composition and thoughtful and timely reflection on its structure, wording, and message. John may certainly have experienced visions on Patmos that inspired the writing of Revelation (as the work claims in Rev 1.9, and which corresponds to the named locations of other visionary experience [cf. Dan 10 and Ezek 1]), and the technical nature of the discussion in this study should not cast doubt on this claim. But the Apocalypse need not have been composed during John's sojourn on Patmos, and if genuine visionary or mystical experiences do lurk behind the Apocalypse, these visions were

---

[189] See Charles, *The Revelation*, 1.cvi–cvix. Additionally, literary composition in antiquity should not be considered as an isolated task, since the majority of works seem to have been dictated to scribal craftsmen for inscription (cf. Hezser, *Literacy*, 474–476).

exegetically processed before inscription. Indeed, the evidence that follows in this discussion suggests that, in accordance with potential visionary experiences, intensive and learned exegetical appropriate of the wording and thematic substance of scriptural traditions is constitutive of Revelation's composition, suggesting a lengthy and careful literary process.[190] John's potential visionary experiences and the divine commands to him to 'write' what he see and hears (e.g. 1.11; 2.1; 14.13; 19.9; 21.5) may have occurred on Patmos, but Revelation itself is mute as to its place of composition, which could have easily occurred in a more urban environment and known location of literary production like Ephesus, Pergamum, or Sardis possibly increasing the author's access to texts, manuscripts, and locations of learning or oral discourse.[191] And if the material from the Judean Desert is truly representative of the textual culture of Judaism more generally (even perhaps to some degree beyond the immediate borders of Palestine in some locations), it is not impossible to imagine that John may have had direct access to a Hebrew form of the Twelve among other potential Greek traditions, although little is known of the text of the HB in the diaspora in this period. An ecstatic experience may have been an impetus for the author of Revelation to write, but it does not account for the complex and intricate composition of the work, including John's use of scripture and reuse of exegetical traditions. The seer presents himself as a scribal copyist, but the composition of the work is much more involved. Regardless of the historical veracity of work's claim to visionary experiences, it is certain that the textual culture of early Judaism had a profound impact on the shape of the Apocalypse.

2.7 Possible Textual Sources for the Book of Revelation

Based on the preceding discussion one is forced to posit that John may plausibly have had different sources at his disposal from which he could have crafted his references to Zechariah. The task of identifying these sources is complicated by the fact that he could have used

---

[190] Although I am not convinced by Fekkes's overarching model, he does acknowledge a lengthy process of composition (*Isaiah*, 289).

[191] The large synagogue located in Sardis (second century CE) indicates the wealth of the Jewish community there, suggesting that the city may have held manuscripts at a centralized location. And the presence of Melito of Sardis (mid-second century CE) demonstrates that Sardis was a location of literary production in early Christianity. See Paul R. Trebilco, *Jewish Communities in Asia Minor* (SNTSMS 69; Cambridge: Cambridge University Press, 1991), 37–54 for an overview of the synagogue in Sardis and the city as a location of literary activity.

multiple different text forms, even of one scriptural work, as we saw in the previous examples of scriptural reuse in the Fourth Gospel, Romans, and Mark. Moreover, just because the wording of one of John's allusions follows a particular textual form, it does not necessarily mean that direct access to the scriptural tradition was John's source. The questions of source and form, while interrelated, are not always identical. We must start by ascertaining the form of an allusion before positing a plausible source. There are twelve options as it applies to textual form to consider:[192] 1. a translation of proto-MT; 2. a translation of the *Vorlage* of OG/LXX; 3. a translation of another Hebrew text; 4. Old Greek; 5. the καιγε recension (8HevXIIgr);[193] 6. a (proto-) Hexaplaric recension; 7. a translation of a Hebrew text (options 1–3) with adaptations; 8. an adaptation of a Greek version (options 4–6); 9. a free paraphrase[194] of a Hebrew text; 10. a free paraphrase of OG/LXX; 11. a Greek text influenced by memory of a Hebrew text;[195] 12. a quotation from memory.[196]

---

[192] I have also noted these options in Garrick V. Allen, 'Textual Pluriformity and Allusion in the Book of Revelation. The Text of Zechariah in the Apocalypse', *ZNW* 106 no 1 (2015): 137–138.

[193] Norton, *Contours*, 3 connects the καιγε recension and 8HevXIIgr manuscript in reference the Book of the Twelve. See also Siegfried Kreuzer, 'Der Antiochenische Text der Septuaginta Forschungsgechichte und eine neue Perspektive', in *Der Antiochenische Text der Septuaginta in seiner Bezeugung und seiner Bedeutung* (DSI 4; ed. S. Kreuzer and M. Sigismund; Göttingen: Vandenhoeck & Ruprecht, 2013), 23–56 and Natalio Fernández Marcos, 'The Antiochene Edition in the Text History of the Greek Bible', in ibid., 58–59. For the Book of the Twelve, the καιγε recension is closely identified with the Antiochene text. As such, and because this textual form is most discernible in 1–4 Kingdoms and in certain Psalter manuscripts, this early Greek revising tradition will not be explored. However, there is textual evidence that Josephus accessed the Antiochene text, as well as other NT authors. See Victoria Spottorno, 'The Status of the Antiochene Text in the First Century A.D.: Josephus and the New Testament', in ibid., 74–83 and Martin Meiser, 'Antiochenische Textformen in neutestamentlichen Psalmzitaten in der Rezeption der christlichen Antike – eine textkritische Spurensuche', in ibid., 179–196.

[194] Molly M. Zahn, *Rethinking Rewritten Scripture: Composition and Exegesis in the 4QReworked Pentateuch Manuscripts* (STDJ 95; Leiden: Brill, 2011), 18 defines paraphrase as '[reflecting] the same basic content as the source passage, and may incorporate some of its significant terms, but otherwise *is formulated differently*'.

[195] A possibility proposed by Labahn, 'Die Macht', 385–416.

[196] George J. Brooke, 'Aspects of Matthew's Use of Scripture in Light of the Dead Sea Scrolls', in *A Teacher for All Generations: Essays in Honor of James C. VanderKam* (ed. E. F. Mason et al.; JSJsup 153.2; Leiden: Brill, 2012), 828–829 suggests that the textual variation in the scriptural texts from Qumran have raised 'an intriguing set of

John certainly did not conceive of his scriptural sources in these text-critical categories, but just because this is so does not mean that he was not aware of textual pluriformity or fluidity as phenomena associated with ancient scriptural encounters. His engagement with the literary work Zechariah occurred through various points of access, entry points that consisted of varying expressions (preserved in various wordings and languages) of a single prophetic work. Untangling this text-critical web of possibilities is relatively straightforward and provides evidence that allows us to describe the shape of John's reading experience in less anachronistic terms at a later stage. The texts from Revelation which reference Zechariah will be analysed and compared to the proto-MT and OG/LXX, with special reference to relevant ancient manuscripts (see Section 2.6), to identify *which* possible textual form is preserved in John's reference.

Due to the lack of attestation for a non proto-MT Hebrew form in the manuscript evidence, option 3 is difficult to substantiate. Similarly, if only a single (albeit fluid) Hebrew form of Zechariah circulated in antiquity, it is likely that options 1 (proto-MT) and 2 (*V*OG) refer to the same text form. Option 2 is examined below, but the prospect of identifying an alternative Hebrew form behind the OG is unlikely. If the instances of reuse correspond closely with any of these texts, many of the possible options are eliminated (8–12). Because the *V*OG and proto-MT are mostly synonymous, option 2 is eliminated leaving only options 1, 4–7. From here, an evaluation of the linguistic and syntactic features of the various traditions will lead to the primary source text where the evidence allows for such a conclusion to be drawn. This preliminary task of identifying *Vorlagen* of references is often overlooked, especially in the discussion of scriptural references in Revelation.[197] However, as Gert Steyn observes,

possibilities' when it comes to the form of the source text quoted in Matthew, indicating that there are many potential forms available in a text-critical sense. This is not just the case for Matthew, but for the entirety of the NT, including Revelation, and I have attempted to articulate them in text-critical terms here.

[197] In addition to the discussion in the previous chapter, it ought to be noted that Beale, *John's Use*, 61–62 bestows all of one paragraph to a discussion on the text form that John uses, suggesting simply that he used the 'proto-Theodotion' Greek text. Although Beale does undertake more substantive investigations into the *Vorlagen* of scriptural references in Revelation elsewhere (see especially 'Reconsideration', 539–543 and 'The Origins of the Title "King of Kings and Lord of Lords" in Revelation 17.14', *NTS* 31 [1985]: 618–620, and, to a lesser degree, *Revelation*, 76–79), his unwillingness

before one can thus attempt to discuss the place, function, interpretation, or exegetical method of explicit quotations with the NT itself, proper attention should be given first and foremost to the *Vorlage* . . . behind these quotations.[198]

In order to understand *how* or *why* the author of Revelation made use of Zechariah, it is first essential to identify *which* textual form he referenced.

Again, it is not as if John perceived his scriptural sources in these categories and the fact that he may have accessed different forms of Zechariah does not necessarily entail that he compared copies or evaluated readings (although this also cannot be ruled out). The eclecticism of the Greek tradition, consisting of variously integrated readings from OG, Hebraizing revisions, or inner-Greek stylistic changes indicates that various 'forms' as conceived of by text critics may have been preserved in a single copy.[199] The textual question of form should not be confused with historical and social question of access to copies. Moreover, instances where the evidence indicates that John was aware of Hebrew textual traditions might theoretically reflect his use of now lost Greek traditions. However, barring another sensational find like 8HevXIIgr, the lack of any direct substantiation of these lost traditions supports the argument that John at times used Hebrew texts. If further Greek texts are discovered all discussions of textual form will require revision.

Additionally, the question of textual form illuminates further the question of source (manuscript, memory, pre-existing interpretative tradition, or a combination of similar options), which in turn provides information about the social realities that stand behind the composition of the Apocalypse.

---

to undertake this task in a monograph devoted to the reuse of scriptural traditions in Revelation illustrates a larger lacuna in the field.

[198] Steyn, 'Which "LXX"', 700. Steyn's sentiment is echoed also by Ronald van der Bergh, 'Differences', 160 and Jon Paulien, 'Elusive Allusions: The Problematic Use of the Old Testament in Revelation', *BR* 33 (1988): 46.

[199] For example, when I argue that John sometimes translated the proto-MT of Zechariah independent of a Greek tradition, I make the judgement because there are no Hebraizing Greek readings that correspond to John's wording in these instances. Additionally, the exegetical changes sometimes introduced by John are dependent on Hebrew words. This is not to say that John may not have accessed a hitherto unknown Greek Hebraizing version of Zechariah, but to suggest that the evidence points forcefully in the direction of a Hebrew form.

These realities include the question of the mechanics of text production, textual culture, and the existence and circulation of distinct exegetical traditions relating to particular texts. To my mind, it is possible that John accessed distinct forms of scriptural texts from three principle sources. First, John may have accessed the text of Zechariah, and other works, through the medium of written Hebrew manuscripts like the 4QXII manuscripts from Qumran or Greek manuscripts similar to 8HevXIIgr. Despite the potentially cumbersome reality of working with manuscripts of the various scriptural works that John engages with (a reality that may not have been perceived as cumbrous by many ancient text users), his knowledge of the minute details of the scriptural tradition in conversation with other coordinated texts indicates that the author had recourse to the graphic shape of written sources. Memory of particular textual forms certainly played a role in shaping John's textual encounter, but not necessarily at the expense of access to textual artefacts. Memory and manuscript cannot be polarized.[200] The function of manuscripts varied in this period, but it is clear that Jewish exegetes of the late Second Temple period had access to scriptural manuscripts, as is illustrated by the production of the Greek scriptural tradition (OG/LXX), a translation that preserves evidence of both precise *Übersetzungsweisen* and more exegetically inclined renderings. It is relatively uncontroversial that translators of this tradition worked with Hebrew copies of the work they produced in Greek even though the precise mechanics of artefactual use are debated. This observation is all the more true in revising traditions, since their revision moved in the direction of a particular Hebrew text form, presumably accessed through artefactual means. The evidence from Qumran and the Septuagint suggests that exegetes and text producers from various locations, both within Palestine and beyond (at least Khirbet Qumran and Alexandria), worked directly with written copies. Education-enculturation in Jewish scriptural traditions had, by this time, extended beyond the priestly realm into parts of the diaspora and remote locations in Palestine, broadening the reach of texts inscribed on writing surfaces.[201]

Additionally, in what amounts to a critique of performance criticism, Larry Hurtado has recently pointed out that objections to the perspective that NT writers directly accessed Jewish scriptural

[200] See Norton, *Contours*, 25–30.
[201] Carr, *Writing*, 219–220.

works through manuscripts – including the dominance of oral performance, lack of readerly helps in manuscript format (*scriptio continua*), and the awkwardness associated with handling scrolls – are often distortions of the actual evidence.[202] There is ultimately little reason to dismiss *a priori* the possibility that John accessed scriptural traditions through manuscripts. This is not to downplay the dominant oral/aural dimension of literary encounters in this period, but to note that these encounters were controlled and influenced by access to textual artefacts.

A second source for John's access to particular forms of Jewish scriptural texts is that of memory (either of text or aural experience), a feature of ancient education-enculturation and text production highlighted in a clear fashion by David Carr. Carr notes that the written-oral/aural interaction with scripture was the primary point of engagement with sacred texts in antiquity generally,[203] and in the Second Temple period more specifically – although a move towards more direct engagement with written texts took place in this later period. He argues that manuscripts functioned as memory aides and that their lack of readerly helps point to their subordinate role in connection with memory. He also reasons that transcriptional errors and examples of imperfect replication of wording in allusions and quotation suggest that authors used their memory as the source of these flawed reproductions, pointing to evidence from Sumerian literature through to the end of the Second Temple period.[204]

Carr is correct to highlight the role of memory and aural/oral learning as a foundational feature of textual culture in this period. Indeed, it possible (though, I think, rather unlikely), as some have argued,[205] that the author of Revelation's reuse of scripture is so allusive because he subconsciously drew on his memory as a scriptural resource.[206] Moreover, it is clear that the structure of Revelation, like many ancient literary works, was designed to enhance its own memorability

---

[202] See Larry W. Hurtado, 'Oral Fixation and New Testament Studies? "Orality", "Performance" and Reading Texts in Early Christianity', *NTS* 60 no 3 (2014): 321–340.

[203] E.g. Carr, *Writing*, 7–8, 74, 127–128, 159–160.

[204] See ibid., 36, 229–230, 241–244, 268–269.

[205] Schüssler Fiorenza, *Justice and Judgment*, 17–18.

[206] When I appeal to memory as a source, I am referring to the conscious accessing of the remembrance of a scriptural utterance, not the subconscious mimicking of traditions. Even allusions preserve significant elements of intention, a reality noticed in the Damascus Document by Jonathan G. Campbell, *The Use of Scripture in the Damascus Document 1–8, 19–20* (BZAW 228; Berlin: De Gruyter, 1995), 176–177, 206.

and encourage the internalization of its message, especially its con-
centric circles of sevens, repeated phraseology and locutions, songs
(e.g. Rev 5.9–10), the various 'ear to hear' asides (e.g. Rev 3.13), and the
vivid image of the eaten scroll (Rev 10.8–10; cf. Ezek 2.9–3.3). However,
there are difficulties with suggesting that the reuse of a particular text
was derived from the author's memory beyond the obvious objection
that it is impossible to access the mind of a long-past author (see also
Excursus 1 for a fuller discussion of memory). Even if memory was
the source of John's allusions, it is the memory of a particular textual
form, perhaps even an 'eclectic' textual form that is no longer extant.
In this way, the role of memory in Jewish education-enculturation
matrices in this period contributed to the pluriform scriptural tradition as remembered texts became inscribed and transmitted alongside
other copies. If memory is a source, it is the memory of a particular
textual form.

Moreover, the imperfect replication of wording in reproduction
(including in translation, allusion, and citation) does not necessarily give decisive evidence for the role of memory as a source. When
clear exegetical goals or more complex changes occur, especially har-
monizations to distant contexts, it is more likely that alterations of
wording are the result of intentional cognitive processes, even if the
wording in a target text differs from its source. Many of the changes
that occur in Revelation point in this direction – that John altered
the wording of his reused scriptural texts, whether subconsciously
as the result of the omnibus of scriptural encounters or consciously
as a voluntary act of interpretation. For ancient tradents, especially
as illuminated by material from Qumran, the wording of a work was
often subservient to the perceived goals and function of the work
itself, and, thus, subject to change in ways that enhanced the overarching agenda of the work as perceived by the one making the
changes. The author of Revelation was certainly an erudite member of the literati – a learned, multilingual presumably well versed
in Jewish scripture, learned through a combination of written-oral
mediums.[207] However, while conscious access to memory remains a
possible source for scriptural engagement for John, the problems outlined above create issues in identifying memory as a distinct source,

---

[207] For more on the interplay of oral and written traditions in early Christianity
from a form critical perspective, see Werner H. Kelber, *The Oral and Written
Gospel: The Hermeneutics of Speaking and Writing in the Synoptic Tradition, Mark,
Paul, and Q* (Philadelphia: Fortress, 1983), esp. 90–139.

particularly as modern access to memory is mediated through the *realia* of texts preserved on writing surfaces. Nonetheless, we should not polarize memory against access to manuscripts. The oral culture of the eastern Mediterranean at the end of the first century, and what is known about educational systems in multiple cultures, suggests that inscribed texts and remembered or experienced texts coalesced in the reading experience of text producers to create meaning and interpretations which led to exegetical engagement and reuse.

Finally, John may have accessed Zechariah traditions through the medium of pre-existing exegetical traditions, transmitted orally and/or via written mediums (*excerpta* collections or the like). The most recent proponent of this source as an access point of scriptural tradition in early Christianity is Martin C. Albl, who argues that the *testimonia* collections – collections of scriptural utterances combined to make certain theological or apologetic points – served as the primary channel of transmission for scriptural quotations preserved in early Christian writings. While Albl, following the previous work of C. H. Dodd and other influential critics, emphasizes the function of excerpted collections of scriptural utterances as independent artefacts functioning as apologetic tools for early Christianity, it is not clear that circulating exegetical traditions always functioned in this manner. In fact, a textually focused education-enculturation model accounts more fully for this evidence, as Albl himself mentions.[208] In other words, the source need not be a *testimonia* collection, but may reflect a pre-existing exegetical tradition that juxtaposed two or more distinct texts, texts encoded in a particular wording and language. The wording of these developed traditions often differed from the wording of other, better-attested textual streams (sometimes referred to as 'LXX-deviant'). Nonetheless, it is clear that groupings of particular texts, often fixed in certain

---

[208] See M. C. Albl, *'And Scripture Cannot be Broken': The Form and Function of Early Christian Testimonia Collections* (NTsup 96; Leiden: Brill, 1999), 7–69 for a succinct overview of scholarly discourse of *excerpta* or *testimonia* collection in early Christianity. See also C. H. Dodd, *According to the Scriptures: The Sub-Structure of New Testament Theology* (London: Nesbit & Co., 1952) and, previously, the influential essays of Edwin Hatch, 'On Early Quotations from the Septuagint' and 'On Composite Citations from the Septuagint' reprinted in *Essays in Biblical Greek* (Amsterdam: Philo, 1970), 131–214 (esp. 203–204), and Rendel Harris's collection of articles *Testimonies* (2 vols.; Cambridge: Cambridge University Press, 1916–1920) wherein he argues for the existence of a single (authoritative) testimony book in wide circulation in early Christianity.

wordings that at times deviated from OG/LXX traditions, circulated in early Christianity and became embedded both in the NT and other early Christian works. For the purposes of this discussion, the functions or mediums (oral and/or written) of these collections are not of primary import. What matters is that the author of Revelation may have had an additional access point to Zechariah traditions in a form already entangled with exegetical traditions or juxtaposed with other scriptural texts. In these cases, the term 'reuse' can be emphasized, as John drew not directly from scriptural manuscripts, interpreting them anew, but from pre-existing interpretative traditions attached to particular texts.

These traditions are distinct from so-called Christian *testimonia* collections, which are often pointed to as the source for Paul's quotations, particularly in Romans.[209] Albl points to seven criteria for identifying the use of extract collections in examples of scriptural reuse:[210]

(1)   quotations that deviate considerably from known scriptural texts (LXX or LXX recensions, MT);

(2)   composite quotations;

(3)   false attributions;

(4)   use of the same series of texts in independent authors;

(5)   editorial or interpretative comments indicative of a collection;

(6)   evident lack of awareness of the biblical context of the quotation;

(7)   use of exegetical comments in independent authors.

I will not examine each of these points here, but briefly note that each criterion need not *necessarily* indicate the existence of an excerpted collection. Independently they are in fact unconvincing. Authorial awareness of the textual details of the breadth of the scriptural tradition indicates that composite quotations, alterations of wording from known traditions,

---

[209] E.g. J. Ross Wagner, *Heralds of the Good News: Isaiah and Paul 'in Concert' in the Letter to the Romans* (NTsup 101; Leiden: Brill, 2002), 20–21, although Wagner is careful to avoid the normal apologetic concerns that usually attached to these collections in the literature. The suggestion that Paul, a widely itinerant missionary who often explicitly quoted texts at length, used *excerpta* collections is much more appealing than it is in the case of John, the author of Revelation. Although one should not completely exclude the possibility that John also, at times and for certain texts, had access to such a collection.

[210] Albl, *Form and Function*, 66.

thematic grouping, and other editorial activity could have been (and often was) accomplished *de novo* – that is, directly from scriptural manuscripts independent of inscribed exegetical traditions – *or* through knowledge of an existing exegetical tradition attached to certain texts. The strongest criterion for establishing the use of a circulating exegetical or juxtaposing tradition is the common usage of composite tradition and its distinctive features by multiple authors. This becomes especially poignant when these traditions share constellations of readings that differ from other known textual traditions. In this way, Albl's criteria 1 and 4 coalesce to point in the direction of an *excerpta* collection despite the fact that on their own they are relatively unpersuasive and that they need not have existed as written *testimonia* source. Despite the issues with *testimonia* hypotheses, I think that it is helpful to acknowledge the existence of pre-circulating exegetical traditions (transmitted orally and/or textually). The reality of shared exegetical or conceptual traditions between Qumran literature and the NT has been emphasized strongly by George Brooke, Jörg Frey, and others,[211] and it should not be surprising if the author of Revelation, too, drew from a common well of interpretative tradition attached to particular scriptural texts. A large quantity of the exegetical traditions embedded in the NT are borrowed and/or modified from antecedent Jewish traditions.

To sum up, John could have accessed Zechariah tradition through various mediums including direct access to manuscripts, the memory of the wording of manuscripts and/or oral/aural scriptural experience, and pre-existent exegetical traditions. Additionally, each of these points of access may have contained various forms of Zechariah. John may have accessed a manuscript containing the OG text of Zechariah, a revising Greek tradition, or a fluid proto-MT tradition. Or he may have reused an exegetical tradition encoded in a particular textual form or forms, one that potentially differed from the form of Zechariah accessed through the medium of a manuscript. While

---

[211] See e.g. George J. Brooke, *The Dead Sea Scrolls and the New Testament* (Minneapolis: Fortress, 2005), 217–297; Jörg Frey, 'The Notion of "Flesh" in 4QInstruction and the Background of Pauline Usage', in *Sapiential, Liturgical & Poetical Texts from Qumran: Proceedings of the Third Meeting of the International Organization for Qumran Studies, Published in Memory of Maurice Baillet* (STDJ 35; ed. D. K. Falk, F. García Martínez, and E. M. Schuller; Leiden: Brill, 2000), 197–226; Campbell, *Damascus Document*, 195–200; and many of the articles in Rey, ed., *The Dead Sea Scrolls and Pauline Literature*.

the difference between form and source has not always been observed in the 'NT in the OT' studies (cf. Section 1.4.1.3), the distinction remains important for how we conceptualize the processes of text production in the textual culture of which John is a part.

2.8 The Text of the Book of Revelation

Another facet of analysing scriptural reuse is the level of variability present in the text of the target composition. Of the works preserved in the NT, the book of Revelation has a complicated and unique textual history.[212] The peculiarity of the text of this work is exacerbated by the general paucity of ancient Greek witnesses and its late acceptance in eastern Christian traditions in contrast to other NT works.[213] The text of the Apocalypse has been previously examined in the monumental works of Hoskier and Schmid (among others),[214] but Karrer has recently questioned the authoritative status of previous research, and called for a new appraisal of the data: the text of the Apocalypse as printed in modern critical editions is far from secure.[215] Moreover, David Parker's general warning for NT studies is instructive in light of the detailed textual analyses in the following chapters. He notes that in NT studies

> debate has centred on the meaning of a single authoritative text . . . such a text does not exist today, and has never

---

[212] The possible exception to this statement is Luke-Acts, which is complicated by the so-called 'Western Text' tradition preserved in Codex Bezae. See D. C. Parker, *Codex Bezae: An Early Christian Manuscript and its Text* (Cambridge: Cambridge University Press, 1992); R. H. van der Bergh, 'The Textual Tradition of Explicit Quotations in Codex Bezae Cantabrigiensis of the Acts of the Apostles' (PhD Diss., University or Pretoria, 2013).

[213] On this latter point, see Boxall, *Patmos*, 105.

[214] H. C. Hoskier, *Concerning the Text of the Apocalypse* (2 vols.; London: Quaritch, 1929); J. Schmid, *Studien zur Geschichte des Griechischen Apokalypse-Textes* (vol. 2; Munich: Karl Zink, 1956). See also J. K. Elliott, *New Testament Textual Criticism: The Application of Thoroughgoing Principles: Essays on Manuscripts and Textual Variation* (NTsup 137; Leiden: Brill, 2010), 145–155; Markus Lembke, 'Beobachtungen zu den Handschriften der Apokalypse des Johannes', in *Die Johannesoffenbarung: Ihr Text und ihre Auslegung* (ABG 38; ed. M. Labahn and M. Karrer; Leipzig: Evangelische Verlagsanstalt, 2012), 19–69.

[215] Karrer, 'Angels', 57–84; Karrer, 'Der Text', 43–78. A fresh evaluation of the textual traditions of the Apocalypse is currently underway at the Kirchliche Hochschule Wuppertal/Bethel, where the *Editio Critica Maior* of Revelation is in preparation (expected 2021).

existed, and that therefore the theological arguments built on such a text are castles in the air.[216]

In what follows, I endeavour to construct a humble home on solid textual ground. Variation in the Greek tradition of the book of Revelation is heeded in this study to the extent that is necessary. These comments are usually located in footnotes. The main text of NA[28] is not taken for granted, and variants in locutions that borrowed material from Zechariah are incorporated and evaluated in the following discussion.[217]

2.9 Conclusion

In the first century CE Jewish scriptural works existed in multiple textual forms and circulated in various sources (manuscripts, exegetical traditions, memory). Long before the discoveries at Qumran, the available textual evidence led scholars to posit that the HB, and its early Greek versions, existed in pluriformity in antiquity. This phenomenon was viewed negatively, especially in light of the well-attested Masoretic *textus receptus*. The discovery of the scriptural manuscripts at Qumran, and the pluriform textual traditions they witnessed, revolutionized perceptions of the shape of the HB, shattering the previous consensus that the form of the scriptural works collected in the MT were the best and most original form of each work. The fact that the Qumran library contained multiple forms of the same books, sometimes in the same cave, and that multiple forms of texts are cited within single Qumran compositions demonstrates that the members of the *Yaḥad*, and early Jewish readers generally, encountered a pluriform scriptural tradition. The perdurance and tolerance of pluriformity was an ambient feature of Jewish textual culture that extended to portions of the NT as well. The Johannine evangelist is aware of multiple forms of the Psalter: both the OG tradition and a Hebrew text. Likewise, in Rom 9, Paul cites from both the OG and

---

[216] Parker, *Living Text*, 76, 203.

[217] Dochhorn, *Prophetie*, 30–36 takes a more aggressive stance towards textual variation in Rev 12, tracing the textual history of Revelation generally and the relevant traditions for chapter 12 specifically. It is becoming more and more apparent that textual criticism remains a critical baseline for good exegesis and evaluations of scriptural reuse. Dochhorn exemplifies this to the utmost degree in his extensive text-critical reconstruction of Rev 12 (pp. 171–184).

proto-MT of Isaiah, referencing both forms not only within a single discourse segment, but also within a single quotation. And the Markan evangelist exhibited an awareness of multiple textual forms of Isaiah.

The textual milieu in which the book of Revelation was composed is one in which the text of scriptural works was both pluriform and fluid. The ancient evidence of the Twelve, and Zechariah specifically, witnesses a Hebrew tradition that is more stable than that of Jeremiah, Isaiah, Daniel, Exodus, Psalms, or Deuteronomy. Even so, the evidence suggests that the Hebrew tradition, while related to the proto-MT family, remained fluid. Textual variation is also present in the early Greek traditions of the Twelve. It is an obligation to investigate the source text(s) for the references to Zechariah in Revelation because there is copious evidence that John's contemporaries regularly utilized multiple forms of the same text within a single composition, pericope, and locution. If one does not know which text form John referenced, it is impossible to say how he altered and interpreted that source text: the search for the *Vorlagen* of scriptural references is an essential preliminary exercise.[218]

---

[218] See Gert J. Steyn, 'The Text Form of the Isaiah Quotation in the *Sondergut Matthäus* Compared to the Dead Sea Scrolls, Masoretic Text and Septuagint', in *Text-Critical and Hermeneutical Studies in the Septuagint* (VTsup 157; ed. J. Cook and H. Stipp; Leiden: Brill, 2012), 428 where he states that 'one cannot simply attempt to discuss the *function* of such OT material unless at least the range of available Hebrew and Greek *textual witnesses* were first identified and assessed in order to determine the . . . text form that was at the disposal of the NT author.' Labahn, 'Ausharren im Leben', 293 confirms that the identification of the *Vorlage* of a scriptural reference is the first step in analysing the manner in which a NT author reused antecedent traditional material.

3

BORROWING PROPHETIC WORDS: TEXTUAL FORM AND ACCESS TO TRADITIONS

3.1 Introduction

The discussion in the preceding chapter has demonstrated that in the late Second Temple period the majority of Jewish scriptural works were textually fluid and pluriform. Modes of transmission varied, and the precise reproduction of wording was not necessarily the goal of manuscript production or forms of reuse. Zechariah, too, circulated in a fluid Hebrew tradition, closely aligned with the proto-MT, and a pluriform Greek tradition. This consideration leaves open the possibility that the author of Revelation may have referenced multiple textual forms of Zechariah, potentially accessing them from different sources. Several scholars have in fact already concluded that John accessed different forms of a single work within Revelation, although not Zechariah.[1]

---

[1] (Genesis): Labahn, 'Ausharren im Leben', 293. (Ezekiel): Karrer, 'Von der Apokalypse', 118, 'Der Apk-Autor kannte das Ezechielbuch auf griechisch und mutmaßlich zusätzlich hebräisch'. (Isaiah): Karrer, 'Die Rezeption des Jesajabuches in der Johannesoffenbarung', in *Überlieferung und Auslegung des Jesajabuches in intra- und interreligiösen Spannungsfeldern* (BETL; ed. F. Wilk; Leuven: Peeters, forthcoming). (Daniel): Beale, *John's Use*, 62; Beale, *Jewish Apocalyptic*, 311–312. (Psalter): J. De Vries, 'Ps 86^MT/Ps 85^LXX in Apk 15,4bß: Anmerkungen zum Text von Psalter und Johannesoffenbarung', in *Von Der Septuaginta zum Neuen Testament: Textgeschichtliche Erörterungen* (ANTF 43; ed. M. Karrer, S. Kreuzer, and M. Sigismund; Berlin: De Gruyter, 2010), 417–423. See also the more general comment in Lichtenberger, 'Die Schrift', 386: 'Der Verfasser kombiniert hebräisch-aramäische und griechische Textformen, da er in beiden zuhause ist'. Daniele Tripaldi, '"Discrepat evangelista et Septuaginta nostraque translatio" (*Hieronymus*, Briefe 57,7,5): Bemerkungen zur Textvorlage des Sacharja-Zitats in Offb 1,7', in *Die Johannesoffenbarung: Ihr Test und ihre Auslegung* (ABG 38; ed. M. Labahn and M. Karrer; Leipzig: Evangelische Verlagsanstalt, 2012), 138–139 argues that the reuse of Zech 12.10 in Rev 1.7 does not provide enough clear data to identify a discrete textual form.

The primary task of this chapter is to examine the *Vorlage(n)* of John's references to Zechariah and to identify the textual form(s) of his sources and points of access to those various sources. This comparative text-critical assessment builds the foundation for examining John's techniques of reuse and interpretive strategies – only once the form of John's source tradition is identified, can one properly examine the textual differences between source and target text, describe the way that he reused scriptural traditions, or construct a picture of the social reality of literary composition. The subsequent textual analyses intimate that, while John often reused a Hebrew form of Zechariah (esp. when referencing Zech 1–8), he was also familiar with exegetical traditions transmitted in a Greek form revised towards the proto-MT stream. John prefers the semantics preserved in the proto-MT stream of Zechariah (= 8HevXIIgr, Hexaplaric traditions) and only rarely used the wording of Zechariah preserved only in the OG tradition.

The textual options presented in the previous chapter remain at the forefront of this discussion, and it is helpful here to reiterate the possibilities. It is conceivable that John could have used one or a combination of the following twelve forms of Zechariah: 1. a translation of the proto-MT family; 2. a translation of the *V*OG/LXX; 3. a translation of another Hebrew text; 4. OG; 5. καιγε recension (8HevXIIgr); 6. a (proto-)Hexaplaric recension; 7. a translation of a Hebrew text (options 1–3) with adaptations; 8. an adaptation of a Greek version (options 4–6); 9. a free paraphrase of a Hebrew text; 10. a free paraphrase of OG/LXX; 11. a Greek text influenced by memory of a Hebrew text; 12. a quotation from memory.

As noted above, a multiplicity of these textual traditions might be preserved in an eclectic way (at least as perceived by our text-critical categories) in a single manuscript. The goal of this chapter is to determine which of these possible forms of Zechariah John reused by examining instances of reuse in the order that they occur in the narrative of Revelation and to identify John's possible points of access (manuscripts, memory, existing exegetical traditions) to these textual forms.

Excursus 1: Michael Labahn and the Influence of Memory

Before moving on, however, it is helpful here to briefly revisit issues related to the claim that John accessed scriptural traditions through the medium of memory. In his article 'Die Macht des

Gedächtnisses: Überlegungen zu Möglichkeit und Grenzen des Einflusses hebräischer Texttradition auf die Johannesapokalypse' (The Power of Memory: Reflections on Possibilities and Limits of the Influence of a Hebrew Textual Tradition on the Apocalypse of John), Michael Labahn assumes that the *Vorlage(n)* of John's references were Greek. Additionally, he contends that John was influenced by the *memory* of Hebrew texts, mediated through 'aspects of orality', which Labahn understands through the lens of cognitive psychology, referring to John's past aural experiences of Hebrew Zechariah.[2] For Labahn, the influence of Hebrew is located in John's Greek syntax, but not in his choice of *Vorlagen*.

In another article, he rephrases his case: 'The Hebrew acts as the memory space of the seer's collective memory and, therefore, influences the text of the Apocalypse of John.'[3] He goes on: 'therefore, it is objectively necessary to compare the Greek text tradition in all its breadth. Thus, the Greek textual tradition forms, in all its breadth, the primary context in which the reception of scripture in the Apocalypse of John is formed.'[4] I affirm the first part of Labahn's second quotation: all relevant, pre-Hexaplaric Greek textual forms must be analysed to measure correspondence to John's scriptural references, since early Christian authors most often appropriated Jewish scripture in its various Greek forms. This approach is adopted in the current study. However, I am not yet convinced that the OG/LXX tradition is the author's 'primary framework', as Labahn describes it. The textual pluriformity of Jewish scriptural works (and their exegetical traditions) in the first century CE makes any assumptions regarding the language of any author's scriptural *Vorlagen* perilous. Although Labahn has adopted a middling view on the influence of memory, against those who assert that John never used immediate textual material to construct allusions,[5] arguing that textuality and memory worked hand in hand to shape

---

[2] Labahn, 'Die Macht', 387.

[3] 'Das Hebräische wirkt als im Gedächtnisraum des Sehers bewahrte Erinnerung einflussreich auf den Text der Johannesapokalypse ein.' M. Labahn, 'Geschrieben', 366. Labahn's use of cultural memory theory is more fully developed in 'Griechische Textformen', 529–560.

[4] 'Es ist daher sachlich notwendig, die griechische Textüberlieferung in aller Breite zu vergleichen. Somit bildet *die griechische Texttradition in ihrer ganzen Breite den primären Rahmen, in den die Schriftrezeption der Johannesapokalypse einzuordnen ist.*' M. Labahn, 'Die Macht', 386–387 (emphasis original).

[5] See Trudinger, 'Text', 159.

the presentation of John's scriptural use, his specific assumption that the Greek scriptural tradition is John's foundational textual form is difficult to substantiate. As the data below intimates, John was aware of *both* the wording of Greek traditions that that stand within the proto-MT stream *and* Hebrew scriptural manuscripts themselves. In some instances (e.g. the horse visions in Rev 6.1–8), the wording of John's allusion only makes sense if he had direct access to a Hebrew textual tradition since no Greek traditions exist that correspond to John's presentation of colour lexemes.

In reference to Labahn's analysis of the use of Zech 4.10b in Rev 5.6b (see Section 3.2.2), he concludes that the 'exotic images' of the seven eyes would have left a permanent impression on the author, leading John to correct the OG to a semantic sense of the locution that is more fully preserved in the proto-MT.[6] This conclusion is suggestive, but only necessary if one assumes that John did not work directly with Hebrew texts. If one operates without this assumption, Labahn's analysis of the textual data supports the conclusion that John alluded to Hebrew Zech 4.10b. The following data intimates that, at least in some cases, John had direct access to a Hebrew text of Zechariah similar to the proto-MT, apart from simple recourse to the memory of past experiences with Hebrew texts.[7]

It is undeniable that memory played a major role in education, textual transmission and production, and the reuse of antecedent textual traditions, and that orality was the primary medium of textual knowledge.[8] Even in textual encounters, once an author's eye moves from the source manuscript to the target text, memory becomes

---

[6] Labahn, 'Geschrieben', 408.

[7] See Allen, 'Textual Pluriformity', 136–145.

[8] Carr, *Writing*, 98–99, 128–129, 137 notes that much of ancient Greek and Egyptian literature and the HB were originally composed with an eye towards 'memorizability'. Jan Assmann, *Cultural Memory and Early Civilization: Writing, Remembrance, and Political Imagination* (Cambridge: Cambridge University Press, 2011), 37 highlights the 'mnemotechnical function' of certain objectifications of both linguistic (inscriptions, mythic literature) and non-linguistic (ritual, jewellery, dance, etc.) aspects of ancient cultures, suggesting that writing in the ancient world originated as a mnemonic device. There is little doubt that the bodies of literature which Assmann and Carr analyse originated in largely oral cultures. However, imposing this perspective on the late Second Temple period cannot be fully sustained in light of the manuscript evidence of the period. In terms of 'intertextuality' in antiquity generally, Michaela Bauks, 'Intertextuality in Ancient Literature in Light of Textlinguistics and Cultural Studies', in *Between Text and Text: The Hermeneutics of Intertextuality*

an intrinsic part of the procedure; memory and direct access to textual artefacts cannot be so easily polarized in discussions regarding the social reality of literary composition in early Jewish textual culture. Nonetheless, the burden of proof lies with the one who argues that an ancient author reused a text from memory if evidence indicates that the author or scribe had immediate access to a manuscript – especially if hermeneutical assumption, exegetical reasoning, or graphic similarity explain the variation between source and target text. The imperfect reproduction of wording does not necessarily indicate comprehensive reliance on the faculty of memory; instead, imperfect reproduction suggests, in certain instances, access to the precise wording of source texts if exegetical reasoning or transcriptional probabilities exist that account for the alteration. If one can establish that an author augmented source material based on certain textual cues – especially if these cues are graphic in nature[9] – the burden of proof becomes heavy for one that claims that the variation between source and target text are due *exclusively* to an author's (faulty) memory.

Norton has also argued that, when exegetical logic behind the alteration of lexical or linguistic material from a specific textual tradition of a source text is present, it is difficult to attribute these changes to residual memory.[10] Such alterations likely result from sustained attention to the textual features and internal discourse of the source text in conversation with other connected texts and traditions. Labahn's theory of memory influence may be valid for the reuse of traditional material elsewhere in Revelation, but his argument is inconclusive concerning John's use of Zechariah. The phenomenon of scriptural reuse in Revelation, and the abidingly allusive

---

in *Ancient Cultures and Their Afterlife in Medieval and Modern Times* (JAJsup 6; ed. M. Bauks, W. Horowitz, and A. Lange; Göttingen: Vandenhoeck & Ruprecht, 2013), 37 notes that many source texts were transmitted orally. Nonetheless, our access to this oral data is only tentative and reconstructed, and the only access modern researchers have to this traditional oral textual data is mediated through extant manuscript evidence. These two options must be held in a mutually illuminating tension, although texts like 2 Macc 2.25 and Eusebius' account of Papias' preference for the 'living voice' (*Hist. eccl.* 3.39.4; also 2.15.1; but contrarily 3.36.4) demonstrate a preference for memory and aural learning as a mode of transmission.

[9] For example: interchange of visually similar graphemes, metathesis (although this can also be explained phonologically), parablepsis, haplography, etc.

[10] Norton, *Contours*, 153. In reference to Paul's use of Isa 25.8pM in 1 Cor 15, he notes that '[Paul's] preference for the pM-form of Isa. 25.8 would not amount to an arbitrary and isolated item of residual lexical detail in Paul's memory, but to his engagement with the exegetical discussion reflected in his literary sources.'

nature of this reuse, cannot be accounted for *in toto* by appeals to memory, although neither can the influence of memory and memorization as a practice of reading be ignored.[11] Nonetheless, Labahn's work provides important contributions to the question of textual culture, since he observes the influence of various forms of scriptural works in the undercurrents of John's wording. This points to the reality of a textual polyculture, wherein various sources (transmitted in various forms) influenced the process of literary construction in early Christianity, not unlike the culture of early Judaism described recently by Teeter.[12]

The following data illustrates that John likely worked with textual forms representative of the proto-MT stream, usually in Hebrew but also transmitted in Greek, embedded in scriptural manuscripts (or the immediate memory of a specific textual tradition) and in pre-existing exegetical traditions. Although they are theoretical possibilities, options 11 and 12 (a Greek text influenced by memory of a Hebrew text and a quotation from memory) are ultimately impossible to measure against the extant physical *realia* of ancient textual production. Additionally, they represent categories that do not accurately reflect the social reality of literary encounters (both textual and aural). The memory of distant and immediate literary encounters *always* plays a role in reading, comprehension, and reuse. These options are omnipresent, leading to their obsolescence. Moreover, the textual differences between the wording of John's allusions and the extant forms and sources of Zechariah can be accounted for by other, more concrete explanations. None of the following analyses necessitate that John referenced Zechariah only from distant memory. Options 11 and 12 are not considered further in the subsequent discussion, although memory (whether of a distinct encounter or an omnibus of experiences) *always* plays a role in procedures of reuse. It is more helpful to construe the role of memory as an intrinsic part of accessing texts, in any form via any medium, instead of a category diametrically opposed to textuality and artefactual reading. Therefore, appealing to memory as a source distinct from texts (found in whatever medium) represents a

---

[11] Cf. Wagner, *Heralds*, 26–28.
[12] Teeter, *Scribal Laws*, 254–257.

polarizing appeal to anachronism in terms of the textual culture of early Judaism.

***

As a final prolegomenon, I must note that the examples of redeployments of wordings from Zechariah in Revelation that I have chosen in this chapter represent the clearest examples of direct dependence based on inductive study of the texts in conversation with the copious secondary literature on the reuse of scripture in Revelation. Numerous other texts from Zechariah might have been examined here; however, for the sake of isolating the least controversial examples of reuse, I have exiled texts that share only thematic threads, non-unique lexical items, or which 'influenced' Revelation to Appendix 1. This separation of demonstrable instances of reuse and interpretative engagement from other *potentia* permits the evidence gathered below to speak directly to the questions at the heart of this discussion: John's practices of reuse, his access to scriptural sources, the social realities of literary composition, and his textual hermeneutics.

Some will no doubt point to lists like those in the Nestle-Aland hand editions and suggest that I have not done justice to the quantity of allusions in this study. However, the principles that stand behind the list in NA[28], for example, are not clearly articulated and most often reflect (non-unique) thematic correspondences (e.g. the measuring of the New Jerusalem in Rev 21.15 and Zech 2.6 [cf. Ezek 40–48], the description of the throne in Rev 4.4 and the stones of the crown made in Zech 6.11, and the result of the first trumpet in Rev 8.7 and the oracle in Zech 13.9). These are at most thematic resemblances that may or may not share non-unique lexical items. Perhaps they influence the composition of Revelation, but this is not at all clear.[13] I have selected the following examples because the wording of particular segments of Revelation is clearly dependent on the wording

---

[13] Another example of this is the proposed allusion to Zech 12.11 in Rev 16.16 by John Day, 'The Origin of Armageddon: Revelation 16:16 as an Interpretation of Zechariah 12:11', in *Crossing the Boundaries: Essays in Biblical Interpretation in Honour of Michael D. Goulder* (ed. S. E. Porter, P. Joyce, and D. E. Orton; Leiden: Brill, 1994), 315–326. It is possible and indeed likely that John's depiction of Armageddon is derivative of a scriptural tradition. The identification of Zech 12.11 is also heightened by John's awareness of Zech 12.10, 12 in Rev 1.7. Nonetheless, the highly allusive nature of this proposal, in comparison to other examples selected for this study, does not allow for its examination in this context.

of antecedent Zechariah texts, and because they are representative of John's direct engagement with Zechariah traditions. While I do not always concur with Jauhiainen's judgements, the main portion of his study is valuable in that it collects and evaluates the majority of proposed allusions to Zechariah in preserved in Revelation.[14] I direct readers to his work for a full evaluation of the evidence in a general sense.

3.2 The Textual Form of Zechariah in Revelation

3.2.1 Revelation 1.7 and Zechariah 12.10 (Daniel 7.13)

The first examination of the textual form of Zechariah embedded in Revelation begins with Rev 1.7, where material from Daniel and Zechariah are combined in a single utterance. This utterance immediately follows the epistolary introduction (1.1–3), John's initial address to the seven churches (1.4), and the extended doxology to God, the seven spirits, and Jesus Christ (1.4–6). This doxology emphasizes Jesus' role in making his people a kingdom and priests. Rev 1.7–8 then adopts a governing voice that is different from the preceding introduction (1.1–6) and John's following description of his initial visionary experience (1.9–20),[15] devolving into first-person divine speech that conflates Jesus traditions (1.7) with various divine epithets (1.8). These verses (esp. v. 8), along with others in the Apocalypse (2.1–3.22; 16.15; 22.7, 12–16, 20), constitute 'the only undisputed example from the first century of prophetic utterances made in the name of Christ in the first person'.[16] The locution in 1.7 preserves material from Zech 12.10.[17]

---

14 See Jauhiainen, *The Use*, 62–135.

15 See especially the contrasting ἐγώ clauses of vv. 8–9: Ἐγώ εἰμι τὸ ἄλφα καὶ τὸ ὦ, λέγει κύριος ὁ θεός . . . and Ἐγὼ Ἰωάννης, ὁ ἀδελφὸς ὑμῶν καὶ συγκοινωνὸς ἐν τῇ θλίψει καὶ βασιλείᾳ καὶ ὑπομονῇ ἐν Ἰησοῦ . . .

16 Bauckham, *Climax*, 92.

17 See the extended discussion of this text in Vos, *Synoptic Traditions*, 60–71 and Paul Penley, *The Common Tradition behind Synoptic Sayings of Judgment and John's Apocalypse: An Oral Interpretive Tradition of Old Testament Prophetic Material* (LNTS 424; London: T&T Clark, 2010), 125–130; Labahn, 'Die Septuaginta', 184–188.

Rev 1.7   Ἰδοὺ ἔρχεται μετὰ[18] τῶν νεφελῶν, καὶ ὄψεται[19] αὐτὸν
πᾶς ὀφθαλμὸς καὶ οἵτινες αὐτὸν ἐξεκέντησαν, καὶ
κόψονται ἐπ᾽ αὐτὸν πᾶσαι αἱ φυλαὶ τῆς γῆς.
ναί, ἀμήν

Behold, he is coming with the clouds and every eye will
see him, even those that pierced him and all the tribes
of the earth will wail on account of him. Truly, amen

Zech 12.10[OG]   καὶ ἐκχεῶ ἐπὶ τὸν οἶκον Δαυιδ καὶ ἐπὶ τοὺς
κατοικοῦντας Ιερουσαλημ πνεῦμα χάριτος καὶ
οἰκτιρμοῦ, καὶ ἐπιβλέψονται πρός με ἀνθ ὧν
κατωρχήσαντο καὶ κόψονται ἐπ᾽ αὐτὸν κοπετὸν ὡς
ἐπ᾽ ἀγαπητὸν καὶ ὀδυνηθήσονται ὀδύνην ὡς ἐπὶ
πρωτοτόκῳ

And I will pour out on the house of David and on
the inhabitants of Jerusalem a spirit of grace and
compassion, and they will look upon me because they
have danced triumphantly, and they will wail over
him a lamentation as if for a loved one and they will
be pained with pain as if for a firstborn

Zech 12.10[LXX]
(8HevXIIgr[rec]/
Hexaplaric
Traditions)[20]   καὶ ἐκχεῶ ἐπὶ οἶκον Δαυιδ καὶ ἐπὶ τοὺς κατοικοῦντας
Ιερουσαλημ πνεῦμα χάριτος καὶ οἰκτιρμοῦ καὶ
ἐπιβλέψονται πρός με εἰς ὃν ἐξεκέντησαν καὶ
κόψονται αὐτὸν ὡς κοπετὸν ἐπ᾽ ἀγαπητὸν καὶ
ὀδυνηθήσονται ἐπ᾽αὐτὸν ὡς ὀδύνη ἐπὶ πρωτοτόκῳ

And I will pour out on (the) house of David and on
the inhabitants of Jerusalem a spirit of grace and
compassion, and they will look upon me, to the one
that they pierced and they will wail over him like a
lament over a loved one and they will be pained over
him like a lamentation for a firstborn

Zech 12.10[PM]   ושפכתי על־בית דויד ועל יושב ירושלם רוח חן ותחנונים והביטו
אלי את אשר־דקרו וספדו עליו כמספד על־היחיד והמר עליו
כהמר על־הבכור

And I will pour out over (the) house of David and over
the inhabitants of a Jerusalem a spirit of grace and
supplication, and they will look to me, to the one
they pierced, and they will wail like a lament over
something of value and become bitter over him like
the bitterness for a firstborn

---

[18] ἐπί (=Dan 7.17[OG]) in C 2053 Sa.
[19] ὄψονται (= Matt 24.30 and John 19.37) in א 1611 2351.
[20] See Appendix 2 for editorial decisions in reconstructing 8HevXIIgr.

Dan 7.13^{OG}

ἐθεώρουν ἐν ὁράματι τῆς νυκτὸς καὶ ἰδοὺ ἐπὶ τῶν
νεφελῶν τοῦ οὐρανοῦ ὡς υἱὸς ἀνθρώπου ἤρχετο,
καὶ ὡς παλαιὸς ἡμερῶν παρῆν, καὶ οἱ παρεστηκότες
παρῆσαν αὐτῷ

I saw in a vision of the night and behold on the clouds
of heaven one like a son of man was coming, and with
the Ancient of Days he was present and the attendants
were present with him

Dan 7.13^{Theo}

ἐθεώρουν ἐν ὁράματι τῆς νυκτὸς καὶ ἰδοὺ μετὰ τῶν
νεφελῶν τοῦ οὐρανοῦ ὡς υἱὸς ἀνθρώπου ἐρχόμενος
ἦν καὶ ἕως τοῦ παλαιοῦ τῶν ἡμερῶν ἔφθασεν καὶ
ἐνώπιον αὐτοῦ προσηνέχθη

I saw in a vision of the night and behold with the clouds
of heaven was coming one like a son of man, he went
as far as the Ancient of Days and was presented before
him

Dan 7.13^{pM}

חזה הוית בחזוי ליליא וארו עם־ענני שמיא כבר אנש אתה הוה
ועד־עתיק יומיא מטה וקדמוהי הקרבוהי

I saw in a vision of the night and behold, with the
clouds of heaven was one like a son of man. And he
came until he reached the Ancient of Days and he
presented himself

The first clause of Rev 1.7 (Ἰδοὺ ἔρχεται μετὰ τῶν νεφελῶν) preserves
material from Dan 7.13. Both the Theodontic and OG version of the
material are similar,[21] and stand within the textual stream represented
by the Aramaic in the proto-MT. The presentation of material in Rev
1.7 differs in two small-scale ways from both versions: the location and
morphology of the verb, and the omission of 'like a son of man' (ὡς
υἱὸς ἀνθρώπου).[22] Nonetheless, it is uncontroversial that opening clause
of Rev 1.7 reuses Dan 7.13, and that a Greek form of Daniel (likely
Theodotion since its verbal form of ἐρχόμενος ἦν corresponds more
closely to the present tense verb in Rev 1.7) stands behind the form of
the text in Rev 1.7 (even though it is similar to the Aramaic as well).[23]

[21] Differences include the choice of preposition (μετὰ or ἐπί, both of which
find attestation in Revelation's textual history) and the form of ἔρχομαι. The
versions differ also in their representation of the second clause in Dan 7.13
(הוה ועד־עתיק יומיא מטה וקדמוהי הקרבוהי), but both are reasonable representations of the
Aramaic. Dan 7.13 is not preserved in the Judean Desert material.

[22] Perhaps implied in the subject of ἔρχεται, supported by the visionary description
in Rev 1.13.

[23] So Beale, *Jewish Apocalyptic*, 154–156; Beale, *John's Use*, 100–105; Aune,
Revelation 1–5, 54–55; Koester, *Revelation*, 218–219.

The next clause, 'and every eye will see him, even those that pierced him' (καὶ ὄψεται αὐτὸν πᾶς ὀφθαλμὸς καὶ οἵτινες αὐτὸν ἐξεκέντησαν), follows the wording of a Greek form of Zech 12.10 revised towards the proto-MT. The pertinent phraseology in Zech 12.10^OG, 'and they will look upon me because they have danced triumphantly' (καὶ ἐπιβλέψονται πρός με ἀνθ ὧν κατωρχήσαντο) is markedly different in this instance from both its proto-MT *Vorlage* and the wording in Rev 1.7, as a result of the translator's reading רקדו ('they danced') for דקרו ('they pierced').[24] The revisions of OG tradition preserved in the Hexapla, and most likely also the textual stream represented by 8HevXIIgr, each revise this reading to better reflect the semantic sense of the proto-MT: α θ preserve ἐξεκέντησαν ('they pierced').[25] This choice of equivalent for דקרו corresponds to the wording of Rev 1.7, indicating that either the presentation of Rev 1.7 was informed by Zech 12.10^PM or a Greek tradition that stands in the same semantic stream. Based solely on the text-historical information, I am not convinced that Revelation's wording incidentally reflects revising Greek traditions in this instance as a result of John's direct engagement with a Hebrew text. The underlying Hebrew term (דקר) is represented with various Greek terms in the OG/LXX and John might have easily selected another equivalent beyond ἐξεκέντησαν if he had directly accessed a Hebrew text.[26] Thus far, the *Vorlage* of the wording of Rev 1.7 for both Daniel and Zechariah material points in the direction of a Greek tradition revised towards the proto-MT.[27]

The final clause in Rev 1.7, 'and all the tribes of the earth will wail on account of him' (καὶ κόψονται ἐπ' αὐτὸν πᾶσαι αἱ φυλαὶ τῆς γῆς), also derives from Zech 12.10, 12 in the form of a Greek tradition. The first portion of this line (καὶ κόψονται ἐπ' αὐτὸν) follows immediately from the previous line in Zech 12.10, and, in Rev 1.7, it follows

---

[24] So Albl, *Form and Function*, 253–254; Tripaldi, 'Discrepat', 132. Albl attributes the OG reading to 'an attempt to avoid this strongly anthropomorphic reading', but this reasoning is uncertain. The graphic similarity of *dalet* and *resh* and employment of metathesis as a resource for reading might better explain this variation.

[25] σ = ἐπεξεκέντησαν.

[26] Other equivalents for דקר include ἀποκεντεῖν ('to kill') (Num 25.8; 1 Sam 31.4 [2x]); συνποδίζειν ('to bind [feet]') (Zech 13.3); ἡττᾶν ('to be inferior') (Isa 13.15); or κατακεντεῖν ('to pierce [together], cut down') (Ezek 23.47).

[27] Contra Penley, *Common Tradition*, 126 who does not consider the Greek revising traditions, suggesting that the tradition is here dependent on Zech 12.10^PM.

the wording of the OG tradition, preserving the preposition (ἐπ') against the revising Greek traditions that unanimously omit it.[28] The second portion of this verse (πᾶσαι αἱ φυλαὶ τῆς γῆς) corresponds imperfectly to the wording of Zech 12.12–14, a locution that also preserves a form of κόπτω as its main verb, connecting it with v. 10. This verse describes the mourning of different groups, which are condensed into the description 'all the tribes of the earth' in Rev 1.7 (cf. Zech 9.1), and which possibly alludes also to Gen 12.3 (cf. Gen 28.14; Ps 71[72].17).[29] Zech 12.12[OG] is a literal representation of the proto-MT, thus it is somewhat unclear as to which form of the verse is represented in Rev 1.7, especially since Rev 1.7 is more allusive in its representation of this clause.

Taken as a whole, the linguistic evidence indicates that the reused material in Rev 1.7 reflects the wording of a revising LXX tradition. This reality necessitates that the semantics of the material also corresponds quite closely to the proto-MT, but in this case, the fact that Rev 1.7 does not preserve any peculiarities that must have arisen from a particular reading of Hebrew consonants and that ἐξεκέντησαν is deployed indicates that a Greek tradition underlies the wording of this verse.[30]

Despite the fact that Greek scriptural traditions are embedded in Revelation, it is not self-evident that John accessed these traditions (Daniel and Zechariah) through the medium of reading full-text scriptural manuscripts in this instance.[31] Similar combinations of Dan 7.13 and Zech 12.10, 12 in other NT works suggests that this conflation of texts was part of an early Christian exegetical tradition,

---

[28] ℵ* 2050 2344 2351 omit the preposition in Revelation in line with the revising traditions. The textual history of Revelation preserves the reading in the OG and the revising traditions (LXX).

[29] So Bauckham, *Climax*, 321 who notes that both Zech 12.12 and Gen 12.3 share the similar phrases משפחות הארץ and משפחת האדמה, a connection also to Ps 71(72).17. Beale, *John's Use*, 100–105 argues that the inclusion of the phrase 'all the tribes of the earth' is part of John's 'universalizing' hermeneutic towards the OT. A better explanation for the wording of Rev 1.7 lies in examining the internal logic of Zech 12 as the compiler of this tradition understood it. Additionally, if John inherited this Daniel/Zechariah exegetical tradition, he is actually doing very little hermeneutically.

[30] So Barnabas Lindars, *New Testament Apologetic: The Doctrinal Significance of the Old Testament Quotations* (London: SCM, 1961), 122–124; Bauckham, *Climax*, 320.

[31] Contra Jauhiainen, *The Use*, 103–104 who argues that John reused material directly from Hebrew Zechariah and was, perhaps, influenced by Matt 24.30.

a tradition (preserved most clearly in Matt 24.30 and John 19.36–37) that is likely John's source for this material (as opposed to directly accessing copies of Zechariah and Daniel, although it is possible that John also accessed these texts in this manner).

Matt 24.30[32]   καὶ τότε φανήσεται τὸ σημεῖον τοῦ υἱοῦ τοῦ ἀνθρώπου
ἐν οὐρανῷ, καὶ τότε κόψονται πᾶσαι αἱ φυλαὶ τῆς γῆς
καὶ ὄψονται *τόν υἱόν τοῦ ἀνθρώπου ἐρχόμενον ἐπὶ τῶν*
νεφελῶν τοῦ οὐρανοῦ μετὰ δυνάμεως καὶ δόξης πολλῆς

John 19.36–37   ἐγένετο γὰρ ταῦτα ἵνα ἡ γραφὴ πληρωθῇ· ὀστοῦν οὐ
συντριβήσεται αὐτοῦ. καὶ πάλιν ἑτέρα γραφὴ λέγει·
ὄψονται εἰς ὃν ἐξεκέντησαν.

The agreement in wording between Rev 1.7 and Matt 24.30 in particular points to the fact that the author of Revelation did not independently access material from Hebrew Zechariah, but was dependent on an already existing tradition common also to apocalyptic discourse in the Gospels. Notably, the presence of forms of ὄψεται/ὄψονται and the verbatim repetition of πᾶσαι αἱ φυλαὶ τῆς γῆς, both of which Matt 24.30 and Rev 1.7 have in common against Zechariah's Greek versions points to a common exegetical tradition and source.[33] John 19.37 also shares these peculiarities even though it does not preserve material from Daniel, but is instead prefaced by a separate quotation of Ps 34.21 in v. 36.[34]

Since these texts share agreements that are not preserved in any known textual tradition, the question of the source of these Gospel quotations and the reference in Rev 1.7 naturally arises. First, the quotation in John 19.37 is somewhat anomalous, a reality that might point to an alternative source. The quotation is not employed in the context of first-person sayings of Jesus, but as a proof text for details surrounding Jesus' death. Additionally, this quotation is not conflated with Daniel material. These facts have led Bynum to argue

[32] Cf. Mark 13.26 // Luke 21.27.
[33] Wilcox, 'Text Form', 201–202; Bauckham, *Climax*, 319–320, 322; Albl, *Form and Function*, 253; Bynum, *Fourth Gospel*, 150.
[34] M. J. J. Menken, 'The Textual Form and the Meaning of Zech 12:10 in John 19:37', *CBQ* 55 (1993): 494–509 (esp. 504) argues that the Johannine evangelist did not access a Hebrew text of Zechariah directly, but instead a Christian exegetical tradition encoded in Greek. See Bynum, *Fourth Gospel*, 2–5 for a brief survey of this history of understanding Zech 12.10 in John 19.37.

that the Johannine evangelist used a form of Zechariah preserved in 8HevXIIgr, independent of any circulating Jesus traditions or exegetical collections (*testimonia* or the like).[35] While I am hesitant to identify the textual tradition of a particular manuscript, the relevant portion of which is not extant, as the source for a quotation, Bynum does recognize that the textual form of the quotation corresponds to features of the early revising tradition of which 8HevXIIgr is the earliest witness. It is possible that the source of the quotation in John is a scriptural text like that once preserved in 8HevXIIgr, a text that stands well within the semantic stream anchored by the proto-MT.

However, when it comes to Matt 24.30 and Rev 1.7, the shared features of these texts against known forms strongly suggest that they are undergirded by a shared exegetical tradition that combined material from Daniel and Zechariah,[36] a tradition that couched Jesus sayings in exegetically sophisticated scriptural language associated with the *parousia*.[37] Despite this common underlying tradition, the wording of the traditional conflation remained malleable. Matthew cites Zechariah first, then includes wording from Daniel, an inversion of the ordering in Revelation. Additionally, Matthew includes more material from Daniel than Zechariah, again, the inverse of the situation in Rev 1.7. In this manner, the source of Rev 1.7 (an exegetical tradition whose wording reflects a revised and interpreted Greek textual form) remained fluid in its wording, even though its deployment in apocalyptic discourses is similar in both Matthew and Revelation. The transmission and use of exegetical traditions corresponds closely to the way that scriptural manuscripts were handled in this period: they were fluid and remained supple to a certain extent.

The question of the transmission of this tradition is further problematized by its purported medium. Did the author of

---

[35] Bynum, *Fourth Gospel*, 161–169, following the assertion of Robert Hanhart, Introduction to *The Septuagint as Christian Scripture*, by Martin Hengel (trans. M. E. Biddle; Edinburgh: T&T Clark, 2002), 7.

[36] Contra Charles, *The Revelation*, 1.lxxxiv who suggests that John borrowed directly from Matthew.

[37] As an aside, this observation supports Chris Keith's argument that, although Jesus was not a scribal-literate teacher, his followers sometimes remembered him as such (*Jesus' Literacy: Scribal Culture and the Teacher from Galilee* [LNTS 413; London: T&T Clark, 2011]).

Revelation access this tradition, the wording of which was encoded in the form of revising Greek traditions, through oral or textual sources? The majority of scholars have argued for an oral medium of transmission of these common traditions,[38] while Menken and Albl have argued forcefully for a written medium.[39] There are benefits and issues with both positions. First, those that argue for an oral medium are right to note that *verbum Christi* traditions likely had wide currency in oral/aural settings, including early liturgical locations embedded in hymns, homiletic discourses, or apologetic/doctrinal formulations. The majority of early Christians would have encountered these traditions only through oral performance. Some support for the existence of Daniel/Zechariah tradition in this setting is found in quotations from Justin (*Dial.* 14.8; *1 Apol.* 52.12) and other early Christian literature (*Did.* 16.8; *Barn.* 7.9; *Apoc. Pet.* 6),[40] although the tradition's inscription in these works and its NT instantiations demonstrates that it was inscribed in a textual medium from an early stage. This observation brings up the obvious issue with assuming that John had access to this tradition via non-textual sources: the tradition is encoded textually at an early juncture in various written works. Perhaps the question of aural vs. written medium also assumes a particular social status and literary capability for the author of Revelation. If John was a highly educated and textually competent person who had developed a set of 'scribal' or literary skills, there is no reason to assume that he did not read this tradition. Regardless of the question of John's social standing among the scribal elite (a topic of conversation to which we will return), the tradition's presence in Matthew demonstrates that by the end of the first century this specific Daniel/Zechariah conflation was transmitted textually as well as orally.

However, this point does not necessarily prove that John accessed this tradition via written sources, although it does gesture in this direction. The main problem with the previous arguments that John encountered this tradition textually is that scholarly portraits

---

[38] Stendahl, *The School*, 212–215; Lindars, *Apologetic*, 122–127; Vos, *Synoptic Traditions*, 22–24; Bauckham, *Climax*, 318–326; Penley, *Common Tradition*, 163.

[39] Menken, 'The Form and the Meaning', 504; Albl, *Form and Function*, 254–265.

[40] See Tripaldi, 'Discrepat', 131–143 for more on the early Christian reception of this tradition.

of early Christian textual encounters have been wrapped up with *testimonia* hypotheses, a perspective best illustrated by Albl's work, whose underlying model of the common existence and use of textualized *testimonia* collections in early Christian literature is problematic for numerous reasons. In addition to other objections,[41] his conception of early Christian engagements with Jewish scripture only partially accounts for the evidence in NT works. He argues that the 'core of all *testimonia* hypotheses is the claim that early Christians did not use Jewish scripture as an undifferentiated whole, but rather selected, shaped, and interpreted certain passages in support of emerging Christian beliefs'.[42] It is self-evident that particular scriptural works were more widely used in early Christianity (as was true also in the *Yaḥad*), but the shaping and selection of theologically pertinent passages that Albl envisions cannot account for the variety of reused material in the NT, especially the more allusive referencing habits that demonstrate awareness of more than isolated and thematically linked texts.

Direct access to scriptural texts through both oral and textual channels without the help of written *testimonia* collections certainly occurred in this period. Nonetheless, based on the competing scholarly perspectives and mixed evidence, I suggest that John's engagement with this particular exegetical tradition in

---

[41] Including: the lack of clear physical evidence (although some manuscripts have been argued to function in this manner, e.g. P. Rylands Greek 460) and the assumed apologetic setting for these collections. Furthermore, the Jewish evidence that Albl offers for existence of these *excerpta* collections is unconvincing (cf. *Form and Function*, 84–93). He suggests that paratextual markers in 1QIsaᵃ and allusions/quotations in CD 6–7, 4QRPᵃ, and portions of the Temple Scroll (11QTemple 19–20) are evidence of *excerpta* collections (among other examples). These examples are better evidence for scriptural interpretation, even if the traditions were drawn from existing sources, than evidence for the existence of written *excerpta* collection. This is a confusion of medium and exegesis. Additionally, Albl (*Form and Function*, 97–158) argues that the primary channel of transmission of quotations of Jewish scripture in early Christianity was written *testimonia* sources, as opposed to direct access to manuscripts, borrowing from other early Christian traditions, or oral/aural experience and memory. I am unconvinced by this assertion, primarily because the explanation is too all encompassing, although a step forward from Harris's less nuanced approach a century earlier. A broader and more complex stream of tradition and transmission must be at play and (perhaps) written *testimonia* are a part of this tradition. Yet, Albl confuses the medium of the scriptural utterance with the utterance itself – its form and function within the tradition to which it belonged (e.g. p. 158).

[42] Albl, *Form and Function*, 65.

Rev 1.7 arose through a combination of oral and textual channels pertaining to an exegetical tradition of Jesus sayings. He may have encountered this *parousia* tradition through oral communication or other liturgical/homiletical avenues, in addition to textual encounters, reading the composite citation in other early Christian works. As the evidence in the following examples demonstrates, John was acutely aware of the details of the scriptural traditions themselves (including Zechariah), even when they are not part of a known exegetical tradition, indicating that he was independently aware of the texts combined in this tradition, probably through access to written texts. John may have accessed the tradition through numerous points of contact, both aural and graphic. The many channels of possible access reflect more broadly the mediating points of contact between readers and scripture in this period. Some scriptural texts were collected into traditions pertaining to certain doctrinal issues, but early Christian writers also accessed Jewish scripture directly.

Ultimately, the textual form of Dan 7.13 and Zech 12.10, 12 in Rev 1.7 best reflects a Greek tradition revised towards the proto-MT, corresponding either to option 5 (καιγε recension [8HevXIIgr]) or 6 (proto-Hexaplaric recension) articulated above (Section 3.1), although he does not aim at isomorphic reproduction of the wording of these traditions, as is his habit. However, the presence of a similar combination in other early Christian texts suggests that John may not have accessed these text forms directly, but through the mediating presence of an exegetical tradition pertaining to Jesus' *parousia* sayings that was already encoded the combination in a revising Greek form, perhaps in some form of *excerpta* collection, although I think it best to remain agnostic on this point. It is not uncommon for John to deploy traditions that have wide currency in early Judaism and Christianity. Rev 5.5 and 22.16 preserve material from Gen 49.9, Isa 11.1, 10, and Num 24.17, texts that coalesce in different combinations (occasionally in combination with Zech 6.12) in many other works to support messianic ideologies (e.g. *4 Ezra* 13.10; *1 En.* 49.3–4; CD 7.18–21; 1QM 11.5–7; *T. Jud.* 24; Heb 7.14; Justin, *Dia.* 32, 120–121).[43] Moreover, the use of Ps 110.1 in Rev 3.21 also corresponds to the many other uses of this locution in early Christian literature to describe Jesus'

---

[43] Although his insistence that these three texts circulated in a written *testimonia* collection is far from certain, Albl, *Form and Function*, 208–216 gathers much of the relevant data pertaining to the reuse of these texts in early Judaism and Christianity.

exaltation,[44] and the use of material from Ezek 1 and 10 (cf. Isa 6.2–3) to describe heavenly beings in Rev 4 corresponds to similar formulations in 4Q385.[45]

The author of Revelation partakes in early Jewish and Christian textual culture as it relates to exegetical traditions. Scriptural encounters inherently constituted exegetical encounters, but this particular encounter is forcefully shaped by antecedent interpretative traditions. In the case of Rev 1.7, it is possible that the Daniel/Zechariah exegetical tradition itself (independent of John's reuse of it) represents a *de novo* translation of the proto-MT that is independent of both the OG and revising traditions,[46] but this is ultimately uncertain. All that can be said with certainty is that John was aware of a revised Greek form of Zechariah that circulated in the form of an exegetical tradition connected to Jesus sayings. The tradition was, by this time, circulating in a Greek form that closely resembled the proto-MT stream, representing a 'set but independent text form'.[47]

3.2.2 Revelation 5.6b and Zechariah 4.10[48]

Next, our analysis moves on to the redeployment of Zech 4.10 in Rev 5.6b, the fourth and final reference to the seven spirits 'before God's throne' (1.4) or 'of God' (3.1; 4.5; 5.6). The locution examined here is the culmination of the extended description of the heavenly court and its ministers in Rev 4.2–5.6. The picture of heavenly worship climaxes with the image of the slain, yet standing lamb among the throne and twenty-four elders, a picture prefaced by the proclamation that the 'lion of the tribe of Judah, the root of David' is coming to take the scroll from the one who sits on the throne (5.5; cf. Isa 11.1–3, 10).[49] The reference in 5.6 is analysed in this section among the other 'seven spirits' locutions because it includes the phrase ἀπεσταλμένοι εἰς πᾶσαν τὴν γῆν ('having been sent into all the earth'), a phrase

---

[44] See Albl, *Form and Function*, 217–219.

[45] See Brooke, *The Dead Sea Scrolls and the New Testament*, 86–89. He notes, 'there is no literary dependence here, but a complex variable exegetical representation of a scriptural experience which can only be adequately expressed by reference to more than one biblical text' (89).

[46] So Menken, 'The Form and the Meaning', 504.

[47] Wilcox, 'Text Form', 201.

[48] I have examined this text elsewhere in some depth. See Allen, 'Textual Pluriformity', 136–145.

[49] For the role of Isaiah traditions in this pericope, see Dochhorn, *Schriftgelehrte Prophetie*, 69.

that elucidates the source of the reference. Each of the references to the 'seven spirits' is interconnected,[50] but I focus on the reference in 5.6b because it contains the locution which identifies the source text for this pattern of references.[51] The overwhelming scholarly consensus and close linguistic relationship between Zech 4.10 and Rev 5.6b, indicate that John reused material from Zechariah.[52]

---

[50] See Bauckham, *Climax*, 162–163.

[51] See Appendix 1 for an overview of the mechanics of reuse pertaining to the other 'seven spirits' texts.

[52] See Lohmeyer, *Die Offenbarung* (1927), 52–53; Franz Tóth, 'Von der Vision zur Redaktion: Untersuchungen zur Komposition, Redaktion und Intention der Johannesapokalypse', in *Die Johannesapokalypse* (ed. J. Frey, J. A. Kelhoffer, and F. Tóth; WUNT 287; Tübingen: Mohr Siebeck, 2012), 348; Koester, *Revelation*, 377; Labahn, 'Die Macht', 406–407; Brian K. Blount, *Revelation: A Commentary* (NTL; Louisville: WJK, 2009), 112; Wilfrid J. Harrington, *Revelation* (SP 16; Collegeville, MN: Liturgical Press, 1993), 84–85; Richard Bauckham, *The Theology of the Book of Revelation* (Cambridge: Cambridge University Press, 1993), 110–115; Jürgen Roloff, *The Revelation of John* (trans. J. E. Alsup; Minneapolis: Fortress, 1993), 79; Maier, *Die Offenbarung*, 1.300; Heinz Giesen, *Die Offenbarung des Johannes* (RNT; Regensburg: Pustet, 1997), 168; Leonard L. Thompson, *Revelation* (ANTC; Nashville: Abingdon, 1998), 95; George E. Ladd, *A Commentary on the Revelation of John* (Grand Rapids: Eerdmans, 1972), 88; R. Dean Davis, *The Heavenly Court Judgment of Revelation 4–5* (London: University Press of America, 1992), 138; Ronald L. Farmer, 'Undercurrents and Paradoxes: The Apocalypse of John in Process Hermeneutic', in *Reading the Book of Revelation* (RBS 44; ed. D. Barr; Atlanta: SBL, 2003), 115; Smalley, *The Revelation*, 133; Moyise, *Old Testament*, 33; J. Massyngberde Ford, *Revelation* (AB 38; Garden City, NY: Doubleday, 1975), 377; Jonathan Knight, *Revelation* (Sheffield: Sheffield Academic Press, 1999), 34, 60; Beale, *Revelation*, 355; Beale, *John's Use*, 106; Aune, *Revelation 1–5*, 353–354; G. B. Caird, *The Revelation of St John* (BNTC; Peabody, MA: Hendrickson, 1966), 75; G. R. Beasley-Murray, *The Book of Revelation* (NCB; London: Oliphants, 1974), 124–126; John Sweet, *Revelation* (London: SCM, 1979), 65; Pierre Prigent, *L'Apocalypse de Saint Jean* (Geneva: Labor et Fides, 2000), 193; Martin Karrer, *Die Johannesoffenbarung als Brief: Studien zu ihrem literarischen, historischen und theologischen Ort* (FRLANT 140; Göttingen: Vandenhoeck & Ruprecht, 1986), 237; Ian Boxall, *The Revelation of Saint John* (BNTC; London: Continuum, 2006), 99; Kelley Coblentz Bautch, 'Putting Angels in Their Place: Developments in Second Temple Angelology', in *With Wisdom as a Robe: Qumran and Other Jewish Studies in Honour of Ida Fröhlich* (HBM 21; ed. K. D. Dobos and M. Kőszeghy; Sheffield: Sheffield Phoenix, 2009), 180 n. 23; Austin Farrer, *The Revelation of St. John the Divine* (Oxford: Clarendon, 1964), 95; Grant R. Osborne, *Revelation* (BECNT; Grand Rapids: Baker, 2002), 257; Leon Morris, *Revelation* (TNTC 20; Grand Rapids: Eerdmans, 1984), 97; A. Tauschev and S. Rose, *The Apocalypse in the Teachings of Ancient Christianity* (2nd edn; Platina, CA: St. Herman of Alaska Brotherhood, 1998), 119; Swete, *The Apocalypse*, 78; Charles, *The Revelation*, 14; Beckwith, *The Apocalypse*, 510; Furthermore, many of the earliest commentators on Revelation identify this reference, including Oecumenius and Andrew of Caesarea. The primary dissenter in this

Rev 5.6b[53]   ἀρνίον . . . ἔχων κέρατα ἑπτὰ καὶ ὀφθαλμοὺς ἑπτὰ οἵ εἰσιν
                τὰ [ἑπτὰ] πνεύματα τοῦ θεοῦ ἀπεσταλμένοι εἰς πᾶσαν
                τὴν γῆν

                a lamb . . . having seven horns and seven eyes, those which are
                the seven spirits of God going about in all the earth

Zech 4.10b[PM]   שבעה־אלה עיני יהוה המה משוטטים בכל־הארץ

                These seven are the eyes of YHWH, they go eagerly about in all
                the earth

While these texts are semantically similar, the representation of this
locution in Rev 5.6b witnesses some lexical differentiation. The first difference between traditions is the substitution of 'spirits' (πνεύματα) for
'eyes' (עיני). While morphologically similar, there is no example of πνεῦμα
as an equivalent of עין in the OG/LXX tradition; πνεῦμα is almost exclusively a translation of רוח.[54] The presence of πνεῦμα in Rev 5.6b may
derive from Zech 4.6, an oracle in which Zerubbabel is told that he will
rebuild the temple 'by my *spirit* (ברוחי)'. The artistry of the conflation
of material in Zech 4 is even clearer when one notes that the slain lamb
(Rev 5.6a) is described as having ὀφθαλμοὺς ἑπτά ('seven eyes') immediately preceding the reference proper. The 'eyes' of the lamb are identified as 'spirits'. Interestingly, 'eyes' is precisely the term that is present in
Zech 4.10, but altered in Rev 5.6. All the material from Zech 4.10b[PM] is
present, but one lexeme (עין) has been substituted for a contextually local
word that John has, for some reason, conflated (ברוחי).

discussion is Ben Witherington III, *Revelation* (NCBC; Cambridge: Cambridge University
Press, 2003), 75. He argues that the seven spirits correspond to the seven archangels surrounding God's throne and sees this fourfold reference as a reference to Tobit 12.15, *1 En.*
20.1–8, and 4Qserek. He does not identify to which text the author is actually alluding.
Joseph A. Fitzmyer, *Tobit* (CEJL; Berlin: De Gruyter, 2003), 296 suggests that the author
of Tobit's conception of seven angels derives from Zech 4.10 and Robert J. Littman, *Tobit*
(SC; Leiden: Brill, 2008), 146 identifies traditions relating to Tobit's seven angels in Rev
8.6. Bogdan G. Bocur, *Angelomorphic Pneumatology: Clement of Alexandria and Other
Early Christian Witnesses* (VCsup 95; Leiden: Brill, 2009), 98–99, also fails to connect the
'seven spirits' to Zech 4. Margaret Barker, *The Revelation of Jesus Christ* (Edinburgh: T&T
Clark, 2000), 131 suggests that the seven eyes of the lamb (5.6) and the menorah lamps
(1.4) are both the seven archangels and the fullness of God's spirit. She recognizes the connection to Zech 4.10, but uses Col 1.19 to elucidate the passage.

[53] The bracketed word (ἑπτά) is absent in some textual witnesses. The two earliest
witnesses of this verse both include ἑπτά (P24 ℵ), and its absence in 02 is the only early
manuscript that does not witness it.

[54] See HRCS, 1151–1153.

Table 3.1 *Textual difference between Rev 5.6b and Zech 4.10b^PM*

Rev 5.6b	Zech 4.10b
πνεύματα	עיני

Beyond this lexical substitution, the wording of Rev 5.6b is nearly identical to Zech 4.10b^PM (see Table 3.1). The nearly unanimous scholarly consensus and the semantic, syntactic, and serial similarities between Zech 4.10b^PM and Rev 5.6b affirm that Rev 5.6b is in fact a reference to Zech 4.10b. Although the relationship between these texts has been firmly established, it remains possible that John used an OG/LXX version. First, however, it is helpful to examine the relationship between the proto-MT and *V*OG of Zechariah to determine the viability of option 2 as a source for John's scriptural reference. If the *V*OG and the proto-MT are similar, as I argued on a large scale in the previous chapter (Section 2.7), option 2 becomes redundant. The following investigation confirms that, in the case of Zech 4.10b, the *V*OG is very similar, if not identical, to the proto-MT.

Zech 4.10b^OG55   ἑπτὰ οὗτοι ὀφθαλμοὶ κυρίου εἰσὶν οἱ ἐπιβλέποντες ἐπὶ πᾶσαν τὴν γῆν

These seven eyes of the Lord are the ones looking about on all the earth

Zech 4.10b^PM   שבעה־אלה עיני יהוה המה משוטטים בכל־הארץ

These seven are the eyes of YHWH, they go eagerly about in all the earth

The OG translation is a literal rendering of a proto-MT *Vorlage.*[56] Each Greek word corresponds to a Hebrew equivalent, and the traditions share precise serial fidelity. There is no quantitative difference

---

[55] In this locution, W stands within the OG stream.

[56] I use 'literal' in the same sense as defined by Barr, *Typology of Literalism* (1979). He argues that there are 'different kinds of literality, diverse levels of literal connection, and

Table 3.2 *Textual difference between Zech 4.10b^OG and Zech 4.10b^pM*

OG	Proto-MT
ἐπιβλέποντες	משוטטים

between the texts (see Table 3.2). In addition, the figurative phrase 'eyes of theLord' is literally translated into Greek (οὗτοι ὀφθαλμοὶ κυρίου). The only difference between the proto-MT and the OG is the translation of משוטטים as ἐπιβλέποντες, a unique rendering in the OG/LXX tradition.[57] Syntactically the words are identical, but the semantic meaning has changed from 'to go eagerly'[58] to 'to look intently'.[59] There are three possible options that explain the translator's divergence from the proto-MT: 1. a purposeful change to reflect more appropriately the actions of the 'eyes'; 2. a change resulting from a contextual deciphering of a rare word that was unknown to the translator (ממשושטים); 3. the 'change' actually reflects a non proto-MT *Vorlage*. There are no extant variant readings of משוטטים and, because the syntax of the rest of the locution is identical to the proto-MT, there is little evidence to indicate a *Vorlage* other than the proto-MT. Most likely, this translation reflects an attempt to decipher a rare and difficult verb based on its nominal subject.[60] Despite this difference, the syntax of Zech 4.10b^OG is identical to the syntax of the proto-MT. This suggests the proto-MT is identical to the *Vorlage* of Zech 4.10b^OG. This equation eliminates option 2, insofar as it is identical to option 1. The proto-MT and *V*OG reflect identical traditions in this locution.

It is clear that both Rev 5.6b and Zech 4.10b^OG correspond closely to Zech 4.10b^pM. Even so, we must ask how Zech 4.10^OG and Rev 5.6b relate to each other.

---

various kinds of departure from the literal' (7). He goes on to chart the 'distinguishable modes of difference between a more literal and a less literal rendering of a Hebrew text' (20).

[57] Cf. Dan 12.4; Amos 8.12; Jer 5.1.

[58] BDB, 1002. *HALOT*, 1440 suggests 'to roam about'.

[59] BDAG, 368; LSJ, 625.

[60] J. Ross Wagner, *Reading the Sealed Book: Old Greek Isaiah and the Problem of Septuagint Hermeneutics* (Waco: Baylor University Press, 2013), 198 identifies a similar approach by the translator of Isa 1^OG where this scribe 'seeks to iron out the awkward wrinkle in his *Vorlage* by harmonising the verbs in vv. 29–30'.

Rev 5.6b ἀρνίον . . . ἔχων κέρατα ἑπτὰ καὶ ὀφθαλμοὺς ἑπτὰ οἵ εἰσιν
τὰ [ἑπτὰ] πνεύματα τοῦ θεοῦ ἀπεσταλμένοι εἰς πᾶσαν
τὴν γῆν

a lamb . . . having seven horns and seven eyes, those which
are the seven spirits of God going about in all the earth

Zech 4.10b^OG ἑπτὰ οὗτοι ὀφθαλμοὶ κυρίου εἰσὶν οἱ ἐπιβλέποντες ἐπὶ
πᾶσαν τὴν γῆν

These seven eyes of the Lord are the ones looking about on all
the earth

There are four differences that distinguish these texts (see Table
3.3). First, Rev 5.6b reads πνεύματα ('spirits') while the OG witnesses
ὀφθαλμοί ('eyes' = proto-MT). In this case, the textual history of Zech
4.10b is united against the text of Rev 5.6b. Second, Rev 5.6b reads θεοῦ for יהוה while Zech 4.10b^OG reads
κυρίου. The difference in Revelation might be explained as a pur-
poseful modification as each of the other three references to 'seven
spirits' includes θεοῦ in its surrounding context, although θεός is not
an uncommon translation of יהוה.[61]

The third difference between Zech 4.10b^OG and Rev 5.6b is the
translation of משוטטים: ἀπεσταλμένοι in Revelation and ἐπιβλέποντες
in the OG.[62] The semantics of ἀπεσταλμένοι suggest a gloss similar
to 'going about',[63] a reading that is more closely related to the idea
of 'going' (משוטטים) than the OG translation of 'looking intently'
(ἐπιβλέποντες). Syntactically, the words also differ. Both are masculine plural participles, but ἀπεσταλμένοι is a perfect passive construction and ἐπιβλέποντες is in the present tense and active voice.
Finally, the texts differ in their translation of the preposition ב. Rev
5.6b presents εἰς, while Zech 4.10b^OG preserves ἐπί. This difference is
attributed to the polysemic nature of ב and influenced by the prefix
of each verb each used to represent משוטטים.

The reconstruction of Zech 4.10b in 8HevXIIgr may witness εἰς
against the OG (ἐπί), in agreement with Rev 5.6b (see Appendix 2),
but this reconstruction does not intimate that the καιγε recension might represent the underlying textual form of the *Vorlage* of
this scriptural reference. Three textual differences remain between

---

[61] See John W. Wevers, 'The Interpretive Character and Significance of the Septuagint
Version', in *HB/OT*, 105.
[62] OG/LXX 538 reads βλεποντες.
[63] BDAG, 120–121; LSJ 219.

Table 3.3 *Textual difference between Rev 5.6 and Zech 4.10b^{OG}*

Rev 5.6	Zech 4.10b^{OG}
πνεύματα	ὀφθαλμοί
θεοῦ	Κυρίου
ἀπεσταλμένοι	ἐπιβλέποντες
εἰς	ἐπί

8HevXIIgr and Rev 5.6b in contrast to the single example of variation preserved between the proto-MT and Rev 5.6b. These differences suggest that the OG and/or the καιγε recension (Options 4–5) of Zech 4.10b were not the textual forms that stand behind the presentation of reused material in Rev 5.6b. Zech 4.10b^{OG} and Rev 5.6b are closely related to the proto-MT (one difference each) but differ from each other (four differences), implying that these traditions are independent translations of proto-MT. Within this scheme, the reconstructed text of Zech 4.10b in 8HevXIIgr stands between the OG and proto-MT traditions.[64] Besides the modification of πνεύματα as a translation equivalent for עיני,[65] the only semantic or syntactic difference between Rev 5.6b and proto-MT is the passive voice used to translate the active participle in the Hebrew sentence (משוטטים). However, the consonantal Hebrew text is ambiguous in terms of voice, and the participle can be translated, depending on the reading tradition, as either active *or* passive. John read this verb with a reading tradition that differed from the traditions preserved by the Masoretes and the OG translator (MT/*V*OG: מְשׁוֹטְטִים; Rev 5.6: מְשׁוּטָטִים). Rev 5.6b is a near verbatim translation of Zech 4.10b^{pM}. The textual evidence compels the conclusion that the primary source text that John used to craft his reference in Rev 5.6b is the proto-MT, although small alterations are present. Because Rev 5.6b is nearly identical to Zech 4.10b^{pM}, the options for source text have been winnowed down to options 1 and 7. The evidence suggests that John used a combination of these two options: he translated the proto-MT (Option 1), but made small alterations to the text in the process of incorporating linguistic material into his composition (Option 7). A Hebrew text of Zech 4.10b underlies this scriptural reference.

[64] There is no Hexaplaric evidence that stands against OG in Zech 4.10b. See F. Fields, *Origenis Hexaplorum* (vol. 2; Oxford: Benediction Classics, 2010), 1020 (Option 6).

[65] The inclusion of ὀφθαλμοὺς ἑπτά ('seven eyes') immediately preceding the reference (Rev 5.6a) accounts for the absence of עיני in Rev 5.6b.

Moreover, the discreetness of the lemma from its surrounding discourse, bracketed by a relative pronoun marker (οἵ) and conjunction (καί), paired with the level of quantitative, serial, lexical, and syntactic fidelity to its source, indicating that Rev 5.6b *quotes* Zech 4.10b, although implicitly. The use of subtle cues to introduce linguistic material external to that of the narrative itself is well catalogued with the HB,[66] in other Second Temple Jewish texts,[67] and in other NT works.[68] This phenomenon is widespread in John's textual milieu. The surface features of these two locutions differ in places, but their high level of correlation indicates literary independence.

In terms of access to this Zechariah material, there exists no clear exegetical tradition associated with seven eyes or spirits in the Second Temple period that indicates that John borrowed an antecedent tradition in this instance. The only possible evidence in this direction is the allusion to Isa 11.1–3, 10 that is also embedded in Rev 5.5–6. The phrase 'root of David' (ἡ ῥίζα Δαυίδ) in Rev 5.5, coupled with leonine titular imagery reminiscent of Gen 49.9, initially recalls the twin references to the 'shoot/root of Jesse' in Isa 11.1, 10 (τῆς ῥίζης Ιεσσαι, ἡ ῥίζα τοῦ Ιεσσαι// ישׁי מגזע ישׁי שׁרשׁ).[69] We meet the bearer of these titles in Rev 5.6 – the lamb, who has seven eyes 'which are the seven spirits of God'. As some have argued,[70] the seven spirits represent a continuation of the allusion to Isa 11.1, since Isa 11.2 enumerates seven spirits (πνεῦμα//רוח) that rest upon the root of Jesse (spirits of God, wisdom, understanding, counsel, might, knowledge, and fear of the Lord).[71] Rev 5.5–6 seems to be arranged in a way that is, at

---

[66] See Fishbane, *Biblical Interpretation*, 44–55.

[67] For example, M. Bernstein, 'The Genesis Apocryphon', in *CBIEJ*, 168 notes that the scribe(s) who produced the *Genesis Apocryphon* keyed on זה in Gen 5.29 to drastically expand the narrative. See also 1QS IX 19 as noted by S. Tzoref, 'The Use of Scripture in the Community Rule', in *CBEIJ*, 211.

[68] De Vries and Karrer, 'Early Christian Quotations', 8 note that a 'wide stylistic range of such markers are found within the New Testament; the authors utilize different semantic fields like writing, speaking, witnessing and sometimes very short signals (ὅτι or similar).' Müller, 'Zitatmarkierungen', 189–199 catalogues some of these signals for NT texts that quote the HB and its Greek versions. Müller notes that Greek particles serve as explicit citation markers in Matt 18.16; Mark 12.32; Rom 11.34; 13.9; 1 Cor 2.16; 10.26; 2 Cor 9.7; Heb 10.37; 1 Pet 1.24; 2.23; 4.8, 14; 5.5.

[69] So also Beale, *Revelation*, 349–350.

[70] Fekkes, *Prophetic Traditions*, 154–156 also notes a potential connection to Isa 53.7, connecting the lamb imagery of the Apocalypse to Isaianic traditions. Cf. also Beale, *Revelation*, 355.

[71] Two of these characteristics (wisdom and might) are also ascribed to the lamb in the song located at Rev 5.12.

least in part, controlled by the structure of Isa 11.1–2. John has combined potent messianic texts (Gen 49.9; Isa 11.1, 10) with texts that pertain to seven spirits (Isa 11.2 and Zech 4.10b), with Isa 11 serving as the lynchpin for the arrangement. The final portion of the description of the heavenly court is dense with complex exegetical reasoning that does not seem to have any obvious traditional precursors. As far as I am aware, neither Gen 49.9 nor Zech 4 is conflated with material from Isa 11 prior to the book of Revelation. Numerous other texts allude to or are influenced by Isa 11.1–2 (cf. *1 En.* 49.3–4; 71.11; *Aramaic Levi Document* Prayer and Ablutions viii; *Pss. Sol.* 17.37; *T. Levi* 18.7; 1QS IV 3; 1QSb V 24–26 [cf. Ps 2.9]; 4Q444), but none of them are composed with material taken from either Zech 4 or Gen 49.9. Although it is possible that John borrowed this tradition from antecedent exegetical sources accessed aurally, there is no evidence to point in this direction beyond the assertion that John must not have read texts.

John accessed Zechariah directly through a textual encounter with a manuscript, perhaps influenced by his previous hearing of these texts read aloud, deploying this borrowed wording along with other similar traditions from other scriptural works, to describe the appearance and import of the slain-but-standing lamb. This example of reuse illustrates John's awareness of the minute features of Zech 4.1–14, not just 4.10, further signifying that a direct graphic-textual encounter stands behind John's close reading of Zech 4. There is no reason not to assume that this exegetical coup is the work of the author of Revelation, arrived at through detailed engagement with the text of these scriptural traditions.

3.2.3 Revelation 6.1–8 and Zechariah 1.8; 6.1–5

There is wide agreement that the vision in Rev 6.1–8 is, in part, based on the horse visions of Zech 1.8; 6.1–5.[72] The following analysis, beginning with the relationship of the OG and proto-MT, affirms this consensus.

---

[72] Cf. Aune, *Revelation*, 2.390; Osborne, *Revelation*, 274; Beale, *Revelation*, 372; Ferrell Jenkins, *The Old Testament in the Book of Revelation* (Grand Rapids: Baker,

1972), 42–43; Robert H. Mounce, *The Book of Revelation* (NICNT; Grand Rapids: Eerdmans, 1977), 152; Caird, *The Revelation*, 79–80; Traugott Holtz, *Die Offenbarung des Johannes* (NTD 11; Göttingen: Vandenhoeck & Ruprecht, 2008), 64; Smalley, *The Revelation*, 147; Koester, *Revelation*, 393; Giesen, *Die Offenbarung*, 174; Morris, *Revelation*, 102; Hermann Lichtenberger, *Die Apokalypse* (TKZNT 23; Stuttgart: Kohlhammer, 2014), 139; Thompson, *Revelation*, 100–101; Ladd, *Revelation*, 96; Martin Kiddle, *The Revelation of St. John* (MNTC; London: Hodder and Stoughton, 1940), 111; Kraft, *Die Offenbarung*, 114–115; Henri Volohonsky, 'Is the Color of That Horse Really Pale?', *IJTS* 18 no 2 (1999): 167–168; Witherington, *Revelation*, 133; Barry F. Peachey, 'A Horse of a Different Colour: The Horses in Zechariah and Revelation', *ET* 110 no 7 (April 1999): 214–216; Alfred Wikenhauser, *Die Offenbarung des Johannes* (RNT 9; Regensburg: Pustet 1959); Ford, *Revelation*, 103–104; Beasley-Murray, *Revelation*, 131; M. D. Goulder, 'The Apocalypse as an Annual Cycle of Prophesies', *NTS* 27 no 3 (1981): 362; Matthew Streett, *Here Comes the Judge: Violent Pacifism in the Book of Revelation* (LNTS 462; London: T&T Clark, 2012), 59; Stephen Finamore, *God, Order and Chaos: René Girard and the Apocalypse* (PBM; Milton Keynes: Paternoster, 2009), 196; Blount, *Revelation*, 121; Eugene M. Boring, *Revelation* (Interpretation; Louisville: WJK, 1989), 123; Sweet, *Revelation*, 140; Judith Kovacs and Christopher Rowland, *Revelation* (BBC; Oxford: Blackwell, 2004), 78; Boxall, *The Revelation*, 104–105; Beckwith, *The Apocalypse*, 517; Prigent, *L'Apocalypse*, 203; Roloff, *Revelation*, 86; Vos, *Synoptic Traditions*, 181; Edmondo F. Lupieri, *A Commentary on the Apocalypse of John* (M. P. Johnson and A. Kamesar, trans.; Cambridge: Eerdmans, 2006), 142; John E. Hartley, *The Semantics of Ancient Hebrew Colour Lexemes* (ANESsup 33; Leuven: Peeters, 2010), 155; Ulrich B. Müller, *Die Offenbarung des Johannes* (OTKNT 19; Würzburg: Gütersloh, 1984), 166; Jörg Frey, 'Was Erwartet die Johannesapokalypse? Zur Eschatologie des letzten Buchs der Bibel', in *Die Johannesapokalypse* (WUNT 287; ed. J. Frey, J. A. Kelhoffer, and F. Tóth; Tübingen: Mohr Siebeck, 2012), 503; W. D. McHardy, 'The Horses in Zechariah', in *In Memoriam Paul Kahle* (ed. M. Black and G. Fohrer; Berlin: Töpelmann, 1968), 177; Peter R. Carrell, *Jesus and the Angels: Angelology and the Christology of the Apocalypse of John* (SNTSMS 95; Cambridge: Cambridge University Press, 1997), 204–205; Blount, *Revelation*, 121; William H. Shea, 'Zechariah's Flying Scroll and Revelation's Unsealed Scroll', *JATS* 14 no 2 (Fall 2003): 96; Mathias Rissi, 'The Rider on the White Horse: A Study of Revelation 6:1–8', *Interpretation* 18 no 4 (1964): 407–418; J. S. Considine, 'The Rider on the White Horse', *CBQ* 6 no 4 (1944): 410–411, 414; Pierre Sauzeau and André Sauzeau, 'Les chevaux colorés de l'Apocalypse I: L'Apocalypse de Jean, Zacharie et les traditions de l'Iran', *Revue de l'Histoire des Religions* 212 no 3 (1995): 259–298 note the connection between Rev 6.1–8 and Zechariah's horse visions, but suggest that the horse described as χλωρός (Rev 6.8) derives from Iranian sources. The latest dissenter in this discussion is Jauhiainen, *The Use*, 63–65. He notes, 'neither the number of horses in Zechariah, nor their colours, corresponds to those in Revelation' (63). If Zechariah's horse visions are read in isolation, this statement is true. However, Jauhiainen does not consider that John may have coordinated both of Zechariah's horse visions. Based on his approach, he does not see how the audience of Revelation would have noticed the 'marked' text.

Zech 1.8; 6.1–5[PM73]   I saw in the night and behold a man riding on a red horse
(על־סוס אדם) and he was standing between myrtles which
were in a glen and after him: horses red
(אדמים סוסים), light green (שרקים) and white (לבנים) . . .
And I turned and I lifted up my eyes and I saw and behold
four chariots (ארבע מרכבות) coming from between two
mountains and the mountains were mountains of bronze.
With the first chariot red horses (סוסים אדמים) and with
the second chariot black horses (סוסים שחרים) and with the
third chariot white horses (סוסים לבנים) and with the fourth
chariot strong spotted horses (סוסים ברדים אמצים). And
I answered and I said to the angel speaking with me, 'what
are these, my lord?' And the angel answered and he said
to me, 'these are the four winds of heaven going out from
being stationed before the Lord of all the earth' (אלה ארבע
רחות השמים יוצאות מהתיצב על אדון כל הארץ).

Zech 1.8; 6.1–5[OG74]   I saw the night and behold a man riding on a red horse
(ἵππον πυρρόν) and this man was standing in the
middle of two overshadowing mountains and after
him horses red (ἵπποι πυρροί), dappled (ψαροί),
many-coloured (ποικίλοι,) and white (λευκοί) . . . And
I turned and I lifted my eyes and I saw and behold
four chariots (τέσσαρα ἅρματα) coming out from the
middle of two mountains and the mountains were
mountains of bronze. With the first chariot red horses
(ἵπποι πυρροί), and with the second chariot black
horses (ἵπποι μέλανες) and with the third chariot white
horses (ἵπποι λευκοί) and in the fourth chariot dappled
and many-coloured horses (ἵπποι ποικίλοι ψαροί). And
I answered and I said to the angel who was speaking
to me, 'What are these, lord?' And the angel who was
speaking to me answered and he said, 'These are the four
winds of heaven, coming out to stand before the Lord
of all the earth' (Ταῦτά ἐστιν οἱ τέσσαρες ἄνεμοι τοῦ
οὐρανοῦ, ἐκπορεύονται παραστῆναι τῷ κυρίῳ πάσης
τῆς γῆς).

The primary difference between the proto-MT and the OG translation
is the number and colour of horses in each vision. The differences arise
as a result of the OG translator's coordination of both of Zechariah's

---

[73] The text of Zech 1.8; 6.1–5 is not reconstructed in Appendix 2 because the analysis
of these locutions in this study relates only the colours and number of the various horses.

[74] W largely agrees with OG preserved in Ziegler's edition, although some minor
diversions are present. Some are orthographic: εορακα | εωρακα (1.8); ιστηκει | εισ–
τηκει (1.8); ειπεν | ειπε (6.5). W adds a word (και) at the beginning of 6.2.

Table 3.4 *Horse colours in Zech 1.8*

Proto-MT	OG
Red (אדם)	Red (πυρρόν)
Red (אדמים)	Red (πυρροί)
Vine-tendril coloured (שרקים)	Pale (ψαροί)
	Spotted (ποικίλοι)
White (לבנים)	White (λευκοί)

horse visions. In Zech 1.8, the translator inserted another horse to correspond to his translation of ברדים אמצים in Zech 6.3.

The obscure Hebrew word שרקים is omitted in the OG translation and the two adjectives that describe the fourth group of horses in the second vision (6.3) are inserted. ψαροί and ποικίλοι share no sematic value with שרקים and this 'translation' is the only instance in the OG/LXX tradition in which either of these Greek words represent שר"ק. With the exception of the black horses (6.2), which are not witnessed in any version of 1.8, the colours from 1.8 and 6.2–3 correspond in the OG translation. The insertion of an extra substantive adjective in 1.8 follows the pattern employed to describe the fourth horse in Zech 6.3. This translation harmonizes both visions and sidesteps a rare Hebrew word: שרקים (1.8). This translation conflates the 'vine-tendril coloured' horse and the 'spotted strong' horses in both visions, drawing a direct connection between these groups of horses.

Another feature of Zech 6.1–5ᴾᴹ that is retrojected to Zech 1.8 in the OG is the backdrop upon which the riders are introduced. The rare word ההדסים ('myrtles') is replaced with the phrase τῶν δύο ὀρέων τῶν κατασκίων ('two overshadowing mountains') in Zech 1.8. The Greek phrase is influenced by a similar expression in Zech 6.1 that introduces the location, from which the heavenly horses come: שני ההרים וההרים הרי נחשת.[75] The alteration of Zech 1.8 coordinates both horse visions and allows the translator to avoid another rare word in 1.8 (ההדסים). Like the colour of the horses, the translator imposed the context and visionary reality of the second horse vision (Zech 6.1–5) onto the first (Zech 1.8).[76]

---

[75] The mountains are 'bronze' (χαλκᾶ) in 6.1 and 'overshadowing' (κατασκίων) in 1.8ᴼᴳ.

[76] A similar phenomenon occurs also in the early versions, where Zechariah's horsemen are coordinated with creatures in Ezekiel. Cf. William A. Tooman, '"To do the Will of Their Master": Re-envisioning the *ḤAYYÔT* in Targum Jonathan of Ezekiel', in *'I Lifted My Eyes and Saw': Reading Dream and Vision Reports in the Hebrew Bible* (LHBOTS 584; ed. E. Hayes and L.-S. Tiemeyer; London: T&T Clark, 2014), 221–233.

Another difference between texts consists of variation in metadiscourse that cannot be attributed to the translators harmonizing tendencies.

Zech 6.5ᴾᴹ

ויען המלאך ויאמר אלי אלה ארבע רחות השמים יוצאות מהתיצב על־
אדון כל־הארץ

And the angel answered and he said to me, 'these are four winds of heaven sent out from presenting themselves before the lord of all the earth.'

Zech 6.5ᴼᴳ

καὶ ἀπεκρίθη ὁ ἄγγελος ὁ λαλῶν ἐν ἐμοὶ καὶ εἶπε Ταῦτά ἐστιν οἱ τέσσαρες ἄνεμοι τοῦ οὐρανοῦ, ἐκπορεύονται παραστῆναι τῷ κυρίῳ πάσης τῆς γῆς

The angel who was speaking with me answered and he said, 'These are the four winds of heaven sent out to stand before the lord of all the earth.'

The OG specifies which angel was speaking in this locution: 'the one who was speaking with me'. In this manner, אלי does not refer to the direction of speech, as in proto-MT, but specifies the speaker. The phrase המלאך הדבר בי ('the angel who was speaking with me') is common in Zechariah (1.9, 13, 14; 2.3; 4.1, 4; 5.5, 10; 6.4), and the inclusion of the phrase (ὁ ἄγγελος ὁ λαλῶν ἐν ἐμοί) in the OG may have been the result of unconscious habit. The translator's *Vorlage* may have included this phrase but, based on the prominence of this phrase in the visionary material, the variation is likely a change introduced in translation, altering the style of the dialogue to cohere with similar dialogue patterns. Beyond this variation, the OG is a literal translation of the proto-MT. The translation retains fidelity to its *Vorlage* in terms of serial arrangement, quantitative elements, syntax, semantics, and style.

Minor differences between proto-MT and *V*OG may have existed but, even if these divergences are not a reflection of translation technique or the translator's tendency to harmonize similar visionary accounts, a strong relationship binds the proto-MT and Zechariahᴼᴳ in the horse visions. The differences in this case are likely related to the *Übersetzungsweise* of the translator, which included a tendency to smooth the rutted narrative texture of a gapped consonantal Hebrew source text. With this information in hand, I now turn to the relationship of these versions to Rev 6.1–8. Does John draw material from a particular form of Zechariah's horse visions?

Rev 6.1–8[77]   And I saw when the Lamb opened one of the seven seals and
I heard one of the four living creatures saying in a loud voice,
'Come!' *And I saw and behold a white horse* (ἵππος λευκός),
and the one seated on it had a bow and a crown was given to
him and he went out conquering and in order to conquer.
And when he opened the second seal, I heard the second living
creature saying, 'Come!' *And another red horse went out* (ἵππος
πυρρός), and the one sitting on it was allowed to take peace
from the earth and so that they might slay one another and a
great sword was given to him. And when he opened the third
seal, I heard the third living creature saying 'Come!' *And I saw,
and behold a black horse* (ἵππος μέλας), and the one sitting
on it had a balance in his right hand. And I heard something
like a voice in the middle of the four living creatures saying,
'a quart of wheat for a denarius and three quarts of barley
for a denarius, and the olive oil and the wine do not harm.'
And when he opened the fourth seal, I heard the voice of the
fourth living creature saying, 'Come!' *And I saw and behold a
green horse* (ἵππος χλωρός), and the one sitting on it is named
Death, and Hades follows with him and authority of a fourth
of the earth was given to him to kill by the sword and by
famine and by death and by the beasts of the earth

OG   I saw the night and behold a man riding on a red horse (ἵππον
πυρρόν) and this man was standing in the middle of two
overshadowing mountains and after him horses red (ἵπποι
πυρροὶ), dappled (ψαροὶ), many-coloured (ποικίλοι,) and white
(λευκοί) . . . And I turned and I lifted my eyes and I saw and
behold four chariots (τέσσαρα ἅρματα) coming out from the
middle of two mountains and the mountains were mountains
of bronze. With the first chariot red horses (ἵπποι πυρροί), and
with the second chariot black horses (ἵπποι μέλανες) and with
the third chariot white horses (ἵπποι λευκοί) and in the fourth
chariot dappled and many-coloured horses (ἵπποι ποικίλοι
ψαροί). And I answered and I said to the angel who was
speaking to me, 'What are these, lord?' And the angel who was
speaking to me answered and he said, 'These are the four winds
of heaven, coming out to stand before the Lord of all the earth'
(Ταῦτά ἐστιν οἱ τέσσαρες ἄνεμοι τοῦ οὐρανοῦ, ἐκπορεύονται
παραστῆναι τῷ κυρίῳ πάσης τῆς γῆς)

---

[77] Textual variation exists in the manuscript tradition of Rev 6.1–8, none of which
weighs on this discussion. See Metzger, *Textual Commentary*, 737–739 for further
comment.

Proto-MT   I saw in the night and behold a man riding on a red horse (עַל־
סוּס אָדֹם) and he was standing between myrtles which were
in a glen and after him: horses red (סוּסִים אֲדֻמִּים), light green
(שְׂרֻקִּים) and white (לְבָנִים) . . . And I turned and I lifted up
my eyes and I saw and behold four chariots (אַרְבַּע מַרְכָּבוֹת)
coming from between two mountains and the mountains were
mountains of bronze. With the first chariot red horses (סוּסִים
אֲדֻמִּים) and with the second chariot black horses (סוּסִים שְׁחֹרִים)
and with the third chariot white horses (סוּסִים לְבָנִים) and with
the fourth chariot strong spotted horses (סוּסִים בְּרֻדִּים אֲמֻצִּים).
And I answered and I said to the angel speaking with me, 'what
are these, my lord?' And the angel answered and he said to
me, 'these are the four winds of heaven going out from being
stationed before the Lord of all the earth' (אֵלֶּה אַרְבַּע רֻחוֹת הַשָּׁמַיִם
יוֹצְאוֹת מֵהִתְיַצֵּב עַל אֲדוֹן כָּל הָאָרֶץ)

Table 3.5 *Horse colours in Zech 1.8; 6.2 and Rev 6.1–8*

Proto-MT	OG	Revelation
Red (אָדֹם)[1] 1.8	Red (πυρρόν) 1.8	Red (πυρρός) 6.4
Red (אֲדֻמִּים) 1.8; 6.2	Red (πυρροί) 1.8; 6.2	
Vine-tendril coloured (שְׂרֻקִּים)[2] 1.8	Dappled (ψαροί)Spotted (ποικίλοι) 1.8; 6.3	Green (χλωρός) 6.8
Spotted (בְּרֻדִּים) Strong (אֲמֻצִּים) 6.3		
White (לְבָנִים) 1.8; 6.3	White (λευκοί) 1.8; 6.3	White (λευκός) 6.2
Black (שְׁחֹרִים) 6.2	Black (μέλανες) 6.2	Black (μέλας) 6.5

[1] See Hartley, *Colour Lexemes*, 73–78, 97–106, 112–119, 152–156, 168–174, 214–217 for a full
discussion of these Hebrew colour lexemes. See also Athalya Brenner, *Colour Terms in
the Old Testament* (JSOTsup 21; Sheffield: Sheffield University Press, 1982) and Roland
Gradwohl, *Die Farben im Alten Testament: Eine Terminologische Studie* (BZAW 83;
Berlin: Töpelmann, 1963).

[2] I have translated this word as 'vine-tendrils' in line with BDB. Hartley, 173 notes that
שׂר"ק has numerous Semitic cognates that suggest a reddish hue. However, I retain
the semantic sense in BDB because this translation connects Zech 1.8 with Isa 16.8 (a
connection that Théophane Chary, *Aggée-Zacharie Malachie* [Paris: Lecoffre, 1969], 59
argues is implicit within Zechariah^PM itself) which provides the logical connection for the
author of Revelation's rendering of שׂרק: χλωρός. In other words, the author of Revelation
likely understood the semantics of שׂר"ק to be related, in some way, to 'vine-tendrils'.

The primary textual connection between Rev 6.1–8 and Zech 1.8; 6.1–5 is the four coloured horses that appear at the opening of the first four seals. In terms of which textual form of Zech 1.8; 6.1–5 John reused, the colour of the fourth horse (χλωρός) in Rev 6.8 is the key piece of evidence. First, like the OG translator, the colours of John's horses differ from the list of horses in Zech 1.8; 6.1–5ᵖᴹ. The evidence suggests that John derived the description of the four horsemen from both of Zechariah's horse visions, borrowing unique lexical material from Zech 1.8 *and* 6.1–3. White and red horses appear in the proto-MT *and* OG Zech 1.8; 6.2 and Rev 6.2, 4. However, black horses (שחרים//μέλανες) only appear in the second horse vision (Zech 6.2). John's inclusion of this horse (Rev 6.5) indicates that he derived these equine images from Zech 6.1–5 alone. Also, thus far, it is unclear which textual form John reused. All textual evidence of the colour of these three groups of horses is consistent across the Greek and Hebrew witnesses.

The trouble arises with John's fourth horse (χλωρός), the horse that parallels the harmonized animals in the OG. Did John derive χλωρός from a particular textual form? The word χλωρός itself is semantically opaque. In classical Greek poetry, as well as in contemporary usage in the first century CE, χλωρός often referred to fresh cut wood, leafy tress, and growing things, or to their colour: 'yellowish-green; light green; greenish gray'.[78] In comparison to Zech 1.8; 6.3ᴼᴳ, χλωρός does not correspond textually or semantically to ψαροί, ποικίλοι, or a collocation of the terms. If John utilized the OG here, his presentation of this text diverged from the colours that the OG translator harmonized in both visions.[79]

Based on the text of the OG translation, I see no exegetical move that could lead from ψαροί ποικίλοι to χλωρός. This leaves the two visions in the proto-MT as our last options: שרקים (1.8) and ברדים אמצים (6.3). There is no example of ברדים, אמצים, or a combination of these words underlying a form of χλωρός in the OG/LXX, and there is no

---

[78] See Eleanor Irwin, *Colour Terms in Greek Poetry* (Toronto: Hakkert, 1974), 31–78. Irwin notes that χλωρός can also connote fear or other emotions (62–68). This identification is also fitting for the fourth horse in Rev 6.7–8 as its rider is 'Death', and 'Hades' follows after it.

[79] The horse colours are consistent in the OG/LXX manuscript tradition except for manuscript 130 which reads πυρινον for πυρρον. Manuscript 410 and the Boharic version omit ποικίλοι in Zech 6.3. The harmonization of both of Zechariah's horse visions is present in each LXX revision except for the Aquilanic recension. This text represents שרקים (Zech 1.8) with ξανθοί ('yellow').

possible misreading of the consonantal Hebrew text (in any script)[80] that might lead to χλωρός as a reasonable translation equivalent of ברדים אמצים. The final option within Zechariah's horse visions that could underlie χλωρός is the horses described as שרקים in Zech 1.8[PM]. שר"ק ('sorrel; vine-tendrils')[81] is translated by multiple words in the OG/ LXX tradition: ποικίλος and ψαρός in Zech 1.8 and three times as a form of ἄμπελος in Isa 5.2; 16.8 and Jer 2.21.[82] The representation of שר"ק with ἄμπελος in Isa 5.2; 16.8 and Jer 2.21, and the connection between χλωρός and plant life or living things, indicates that, in Rev 6.8, χλωρός functions as a translation equivalent for שר"ק.[83] John conflated the horse visions (including unique lexical material from both)[84] by utilizing χλωρός as a translation equivalent for שרקים. In support of this conclusion, χλωρός is occasionally used adjectivally to describe an ἄμπελος (the most prevalent translation equivalent in the OG/LXX traditions) or the leaves of an ἄμπελος in contemporary literature.[85] Also, within Revelation, χλωρός refers to grass or living/green things (Rev 8.7: πᾶς χόρτος χλωρός; Rev 9.4: ἀδικήσουσιν τὸν χόρτον τῆς γῆς οὐδὲ πᾶν χλωρὸν οὐδὲ πᾶν δένδρον). It is not unreasonable to represent שרקים with a form of χλωρός in translation.

This translation choice connects each of the four horses in Rev 6.1–8 to the proto-MT of both of Zechariah's horse visions. The first colours of the horses in Rev 6.1–8 correspond to both the OG and the proto-MT, but the only possible extant textual tradition that can account for the fourth horse (χλωρός) is the Hebrew word used to describe the third group of horses in Zech 1.8 (שרקים). Because the VOG of Zechariah's horse visions corresponds closely

---

[80] See HRCS, 1471. Emanuel Tov, *The Text-Critical Use of the Septuagint in Biblical Research* (2nd edn; JBS 8; Jerusalem: Simor, 1997), 149–150 notes that the *Vorlage* of some books of the OG/LXX may have been written in the pre-Assyrian palaeo-Hebrew script. The presence of palaeo-Hebrew scriptural manuscripts at Qumran raises the possibility that these works were read during the composition of the NT. See 1Q3; 2Q5; 4QpaeloGen-Exod[l]; 4QpaleoGen[m]; 4QpaleoExod[m]; 4QpaeloDeut[r, s]; 4QpaleoJob[c]; 4Q123–125; 6Q1; 6Q2; 11Q1.

[81] BDB, 977.

[82] The rendering in Zech 1.8[OG] is likely not a direct translation of שרק, but a harmonization to ברדים אמצים in Zech 6.3.

[83] Noted also by Lohmeyer, *Die Offenbarung* (1927), 59.

[84] The black horses from Zech 6.2 and the 'vine-tendril' coloured horses from 1.8.

[85] E.g. Galen, *Comp. Med. Loc.* 12.791.8; 13.171.1.

to the proto-MT, an alternative Hebrew textual form need not be sought, eliminating option 2 (*V*OG). Also, Zech 1.8; 6.1–5 are not extant in 8HevXIIgr and there is no revising impulse within the manuscript that would suggest that the scribe altered the OG translation of the horse colours, eliminating option 5 (καιγε recension [8HevXIIgr]). Option 6 (a proto-Hexaplaric revision) is also unlikely since the horse colours in Rev 6.1–8 do not match any of the minor alterations in the variant witnesses to the Greek tradition.[86] Additionally, as discussed above, the OG is not the source for the four horsemen based on John's use of χλωρός, eliminating options 4 (OG) and 8 (OG/LXX with adaptations).[87] There is no evidence of an alternative Hebrew textual form of the horse visions beyond proto-MT (= *V*OG).[88] The colour of the horses in Rev 6.1–8 indicates that John referenced the proto-MT (Option 1).

The composition of Rev 6.1–8 is complex, and John did not simply transpose the Hebrew text of Zechariah. Instead he borrowed lexical material from the proto-MT, greatly expanding the role of Zechariah's horsemen for his own vision. A conflation of options 1 and 7 is the best textual option: John used Zech 1.8; 6.1–5[PM] as the foundation from which to depict his own horse vision, especially in terms of colour lexemes, but not without further reflection. John's use of Zechariah as a structural frame for his own horse visions, indicated by the borrowing of colour lexemes, only makes sense if he used a Hebrew text.

Additionally, like the previous example (Section 3.2.2), it is probable that John directly accessed the Hebrew text of Zechariah on a graphic writing surface, although he likely also encountered this these equine visions in aural environments and through access to the memory of past encounters with this text. When translation is involved, as it likely is here, the chances of a textual encounter

---

[86] The Aquilanic version preserves a variant in Zech 1.8 against the OG translation of ψαροὶ καὶ ποικίλοι for שׁרקים: ξανθόι (cf. Josephus, *Ant.* 4.79). The Hebrew phrase ברדים אמצים in Zech 6.3 is also revised towards proto-MT by Symmachus and Theodotion: ברדים (ποικίλοι) to πελιδνοί ('livid'). Aquila also revised the OG rendering of אמצים (ψαροί) to καρτεροί ('strong'). None of these revisions match the colour of the fourth horse in Rev 6.8.

[87] The text of W is not sufficiently different from OG in these sections to suggest that the tradition preserved in this manuscript is independent of OG.

[88] Zech 1.8 is not witnessed in Qumran manuscripts and the text of Zech 1.9–10, 13–14 in fragments 4–5 of 4QXII[c] are damaged and very difficult to read. The only visible difference seems to be a fuller orthography of נחומים in Zech 1.13. The only

generating the presentation of reused material becomes more likely. Moreover, outside of the early Greek and Aramaic versions of Zechariah, there is little engagement with his horse visions in Jewish antiquity: there was no existing tradition for John to draw upon, although his approach to understanding Zechariah's horse visions is similar to that employed in the early versions while retaining a level of independence (see Section 5.4). Although the depiction of four horsemen also draws on material reminiscent of other texts (cf. 2 Kgs 7.1 [Rev 6.6]; Hos 13.14; Ezek 5.12–17; 14.21; 33.27; Jer 14.12; 21.7 [Rev 6.7–8])[89] and their actions are similar to events described in the Synoptic apocalyptic traditions (cf. Matt 24//Mark 13//Luke 21),[90] there is nothing to indicate that these texts were previously connected in an existing exegetical tradition to Zechariah. The intricacies of this example point to a direct textual encounter, perhaps influenced by the memory of past experiences (aural or otherwise) with the text, as the point of access to Zechariah traditions.

3.2.4   Revelation 11.2 and Zechariah 12.3

Following the description of the seer's encounter with a sweet tasting, but ultimately bitter scroll (Rev 10.8–11), a new vision ensues, framed as the words of an angelic interpreter (Rev 11.1–13). Portions of this discourse are reliant upon the wording of passages from Zechariah (in combination with material from Dan 8.10–14), the first instance of which occurs in Rev 11.2. Zechariah is not the dominant tradition in this pericope (cf. the prophetic commissioning in Ezek 2–3, the temple vision in Ezek 40–48, and the reflections on the temple in Dan 10–12),[91] but material from Zechariah plays a role in constructing the vision nonetheless. It is not surprising that material from Zech 12.3 is used in this setting, since the unrelenting focus of the chapter is YHWH's interaction with Jerusalem.

---

differences between fragments 14–15 of 4QXIIᵉ and proto-MT in Zech 6.1–5 are orthographic: inconsistent spellings of *wayiqtol* of אמר (cf. Zech 4.4; 5.10; 6.5 in 4QXIIᵉ) and a full orthographic spelling of כול in 6.5. There is also a *possible* variant for the word אמיצים: אמצים.

[89] Kowalski, *Rezeption*, 125–128 examines these non-Zecharian texts in detail, especially the *Mischanspielung* in Rev 6.8.

[90] Cf. Vos, *Synoptic Traditions*, 181–192

[91] So Koester, *Revelation*, 494.

Rev 11.2

καὶ τὴν αὐλὴν τὴν ἔξωθεν τοῦ ναοῦ ἔκβαλε ἔξωθεν καὶ μὴ αὐτὴν μετρήσῃς, ὅτι ἐδόθη τοῖς ἔθνεσιν, καὶ τὴν πόλιν τὴν ἁγίαν πατήσουσιν μῆνας τεσσεράκοντα [καὶ] δύο.

And the outer court of the temple, exclude it, and do not measure it, for it has been given to the nations, and they will trample the holy city forty-two months

Zech 12.3^OG/LXX92

καὶ ἔσται ἐν τῇ ἡμέρᾳ ἐκείνῃ θήσομαι τὴν Ιερουσαλημ λίθον καταπατούμενον πᾶσιν τοῖς ἔθνεσιν, πᾶς ὁ καταπατῶν αὐτὴν ἐμπαίζων ἐμπαίξεται, καὶ ἐπισυναχθήσονται [θ: πᾶς ὁ βαστάζων αὐτὸν σπαρασσόμενος ἀμυχθήσεται] ἐπ᾿ αὐτὴν πάντα τὰ ἔθνη τῆς γῆς

And it will be in that day, I will set Jerusalem a stone trampled by all the nations, all those who trample her will surely mock [θ: all those who bear it, shaking, will be scarred] and all the nations of the earth will be gathered to her

Zech 12.3^PM

וְהָיָה בַיּוֹם־הַהוּא אָשִׂים אֶת־יְרוּשָׁלַ͏ִם אֶבֶן מַעֲמָסָה לְכָל־הָעַמִּים כָּל־עֹמְסֶיהָ שָׂרוֹט יִשָּׂרֵטוּ וְנֶאֶסְפוּ עָלֶיהָ כֹּל גּוֹיֵי הָאָרֶץ

And it will be in that day, I will set Jerusalem a stone of burden to all the peoples, all those who bear her will surely be lacerated and all the nations of the earth will be gathered to her

Dan 8.13^OG93

καὶ ἤκουον ἑτέρου ἁγίου λαλοῦντος, καὶ εἶπεν ὁ ἕτερος τῷ φελμουνι τῷ λαλοῦντι Ἕως τίνος τὸ ὅραμα στήσεται καὶ ἡ θυσία ἡ ἀρθεῖσα καὶ ἡ ἁμαρτία ἐρημώσεως ἡ δοθεῖσα, καὶ τὰ ἅγια ἐρημωθήσεται εἰς καταπάτημα

And I heard one of the holy ones speaking, and the other one said to Phelmouni who was speaking, 'How long will the vision stand: even the sacrifice which has been taken away and the sin of desolation has been given and the holy things will be made desolate unto trampling?'

Dan 8.13^PM

וָאֶשְׁמְעָה אֶחָד־קָדוֹשׁ מְדַבֵּר וַיֹּאמֶר אֶחָד קָדוֹשׁ לַפַּלְמוֹנִי הַמְדַבֵּר עַד־מָתַי הֶחָזוֹן הַתָּמִיד וְהַפֶּשַׁע שֹׁמֵם תֵּת וְקֹדֶשׁ וְצָבָא מִרְמָס

And I heard one of the holy ones speaking, and one of the holy ones said to the certain one who was speaking, 'How long will the vision continue and the transgression of desolation given and the sanctuary and host trampled?'

---

[92] Zech 12.3 is not preserved in 8HevXIIgr and (perhaps) one grapheme from this verse is present in 4QXII^g.

[93] The other Greek versions of this verse (esp. θ) stand in the same stream as the OG, despite minor variations in wording and morphology.

The first question that requires attention is that of the textual form of Zechariah embedded in Rev 11.2. In this case, John reused a Greek form of Zechariah.[94] There are numerous points of correspondence between Zech 12.3 (in both Hebrew and Greek) and Rev 11.2 that demonstrate literary dependence, including the shared reference to Jerusalem (or the holy city [Rev 11.2]) and many nations ('the nations' [Rev 11.2] or 'all the nations of the earth' [Zech 12.3]). Moreover, the form of Zechariah represented by the proto-MT differs significantly from the OG stream. In Hebrew, Jerusalem is made a 'stone of burden' (אבן מעמסה) that injures 'all those who bear her' (כל־עמסיה). The Greek revising versions also stand in this stream (e.g. θ: ὁ βαστάζων αὐτον σπαρασσόμενος ἀμυχθήσεται): Jerusalem is not the one inflicting injury in the OG translation, but the passive victim of the nations, a 'stone trampled' (λίθον καταπατούμενον). Those who trample will mock her (πᾶς ὁ καταπατῶν αὐτὴν ἐμπαίζων ἐμπαίξεται). The primary difference between traditions lies in the fact that the Hebrew underlying the OG translation (whether this was inscribed or in the mind of the translator) read מרמס ('trampling') where the proto-MT preserves מעמסה ('burden').[95] Ultimately the OG tradition responded to a different sense contour activated by graphic similarities made possible by ambiguous Hebrew consonantal arrangements.

For Bauckham, the fact that Rev 11.2 preserves the reading associated with OG tradition, in which the nations trample (πατήσουσιν) the holy city for forty-two months, signals that John associated the Hebrew texts of Zech 12.3 (reading מרמס, 'trampling') with Dan 8.10–14 (esp. v. 13) based upon 'the kind of Jewish exegetical practice that John follows'.[96] In this way, Bauckham envisions John working innovatively with the same Hebrew text that stands behind the Greek tradition. If this is so, then the OG tradition and the allusion in Rev 11.2 work together to suggest that some Zechariah manuscripts may have actually preserved מרמס in place of the unanimously attested מעמסה, pointing to the conclusion that John used option 2 (translation of the VOG/LXX) as the textual form of Zech 12.3.

However, Bauckham's argument falters on two fronts. First, it is not necessary to posit that the correlation of Dan 8.10–14 and Zech 12.3

---

[94] So also Aune, *Revelation*, 2.608; Beale, *Revelation*, 569; Jauhiainen, *The Use*, 108–109.

[95] The only time in the OG/LXX tradition where מעמסה underlies a form of πατέω or its compounds occurs in Zech 12.3.

[96] Bauckham, *Climax*, 268–273 (here 271).

occurred at the Hebrew level. The two texts are much more closely related in their Greek instantiations, sharing language of trampling and descriptions of the oppression of Jerusalem by gentiles. None of these features are shared in their respective Hebrew traditions (unless of course one posits an alternative Hebrew tradition to Zechariah as Bauckham has). It is more likely that these texts were exegetically intertwined after reflection on their Greek texts. This suggests that John was aware of and deployed a Greek text of Zech 12.3 associated with the OG stream (option 4). Second, while pointing to other texts that combine material from Dan 8.10–14 and Zech 12.3, Bauckham implies that John is ultimately responsible for the exegetical tradition embedded in Rev 11.2.[97] It is possible that John created a new exegetical connection between Daniel and Zechariah traditions, but other indicators insinuate that John, very much like his use of Daniel/ Zechariah traditions in Rev 1.7, accessed these texts (encoded in their Greek forms) through a pre-existing exegetical tradition.

Though the form of Zech 12.3 used by John is closely aligned with the OG tradition, it is not at all self-evident that John accessed this text, in combination with Dan 8.10–14, in full-text Greek manuscripts. To begin, John's use of an antecedent Daniel/Zechariah tradition in Rev 1.7 hints that he may have had access to other exegetical traditions associated with these two works. Additionally, the combination of these texts in other early Jewish and Christian texts indicates that this exegetical tradition pre-dates Revelation and that John made use of a traditional textual combination with wide currency. The text that provides the clearest view on this tradition beyond Rev 11.2 is Luke 21.24.[98]

Luke 21.24   καὶ πεσοῦνται στόματι μαχαίρης καὶ αἰχμαλωτισθήσονται
εἰς τὰ ἔθνη πάντα, καὶ Ἰερουσαλὴμ ἔσται πατουμένη
ὑπὸ ἐθνῶν, ἄχρι οὗ πληρωθῶσιν καιροὶ ἐθνῶν

This utterance attributed to Jesus in Luke 21.24 (a saying that does not have any direct support from the other Synoptics) is part of the Lucan Jesus' apocalyptic discourse, a string of sayings that is also related to Rev 1.7 (cf. Luke 21.27, Section 3.2.1). According to Vos, the multiple similarities between these texts suggest that the use of Zech 12.3 in Rev 11.2 reflects John's appropriation of an exegetical tradition

---

[97] Ibid.
[98] See the extended exposition of this relationship in Vos, *Synoptic Traditions*, 120–125 and Penley, *Common Tradition*, 120–122.

attributed to Jesus: 'it would seem that John was either acquainted with the Gospel of Luke . . . or both Luke and the Apocalyptist were acquainted with a separate tradition in which this specific prediction of Jesus was found.'[99] Both texts refer to Jerusalem's trampling (πατέω) by the nations and offer limits to the time of trampling (forty-two months and 'until the times of the Gentiles are fulfilled'), similarities that are undergirded by their shared reliance on Greek traditions of Dan 8.13 and Zech 12.3.[100] Both Rev 11.2 and Luke 21.24 preserve Jesus traditions circulating in Greek that reflect exegetical attention to Daniel and Zechariah traditions. It is unlikely (or, at least, remains to be demonstrated) that John had at his disposal the book of Luke in any form that resembles the work as we now know it. The more likely scenario is that both the author of Revelation and Luke had access to early exegetical traditions associated with Jesus, probably through both oral (liturgical, homiletical, or eyewitness testimony in Luke's case) and written mediums (graphic representation of Jesus *logia*), that they accessed independent of one another. The path of transmission that I offer here indicates the wide currency of Jesus traditions in early Christianity beyond the Gospel texts. John apparently accessed these traditions (see also Rev 1.7), transmitted to him in Greek, in the process of composing the Apocalypse.

The combination of Dan 8.13 and Zech 12.3 in Rev 11.2 is part of a broader phenomenon that partially distinguishes Revelation from a distinctly Jewish textual culture. Exegetical traditions attributed to Jesus are influential sources for our author and, although access to this tradition at an early stage was likely perceived to stand within a Jewish textual culture, the importance and high regard for traditions associated with Jesus begin to be distinguishing features of composition that delineated the identity of a Christian textual culture distinct from Jewish literary currents as they evolved over the intervening centuries in the aftermath of 70 CE. However, access to Jesus traditions within a Jewish textual culture indicates that, at least for a time, exegetical traditions connected to Jesus were part of a specific subset of this broader culture, and these traditions were handled in ways similar to other scriptural texts. Overall, John accessed the exegetical tradition that combined Dan 8.13 and Zech 12.3 in Greek, not necessarily independently examining these texts in various manuscripts.

---

[99] Vos, *Synoptic Traditions*, 122–125 (here 125).

[100] So also J. A. Fitzmyer, *The Gospel According to Luke* (AB 28A; 2 vols.; Garden City, NY: Doubleday, 1985), 2.1346–1347.

3.2.5 Revelation 11.4 and Zechariah 4.14

Following the reuse of Zechariah traditions in Rev 11.2, the majority of commentators agree that Rev 11.4 also redeploys material from Zech 4.14.[101] The close semantic and syntactic relationship between the proto-MT and Rev 11.4 and the scholarly consensus on the issue support this conclusion. This locution is one of the most direct examples of reuse in Rev 11.1–13 and it reinforces John's close attention to the intriguing and grammatically complex vision of Zech 4.

[101] D. B. Weiss, *Die Johannes-Apokalypse: Textkritische Untersuchungen und Textherstellung* (Leipzig: Hinrichs'sche, 1891), 185; J. Cambier, 'Les images de l'Ancien Testament dans l'Apocalypse de saint Jean', *NRT* 2 (1955): 115; Allen, 'Textual Pluriformity', 136–145; Koester, *Revelation*, 498; Cullen Tanner, 'Climbing the Lampstand-Witness-Trees: Revelation's Use of Zechariah 4 in Light of Speech Act Theory', *JPT* 20 (2011): 81–92; Thomas Edward McComiskey, 'Alteration of OT Imagery in the Book of Revelation: Its Hermeneutical and Theological Significance', *JETS* 36 no 3 (1993): 309; Lohmeyer, *Die Offenbarung* (1927), 89; Gregory Stevenson, *Power and Place: Temple and Identity in the Book of Revelation* (BZNW 107; Berlin: De Gruyter, 2001), 260; Marko Jauhiainen, 'The Minor Prophets in Revelation', in *The Minor Prophets in the New Testament* (LNTS 377; ed. M. J. J. Menken and S. Moyise; London: T&T Clark, 2009), 159–160, 165–167; Jauhiainen, 'Revelation and Rewritten Prophecies', in *Rewritten Bible Reconsidered* (SRB 1; ed. A. Laato and J. van Ruiten; Winona Lake: Eisenbrauns, 2008), 187–188; Lichtenberger, *Apokalypse*, 169; Smalley, *The Revelation*, 277; Giesen, *Die Offenbarung*, 250; Maier, *Die Offenbarung*, 464; Craig A. Evans, '"The Two Sons of Oil": Early Evidence of Messianic Interpretation of Zechariah 4:14 in 4Q254 4 2', in *The Provo International Conference on the Dead Sea Scrolls* (STDJ 30; ed. D. W. Parry and E. Ulrich; Leiden: Brill, 1999), 567; T. Holtz, 'Gott in der Apokalypse', in *L'Apocalypse Johannique et l'Apocalypse dans le Nouveau Testament* (BETL 53; ed. J. Lambrecht; Leuven: Leuven University Press, 1980), 257; Blount, *Revelation*, 209; VanderKam, '1 Enoch, Enochic Motifs, and Enoch in Early Christian Literature', in *The Jewish Apocalyptic Heritage in Early Christianity* (CRINT 3.4; ed. J. C. VanderKam and W. Adler; Assen: Van Gorcum, 1996), 90; David A. deSilva, *Seeing Things John's Way: The Rhetoric of the Book of Revelation* (Louisville: WJK, 2009), 154; Ford, *Revelation*, 171; Beale, *Revelation*, 576–579; Aune, *Revelation 6–16*, 612; Aune, *Apocalypticism, Prophecy and Magic*, 133; Caird, *Revelation*, 134; Beasley-Murray, *Revelation*, 183–185; Sweet, *Revelation*, 184–185; Prigent, *L'Apocalypse*, 271; Boxall, *Revelation*, 163; Collins, *Scepter and the Star*, 135; Felise Tavo, *Woman, Mother and Bride: An Exegetical Investigation into the 'Ecclesial' Notions of the Apocalypse* (BT 3; Leuven: Peeters, 2007), 205, 221; Kiddle, *The Revelation*, 194; Farrer, *Revelation*, 133; Osborne, *Revelation*, 420–422; Swete, *The Apocalypse*, 135; Charles, *The Revelation*, 282; Michael R. Stead, *The Intertextuality of Zechariah 1–8* (LHBOTS 506; London: T&T Clark, 2009), 256; Israel Knohl, 'The Gabriel Revelation', in *The Dead Sea Scrolls and Contemporary Culture: Proceedings of the International Conference held at the Israel Museum, Jerusalem (July 6–8, 2008)* (STDJ 93; ed. A. D. Roitman, L. H. Schiffman, and S. Tzoref; Leiden: Brill, 2011), 453.

Rev 11.4

οὗτοί εἰσιν αἱ δύο ἐλαῖαι[102] καὶ αἱ δύο
λυχνίαι αἱ ἐνώπιον τοῦ κυρίου τῆς
γῆς ἑστῶτες

These are the two *olive trees and the two
lampstands* standing before the Lord
of the earth

Zech 4.14[PM]

אלה שני בני־היצהר העמדים על־אדון
כל־הארץ

These are the two sons of oil standing
before the Lord of all the earth.

The manner in which Rev 11.4 is constructed corroborates its connection to Zech 4.14, although minor differences are present. First,
the phrase καὶ αἱ δύο λυχνίαι and its retroverted equivalent, ושני מנורות,
are not reflected in any OG/LXX tradition or Hebrew form of Zech
4.14. However, the word λυχνίαι ([ה]מנורת) does occur in Zech 4.2, 11.[103]
This phrase in Rev 11.4 is a conflation of Zech 4.2, 11, and 14 where

---

[102] Codex Alexandrinus (A02) preserves a singular reading here that is not noted in the
apparatus of NA[28] or UBS[3-4]. A02 reads ΑΥΛΑΙΑΙ ('curtains') while all other textual witnesses
preserve the word included in the main text of all modern critical editions: ἐλαῖαι. This singular reading is intricate in that it corresponds morphologically with and is phonologically
similar to ἐλαῖαι and Karrer has suggested that transcriptional probability makes it possible
that this reading is the original. Forms of αὐλαία occur almost exclusively as descriptions
of the curtains of the desert tabernacle in Exod 25–26; 37. This reading is explicable based
on two considerations. First, the word is morphologically, graphically, and phonological
similar reading present in all other witnesses. Second, the cultic imagery that pervades Rev
11 recalled for this scribe the tabernacle account in Exod 25–26; 37[OG], causing this scribe to
correlate these two accounts further. The lexical overlap between Rev 11 and Exodus[OG] evi-
denced by the measuring of the temple (Rev 11.1–2), the mention of lampstands (Rev 11.4;
cf. Exod 25.30–35[31–36]; 26.35; 30.27; 31.8; 35.16[14]; 38.13[37.17]), and the opening of
the heavenly temple to reveal the ark of the covenant (Rev 11.19: ἡ κιβωτὸς τῆς διαθήκης; see
Exod 25.9[10], 13–15[14–16], 20–21[21–22]; 26.33–34; 30.6; 31.7; 35.11[12]; 38.1[37.1]) may
have guided the scribe to make this alteration based on an acute awareness of the Exodus[OG]
(see also the juxtaposition of tabernacle curtains and a lampstand in *Massekhet Kelim* §1).
Although this singular reading is suggestive, it will not be analysed here as the manuscript
evidence is overwhelmingly in favour of ἐλαῖαι. αυλαια is more easily explained as an alteration of ἐλαῖαι, and Revelation in A02 evidences other scribal particularities that would
suggest the reading here is secondary. Martin Karrer, 'Der Text der Johannesoffenbarung –
Varianten und Theologie', *Neotestamentica* 43 no 2 (2009): 383–388 notes that certain readings in A02 highlight the cultic framework of the Apocalypse (see also A02 Rev 4.3; 14.4,
9). For 11.4 specifically, see Juan Hernández Jr., *Scribal Habits and Theological Influences in
the Apocalypse* (WUNT 2.218; Tübingen: Mohr Siebeck, 2006), 119 n.110. See also parallels between Rev 11 and 1 Macc 7.17.

[103] For a detailed account of menorah imagery in Zechariah, see Jens Voß, *Die
Menora: Gestalt und Funktion des Leuchters im Tempel zu Jerusalem* (OBO 128;

Table 3.6 *Quantitative divergences between Rev 11.4 and Zech 4.14ᴾᴹ*

Rev 11.4	Zech 4.14ᴾᴹ
καὶ αἱ δύο λυχνίαι	Absent
Absent	כל

the reference to 'two sons of oil' has been replaced by the 'two olive trees' (זיתים; 4.2, 11).[104] Also, a word from the source text is absent in the target text. כל is not represented in Rev 11.4,[105] constituting the only omission between locutions (see Table 3.6). Beyond this exclusion, *every* other syntactic element of Zech 4.14ᴾᴹ is represented in Rev 11.4. The lone verbs in each phrase (עמדים/ἑστῶτες) are masculine plural participles and ἵστημι stands well within the semantic range of עמ"ד. Moreover, the construct phrase בני־היצהר is translated as ἐλαῖαι. This translation represents the rare word יצהר and, in this sense, condenses the Greek locution by omitting an equivalent for בני. The translation of יצהר is consistent with every other translation of this word in the rest of the OG/LXX, except in Zech 4.14.[106] The syntactic, grammatical, and semantic overlap between Rev 11.4 and Zech 4.14ᴾᴹ indicates literary dependence.[107] Nonetheless, the examination must move on to the relationship between the proto-MT and *VOG*, in order to

Göttingen: Vandenhoeck & Ruprecht; 1993) and Rachel Hachlili, *The Menorah, the Ancient Seven-Armed Candelabrum: Origin, Form and Significance* (JSJsup 68; Leiden: Brill, 2001), esp. 18–22. In Zech 4.2ᴹᵀ, מנורת is vocalized as a singular noun in construct. In 4.11 מנורה is also singular.

[104] This same conflation occurs in *b. San* 3.1.

[105] בני is absent as well, but only in the sense that the entire construct phrase (בני־היצהר) has been replaced by ἐλαῖαι.

[106] HRCS, 174, 447, 723, 1135. One other questionable translation occurs in Jer 38(31).12. However, outside of Zech 4.14, the word is always translated (twenty-two times) consistently with forms of ἔλαιον. *TJ* Zech 4.14 translates the term 'sons of the great ones' (רברביא). This is the only instance where רברביא translates היצהר, but, most likely, this reflects a consistent *Vorlage* due to the large semantic range of רברביא. P. S. Alexander, 'The Targumim and Early Exegesis of "the Sons of God" in Genesis 6', *JJS* 23 (1972): 60–71 notes that the expression 'sons of the great ones' is often a translation from the MT 'sons of God'. רברביא translates no fewer than thirty-eight Hebrew equivalents. See J. C. de Moor, ed., *A Bilingual Concordance to the Targum of the Prophets* (vols. 2, 5, 8, 11, 14, 20; Leiden: Brill, 1996–2003).

[107] The phrase אדון כל־הארץ is found elsewhere in the HB (Josh 3.11; Ps 97.5; Mic 4.13) but in all other instances יצהר and the verb עמד are not present.

fully appreciate the textual relationship between the versions and Revelation.

In concert with the preceding observations regarding the relationship between OG and Zech 1–8ᴾᴹ thus far, it is likely that the *Vorlage* of Zech 4.14ᴼᴳ is closely related to the proto-MT. The following evidence also points to this conclusion.

Zech 4.14ᴼᴳ   Οὗτοι οἱ δύο υἱοὶ τῆς πιότητος παρεστήκασι τῷ
κυρίῳ πάσης τῆς γῆς
These are the two sons of wealth standing before the
Lord of all the earth

Zech 4.14ᴾᴹ   אלה שני בני־היצהר העמדים על־אדון כל־הארץ

These are the two sons of oil standing before the Lord
of all the earth

In relation to the proto-MT, the OG translation is rendered with a high level of literalness. All but one Hebrew word is translated with a common Greek equivalent,[108] presented in identical word order. The OG translation even omits the unexpressed verb of being (expressed in Rev 11.4 with εἰσιν). The OG also translates the phrase בני היצהר literally as υἱοὶ τῆς πιότητος, replicating the syntax of the Hebrew metaphor of 'sons of fresh oil'.[109] The *Vorlage* Zech 4.14ᴼᴳ and proto-MT are closely related.

Despite the concord between these texts, two issues require explanation. First, certain Greek manuscripts and other versions do preserve οὗτοί εἰσιν, a reading that agrees with Rev 11.4 against the OG.[110] Second, the translation of πιότητος for יצהר is noteworthy because it is a unique translation in the OG/LXX tradition. πιότητος is most often a translation of דשׁ"ן ('to be fat').[111] However, in the NT, πιότητος does refer to a 'state of oiliness' (cf. Rom 11.17). Moreover, πιότητος is altered in the traditions

---

[108] With the exception of πιότητος for יצהר.

[109] Cécile Dogniez, 'Some Similarities between the Septuagint and the Targum of Zechariah', in *Translating and Translation: The LXX and its Modern Translations in the Context of Early Judaism* (BETL 213; ed. H. Ausloos et al.; Leuven: Peeters, 2008), 97 notes that Zechariahᴼᴳ often preserves the figurative language of its *Vorlage*. See also Barr, *Typology*, 41.

[110] Manuscripts 130 239 393.

[111] BDB, 206. According to LSJ, 1406 πιότης defines either physical 'fattiness' or metaphysical 'wealth, prosperity'.

of Aquila, Symmachus, and Theodotion. Each variant in these traditions describes 'oil' in some sense.[112] Although πιότητος is a unique translation of יצהר, it nonetheless reflects the idea of 'oil', albeit on the fringe of its semantic range.[113] There is a minor loss of semantic fidelity in this translation choice, but the selection of a single equivalent does not necessarily detract from the fact that the syntax of the Greek translation reflects the syntax of the proto-MT exactly. Overall, the differences between the proto-MT and OG can be explained by way of translation technique: the *V*OG does not reflect a Hebrew tradition different from proto-MT.

Although it is clear that Zech 4.14ᴾᴹ and Rev 11.4 are closely related, the question remains as to whether the proto-MT was the only tradition to which John alluded. It is prudent here to examine the relationship of the OG and Rev 11.4.

Rev 11.4   οὗτοί εἰσιν αἱ δύο ἐλαῖαι καὶ αἱ δύο λυχνίαι αἱ ἐνώπιον τοῦ κυρίου τῆς γῆς ἑστῶτες

These are the two olive trees and the two lampstands standing before the Lord of the earth.

Zech 4.14ᴼᴳ   Οὗτοι οἱ δύο υἱοὶ τῆς πιότητος παρεστήκασι τῷ κυρίῳ πάσης τῆς γῆς

These are the two sons of wealth standing before the Lord of all the earth.

There are multiple differences between these Greek texts. As noted above, Rev 11.4 omits a word that is present in the OG: πάσης. Second, Rev 11.4 is moderately expansive, adding the explanatory phrase καὶ αἱ δύο λυχνίαι. Third, Rev 11.4 explicates the meaning of the Hebrew preposition על by translating it with the preposition ἐνώπιον. In contrast, the OG translator employed the dative construction τῷ κυρίῳ to express the position of the two 'sons of oil'. A fourth difference lies in the translation of עמדים: Rev 11.4 preserves ἑστῶτες, and Zech 4.14ᴼᴳ παρεστήκασι. However, despite the attachment of a prefix, the

---

[112] The variants are στιλπνότητος ('to shine'), ἐλαίου, and λαμπρότητος ('brilliance, splendour') respectively.

[113] The usage of πιότης to describe olives or oil of some kind is also found in Judg 9.9ᴼᴳ, *T. Levi* 8.8, and *T. Issachar* 5.5. See BDAG, 814 and R. H. Charles, ed., *The Greek Versions of the Testaments of the Twelve Patriarchs* (Oxford: Clarendon, 1908).

words retain nearly identical semantic value: 'to stand, stand firm'.[114] Fifth, the beginning of Rev 11.4 reads οὗτοί εἰσιν where the majority of exemplars of Zech 4.14[OG] leave the verb unexpressed (following the Hebrew). Sixth, the two translations differ in their representation of בני־היצהר. The equivalent in Rev 11.4 (ἐλαῖαι) is more common than the word choice of the OG translator (υἱοὶ τῆς πιότητος). In this case, the translator chose a word on the outskirts of the semantic range of יצהר (πιότητος), while retaining the figurative language of the source tradition. In contrast, John's translation equivalent is common, but he does not transmit the metaphor. Seventh, the lone verb in each phrase differs syntactically. Zech 4.14[OG] translates העמדים not as a participle, but as a third-person plural verb in the perfect tense. John writes the word as a perfect tense active plural participle.

These six differences indicate that Zech 4.14[OG] is not John's source text in this instance (see Table 3.7). These three traditions do, however, share many characteristics. Both Zech 4.14[OG] and Rev 11.4 betray a close relationship to proto-MT, but differ in multiple ways from each other. If John used a Greek text to craft this reference, he should have adopted some of the peculiarities of his source. Instead, he strays from the OG on semantic and syntactic fronts. Zech 4.14[OG] and Rev 11.4 share a source text but differ in their translation and reading traditions. The textual evidence suggests that Zech 4.14[OG] and Rev 11.4 are independent translations of the proto-MT, which differ in degree of literalness.

However, the possibility remains that John reused a revising Greek tradition. Two notable variants in the Greek tradition agree with the reference in Rev 11.4 against the critical text. First, certain Greek manuscripts do preserve εἰσιν in agreement with Revelation.[115] However, these manuscripts do not evidence any other agreement with Rev 11.4 against the OG. Each still witness five differences with Rev 11.4. Second, the Hexaplaric translations of יצהר differ from OG. The Symmachian reading (ἐλαίου) is similar to the reading in Rev 11.4 (ἐλαῖαι), although not in number. Again, this reading is closer to Rev 11.4 than the OG, but still differs from the reference in five places. Also, if Symmachus

---

[114] See BDAG, 482 and T. Muraoka, *A Greek-English Lexicon of the Septuagint* (Louvain: Peeters, 2009), 535.

[115] Jellicoe, *Septuagint*, 156, 167 categorizes 130 as Lucianic and 239, 393 as Hesychian, although he does not base his categories on textual affinities, but 'historical' citations in Patristic authors.

Table 3.7 *Differences between Rev 11.4 and Zech 4.14^{OG}*

Rev 11.4	Zech 4.14^{OG}
οὗτοί εἰσιν	οὗτοι
ἐλαῖαι	υἱοὶ τῆς πιότητος
καὶ αἱ δύο λυχνίαι	Absent
αἱ ἐνώπιον	τῷ κυρίῳ
ἑστῶτες	παρεστήκασι
Absent	πάσης

does revise the OG towards proto-MT, this is precisely the kind of alteration one envisions: the movement from an obscure translation to a more common translation equivalent. None of the inner-Greek variation necessarily indicates that John referenced one of these traditions.

The six differences between Zech 4.14^{OG} and Rev 11.4 (five if a Greek version is the assumed source) do not reveal a link between John's text and the OG/LXX tradition. This eliminates options 4–6, 8, 10: OG, the καιγε recension (8HevXIIgr),[116] a proto-Hexaplaric recension, an adaptation of a Greek version, and a free paraphrase of OG/LXX. The close correlation between the proto-MT and the *V*OG eliminates option 2 as a category distinct from option 1. It seems, like the preceding analyses, that John utilized a combination of option 1 (a translation of proto-MT [=*V*OG]) and option 7 (a translation of the proto-MT with adaptations). With minor exceptions, the text of Rev 11.4 is a literal representation of Zech 4.14^{PM}.

With the form of Zech 4.14 identified, the question of John's point of access to this text remains. Three factors imply that, like John's use of Zech 4.10, he accessed Zech 4.14 through the medium of a textual encounter with a Hebrew form of Zechariah, in conversation with traditions pertaining to divine messengers. First, while the depiction of the two prophets as those who 'stand before the Lord of all the earth' appropriates other traditions pertaining to angelic beings in the heavenly court (e.g. Job 1.6), there is no direct reuse of material from these other traditions. In other words, Rev 11.4 does not preserve a composite tradition of which Zech 4.14 is a part, but, instead,

---

[116] My reconstruction of Zech 4.14 in 8HevXIIgr is identical to the OG. See Appendix 2.

the entire locution is reused from Zech 4.14. Second, although a segment of Zech 4.14 is preserved in the fragmentary 4Q254 and later rabbinic texts (cf. Section 5.3), v. 14 and the chapter as a whole are not the objects of much exegetical attention outside the book of Revelation. Zech 4 boasts little influence over the shape of Second Temple Jewish exegetical reflection, and other NT authors fail to engage the chapter altogether. There is not a robust or even an identifiable tradition of exegetical engagement with Zech 4 before the book of Revelation, outside of the implied interpretation in Zechariah's early Greek and Aramaic versions. And third, as the discussion of this text in the next chapter demonstrates (Section 4.4.5), the textual differences between Zech 4.14ᴾᴹ and Rev 11.4 are accounted for by John's interpretative encounter with the graphic details of Hebrew consonants and the question of reading tradition associated with those consonants. These points coalesce to indicate that John has access to a textual artefact that preserved Zech 4 in Hebrew, although his interaction with this artefact was likely influenced by past aural encounters with this text, encounters that may have informed the way in which he attached semantic value to the consonants through patterns of vocalization. Again, as the discussion in the next chapter will make abundantly clear, the distinction between textual and aural scriptural encounters cannot be neatly maintained.

3.2.6 Revelation 19.11–16 and Zechariah 1.8; 6.1–6

Another example of John's reuse of Zechariah's horse visions (cf. Section 3.2.3) is located in Rev 19.11–16, a text that represents a conglomeration of multiple antecedent scriptural traditions and which opens a new vision signalled by the words 'and I saw' (καὶ εἶδον). Material from Zech 1.8; 6.1–6 is discernible within this composite passage along with other texts.[117] Scholarly opinion on whether Rev 19.11–16 borrowed material from Zech 1.8; 6.1–6 is, however, largely negative. The majority of commentators do not mention Zechariah in their exposition of Rev 19.11–16,[118] and those who discuss the prospect

---

[117] References to previous passages from Revelation are present – including 1.12–20; 2.17; 14.14–20 – as well as references to other literature including a reference to Ezek 1.1 (Rev 19.11; see Kowalski, *Rezeption*, 208–210, 506), Ps 2.9 (Rev 19.15), and Joel 4.13–14 (Rev 19.15).

[118] See Beale, *Revelation*, 948–964; Koester, *Revelation*, 752–759; Aune, *Revelation*, 1052–1054; Charles, *Revelation*, 2:131; Osborne, *Revelation*, 679–680; Lichtenberger, *Apokalypse*, 248–251; Smalley, *The Apocalypse*, 487–496; Boxall, *The Revelation*,

of a reference to Zechariah reject the possibility.[119] Despite the opposition to the presence of this reference in scholarly opinion, there are multiple textual points of contact between Rev 19.11–16 and Zechariah's horse visions, as well as evidence of internal textual mimesis within Revelation itself.[120] The connections are not as convincing as the preceding examples, but are worthy of further scrutiny since they represent one end of the mimetic spectrum and offer an opportunity (in the next chapter) to closely examine a pericope in which possible Zechariah traditions are closely enmeshed with locutions from other scriptural texts.

Rev 19.11–16	And I saw heaven opened (Καὶ εἶδον τὸν οὐρανὸν ἠνεῳγμένον) and behold a white horse (ἵππος λευκὸς) and the one sitting on it was called faithful and true[121] and in righteousness he judges and makes war. And his eyes are as a burning flame and on his head are many diadems, having a name written which no one knows except him. And he has been clothed in a garment that had been dipped in blood and his name is called the word of God. And the armies which are in heaven follow him on white horses (Καὶ τὰ στρατεύματα τὰ ἐν τῷ οὐρανῷ ἠκολούθει αὐτῷ ἐφ᾽ ἵπποις λευκοῖς), clothed in pure clean linen. And from his mouth comes a sharp sword, so that with it he can smite the nations and he shatters them with an iron rod and he tramples the winepress of the wrath of the anger of God Almighty

272–274; Mounce, *Revelation*, 343–344; Kiddle, *The Revelation*, 383–384; Boring, *Revelation*, 195–196; Blount, *Revelation*, 350–356; Holtz, *Die Offenbarung*, 124–126; Morris, *Revelation*, 229; Caird, *The Revelation*, 240–241; Knight, *Revelation*, 127–128; Ford, *Revelation*, 312; Swete, *Apocalypse*, 250; Beasley-Murray, *Revelation*, 279; Harrington, *Revelation*, 190–195; Witherington, *Revelation*, 242; Sweet, *Revelation*, 281–282. Giesen, *Die Offenbarung*, 420 and Smalley, *The Apocalypse*, 488 connect Rev 19.11–16 and Zech 9.9 based on christological concerns. The lexical and linguistic links between these texts are relatively thin and the horse vision here mirrors the fourth horse in Rev 6.8 which, in turn, is designed in part based on Zech 1.8; 6.1–5.

[119] Rogers, 'John's Use of Zechariah', 115–116; Jauhiainen, *The Use*, 65–66.

[120] Cf. Rev 6.1–8 and 19.11–16. This connection is highlighted by Carrell, *Jesus and the Angels*, 204–205.

[121] The phrase καλούμενος πιστὸς καὶ ἀληθινός exists in multiple forms in the manuscript evidence. Other readings include πιστὸς καλούμενος καὶ ἀληθινός (ℵ), πιστὸς καὶ ἀληθινός καλούμενος, πιστὸς καὶ ἀληθινός, and vocabatur fidelis, et verax vocatur in some Latin witnesses. The textual variation of the locution does not weigh heavily on the present discussion, as the locution is not reliant upon Zechariah. For further comment, see Juan Hernández Jr., 'The Apocalypse in Codex Alexandrinus: Its Singular

Zech 1.8; 6.1–6[OG]   I saw the night and behold a man riding on a red horse (ἵππον πυρρόν) and this man was standing in the middle of two overshadowing mountains and after him horses red (ἵπποι πυρροί), dappled (ψαροί), many-coloured (ποικίλοι,) and white (λευκοί) . . . And I turned and I lifted my eyes and I saw and behold four chariots (τέσσαρα ἅρματα) coming out from the middle of two mountains and the mountains were mountains of bronze. With the first chariot red horses (ἵπποι πυρροί), and with the second chariot black horses (ἵπποι μέλανες) and with the third chariot white horses (ἵπποι λευκοί) and in the fourth chariot dappled and many-coloured horses (ἵπποι ποικίλοι ψαροί). And I answered and I said to the angel who was speaking to me, 'What are these, lord?' And the angel who was speaking to me answered and he said, 'These are the four winds of heaven, coming out to stand before the Lord of all the earth.' And the one with the black horses went to the land of the north and the white ones went behind them (καὶ οἱ λευκοὶ ἐξεπορεύοντο κατόπισθεν αὐτῶν) and the many-coloured horses when to the land of the south

Zech 1.8; 6.1–6[PM]   I saw in the night and behold a man riding on a red horse (על־סוס אדם) and he was standing between myrtles which were in a glen and after him: horses red (סוסים אדמים), light green (שרקים) and white (לבנים) . . . And I turned and I lifted up my eyes and I saw and behold four chariots (ארבע מרכבות) coming from between two mountains and the mountains were mountains of bronze. With the first chariot red horses (סוסים אדמים) and with the second chariot black horses (סוסים שחרים) and with the third chariot white horses (סוסים לבנים) and with the fourth chariot strong spotted horses (סוסים ברדים אמצים). And I answered and I said to the angel speaking with me, 'what are these, my lord?' And the angel answered and he said to me, 'these are the four winds of heaven going out from being stationed before the Lord of all the earth.' And the black horses went to the land of the north and the white ones when behind them (והלבנים יצאו אל־אחריהם) and the spotted ones went to the land of the south

Readings and Scribal Habits', in *Scripture and Traditions: Essays on Early Judaism and Christianity in Honor of Carl R. Holladay* (NTsup 129; ed. P. Gray and G. R. O'Day; Leiden: Brill, 2008), 341–358.

Numerous textual features of Rev 19.11–16 correspond to features of Zechariah. First, both proto-MT and Zech 1.8, 6.3^OG preserve the phrase 'white horses' (סוסים לבנים/ ἵπποι λευκοί). This locution is also present in Rev 19.11 in the singular (ἵππος λευκός) referring to the rider's horse and, in v. 14, in the plural (ἵπποις λευκοῖς), referring to the horses of the heavenly armies that follow the first rider. It is difficult to find a parallel to the collocation 'white horse(s)' in the Second Temple period. The uniqueness of the locution among scriptural traditions indicates that, if John referenced an antecedent textual tradition here, Zech 1.8; 6.3 is the likely candidate.

The second textual connection between these texts is the actions of the white horses in Rev 19.14 and Zech 6.6:

Rev 19.14

Καὶ τὰ στρατεύματα τὰ ἐν τῷ οὐρανῷ ἠκολούθει αὐτῷ ἐφ' ἵπποις λευκοῖς

Zech 6.6^OG

ἐν ᾧ ἦσαν οἱ ἵπποι οἱ μέλανες, ἐξεπορεύοντο ἐπὶ γῆν βορρᾶ, καὶ οἱ λευκοὶ ἐξεπορεύοντο κατόπισθεν αὐτῶν, καὶ οἱ ποικίλοι ἐξεπορεύοντο ἐπὶ γῆν νότου

Zech 6.6^PM

אשר־בה הסוסים השחרים יצאים אל־ארץ צפון והלבנים יצאו אל־אחריהם והברדים יצאו אל־ארץ תימן

The white horses in Zech 6.6 follow the black horses and their chariots to the land of the north, a pattern that followed by the white horses in Rev 19.14. The verb chosen to describe the action of the heavenly cavalry in Rev 19.14 (ἠκολούθει) does not correspond to the verb clause in Zech 6.6^OG (ἐξεπορεύοντο κατόπισθεν), although the semantics are not altogether dissimilar. However, the question remains as to whether ἠκολούθει finds an equivalent in Zech 6.6^PM (יצאו אל־אחריהם). The locution in the proto-MT is grammatically difficult and possibly corrupt,[122] but a connection with Rev 19.14 does exist.

---

[122] Carol L. Meyers and Eric M. Meyers, *Haggai, Zechariah 1–8* (AB 25B; Garden City, NY: Doubleday, 1987), 325–326 argue that the phrase אל־אחריהם is corrupt along with the various directions in which the horses go and the colours of the horses. They suggest that this textual confusion 'occurred very early in the history of the transmission of the MT' (326). Hinckley G. Mitchell, *A Critical and Exegetical Commentary on Haggai and Zechariah* (ICC; Edinburgh: T&T Clark, 1912), 180 and Rex Mason, *The Books of Haggai, Zechariah and Malachi* (CBC; Cambridge: Cambridge University Press, 1977), 60 also previously suggested emending אל־אחריהם ('after them') to 'to the west of them'. Hans-Friedemann Richter, 'Die Pferde in den Nachtgesichten des

While there is no example of a form of ἀκολουθέω serving as a translation equivalent for יצ"א, forms of ἀκολουθέω occasionally serve as equivalents for the preposition אחרי (Deut 12.30; Job 6.7(8); 14.8, 9; 1 Kgs 16.22^A; Prov 20.7). A similar translation is witnessed in the reference to Zech 6.6 (והלבנים יצאו אל־אחריהם) in Rev 19.14 (τὰ στρατεύματα τὰ ἐν τῷ οὐρανῷ ἠκολούθει αὐτῷ). There are significant differences between these two locutions, including the subject and number of the personal pronoun at the end of each phrase; however, it seems that John represented הלבנים with the phrase τὰ στρατεύματα τὰ ἐν τῷ οὐρανῷ, explicating Zechariah's white horses by ascribing a specific identify to them. Additionally, John either omitted יצאו as redundant – translating אל־אחריהם as ἠκολούθει – or condensed the phrase יצאו אל־אחריהם into a single verbal idea represented by ἠκολούθει.[123] Either way, the parallel examples of this translation and the representation of אחרי with a verb in other Greek scriptural texts[124] suggest that it was possible for a form of ἀκολουθέω to serve as a translation equivalent for אחרי, creating another point of textual contact between Zech 1.8; 6.1–6 and Rev 19.11–16.

The third linguistic connection between Rev 19.11–16 and Zech 1.8; 6.1–6 is the internal verbal correlation between Rev 19.11–16 and the previous horse vision (Section 3.2.3). The textual evidence and scholarly opinion support the claim that Rev 6.1–8 references Zech 1.8; 6.1–5. Verbal parallels between Rev 6.1–8 and Rev 19.11–16 suggest that John constructed both visions using a common well of traditional sources. First, the white horse (Rev 6.2) and each of the three following

---

Sacharja', *ZAW* 98 (1986): 98–99 reconstructs Zech 6.6 following E. C. Bissell, 'On Zech. vi. 1–7', *JSBLE* 6 (1886): 117–118, who argues for textual emendation. There is no manuscript evidence available to confirm this claim and, if the proto-MT textual tradition of Zech 6.1–8 is corrupt, the corruption occurred before Zechariah was translated into Greek and well before the composition of the book of Revelation.

[123] According to T. M. Law, 'The Translation of Symmachus in 1 Kings (3 Kingdoms)', in *XIII Congress of the International Organization for Septuagint and Cognate Studies Ljubljana, 2007* (SCS 55; ed. M. K. H. Peters; Atlanta: SBL, 2008), 283 a similar translation approach that intentionally omits linguistic data from a Hebrew source text is witnessed in the Greek version of Symmachus in 3 Kingdoms. He notes that 'Sym communicates the sense of the Hebrew using fewer words than LXX.' Likewise, Joosten, 'Septuagintal', 218 notes that the OG translation of the Twelve tends to systematically eliminate Hebrew linguistic material when 'the source text was perceived to express the same element twice'. A similar pattern may occur in John's translation.

[124] See also this style of representation in Lev 26.33 (ἐπιπορευομένη); Prov 20.7 (καταλείψει); Deut 11.28 (λατρεύειν).

horses (Rev 6.3–8) are introduced after the lamb opens (ἤνοιξεν) one of the seven seals. Similarly, in Rev 19.11, the seer encounters a white horse immediately after seeing heaven opened (ἠνεῳγμένον). The verbal parallels between these scenes are greater still.

Rev 6.2a   καὶ ἰδοὺ ἵππος λευκός, καὶ ὁ καθήμενος ἐπ'
                αὐτὸν ἔχων τόξον . . .

Rev 19.11a   καὶ ἰδοὺ ἵππος λευκὸς καὶ ὁ καθήμενος ἐπ'
                αὐτὸν καλούμενος . . .

The introduction of the rider on the white horse in each passage is identical, although the rider is described differently. This verbal correlation intimates that Rev 19.11–16 and 6.1–8 are related or, at least, that the author designed Rev 19.11–16 to be read in coordination with the previous horse vision.

Overall, the external verbal correlation between Rev 19.11–16 and Zech 1.8; 6.1–6 and the internal verbal correlation with Rev 6.1–6 suggests that the rider of the white horse and his following army in Rev 19.11–16 is, in part, a reference to Zechariah's horse visions. Moreover, the evidence supports the conclusion that John reused a particular textual tradition of Zechariah – the proto-MT. The internal evidence is obviously not reliant upon a Hebrew text, but the connection between Rev 19.14 (ἠκολούθει) and Zech 6.6 (אחריהם) is not tenable if one assumes that the author of Revelation utilized Zech 6.6^{OG/LXX}. Like the reference to Zechariah's horse visions in Rev 6.1–8, John utilized Zech 1.8; 6.1–6^{PM} to help craft his horse vision in Rev 19.11–16.

And like the reuse of Zechariah's horse visions in Rev 6.1–8, it is likely that John engaged this tradition through access to a textual artefact, perhaps influenced by aural experience. The textual detail upon which this encounter is based indicates an awareness of the graphic details and grammatical issues surrounding the consonantal Hebrew text. Additionally, as the discussion of this allusion in the next chapter explores in depth (Section 4.4.6), the larger pericope of Rev 19.11–16 is dependent upon numerous other scriptural texts, texts that are not combined with material Zechariah in any other Second Temple Jewish texts, including the NT. Although John's textual hermeneutics for combining diverse scriptural texts are commensurate with other examples of exegetical rewriting in the period, this particular combination of traditions is unique to the Apocalypse. In this way, John is a creative reader of the scriptural tradition, but only in the sense that he is part of and influenced by a broader tradition of exegesis and reading. Although he engages Zechariah's horse visions through a textual artefact, he does not do so outside of dominant modes of reading and interpretation enshrined in his broader textual culture. Encountering Zechariah traditions through a textual encounter does not mean that John is reading the text apart from his own previous experience of Zechariah (i.e. the memory of previous textual and aural encounters) or the collective memory of Zechariah that influenced these encounters.

3.2.7 Revelation 19–22 and Zechariah 14.7–11

The final example of an interpretative encounter of Zechariah traditions is scattered among texts located in Rev 19–22 (19.6; 21.6/22.1; 21.25; 22.3). It is well known that the final four chapters of the Apocalypse draw unambiguously on numerous scriptural traditions associated with eschatological judgement and divine action embedded in Jewish scripture. In this context, it is not surprising to find material from Zech 14, a text that consistently articulates what will happen 'on that day', and that describes YHWH's return to Jerusalem and secure state of his people. Rev 19–22 does not borrow material from Zech 14.7–11 in chronological order, but a pattern of reuse of the majority of this segment is present, beginning in Rev 19.6.

Rev 19.6	Καὶ ἤκουσα ὡς φωνὴν ὄχλου πολλοῦ καὶ ὡς φωνὴν ὑδάτων πολλῶν καὶ ὡς φωνὴν βροντῶν ἰσχυρῶν λεγόντων· ἁλληλουϊά, ὅτι ἐβασίλευσεν κύριος ὁ θεὸς [ἡμῶν] ὁ παντοκράτωρ
	And I heard a sound like a great crowd and a sound like many waters and a sound like loud thunder saying, 'Alleluia, for the Lord our God, the almighty reigns'
Zech 14.9^pM125	וְהָיָה יְהוָה לְמֶלֶךְ עַל־כָּל־הָאָרֶץ בַּיּוֹם הַהוּא יִהְיֶה יְהוָה אֶחָד וּשְׁמוֹ אֶחָד
	And YHWH will be king over all the land in that day. YHWH will be one, his name one
Zech 14.9^OG/LXX126	καὶ ἔσται κύριος εἰς βασιλέα ἐπὶ πᾶσαν τὴν γῆν, ἐν τῇ ἡμέρᾳ ἐκείνῃ ἔσται κύριος εἷς καὶ τὸ ὄνομα αὐτοῦ ἕν
	And the Lord will be king over all the land in that day. The Lord will be one and his name one

---

125 Zech 14.9 is not preserved at Qumran.

126 The revising Greek forms of Zechariah do not pay much heed to 14.9, likely since it already represents an isomorphic translation of the proto-MT. As such, its text in 8HevXIIgr is not reconstructed in Appendix 2.

The connection between Zech 14.9 and Rev 19.6 (cf. Rev 11.5) rests in the assertion that 'YHWH will be king' (למלך יהוה והיה//καὶ ἔσται κύριος εἰς βασιλέα) in that day and the proclamation 'Alleluia, for the Lord our God, the almighty reigns' (ἐβασίλευσεν κύριος ὁ θεός). A few comments on this example set the stage for the broader discussion pertaining to Zech 14.7–11.

First, the assertion that YHWH will reign is not unique to Zechariah among other Jewish scriptural texts. Numerous psalms (e.g. 93.1; 97.1; 99.1) and other works (e.g. 1 Chr 16.28) extol the kingship of YHWH using similar turns of phrase. The wording of these texts (in their Hebrew and Greek forms) does not correspond directly to the presentation of this exultation in Rev 19.6, but they are, along with Zech 14.9 closely aligned with its general thrust. The non-unique parallel between Rev 19.6 and Zech 14.9 leads Jauhiainen to cast doubt on the presence of an allusion in this instance.[127] However, the linguistic association of these texts, supported by the broader pattern of reference to Zech 14.7–11 and the further connotations of divine disclosure associated with the phrase 'I heard a sound like a great crowd and a sound like many waters and a sound like loud thunder saying' (cf. Isa 17.12–13; Ezek 1.24; 43.2; Dan 10.6) in conversation with broader traditions linked with divine kingship in Jewish scripture, highlights the possibility that John alluded here to Zech 14.9.

Second, if Rev 19.6 does in fact allude to Zech 14.9 it is likely that John referenced a Hebrew tradition. The Greek version of Zech 14.9 is a precise replication of the proto-MT, including the representation of למלך with βασιλέα (=לְמֶלֶךְ). The use of a verbal form in Rev 19.6 (ἐβασίλευσεν) does not correspond to the wording of the Greek tradition. Instead, it corresponds to a reading of למלך as a verbal form (i.e. לְמָלַךְ), a reading that occurs in numerous places in the OG where the MT reads לְמֶלֶךְ.[128] In this way, John follows a minority, but established pattern of translation in representing material from Zechariah. However, the allusive nature of this particular reference does not provide much information in regard to the avenue of access to this tradition. It does not rule out access to a textual artefact, but neither does it point towards a remembrance of a textual or aural encounter. This allusion is best understood within the context of the

---

[127] Jauhiainen, The Use, 123–124.
[128] Cf. Judg 15.9; 2 Sam 2.4; 3.17; 1 Kgs 14.2, 25; Isa 30.33; 36.1.

pattern of reference that is next exemplified in Rev 21.6 and 22.1 (cf. 7.17; 22.17).

Rev 21.6

καὶ εἶπέν μοι· γέγοναν. ἐγώ [εἰμι] τὸ ἄλφα καὶ τὸ ὦ, ἡ ἀρχὴ καὶ τὸ τέλος. ἐγὼ τῷ διψῶντι δώσω ἐκ τῆς πηγῆς τοῦ ὕδατος τῆς ζωῆς δωρεάν

And he said to me: 'it is done. I am the alpha and the omega, the beginning and the end. I will give water to the thirsty from the spring of the water of life as a gift'

Rev 22.1

Καὶ ἔδειξέν μοι ποταμὸν ὕδατος ζωῆς λαμπρὸν ὡς κρύσταλλον, ἐκπορευόμενον ἐκ τοῦ θρόνου τοῦ θεοῦ καὶ τοῦ ἀρνίου

And he showed me a river of living water, clear as crystal, coming out from the throne of God and the lamb

Zech 14.8ᵖᴹ

והיה ביום ההוא יצאו מים־חיים מירושלם חצים אל־הים הקדמוני וחצים אל־הים האחרון בקיץ ובחרף יהיה

And it will be in that day living water will go out from Jerusalem; half to the eastern sea and half to the western sea. This will be so in summer as in winter

Zech 14.8ᴼᴳ/ᴸˣˣ

καὶ ἐν τῇ ἡμέρᾳ ἐκείνῃ ἐξελεύσεται ὕδωρ ζῶν ἐξ Ιερουσαλημ, τὸ ἥμισυ αὐτοῦ εἰς τὴν θάλασσαν τὴν πρώτην καὶ τὸ ἥμισυ αὐτοῦ εἰς τὴν θάλασσαν τὴν ἐσχάτην, καὶ ἐν θέρει καὶ ἐν ἔαρι ἔσται οὕτως

And in that day living water will go out from Jerusalem; half of it to the first sea and half of it to the last sea. And in summer and in spring it will be thus

The second allusion to Zech 14.7–11 occurs in both Rev 21.6 and 22.1 and relates to the image of living water flowing from the throne of God and the lamb. Following the announcement of a new heaven and new earth (21.1–2) and the raucous song from the throne (21.3–4), the one seated upon the throne speaks, enumerating his actions (21.5–6). One of these actions includes the gift of access to 'the spring of living water' (ἐκ τῆς πηγῆς τοῦ ὕδατος τῆς ζωῆς). Additionally, after an extended description of the physical layout of the city (21.9–27), the seer is shown a 'clear river of living water' (ποταμὸν ὕδατος ζωῆς λαμπρὸν) in Rev 22.1, moving outward from the throne. Both of these descriptions of streams of living water that originate in the midst of Jerusalem reflect traditions also found in Zech 14.8, where living water streams from Jerusalem in two directions in all seasons. Similar traditions are associated with 'living water' (e.g. Jer 2.13; 7.17; 21.6; Isa 55.1) and the eschatological river (e.g. Ezek 47.1–12 [cf. Gen 2.10]; Joel 4.18), but only in Zechariah, and then eventually in Revelation, are both of these facets combined. The uniqueness of this tradition in Zechariah suggests that the author of Revelation referenced Zech 14.8 in conjunction with Ezek 47, a connection made manifest in Rev 22.2.[129]

However, it is not at all clear at this point which form of Zechariah John reused or through which point of access he encountered the text. The Greek tradition of the locution is a rather literal representation of the Hebrew (with some minor exceptions)[130] and the Revelation texts couch the descriptions in first-person speech or vision reports, not the oracular form present in Zech 14.8, creating literary dissonance between the representations. If the use of Zech 14.9 in Rev 19.6 hints that John used a Hebrew form of this text, perhaps the same is true here, but this remains uncertain. Nonetheless, the identification of this allusion continues to build a pattern of reference to the oracles preserved Zech 14.7–11, a pattern that provides insight into John's textual hermeneutics and his understanding of deutero-Zechariah. It continues in Rev 21.25 and 22.5.

Rev 21.25   καὶ οἱ πυλῶνες αὐτῆς οὐ μὴ κλεισθῶσιν ἡμέρας, νὺξ γὰρ οὐκ ἔσται ἐκεῖ

And her gates will never be shut by day, for there will not be night there

Rev 22.5   καὶ νὺξ οὐκ ἔσται ἔτι καὶ οὐκ ἔχουσιν χρείαν φωτὸς λύχνου καὶ φωτὸς ἡλίου, ὅτι κύριος ὁ θεὸς φωτίσει ἐπ' αὐτούς, καὶ βασιλεύσουσιν εἰς τοὺς αἰῶνας τῶν αἰώνων

And there will not be night again and they will not have need of the light of a lamp of the light of the sun, because the Lord God will shine upon them, and they will rule forever and ever

---

[129] So also Beale, *Revelation*, 1103; Jauhiainen, *The Use*, 122–123; Kowalski, *Rezeption*, 245–247.

[130] See Fields, *Hexaplorum*, 2.1029.

Zech 14.7[pM] והיה יום־אחד הוא יודע ליהוה לא־יום ולא־לילה והיה לעת־ערב
יהיה־אור

And it will be one day (so knows YHWH) that there will
be neither day nor night, and it will be that there will be
light in the evening

Zech 14.7[OG131] ἔσται μίαν ἡμέραν, καὶ ἡ ἡμέρα ἐκείνη γνωστὴ τῷ κυρίῳ,
καὶ οὐχ ἡμέρα καὶ οὐ νύξ, καὶ πρὸς ἑσπέραν ἔσται φῶς

There will be one day, and that day is known to the Lord,
and (in that day) neither day nor night, and in the
evening there will be light

Material from Zech 14 appears once again in Rev 21.25 and in the
locution that culminates the descriptions of the New Jerusalem in
22.5.[132] The cosmic disorder wrought by the New Jerusalem in Rev
21–22, including the dual references to the lack of night, are drawn
in part from Zech 14.7, in connection with other traditions related to
the future glory of Zion (e.g. Isa 60.11 [cf. 1QM XII 13–15], 19–20
[cf. 1QH[a] XV 28]) and divine rule (e.g. Dan 7.18, 27). Specifically,
the reference to the lack of night in Zechariah, a unique feature
among related traditions, suggests that John drew upon a form of
this particular text.[133] Like the preceding uses of Zech 14, the representation of material in Revelation does not reproduce the wording of the source tradition, but instead alludes to the conflation of
night and day. Because of this situation, it is difficult to identify a
precise form of Zechariah that stands behind these allusions. The
same is true for the point of access to these traditions: it is unclear
if John used existing exegetical traditions associated with Zion or
if he accessed Zech 14.7, combining it with similar texts to create a
portrait of the eschatological city. It is also uncertain if his access to
Zech 14.7 was mediated primarily through a textual encounter or an
aural one. Regardless, there is good reason for John to have created

---

[131] The Greek tradition of Zech 14.6–7 differs somewhat in the later revisions that
combine vv. 6 and 7 to create a single semantic unit. For example, the σ tradition rear-
ranges material from these verses so that a more coherent whole is created. For the present
discussion, the textual differences within the Greek tradition are of minimal significance.

[132] Cf. Paul B. Decock, 'The Scriptures in the Book of Revelation', *Neotestamentica*
33 (1999): 382–383.

[133] Jauhiainen, *The Use*, 121–122 refers to this as an 'echo', but other have found
the connection more appealing. E.g. Mounce, *Revelation*, 388 and Aune, *Revelation*,
3.1172.

a *Mischanspielung* combining Zech 14.7 with Isa 60.11, 19–29 and Dan 7.18, 27 based on the similarities in wording and thematic overlap. Most importantly, the allusions to Zech 14.7 in Rev 21.25 and 22.5 continue to establish a pattern of engagement with Zech 14. The final allusion that fills out the constellation of references to Zech 14 is located in Rev 22.3.

Rev 22.3	καὶ πᾶν κατάθεμα οὐκ ἔσται ἔτι. καὶ ὁ θρόνος τοῦ θεοῦ καὶ τοῦ ἀρνίου ἐν αὐτῇ ἔσται, καὶ οἱ δοῦλοι αὐτοῦ λατρεύσουσιν αὐτῷ
	And every curse will be no more and the throne of God and the lamb will be in her [Jerusalem], and his servants will worship him
Zech 14.11[PM134]	וישבו בה וחרם לא יהיה־עוד וישבה ירושלם לבטח
	And they will dwell in her [Jerusalem] and an accursed thing will not be again, and Jerusalem will dwell in security
Zech 14.11[OG/LXX]	κατοικήσουσιν ἐν αὐτῇ, καὶ οὐκ ἔσται ἀνάθεμα ἔτι, καὶ κατοικήσει Ιερουσαλημ πεποιθότως
	And they will dwell in her [Jerusalem], and there will not be a curse again, and Jerusalem will be inhabited safely

Once again, the author of Revelation alludes to Zech 14 in the description of the New Jerusalem, this time describing the state of divine-human relationship within the city. The assertion that 'every curse will be no more' (πᾶν κατάθεμα οὐκ ἔσται ἔτι), in combination with the depiction of Jerusalem's habitation (by the throne of God and the lamb in Revelation and by an unremunerated 'they' in Zech 14.11),[135] indicates a direct connection to Zech 14.11.[136]

Of the other three allusions to Zech 14, this is the clearest example and provides some interesting evidence regarding the question

---

[134] Like the other texts examined in Zech 14, v. 11 has no attestation at Qumran. It also has very little internal variation in the Greek tradition.

[135] The mystery of the referent of וישבו is further highlighted by the passive use of וישבה at the end of the verse (Al Wolters, *Zechariah* [Historical Commentary on the Old Testament; Leuven: Peeters, 2014], 467). The subject may refer back to the multitudes that will return to Jerusalem depicted in (perhaps) in 12.10. So C. L. Meyers and E. M. Meyers, *Zechariah 9–14* (AB 25c; Garden City: NY: Doubleday, 1993), 448.

[136] So also Aune, *Revelation*, 3.1178–1179; Beale, *Revelation*, 1112; Osborne, *Revelation*, 772–773; Jauhiainen, *The Use*, 125–126; Koester, *Revelation*, 824.

of textual form. While the OG tradition of Zech 14.11 is a fairly straightforward literal rendering of the proto-MT, the Greek of Rev 22.3 differs in an interesting way from the translation. Rev 22.3 preserves a previously unattested word for 'curse' (κατάθεμα) in contrast to the common word preserved unanimously in the OG/LXX (ἀνάθεμα). The semantic distinction between κατάθεμα and ἀνάθεμα is not entirely clear, but there seems to be no reason for John to have changed the accepted wording of Zech 14.11^OG.[137] Instead, it seems likely that John translated חרם ('ban') as κατάθεμα, a conclusion supported by multiple critics. Even Aune, who is reticent to suggest direct literary dependence, notes, 'it appears that κατάθεμα is the author's way of interpreting חרם'.[138] Rev 22.3 also follows the word order of the proto-MT more closely than the OG/LXX, which places its translation of חרם (ἀνάθεμα) after the verb.

Overall, the likelihood that a Hebrew form Zech 14.11 underlies Rev 22.3, in agreement with the previous suggestion that Rev 19.6 preserves a particular vocalization of Zech 14.9 that differs from the received reading tradition in the MT, suggests that John was aware of a Hebrew text of Zech 14, one that closely resembled the proto-MT (option 1). The text of this chapter known to the author was not read in isolation, but in conversation with other Jewish scriptural texts that are linked to Zechariah through similar catchwords and thematic threads. That the presentation of reused material in Rev 19–22 seems to suggest a Hebrew text of Zechariah coheres with other examples of reuse, especially those that use material from Zech 1–8. Moreover, the fact that John alluded, albeit in differ- ent locations, to material from a substantial segment of Zechariah (14.7–9, 11), indicates that he had direct access to a continuous text of Zechariah. The point of access was likely through a textual artefact (manuscript) due to his detailed engagement with minute textual features, although the memory of previous aural encoun- ters may have influenced his choice of implicit reading tradition. There is good reason to think that John read a Hebrew manuscript of Zechariah in the process of composing Rev 19–22, although this text was certainly not the only (or even the primary) tradition from which he drew.

---

[137] There are witnesses that preserve αναθεμα in Revelation's textual history, among other variants. Cf. Hoskier, *Concerning*, 2.619.

[138] Aune, *Revelation*, 3.1179. See also BDAG, 517; Beale, *Revelation*, 1112.

3.3 Conclusion

The preceding examples of textual engagement provide interesting observations and avenues for further enquiry regarding John's reuse of Zechariah traditions, many of which I will examine in the following chapter. First, in most examples, John reused a form of Zechariah that is very closely related to the semantics of the textual stream exemplified by the proto-MT tradition and revising Greek versions (except in 11.2). In Rev 1.7 the wording of John's allusions in Zech 12.10 indicates the use of a Greek form of Zechariah corrected in some readings away from the OG towards the proto-MT. The text of Rev 11.2 is equally close to the OG and revising traditions. In the remaining examples (Rev 5.6; 6.1–8; 11.4; 19.11–16; 19–22) John's lexical choices and the deployment of reading tradition that differ with those embedded in the entire OG/LXX tradition indicate that the textual tradition of Zechariah witnessed in the book of Revelation is the proto-MT (option 1). Furthermore, the *V*OG of each of these passages closely resembles the proto-MT. John had access to Hebrew Zechariah as well as Greek revising traditions. All the evidence here indicates that the Hebrew form of Zechariah known to the OG translator is the same Hebrew form available to John; only in Rev 11.2 is there any evidence that John knew the OG form of Zechariah. In cases where the textual traditions of Zechariah share a common semantic sense or contour, John's lexical choices suggest that he responded to cues in the proto-MT (aside from his reuse of Synoptic traditions in Rev 1.7; 11.2) and that his lexical repertoire and translation patterns differed from the OG translator(s). At times John *translated* a Hebrew form of Zechariah that was closely related to the proto-MT. His strategies of translation retain a level of similarity to the norms of translation in the OG, but his lexical choices, at times, differ. In addition to John's translation of Hebrew, he also accessed Zechariah traditions, exegetically combined with Daniel texts, encoded in a Greek form derived from revising traditions. John referenced Zechariah in two distinct texts forms and languages.

The author's deployment of these two text forms might also be linked to points of access to these traditions. The majority of these examples illustrate that John worked with the Hebrew text of Zechariah. The way in which these references were constructed, including their detailed exegetical appropriation and combination with other traditions, indicates that John likely had access to a textual artefact or manuscript that contained Hebrew Zechariah, and that his interaction with this artefact, perhaps influenced by the totality of previous experiences with Zechariah (both textually and aurally), informed the way he presented reused material in the process of composition. Based on the preceding discussion regarding memory and the social realities of textuality in the late Second Temple period (Section 2.6 and Excursus 1), it is not improbable that he had access to a Hebrew manuscript of Zechariah. Collective memory and past experience, in dialogue with other scriptural traditions, inform the reading experience of a Hebrew manuscript, but it is probable that John worked with manuscripts at some point during the composition of the Apocalypse, which may have been a lengthy process. The correlation between Hebrew Zechariah especially and the scriptural references in the book of Revelation imply a direct textual relationship based on the author's familiarity with this textual tradition.[139]

In addition to working with Hebrew exemplars, John also accessed pre-existent exegetical traditions associated with Jesus that combined texts from Zech 12 and Daniel. It is difficult to discern with certainty if these traditions were available to John in oral[140] or written[141] forms, but it is clear that John was familiar with *logia* traditions also embedded in the Gospels, particularly in the Synoptic apocalyptic discourses. These traditions, unlike John's predominant use of Hebrew Zechariah, were transmitted to John in Greek forms that had been revised towards the semantics of the proto-MT. Like John's point of access to Hebrew Zechariah (textual encounter influenced by past experiences), it is not unlikely that he accessed these traditions through textual means[142] and through aural experience, particularly since Jesus traditions likely boasted wide currency in oral

---

[139] This phenomenon is also noted by Sheree Lear, 'Revelation 19.16's Inscribed Thigh: An Allusion to Gen 49.10b', *NTS* 60 (2014): 280–285 who argues that the reference to Jesus' inscribed thigh is an allusion to an MT-like form of Gen 49. See also Lear, 'Visions of Locusts: The Composition of Revelation 9.7–11', in *'I Lifted my Eyes and Saw': Reading Dream and Vision Reports in the Hebrew Bible* (LHBOTS 584; ed. E. R. Hayes and L.-S. Tiemeyer; London: T&T Clark, 2014), 169–182.

[140] So Penley, *Common Tradition*.

[141] So M.-É. Boismard, 'Rapprochements littéraires entre l'évangelie de Luc et l'Apocalypse', in *Synoptische Studien: Festschrift A. Wikenhauser* (ed. J. Schmid and A. Vöglte; Munich: Karl Zink, 1953), 53–63.

[142] U. Vanni, 'The Apocalypse and the Gospel of Luke', in *Luke and Acts* (trans. M. J. O'Connell; ed. G. O'Collins and G. Marconi; New York: Paulist, 1993), 9–25 argues that John actually reused material from the Gospel of Luke (following Charles, *The Revelation*, 1.lxxxiii–lxxxvi) although this stretches the credulity of the evidence.

communication in early Christianity. John knows both Hebrew traditions and pre-existing Greek exegetical traditions that juxtapose Zechariah with other scriptural texts.

Third, as noted by many, John did not explicitly introduce reused linguistic material from Zechariah via explicit introductory formulae, nor does he aim to reproduce exactly his Hebrew or Greeks texts. Compositional changes exist in each example analysed in this chapter, and it is these changes, along with differences between the various forms of Zechariah, that illuminate the *Vorlagen* that John utilized. Even when circulating exegetical traditions are accessed, John did not reproduce them verbatim, as the differences between John's formulations and the Synoptic Gospels demonstrates. His reuse of Zechariah is occasionally syntactically discreet from surrounding material, but signalled only implicitly.

The analysis of textual form and access to scriptural tradition provides the proper data set from which to analyse the author's techniques of reuse, reading habits, and exegetical resources. The textual pluriformity and fluidity in the late Second Temple period necessitate the identification of the textual form of a given scriptural reference, and, as Norton has noted regarding the reuse of scripture in Paul's letters, 'selection of a particular form of a passage belongs to the exegetical repertoire current in Paul's day'.[143] John's choice of the Hebrew text of Zechariah *and* a Greek exegetical tradition that includes material from Zechariah, too, constitutes an exegetical choice. It is to the consequences of this choice and its insight into John's exegetical practices and social setting that we now turn.

---

[143] Norton, *Contours*, 153.

4

READING ZECHARIAH WITH JOHN: TECHNIQUES OF REUSE, EXEGETICAL RESOURCES, AND TEXTUAL HERMENEUTICS

4.1 Introduction

In the previous chapter I examined the textual forms of Zechariah used by the author of Revelation and his points of access to these traditions. Now that a particular form and source of Zechariah traditions in each example of its reuse in Revelation has been identified where possible, we are able to engage the mechanics by which John incorporated linguistic material from a consonantal Hebrew text and Greek exegetical traditions into the language of the Apocalypse. The author's modes of reformulation (techniques of reuse) and exegetical resources provide evidence for his underlying methods of creating a comprehensible reading of his scriptural texts (textual hermeneutics), a reading that underwrites his changes to inherited traditions. Understanding these processes aids in comprehending not only the contours of Revelation's message in the pericopae where Zechariah is reused, but also the social-historical realities of literary composition in this period and the work's close relationship with Second Temple Jewish literature in terms of reusing scripture in the process of composition (see Chapter 5).

John never isomorphically reproduced material from Zechariah or directly borrowed quantitatively large segments of this work. And material from Zechariah is always interspersed among the wording of other scriptural traditions. This inexactness of reproduction and pastiche-like conflations, modes of composition unexceptional in Jewish literary production of the period, requires an evaluation of the scope of John's practices of reuse. In this chapter, I describe John's techniques of reuse by cataloguing the various points of connection between the borrowing and borrowed traditions, and indicate how these points of connections aid in better understanding the poetics of the composition of the Apocalypse.

Moreover, reading (whether through an immediate textual encounter, a textual encounter in the distant past, or through the aural hearing of the recitation of a written work) is an additional factor that must be considered when creating a portrait of John's textual hermeneutics. Reading a text, usually resulting in comprehension derived from a set of exegetical resources, is a precursor to its reuse, and the presentation of reused material in a target text often betrays the choices employed to make sense of a particular source tradition. The discussion of John's habits of reading – the textual features of a source text that motivated the crafting of connections between the target text and the antecedent tradition – is closely related to an analysis of techniques of reuse. These instances of reuse represent interpretative encounters with Jewish scripture, encounters that are usually important to understanding the message of John's work.

This chapter completes the reverse engineering of scriptural references in Revelation, endeavouring to describe the textual features of Zechariah to which John initially responded. The following analysis delves beyond surface features and enquires into the deep structure of reuse asking, what underlying motivations or mechanics explain the presentation of the surface features of material from Zechariah in Revelation? What textual characteristics of Zechariah traditions stimulated the deployment of particular exegetical resources? This discussion is concerned not only with John's selection and physical arrangement of graphemes, but also with what the given arrangements reveal about how he read his scriptural traditions. In specific instances, reconstructing the reasoning behind John's presentation of reused material leads to a greater appreciation of the message that the author crafted.

4.2 Techniques of Reuse

Before pressing on, the collocation 'techniques of reuse' requires explanation. For quotations, 'techniques of reuse' refers to the expansions, omissions, and alterations which the author made to the quoted source in the process of incorporating material; it is a measurement of the presentation of the surface features of reused material in the target text compared to its instantiation in the source tradition. The terms 'expansion' and 'omission'[1] are commonplace in text-critical and translation studies, and refer to quantitative differences between *Vorlage* and target text. The category 'alterations' is broader, referring to an author's non-quantitative adjustments to the *Vorlage* of a scriptural reference (semantic, lexical, graphic, syntactic, morphological, stylistic, etc.). 'Techniques of reuse' denotes the processes employed by an author to reformulate the surface features of a given source text.[2]

The usefulness of these categories is largely dependent on the level of literalness with which the author reproduced the surface features of his Hebrew text in Greek translation. As I noted, quotations (Section 1.2) are more readily submitted to this type of analysis, since the boundaries of the reused locution are easier to delineate and demonstrable linguistic overlap is present. Explicit allusions can also be submitted to this type of text-critical enquiry, although the level of uncertainty of the result begins to increase as it becomes more difficult to rule out other factors (rhetoric, theology, alternative traditions, internal discourse, etc.) that may have contributed to the shape of the allusion. For implicit allusions, these categories, particularly omission, become less descriptive of actual phenomena. By their very nature implicit allusions differ significantly from their sources. While a similar hermeneutic underlies allusions and other less explicit forms of reuse, it is difficult to describe the divergence of surface features between an allusion and its source in terms of text-critical language. In cases where allusion is the operative form of re-presentation, I discuss John's techniques of reuse by highlighting points of contact between the allusion and

---

[1] I adopt the terminology of expansion, omission, and alteration from Zahn, *Rethinking*, 17–23 with a notable augment. Zahn adopts the category of 'additions', and she distinguishes between additions of new material (A.1) and additions of material from elsewhere (A.2). For her purposes, analysing compositional and exegetical strategies in the Reworked Pentateuch manuscripts (4Q158; 4Q364–367), this nomenclature is apt as the work witnessed in these manuscripts reworks antecedent Pentateuchal traditions, working with a base text that is, at least, similar to the consonantal framework of the MT. John, in contrast, did not rework a single scriptural literary source as a base text. He crafted a new composition, relying upon numerous segments of diverse scriptural works, interwoven into a new composition. The literary and compositional differences between the nature of 4QRP manuscripts and the book of Revelation make the term 'expansions' more appropriate.

[2] For similar approaches to describing the form of examples of reuse, see Teeter, *Scribal Laws*; William A. Tooman, 'The Hermeneutics of Scribal Rewriting in Targum Jonathan Ezekiel 1', *JAJ* 5 no 3 (2014): 393–414 and J. van Ruiten, 'Biblical Interpretation in the Book of Jubilees', in *CBIEJ*, 147.

its source tradition. This catalogue of reused features is essential for comprehending John's habits of reading.

4.3 Habits of Reading

Habits of reading identify the features of a source text that influenced an author's deployment of particular exegetical resources in the process of reuse. What factors involved in reading ancient Hebrew and Greek texts influenced John's comprehension of Zechariah in the face of its inherent ambiguities? These factors may include, but are not limited to:

- the identification of intertextual and intratextual connections within Zechariah and across the author's perceived boundaries of Jewish scripture;
- the polysemic possibility of graphically/phonologically similar letters;
- the polysemic possibility of grapheme arrangement (e.g. metathesis);
- the use of a reading tradition of Hebrew consonants which at times differs from the Masoretic tradition;[3]
- the explicative clarification of perceived incoherence (meaning) or incohesion (grammatical irregularity) in the discourse of the source text.

---

[3] See Schorch, 'Rewritten Bible', 137–151; Schorch, 'Die Rolle des Lesens für die Konstituierung alttestamentlicher Texte', in *Was ist ein Text? Alttestamentliche, ägyptologische und altorientalistische Perspektiven* (BZAW 362; ed. L. Morenz and S. Schorch; Berlin: De Gruyter, 2007), 108–122. 'Reading tradition' refers to the vowel markings that guide a reading of Hebrew consonants. These signs were not present on manuscripts in the first century CE, but were implied in a silent reading or made explicit through a vocalized reading of a consonantal text. John's reading tradition was not graphically affixed to the copy from which he reused material, but was the product of his past experiences in reading or aural experience of a text. James Barr, 'Vocalization and the Analysis of Hebrew Among the Ancient Translators', in *Bible and Interpretation: The Collected Essays of James Barr* (vol. 3; ed. J. Barton; Oxford: Oxford University Press, 2014), 5–6 notes two possible modes of reading tradition in antiquity. *Method A*: The author moves from consonantal graphemes (possibly with *matres lectionis*) to the various lexical options available in the target language. From these possible meanings, one is selected. *Method B*: The translator asks what the fully vocalized form of a Hebrew lexeme is and, thus, creates a translation equivalent in the target language. John's play with the various semantic options of Hebrew lexemes suggests that his method is closer to *Method A*. Barr also notes that issues of differ-vocal have minimal impact on an 'average passage' in Hebrew. However, 'obscure and abnormal locutions often revealed that antiquity lacked a rigorous analysis of Hebrew' (13). Like his translating

These categories describe a range of resources that clarify or disambiguate the source tradition, resources that respond to the latent possibilities native to the forms of Zechariah that John reused. They represent resources potentially deployed in the process of comprehending Jewish scriptural texts in the late Second Temple period.[4] These categories describe types of gaps in a text that may initiate an interpretative response in the quest for coherence, a response predicated upon the heightened ambiguity and polyvalence of vision reports and oracles contained in Zechariah.[5] The function of John's reuse, motivated by his underlying habits of reading, is 'an approach to text handling that is strongly oriented towards the implicit meaning of the transmitted [or, in this case, reused] text' which 'is heavily influenced by verbal and textual parallels, indicative of the influence of the broader collection'.[6] John's perception of the meaning of Zechariah traditions, predicated on his close engagement with its textual features, shapes the role that Zechariah plays in creating meaning in Revelation. Reading is the process through which the signs of the text are comprehended and constructed into a cohesive and coherent whole.[7]

I must note, however, that not every textual difference between the presentation of reused material in Revelation and its corresponding source is explicable by means of the textual triggers. Factors external to source traditions also influenced the presentation of reuse material. Nevertheless, where the particular presentation of reused material is explicable by way of features of the source text, this evidence ought to be heeded. Additionally, the employment of the phrase 'habits of reading' does not imply that John approached Zechariah in a methodical or programmatic manner, with a predetermined set of textual features that would motivate reworking. Alexander Samely's

predecessors of the OG/LXX, John was not a grammarian; he exploited subtle semantic avenues made available by ambiguities preserved in the text of Zechariah. See comment on this issue in Theocharous, *Lexical Dependence*, 15–18. See also Barr's colourful response to Tov's objections (*Text-Critical Use*, 160–165) in 'Guessing in the Septuagint', in *Bible and Interpretation: The Collected Essays of James Barr* (vol. 3; ed. J. Barton; Oxford: Oxford University Press, 2014), 28–43 and 'Translator's Handling of Verb Tense in Semantically Ambiguous Contexts', 195 in the same volume.

   [4] Teeter, *Scribal Laws*, 176–178.
   [5] See Lena-Sophia Tiemeyer, *Zechariah and His Visions: An Exegetical Study of Zechariah's Vision Report* (LHBOTS 605; London: T&T Clark, 2014), 6–11.
   [6] Teeter, *Scribal Laws*, 179.
   [7] Cf. Schorch, 'Rolle des Lesens', 120.

observation pertaining to the reuse of scripture in the Mishnah corresponds generally to John's employment of exegetical resources:

> Rabbinic resources of interpretation are always specific, applied to a concrete biblical text with concrete results. There is also no sign of a rabbinic commitment to a finite set of methods. And rabbinic resources of interpretation have no inbuilt universality, that is, they involve no commitment to treat all similar cases in a similar manner. Under the conditions of reading envisaged here there is a choice of resources for the rabbinic reader; but that choice is not between abstract stratagems of reading, but rather is constrained or triggered by the text's subject-matter and the reader's concern.[8]

As the following discussion indicates, a similarly flexible approach to reading, triggered by particular features of a source text in specific textual encounters, is preserved in John's reuse of Zechariah. John is not constrained to handle reused traditions in a consistent manner. His exegetical repertoire is unarticulated in part because it is undefined.

Finally, the process of reverse engineering concludes by analysing John's exegetical resources. The motivation to expend exegetical energy lies in the realm of reading strategies, rooted in the perceived gaps of the source tradition; the moves that explain John's presentation of reused material are his exegetical resources established by his responses to the source tradition. A textual feature that motivated the use of an exegetical resource is fundamentally different from the resource itself. Likewise, the resource itself is distinct from the outcome that it produces in the target composition. This separation of categories allows us to catalogue reading habits and determine which habits produced the use of particular exegetical resources.

Excursus 2: Audience Reception and Minute Exegesis

Before moving on to examine these features in John's instances of reuse, I must clarify a point that continues to arise, in print and in informal discussions, regarding the efficacy of these types of detailed exegetical procedures for John's message and its reception by its first hearers.[9] It has been argued by some that because these precise

---

[8] Samely, *Rabbinic Interpretation*, 12–13.
[9] This is a point to which I return in Section 6.2.

exegetical processes, some of which depend on John's use of Hebrew scriptural texts and graphic/aural play with Hebrew consonants, would not have been accessible to his audience, they are useless for his literary and rhetorical goals. The inference then follows that John must not have read texts in this way since it does not directly contribute to his communicative strategy. Additionally, the lack of attestation of some of my explanations for John's reuse of Zechariah in the reception history of Revelation, it has been argued, casts doubts on my evaluation of the data in this chapter. Steve Moyise, commenting on one of my recent articles that examines John's use of Zech 4,[10] argues that

> recent studies on literacy in the first century make it almost impossible to imagine how any of John's hearers (Rev 1.3) of the Greek text could have discerned his [Allen's] proposed solution and it has gone unnoticed throughout the reception history of the passage.[11]

I have three brief responses to this type of objection. First, the reuse of scripture in this period is not always employed to strengthen the literary or rhetorical force of a passage, and even if it is, the audience's ability to discern the author's private (unacknowledged) exegetical practices is not necessarily key to the function of the text in its new co-textual environment.[12] In fact, the force of my argument in this book is not that John always reappropriated scriptural traditions for the benefit of his audience, but that his usage of traditions in particular languages and forms was an innate outworking of literary composition in his specific textual culture. In other words, this detailed engagement with scriptural locutions is normal for literary

---

[10] Some material from this article is re-presented in this chapter. See Garrick V. Allen, 'Techniques of Reuse: Reworking Scripture in the Apocalypse', in *The Book of Revelation: Currents in British Research on the Apocalypse* (WUNT 2.411; ed. G. V. Allen, I. Paul, and S. P. Woodman; Tübingen: Mohr Siebeck, 2015), 1–17.

[11] Steve Moyise, 'A Response to *Currents in British Research on the Apocalypse*', in *The Book of Revelation: Currents in British Research on the Apocalypse* (WUNT 2.411; ed. G. V. Allen, I. Paul, and S. P. Woodman; Tübingen: Mohr Siebeck, 2015), 281–288 (here 283).

[12] Thomas Hieke, 'Die literarische und theologische Funktion des Alten Testaments in der Johannesoffenbarung', in *Poetik und Intertextualität in der Johannesapokalypse* (WUNT 346; ed. S. Alkier, T. Hieke, and T. Nicklas; Tübingen: Mohr Siebeck, 2015), 271–290 offers alternative observations for the function of scripture in Revelation, most of which are also related to its communicative strategy.

production in this milieu. John's mode of scriptural engagement is completely unremarkable in light of the transmission of traditions found in contemporaneous works – this type of detailed reworking of scriptural traditions (both those adopted from other sources and those which are original) is the dominant idiom in which early Christian and Jewish literature are composed. Christopher Stanley's 'audience-centred' approach to Pauline citations also relies heavily on the supposition that the author's communicative strategy is primary motivation for scriptural reuse. While this may be true for explicit quotations to higher degree, it is less so for the types of implicit uses of scripture that pervade Revelation. The literary power of reuse does not always lie in the audience's ability to deconstruct the author's exegetical processes, nor is it always the case that the meaning of a text is determined by an audience's ability to do so.[13] This constitutes one of the weaknesses of exclusively adopting an 'audience-centred' approach.

Even if the initial hearers of the Apocalypse did not know Hebrew and failed to recognize the various allusions to Zechariah, the message of the pericopae that contain these references remain comprehensible. Surely a layer of meaning is not accessible to the uninitiated, but the work is not completely unintelligible even if the implied expectations for the audience are high based on the intricate composition of the work. John's use of scripture usually contributes significant depth to a particular image or narrative, but rarely does its surface comprehensibility rest in understanding John's habits of reading or textual hermeneutics. The objection of Moyise assumes that John's processes of reuse are central part of the communication strategy of a work, and not the product of the outworking of a long process of engagement with scriptural traditions and their exegetical instantiations by an author who is a member of a certain literary community with established norms of composition. While beneficial to an audience with ears to hear (perhaps over and over), John's use of scripture is conditioned by his past encounters and conceptions of Zechariah, a consideration that is related to, but distinct from rhetorical intent. Additionally, the volume of references

---

[13] See also Christopher Stanley, *Arguing with Scripture: The Rhetoric of Quotations in the Letters of Paul* (London: T&T Clark, 2004), 55 who notes that 'the bulk of Paul's prior interpretive engagement with the text of Scripture would have been invisible to most of the people in his audiences'.

to Jewish scriptural works invites hearers or readers to re-engage the sources that resonate as they read or hear. As Thomas Hieke states, '*der Text* [der Johannesapokalypse] *zwingt zum Bibellesen*'.[14] Perhaps John's use of scripture secondarily served as a didactic motivation for hearers to encounter the scriptures anew. If so, literary approaches to John's reuse of scripture, especially those that emphasize 'intertextuality', should carefully consider similar interpretative/didactic strategies that are perhaps native to Revelation's composition.

Second, if John's reuse of Zechariah was not always intended for the benefit of his audience,[15] that does not mean that he did not read scriptural texts in the detailed way that I am presenting. As much of the recent scholarship on the literature of the Second Temple period that I have engaged with thus far has made clear, and which the next chapter will crystallize, interpretative moves based on the detailed knowledge of broad swathes of Jewish scripture were commonplace in John's textual culture. The texts of Jewish scripture were central to the composition of literary works, and indeed the jumping off point for the perspectival play that characterizes works like *Jubilees*, Temple Scroll, and *Joseph and Aseneth*, to name only a few. The mode of reading scripture that I attribute to John is part of an ambient mode of literary composition and textual transmission in this period. Unquestionably John's use of scripture does not square with modern exegetical practices; it is 'pre-critical' in the sense that historical-criticism does not tolerate the habits of reading and

---

[14] Hieke, 'Funktion', 290 (emphasis original).

[15] The question of audience is also a problematic construct. We may speculate that the members of the seven churches in Asia Minor were predominantly gentile, Greek-speaking, uneducated, and generally unfamiliar with the Jewish scriptures, let alone in Hebrew. Even if this reconstruction is valid to some extent, we must distinguish between various types of readers or hearers in these communities. The initial hearers of the Apocalypse were a stratified group, a group in which some were more familiar with Jewish scriptural works than others. John's level of erudition was likely shared by relatively few, but we can envision a gradation of familiarity with the texts that John's reused. We may also need to differentiate between the purported audience of the Apocalypse (seven Greek-speaking churches in western Asia Minor) and John's ideal audience. In other words, did John expect the Apocalypse to be read by future communities and was his use of scripture crafted with this broader audience in mind? The *Sicherungsformel* in Rev 22.18–19 suggests that the work was created with its own broader transmission in mind, beyond the confines of the seven churches addressed in chapters 2–3 (so Gamble, 'Book Trade', 32–33). Cf. Section 6.3.

exegetical procedures native to Second Temple Judaism and early Christianity. Nevertheless, this doesn't necessarily discount the fact that John responded to his scriptural traditions in this way. The goal of John's engagement with scriptural traditions was not always for the immediate benefit of his audience or his communication strategy. Finally, while reception history is a powerful control for these types of studies, I am not primarily concerned with how Revelation has been received throughout its history or with 'audience-centred' approaches to reuse, although it is necessary and important also to consider this feature of the work. The assertion that no readers of the Apocalypse have reconstructed John's exegesis of Hebrew Zechariah's horse visions in the way that I have understood them, for example, fails to take into account the implicit parallel readings in antiquity.[16] In the act of crafting the horse vision visions, for example, John was receiving an already existing tradition of comprehending these complex visions witnessed in Zechariah's early Greek and Aramaic versions (see Section 5.4). If sources contemporary to John use the same scriptural texts in similar ways, this significantly supports the argument that John comprehended these texts in this manner, in spite of the lack of explicit reception for these habits in the later tradition.

Overall, the objection raised here by Moyise is predicated on common misconceptions in 'OT in the NT' studies about the nature and purposes of scriptural reuse in this period, a conception undergirded in large part by modern literary theory. Critical theory is certainly a helpful conversation partner for studies that engage reuse, as my own use of literary categories indicates, but one must always remember that ancient authors did not compose with the categories enshrined in literary criticism in mind. To be clear, the burden of proof lies with the one who will claim that John could not have possibly been a sophisticated reader of texts in light of the plethora of parallel evidence found in the Jewish literature of the Second Temple period. Even if these interpretative moves were not the work of the author himself, his awareness and appropriation of exegetical traditions demonstrates firmly his cognizance of texts and their traditions. Text producers were text users.

---

[16] If we understand reception history in its broadest sense, then critical commentaries and modern scholarship are part of an ongoing tradition of reception. In this way, others have suggested that John, for example, interpreted a Hebrew text of Zech 4 (cf. Charles, *The Revelation*, lxx). Reception history is a broad category.

4.4 Zechariah in Revelation

4.4.1 Reading Zechariah in the Context of Jesus Tradition in Revelation 1.7

Rev 1.7

Ἰδοὺ ἔρχεται μετὰ τῶν νεφελῶν, καὶ
ὄψεται αὐτὸν πᾶς ὀφθαλμὸς καὶ
οἵτινες αὐτὸν ἐξεκέντησαν, καὶ
κόψονται ἐπ᾽ αὐτὸν πᾶσαι αἱ φυλαὶ
τῆς γῆς. ναί, ἀμήν

Behold, he is coming with the clouds
and every eye will see him, even
those that pierced him and all the
tribes of the earth will wail on
account of him. Truly, amen

Zech 12.10^{LXX} (revising traditions)

καὶ ἐκχεῶ ἐπὶ οἶκον Δαυιδ καὶ ἐπὶ
τοὺς κατοικοῦντας Ιερουσαλημ
πνεῦμα χάριτος καὶ οἰκτιρμοῦ
καὶ ἐπιβλέψονται πρός με εἰς ὃν
ἐξεκέντησαν καὶ κόψονται αὐτὸν
ὡς κοπετὸν ἐπ᾽ ἀγαπητὸν καὶ
ὀδυνηθήσονται ἐπ᾽αὐτὸν ὡς ὀδύνην
ἐπὶ πρωτοτόκῳ

And I will pour out on (the) house
of David and on the inhabitants
of Jerusalem a spirit of grace and
compassion, and they will look upon
me, to the one that they pierced and
they will wail over him like a lament
over a loved one and they will be
pained over him like a lamentation
for a firstborn

To begin, I must note that it is difficult to measure the techniques of reuse of a tradition that is no longer extant. While it is likely that the form of Zechariah in this tradition was closely related to revising Greek traditions, its text was probably already subject to exegetical alteration as it stood in the tradition.[17] One cannot know the wording of John's source with confidence. However, the use of this tradition in Revelation provides some interesting insights into John's

---

[17] Lindars, *Apologetic*, 24 suggests that the common tradition behind Rev 1.7 was
καὶ ὄψονται εἰς ἐξεκέντησαν καὶ κόψονται ἐπ᾽ αὐτὸν πᾶσαι αἱ φυλαὶ τῆς γῆς.

techniques of reuse and his exegetical resources, as well as the role of the tradition in shaping the meaning of Rev 1. Even though John's avenue of access to Zech 12.10–14 is likely not through immediate access to a manuscript in this occasion, his presentation of the tradition still indicates that he was a careful reader and was aware of the broader literary features of the texts associated with this tradition. First, the deployment of this tradition in Rev 1.7 foreshadows John's description of his encounter with the 'one like a son of man' (Rev 1.12–20), a description that deploys wording from Dan 7.9–14 and 10.5–10 to describe the glorified Jesus.[18]

The fact that the phrase 'son of man', a title present in Matt 24.30 but omitted in Rev 1.7, is present in Rev 1.13 suggests a connection between 1.7 and 1.13. Moving this phrase to description of his first visionary encounter carefully connects the epistolary introduction to the visionary material that follows, creating a heightened sense of coherence between different literary forms. In this way, the deployment of scriptural locutions and play with existing exegetical traditions creates a greater level of literary artistry and functions as a unifying feature of a complex literary work. The reworking of this *parousia* tradition demonstrates again that John retains a high level of flexibility when it comes to the wording of his scriptural traditions and that his deployment of this exegetical tradition serves broader literary goals. These goals are twofold: the reworking of this tradition creates points of contact between disparate literary forms *and* provides a base tradition from which John created his depiction of Jesus in Rev 1, a christological tradition whose imagery is markedly discordant from the slain-but-standing lamb we meet in Rev 5.6. It is interesting that Zechariah is drawn upon in both occasions, in addition to other texts, to craft John's depictions of Jesus. In Rev 1 John's christological conceptions are on display, based partially upon a literarily erudite construal of an existing exegetical tradition. The redeployment of this tradition provides an added layer of theological and literary depth for those familiar with the wording of this tradition.

Additionally, the reuse of locutions from Dan 7 and 10 in Rev 1.12–20 (e.g. ἡ θρὶξ τῆς κεφαλῆς αὐτοῦ ὡσεὶ ἔριον καθαρόν [cf. Dan 7.9[Theo]], ὁ θρόνος ὡσεὶ φλὸξ πυρός [cf. Dan 7.9[OG]], and ἡ δὲ κεφαλὴ αὐτοῦ καὶ αἱ τρίχες λευκαὶ ὡς ἔριον λευκὸν ὡς χιὼν καὶ οἱ ὀφθαλμοὶ αὐτοῦ ὡς φλὸξ πυρός [Rev 1.14]) suggests that John had direct access to Daniel

---

[18] See Beale, *Jewish Apocalyptic*, 156–177.

traditions independent of known exegetical traditions (cf. *1 En.* 46). John intentionally altered the wording of this exegetical tradition, of which Zech 12.10–14 was a part, in a way that demonstrates awareness of other Daniel traditions. Although he knew material from Zech 12.10 in combination with texts from Daniel, he was still able to distinguish between and access the constituent parts of the tradition. Finally, the composition of this tradition in Rev 1.7 suggests that John understood Zech 12.10 – the secondary tradition in this conflation – to refer to the future actions of Jesus.[19] The complex textual history and grammatical structure of Zech 12.10 provided the possibility for early Christian authors, including the original compiler of the Daniel/Zechariah tradition, to understand the first-person speech as divine. This is particularly relevant if John read 'when they look upon *me* (= proto-MT and Greek revising traditions against OG *him*) whom they pierced'.

Additionally, the speaker's pouring out of a 'spirit of grace and compassion' upon the house of David and Jerusalem 'on that day' (Zech 12.10–11) corresponds loosely to John's self-description as 'being in the Spirit on the Lord's Day' (Rev 1.10), providing another allusive connection between the quotation in Rev 1.7 and the introduction of John's vision of the exalted Jesus. This connection implies that John's experience on Patmos on the Lord's Day was informed by the expectation of divine visitation articulated in Zech 12.10–13.9.

John's deployment of this pre-existent exegetical tradition is coupled with his numerous allusions to Daniel and Zechariah located within Rev 1. This use of an anchoring locution (Rev 1.7), in addition to more allusive reuses of similar texts in the vicinity, signposts that John is aware of scriptural works and their accompanying exegetical frames. With reference to Zechariah in particular, John is familiar with a tradition encoded in Greek that corresponds to the peculiarities represented by the semantics of the proto-MT stream and accompanying Greek revisions. Moreover, the deployment of allusions serves a literary purpose, linking the various literary forms and portions of Revelation together. The epistolary introduction and vision of Jesus among the lampstands (and the subsequent letters to the seven churches) are linked by the explicit deployment of the tradition in Rev 1.7 *and* the numerous allusions to Zech 12 and Dan 7 and 10 in the narrative that follows.

---

[19] See also Albl's analysis of the use of Zech 12.10 by Justin (*Form and Function*, 258–259).

4.4.2 Revelation 5.6b and Zechariah 4.10

Rev 5.6b

ἀρνίον . . . ἔχων κέρατα ἑπτὰ καὶ
ὀφθαλμοὺς ἑπτὰ οἵ εἰσιν τὰ [ἑπτὰ]
πνεύματα τοῦ θεοῦ ἀπεσταλμένοι
εἰς πᾶσαν τὴν γῆν

a lamb . . . having seven horns and
seven eyes, those which are the seven
spirits of God going about in all the
earth

Zech 4.10b^PM

שבעה־אלה עיני יהוה המה משוטטים
בכל־הארץ

These seven are the eyes of YHWH,
they go eagerly about in all the earth

When it comes to the reuse of Zech 4.10 in Rev 5.6, John's presentation of this tradition illuminates his reading of the broader context
of Zech 4. While Rev 5.6b is not quantitatively divergent from Zech
4.10b, I have identified two minor alterations. First, the context of the
quotation requires that the stylistics of the reference in Rev 5.6b differ from its source. The demonstrative pronoun in the Hebrew (אלה)
is altered to a relative pronoun (οἵ), a device which functions both as
a linguistic marker introducing antecedent material and subordinates
the reused locution as a description of the lamb (5.6a).[20] This marker
delineates the boundaries of the reused material and, in coordination
with the conjunction (καί) that begins the following locution (Rev 5.7),
creates disjunction at both ends of the locution.[21] This stylistic change
incorporates the reused material into the source text in a manner that is
sensitive to surrounding discourse in Rev 5, yet sets the locution apart.

Second, Zech 4.10b reads 'these seven are the *eyes* (עיני) of YHWH',
while Rev 5.6b reads 'which are the seven *spirits* (πνεύματα) of God'.
John has not omitted a reference to 'eyes' altogether, as material from

---

[20] Cf. Rev 4.5; 6.2, 5, 8; 11.4 where similar markers introduce scriptural references. This list is not exhaustive. See also Fishbane, *Biblical Interpretation*, 44–55 and
Fishbane, 'Inner-Biblical Exegesis', in *HB/OT*, 35–37 for comments on the use of
Hebrew deictic elements that signal editorial activity within the HB. These elements
differ from deictic markers available to Greek authors as the Greek language retains
a wider variety of particles, prepositions, and other linguistic features that serve as
markers of deixis or linguistic intrusion.

[21] The framing of this locution with a linguistic marker and a conjunction creates a
level of implied discreetness between the locution and its surrounding co-texts.

Zech 4.10b describes the 'seven eyes (ὀφθαλμούς)' of the lamb (Rev 5.6a). Additionally, the author's alteration from 'eyes' to 'spirits' suggests that he borrowed material from Zech 4.6 (ברוחי, 'by my spirit')[22] and, thus, modified 4.10b by substituting material from its surrounding co-texts. All the lexical elements of Zech 4.10b are present in Rev 5.6, but some elements have been rearranged to better fit the style, syntax, and logic of Rev 5.6.[23]

John's deployment of πνεύματα as an equivalent for עיני requires special comment. There is no direct example of a form of עין underlying a form of πνεύμα in the OG/LXX tradition.[24] However, John's reading of the immediate co-texts of Zech 4.10, and his use of particular exegetical resources, controlled the form of the quotation of Zech 4.10 in Rev 11.4.

Most commentators tacitly suggest that this discrepancy between quotation and its source is the result of John's theological outlook. For example, referring to Rev 5.6b, Beale suggests that 'as a result of the death and resurrection, these spirits also become Christ's agents throughout the world, who figuratively represent the Holy Spirit himself.'[25] The suggestion that John altered Zech 4.10b to include a reference to the seven spirits based on pneumatological concerns is not uncommon.[26] This perspective suggests that, although John presented his theological point in scriptural language, his presentation of material does not reflect exegetical attention to Zech 4 itself. This implies that John altered his source text based on ideological concerns external to the text of Hebrew Zechariah.

While this perspective is not necessarily problematic, other options have been offered that assume that John's presentation of material

---

[22] Similarly, see Zech 6.8.

[23] Minor modifications and rearrangement of source material is common in the Jewish Greek scriptural tradition. For example, Wagner, *Reading*, 133 identifies this phenomenon in Isa 1.15[OG], noting that '[the translator] also continues to make minor modifications to his source that enhance the logical cohesion and persuasive power of the discourse'.

[24] Additionally, the equivalency of 'eyes' for 'spirit' does not exist in the Aramaic versions.

[25] Beale, *Revelation*, 355.

[26] See Osborne, *Revelation*, 257; Aune, *Revelation 1–6*, 353; Swete, *Apocalypse*, 79; Caird, *Revelation*, 75; Beasley-Murray, *Revelation*, 124; Sweet, *Revelation*, 129; Barker, *Revelation*, 131; Prigent, *L'Apocalypse*, 193–194. Suggestions that this alteration reflects John's Christology are also common. See Boxall, *The Apocalypse*, 99; Jauhiainen, *The Use*, 84–5, 89; Mounce, *Revelation*, 145; Beasley-Murray, *Revelation*, 124; Morris, *Revelation*, 96–97; Farrer, *Revelation*, 94–95.

was based on his reading of the broader context of Zech 4.10. In contrast to the majority of scholarly attempts to understand this complex imagery, Richard Bauckham has suggested that John constructed the image of the lamb and its seven eyes based on an exegetical reading of Zech 4.1–14.[27] Bauckham is ultimately concerned with the theological message of Rev 5.6, but his reconstruction of *how* John read Zech 4 is instructive. He assumes that John read Zech 4[MT] in accordance with the Masoretic reading tradition,[28] which leads him to suggest that 4.10b (שבעה־אלה עיני יהוה המה משוטטים בכל הארץ) is the answer to the seer's question posed in 4.4 (מה אלה אדני).[29] Additionally, in Bauckham's estimation, John incorporates material from the intervening oracle (Zech 4.6[b]–10a), particularly the word בְּרוּחִי, in the quotation in Rev 5.6b, thus accounting for his alteration of 'spirits' for 'eyes'.[30] Bauckham's reconstruction of John's reading habits suggests that the immediate antecedent of 4.10b (אלה) is the seer's question in 4.4 – 'What are these, my lord?' (מה אלה אדני).

This approach, while laudable, is not without problems. If John read the Hebrew text in accordance with MT, בְּרוּחִי (4.6), a singular feminine noun with a first-person singular pronominal suffix, cannot be the antecedent of 4.10b (שבעה אלה), a plural construction. This explanation provides no linguistic solution for the presence of 'spirits' in the quotation. What Bauckham does not notice is that the consonantal text provided John with a more natural linguistic possibility to understand 'eyes' as 'spirits'. Bauckham is right to observe that Zech 4.10b is the answer to the seer's question in Zech 4.4 (מה אלה אדני). However, the intervening oracular material (4.6[b]–10a) is of greater consequence for understanding John's reading habits than he acknowledges. If the assumption is made that John adopted the reading tradition preserved in the MT, there exists no direct answer to the seer's question until 4.10b, a reality that led Bauckham to undervalue the significance of the oracular material.[31]

The consonantal text provides another option that explains John's representation of 'eyes' with 'spirits', based on the reversion of the

---

[27] Bauckham, *Climax*, 162.

[28] This assumption is implicit within his analysis. So also Jauhiainen, *The Use*, 88.

[29] Bauckham, *Climax*, 163.

[30] Ibid.

[31] Are there any plural nouns in the oracular section that might serve as the answer to the seer's question and correspond to the plural demonstrative אלה present in the query (4.4) and answer (4.10b)? In the MT, the only possible option is the locution ליום

statement in (4.10b) to the wording offered by the seer in the original question (4.4). If ברוחי (4.6) is read as a masculine plural noun with a first-person singular pronominal suffix[32] (בְּרוּחַי instead of MT בְּרוּחִי), Zech 4.6b would read: לֹא בְחַיִל וְלֹא בְכֹחַ כִּי אִם־ בְּרוּחַי אָמַר יְהֹוָה צְבָאוֹת ('not by strength and not by power, but by my *spirits* says YHWH Sebaoth'). If John vocalized the word as בְּרוּחַי, it is logical that he understood 'my spirits' as the direct answer to the seer's question in 4.4 ('what are these [olive trees]?'). Zech 4.10b, then, further clarifies the answer to the seer's original question, providing a second answer to the question posed in 4.4: 'these seven [spirits] are the eyes of YHWH, they range throughout all the earth'. Zech 4.10b disambiguates the first answer proffered in Zech 4.6. If, following a non-Masoretic reading tradition, the consonants ברוחי are understood to be plural, the immediate antecedent of אלה is בְּרוּחַי, and two answers to the seer's question in 4.4 are supplied: one in an oracle to Zerubbabel regarding YHWH's spirits (4.6) and the other in the continuation of the visionary discourse in Zech 4.10b, the second answer explaining the opaque oracular response in 4.6.

If this reconstruction of John's reading of Zech 4 is valid, it is natural for him to equate the predicate of 4.10b (עיני) with its immediate antecedent in 4.6 (ברוחי). The exegetical resource that culminated in the representation of 'eyes' with 'spirits' in Rev 5.6b is the disambiguation of a scriptural lemma based on the syntax and textual structure of its co-texts, climaxing in lexical substitution. The narrative logic of Zech 4, tracing the ambiguous web of referent and antecedent, shapes the form of the quotation in Rev 5.6b. Furthermore, John used the polymorphic ambiguity of the consonantal Hebrew

---

קטנות in 4.10a ('for the day of small things'). However, the referent of this locution is unrelated to the question in 4.4. It is a further comment on the prophet's assertion that 'you will know that YHWH Sebaoth sent me to you', linked to 4.9 by כי.

[32] The word could either be understood as a defective feminine plural with first person singular suffix or as a masculine noun with a first person singular suffix. According to Charles A. Briggs, 'The Use of רוח in the Old Testament', *JBL* 19 no 1 (1900): 132–145, of the 378 times רוח occurs in the HB, it has a first person singular pronominal suffix affixed on 22 occasions. Of these instances, none are plurals. In terms of gender, רוח usually adheres to feminine grammatical patterns. However, there are instances in which רוח is collocated with other masculine noun forms (Exod 10.13). Because of this confusion of grammatical gender within the MT, it is possible that John understood the graphemes ברוחי to adhere to masculine pluralization patterns in connection with a first-person singular pronominal suffix, even though רוחות, an unambiguously feminine plural form, appears in Zech 2.10 and 6.5.

text to identify an additional intratextual connection in the grammatical string of Zech 4.4–10, connecting אלה (4.4), ברוחי (4.6), and עיני (4.10b) as a string of related entities. He correlated these lexemes based on the intersection of his reading habits and reading tradition, explicating this connection in his presentation of this material in Rev 5.6b. This reading neutralizes the need to explain John's alteration of his source text by means of his theological/ideological resources, while still allowing for the probability that these had some impact on the shape of reuse. The alteration of the source text preserved in Rev 5.6b is primarily the result of John's text-exegetical habits of reading, understanding Zech 4.10b in light of the narrative flow of its context.[33] This alteration need not be explained by an appeal to John's theological resources, but by his sustained reading of a semantically and syntactically ambiguous Hebrew text.[34]

John's direct correlation of the 'seven eyes of YHWH' (Zech 4.10b) with 'my spirits' (Zech 4.6) is elucidated further in the composition of Rev 5.6. Rev 5.6a presents a slain, yet standing lamb with seven horns and seven eyes (ἀρνίον ἐστηκὸς ὡς ἐσφαγμένον ἔχων κέρατα ἑπτὰ καὶ ὀφθαλμοὺς ἑπτά). Rev 5.6b explicates the significance of the 'seven eyes of the lamb' by suggesting that they are the 'seven spirits'. This is an inverted presentation of Zech 4 where the spirits (4.6) are explained by the phrase 'these are the seven eyes of YHWH'.[35] Both answers to the seer's question in Zech 4.4 (מה אלה אדני – (בְּרוּחִי (4.6) and שבעה־אלה עיני יהוה (4.10b) – are represented in Rev 5.6. This compositional feature inverts the narrative order of the linguistic elements preserved in John's source text, a word substitution made possible by the syntactic ambiguity of the Hebrew consonantal text.[36]

---

[33] For more on the logic of Zech 4, see Tiemeyer, *Zechariah*, 147–180.

[34] This is not to say that the author's theological goals never influenced the presentation of reused scriptural texts, but that, in this instance, the evidence points more forcefully to a primary text-exegetical process. Often these two stimulants for reuse are thoroughly enmeshed.

[35] Yair Zakovitch, 'Through the Looking Glass: Reflections/Inversions of Genesis Stories in the Bible', *Biblical Interpretation* 1 no 2 (1993): 139–152 makes a similar observation regarding characterization in the HB where the characteristics of an antecedent character are inverted to colour the reading of a new character. Zakovitch focuses on the inversion of macro-structural literary elements, but the identification of very small linguistic segments – even the inversion of single words – fits the larger pattern of reading and rewriting noticed by Zakovitch in the reuse of antecedent scripture. See also Lissa W. Wray Beal, 'Blessing Lost: Intertextual Inversions in Hosea', *Didaskalia* (2005): 17–39.

[36] For an extended conversation on the ambiguous nature of the Hebrew consonantal text of Zech 4, see Eibert J. C. Tigchelaar, *Prophets of Old and the Day of the*

Thus far, we can observe the following about John's habits of reading. First, his reading tradition does not always align with the vocalization of the MT. It is possible that reading the same morpheme in accordance with different reading traditions is one of John's exegetical resources.[37] Second, the surrounding context of reused locutions influenced the way that John re-presented this material. The explication of implicit or perceived co-textual syntactic relationships belongs to John's repertoire of exegetical resources.

Additionally, John's reading of Zech 4 clarifies the image of the slain lamb with seven eyes in Rev 5.6. As I mentioned in the previous chapter (Section 3.2.2), the use of Zech 4.10 in this pericope is controlled by material from Isa 11.1–2, where the stump of Jesse (cf. Isa 11.10) that will sprout many roots (cf. 'root of David' in Rev 5.5) is combined with an enumeration of a number of 'spirits' (11.2). The combination of material from Isa 11.1–2, 10 and Zech 4.10 further informs our understanding of the boundaries of John's scriptural reading. Both texts allude to the Davidic dynasty (Jesse in Isaiah and Zerubbabel in Zechariah) and enumerate many spirits insofar as John read ברוחי in Zech 4.6 as a plural. Moreover, both texts reference the 'eyes of YHWH' (Isa 11.3; Zech 4.14).

These features coalesced to suggest to John that they were ultimately connected, accounting for their combination in Rev 5.5–6. The association of these texts indicates John's conception of scripture as an interconnected whole, where texts that share similar features and turns of phrase can be combined to create a new picture of divine action in the world carried out by the lamb in his opening of the seven seals. The juxtaposition of material from Isa 11 and Zech 4 in Rev 5.5–6 is not coincidental, but structured and controlled by John's awareness of like traditions embedded in the scriptural tradition writ large. The use of Davidic language and pneumatological imagery in Rev 5.5–6 provides John the raw material from which to further construct his image of Jesus as the one who is worthy of worship and who enacts divine judgement. Understanding the mechanics behind John's reuse and his habits of scriptural reading further endows our understanding of the vivid christological formulations embedded in his image of the slain-but-standing lamb. However, the semantic value of the

End: Zechariah, The Book of Watchers and Apocalyptic (OS 35; Leiden: Brill, 1996), 16–46 and Bart B. Bruehler, 'Seeing though the עינים of Zechariah: Understanding Zechariah 4', *CBQ* 63 no 3 (2001): 430–443.

[37] See Samely, *Rabbinic Interpretation*, 378.

image as a part of John's message is not bankrupt if John's reading habits are not reconstructed. This example helps us to understand John as a reader of Jewish scripture and as an author deeply engaged in the literary culture of which he was a part.

4.4.3 Revelation 6.1–8 and Zechariah 1.8; 6.1–5

Rev 6.1–8   And I saw when the Lamb opened one of the seven seals and I heard one of the four living creatures saying in a loud voice, 'Come!' *And I saw and behold a white horse* (ἵππος λευκός), and the one seated on it had a bow and a crown was given to him and he went out conquering and in order to conquer. And when he opened the second seal, I heard the second living creature saying, 'Come!' *And another red horse went out* (ἵππος πυρρός), and the one sitting on it was allowed to take peace from the earth and so that they might slay one another and a great sword was given to him. And when he opened the third seal, I heard the third living creature saying 'Come!' *And I saw, and behold a black horse* (ἵππος μέλας), and the one sitting on it had a balance in his right hand. And I heard something like a voice in the middle of the four living creatures saying, 'a quart of wheat for a denarius and three quarts of barley for a denarius, and the olive oil and the wine do not harm.' And when he opened the fourth seal, I heard the voice of the fourth living creature saying, 'Come!' *And I saw and behold a green horse* (ἵππος χλωρός), and the one sitting on it is named Death, and Hades follows with him and authority of a fourth of the earth was given to him to kill by the sword and by famine and by death and by the beasts of the earth

Zech 1.8;   I saw in the night and behold a man riding on a red horse (על־סוס
6.1–5^{PM}   אדם) and he was standing between myrtles which were in a glen and after him: horses red (סוסים אדמים), light green (שרקים) and white (לבנים) . . . And I turned and I lifted up my eyes and I saw and behold four chariots (ארבע מרכבות) coming from between two mountains and the mountains were mountains of bronze. With the first chariot red horses (סוסים אדמים) and with the second chariot black horses (סוסים שחרים) and with the third chariot white horses (סוסים לבנים) and with the fourth chariot strong spotted horses (סוסים ברדים אמצים). And I answered and I said to the angel speaking with me, 'what are these, my lord?' And the angel answered and he said to me, 'these are the four winds of heaven going out from being stationed before the Lord of all the earth' (אלה ארבע רחות השמים יוצאות מהתיצב על אדון כל הארץ)

As the evidence from the preceding chapter suggests, the reuse of material from Zech 1.8; 6.1–5 in Rev 6.1–8 is not a straightforward case of a quotation. Yet John clearly borrowed linguistic material unique to each of Zechariah's horse visions in the processes of crafting his own equine scene.[38] In terms of colour lexemes in Rev 6.1–8, John does not offer any expansions to their representation in Zech 1.8; 6.1–5. Each of the colours of the horsemen corresponds to the consonantal Hebrew text of the author's source. 'White' (λευκός) finds a parallel horse colour in Zech 1.8; 6.3. 'Red' (πυρρός) corresponds to both Zech 1.8; 6.2. The 'black' (μέλας) horse finds a parallel in the second horse vision (Zech 6.2). Finally, the 'green' (χλωρός) horse finds a comparable equivalent in the horses described as שרקים (Zech 1.8). The lexical overlap between works is their primary point of textual connection.

The correlation between colour lexemes is not, however, the only point of contact between traditions. The horse visions of Zechariah and Revelation both appear in the context of heavenly court motifs. In Revelation, the seer's ascent to the heavenly court (Rev 4.1) and the extended description of the scene (Rev 4.2–5.14) clearly locate the four horsemen in this milieu. The backdrop for the four horsemen is the heavenly worship of the lamb and the one who sits upon the throne (Rev 5.9–14). The heavenly court motif in Zechariah is more implicit, but detectable. The patrolling action of the horses in Zech 1.10, and the divine commissioning of their mission (אשר שלח יהוה להתהלך בארץ), indicates that the riders are members of the heavenly entourage (cf. Job 1.6–7; 2.1–2).[39] A number of features in Zech 6.1–8 also suggest that the horses are YHWH's heavenly servants. First, the horses pull chariots, alluding perhaps to other instances of chariots in YHWH's service (cf. Hab 3.8; Joel 2.4–5; Isa 66.15; Hag 2.22–23). Zech 6.8 also describes the horses as instruments of YHWH's judgement (ויזעק אתי וידבר אלי לאמר ראה היוצאים אל־ארץ צפון הניחו את־רוחי בארץ צפון). Finally, the reference to bronze mountains in Zech 6.1, a potential allusion to Isa 45.2,[40] may suggest that the horses come from YHWH's abode. The identification of the horses in both visions as servants of YHWH ties them closely to the heavenly

---

[38] This reuse is part of a larger tradition of heavenly horse visions. See also Joel 2.4–5; 4Q492 I1–3; *T. Adam* 4.7; 2 Macc 3.24–28; 5.1–5; 10.29–31; 4 Macc 4.10–11; *3 En.* 17.8; 18.1; Josephus, *Ant.* 5.284; *T. Abr.*; Eusebius, *Hist. eccl.* 3.8.5. Although not deriving from the Second Temple Period, see *The Simpsons*, 'Tree House of Horror XIX' (2008).

[39] So Stead, *Intertextuality*, 208.

[40] See ibid., 212.

court.[41] Thus, it is clear that John's horse vision shares a similar setting with Zechariah's horse visions.

Second, an additional connection is located in the overlap in wording between Zech 1.8b and Rev 6.4.

Zech 1.8b: ואחריו סוסים אדמים
                       And after him, red horses

Rev 6.4:   καὶ ἐξῆλθεν ἄλλος ἵππος πυρρός
                       And another red horse came out

John expands this introduction by including ἄλλος and by introducing a verb that is, perhaps, implied in the Hebrew ואחריו.[42] Nonetheless, the syntactic similarities suggest that John's introduction to the red horse (Rev 6.4) follows an introductory pattern borrowed from Zech 1.8b. Beyond the reuse of colour lexemes, the arrangement of John's equine vision corresponds to some syntactic patterns located in Zechariah, and the heavenly court motif is present in both works.

John's reuse of material from Zech 1.8–10; 6.1–5 extends beyond the re-presentation of lexical material. He also borrows from the thematic register of the source tradition (heavenly court motif), and some of his introductory comments mimic the syntactic structure of similar locutions in Zechariah. This evidence coalesces to intimate that John alluded to Zech 1.8; 6.1–5. The lexical, topical, and syntactic correspondences between the two texts suggest a connection, but the overlap is not presented in a literal enough fashion to qualify this reference as a quotation. Although allusive, this example of reuse illustrates the breadth of John's exegetical repertoire; he reused embedded lexical items in a similar thematic context, using analogous syntactic patterns to the source tradition.

Moreover, his presentation of Zechariah's horse colours is the result of his coordination of Zechariah's horse visions. The next question that detains us is this: what features of Zechariah motivated John to create an implied analogy between Zech 1.8 and Zech 6.1–3, and which exegetical resources account for the presentation of this

---

[41] The scene in Zech 3 also strengthens the presence of the heavenly court motif in Zech 1–8.

[42] This word is represented with a verb in the OG/LXX multiple times (Deut 12.30; Job 6.7(8); 14.8, 9; 1 Kgs 16.22; Prov 20.7). Perhaps ואחריו is translated twice here, represented by both ἐξῆλθεν and ἄλλος.

correlation in Rev 6.1–8? There are numerous features of Zechariah's horse visions that may have led to their equation. First, the accounts utilize a similar vocabulary, suggesting a connection between pericopae (see Table 4.1). Nearly every significant lexeme in Zech 1.8, 10 is preserved in 6.1–3, 6. The volume and quality of the shared vocabulary of these accounts hints at their connectedness; the lexical overlap and shared imagery of coloured horses/chariots who 'patrol the earth' (התהלך בארץ) forges an implied relationship between the reports. However, the initial commonalities fail to adequately disguise their many and glaring differences. These differences often trouble modern commentators and cause Meyers and Meyers, for instance, to suggest textual emendations to bring the accounts into an even closer relationship.[43] The different colours of the horse groups and their varying number highlight the inconsistencies of these passages despite their strong parallels.

The assumption that these passages describe identical phenomena is the underlying principle behind the desire to create greater coherence between them. However, as we will see (Section 5.4), the inconsistencies of the details present in these passages are not lost on other ancient readers, particularly the translators of Zechariah's early Greek and Aramaic versions. Much of the reworking of scriptural traditions in antiquity revolved around the desire to alleviate implied textual inconsistencies or smooth out rutted narrative

Table 4.1 *Lexical overlap between Zech 1.8 and Zech 6.1–3*[1]

Zech 1.8	Zech 6.1–3
ראיתי	ואראה
והנה	והנה
רכב*	מרכבה*
סוס/סוסים	סוסים
אדם/אדמים	אדמים
בין ההדסים*	מבין שני ההרים*
ואחריו	אחריהם (6.6)
לבנים	לבנים
להתהלך בארץ (1.10)	התהלכו בארץ (6.7)

[1] Lexemes marked with (*) indicate inexact parallels.

[43] Meyers and Meyers, *Haggai*, 112, 326.

Table 4.2 *Correspondence of colour lexemes between Revelation, Zech 1.8, and Zech 6.1–5*

Revelation	Zech 1.8	Zech 6.1–5
White (λευκός) 6.2	White (לבנים) [4][1]	White (לבנים) 6.3 [3]
Red (πυρρός) 6.4	Red (אדם) [1]	Red (אדמים) 6.2 [1]
	Red (אדמים) [2]	
Black (μέλας) 6.5		Black (שחרים) 6.2 [2]
Green (χλωρός) 6.8	Vine-tendril coloured	
	(שרקים) [3]	
		Spotted (ברדים)
		Strong (אמצים) 6.3 [4]

[1] [Numbers] indicate the narrative order of the coloured horses introduced in Zech 1.8; 6.1–5.

texture.[44] With reference to the colour lexemes in Zech 1.8; 6.1–3, John's reading assumes coherence between accounts. In light of the inconsistency of the colour lexemes used to describe the horse groups, he created his own image of coloured horses by utilizing linguistic material that is unique to both accounts (see Table 4.2).

John's selection of material unique to each horse vision is the exegetical resource that indicates his reading habit. His choice of colours illustrates that he read both visions, disparately located in the source tradition, as a unified account describing identical phenomena. The inconsistencies between Zechariah's horse visions (colours and number of horses) are implicitly acknowledged, but not explicitly retained in the text of Rev 6.1–8. He read Zech 1.8; 6.1–8 as parallel accounts which, due to their inconsistencies, required narrative levelling to reconcile their perceived contradictions.

Overall, John's habit of reading reflected in his reuse of Zechariah's horse visions assumes the coherence and consistency of his scriptural texts. For John, the similarities between traditions indicated that the differences in detail between Zech 1.8 and 6.1–5 required resolution. John reconciled these perceived contradictions through the selective deployment of words unique to both visions. For ancient readers, the consistency of the accounts, signalled by significant verbal overlap, trumps any potential inconsistency noted by modern critics.

[44] See James Kugel, 'The Beginnings of Biblical Interpretation', in *CBIEJ*, 11.

The purview of John's reading of Zechariah is broad. In the previous example, John used the narrative structure and linguistic substance of the entirety of Zech 4 to understand its constitutive parts; Zech 4 is, for John, a network of mutually illuminating locutions that constitute a larger narrative whole. The scope of the network is more expansive in this example, stretching across numerous chapters of intervening material. The lexical and thematic parallels between visions enlarged John's associative network.

Understanding the mechanics of reading that stand behind this extended allusion also aids in understanding the function of the horsemen in Rev 6.1–8, in conversation with the other scriptural tradition deployed in this pericope. While material from Zechariah is found throughout the vision to describe the appearance of the horses, the actions of the horsemen correspond to other prophetic traditions of divine judgement, notably Jer 15.2 and Ezek 5.12; 14.12–21. This combination of traditions couches Zechariah material in the context of divine judgement, suggesting that John understood the angelic riders in Zechariah to be instruments of wrath. Divine action in Rev 6.1–8 is rationalized by the depiction of the martyrs under the altar (Rev 6.9–11), a scene that culminates in cosmic catastrophes and the overturn of the social order associated with 'Day of the Lord' traditions (Rev 6.12–17; e.g. Ezek 38.19; Joel 3.4; Hos 10.8; Zeph 1.14; Nah 1.6; Isa 34.4). John has crafted his seven-seals vision primarily from texts located in Jewish prophetic works, juxtaposing locutions from thematically linked textual segments. Not only does this pastiche-like mode of composition place John in continuity with the prophetic tradition, but it also implies that his vision encompasses the entirety of prophetic tradition. The use of Zechariah plays an important role within this ambient literary mode. Much has been made of the connotations that each colour would have activated for the ancient reader,[45] and while it is possible that the colours selected correspond to the actions of the riders in some sense, the important aspect of the use of colours from Zechariah is that John incorporated

---

[45] As a recent example, Lourdes García Ureña, 'Colour Adjectives in the New Testament', *NTS* 61 (2015): 219–238 has argued that the aural affect of colour in the Apocalypse imbues the colours with metaphorical meaning, although she does not venture any indications of the potential meaning of the deployment of colour imagery. See Mounce, *Revelation*, 152 who argues that the colour of the horses in Zechariah have no specific metaphorical meaning, but that the colour of the riders in Rev 6.1–8 'symbolize conquest (white), bloodshed (red), scarcity (black), and death (pale, livid)'.

material from horse imagery located in both of Zechariah's equine visions. John's use of Zechariah traditions, drawing from the breadth of the work, resembles his use of the prophetic tradition (and perhaps the scriptural tradition) as a whole. He is aware of the details of vast swathes of Jewish scriptural texts.

4.4.4 Revelation 11.2 and Zechariah 12.3

Rev 11.2

καὶ τὴν αὐλὴν τὴν ἔξωθεν τοῦ ναοῦ ἔκβαλε ἔξωθεν καὶ μὴ αὐτὴν μετρήσῃς, ὅτι ἐδόθη τοῖς ἔθνεσιν, καὶ τὴν πόλιν τὴν ἁγίαν πατήσουσιν μῆνας τεσσεράκοντα [καὶ] δύο.

And the outer court of the temple, exclude it, and do not measure it, for it has been given to the nations, and they will trample the holy city 42 months

Zech 12.3^{LXX}

καὶ ἔσται ἐν τῇ ἡμέρᾳ ἐκείνῃ θήσομαι τὴν Ιερουσαλημ λίθον καταπατούμενον πᾶσιν τοῖς ἔθνεσιν, πᾶς ὁ βαστάζων αὐτὸν σπαρασσόμενος ἀμυχθήσεται ἐπ᾽ αὐτὴν πάντα τὰ ἔθνη τῆς γῆς

And it will be in that day, I will set Jerusalem a stone trampled by all the nations, all those who bear it, shaking, will be scarred and all the nations of the earth will be gathered to her

Once again, we return to an example where John reused a Greek form of Zechariah that circulated in a pre-existent exegetical tradition. As I commented in the section discussing Rev 1.7 (Section 4.4.1), it is difficult to measure John's techniques of reuse directly, since we cannot be certain as to the precise wording of the tradition he received. However, John's use of this tradition in Rev 11.2 provides a clear picture of his exegetical repertoire, especially the principles that undergird his conflation of numerous Jewish scriptural texts. And his deployment of these texts produces insight into the meaning of Rev 11.1–13, a pericope that can be more fully commented upon after examining the use of Zechariah in Rev 11.4 in the next example.

Beyond the combination with material from Dan 8.10–14 (and other trampling traditions, cf. Isa 63.18; Ps 79.1), Rev 11.2 is prefaced by the command to measure (v. 1) that the seer receives from an angelic mediator. This tradition is borrowed from Ezek 40.3 (cf. Zech 2.1), where the seer is given a linen cord and a measuring reed and commanded to take heed of the features of the city that he beholds. John also draws on Ezek 37.5 and 10 in his depiction of the resurrection of two witnesses in Rev 11.11. And this is only the most direct reference to a number of scriptural texts and traditions that he used in crafting his depiction of the two witnesses (Rev 11.5–10; cf. Exod 7.17–19; 1 Sam 4.8[OG]; 1 Kgs 17.1; 2 Kgs 1.10; Jer 22.6; Ezek 11.6; Pss 97.3; 105.38). Again it is clear that the use of Zechariah is accompanied by a broader stream of traditions that relate to a given portion of John's visions. In this way, John's visionary experiences, at least as they are recorded in Revelation, are controlled by recurrent themes in Jewish scriptural works and his engagement with these traditions.

In this example, John inherited an interpretative tradition of Zechariah combined with Dan 8.10–14 based on their shared similarities. He then embedded the tradition within a pericope that uses other forms of traditional language from numerous works. This represents a proclivity to collect related traditions (whether they are related by wording or thematic content) into his presentation of visionary material. This pericope, along with the seven-seals narrative (Section 4.4.3), constitutes a condensation of relevant scriptural traditions from a diverse collection of works and literary forms into a vision report. This process of broad assimilation indicates that John is a reader of scripture and knowledgeable about its wording and thematic content, regardless of the genre of the scriptural work. Moreover, this exegetical habit indicates that Revelation, although potentially predicated on genuine mystical experiences, is the result of a lengthy process of exegetical reflection and compositional refinement. The use of material from Zechariah is a part of this larger process of scriptural engagement as a mode of literary composition. The deployment of scripture in these pericopae represents more than just the borrowing of scriptural wording, but reflects John's interaction with the breadth of the tradition.

4.4.5 Revelation 11.4 and Zechariah 4.14

Rev 11.4   οὗτοί εἰσιν αἱ δύο ἐλαῖαι καὶ αἱ δύο λυχνίαι αἱ ἐνώπιον τοῦ κυρίου τῆς γῆς ἑστῶτες

These are the two *olive trees and the two lampstands* standing before the Lord of the earth

Zech 4.14[PM]   אלה שני בני־היצהר העמדים על־אדון כל־הארץ

These are the two sons of oil standing before the Lord of all the earth.

Another example of John's use of Zechariah traditions in Rev 11 is found in v. 4, and there is much evidence that indicates that he was exegetically engaged with details of Zech 4, much like in Rev 5.6 (Section 4.4.2). I begin by examining John's techniques of reuse.

Rev 11.4 is quantitatively longer than Zech 4.14, preserving an expansion vis-à-vis its Hebrew source: καὶ αἱ δύο λυχνίαι (retroverted to והשני מנורות). Lampstand (מנורה) occurs in Zech 4.2, 11, but the seer describes only a single lampstand. Also, the word 'two' (שני) occurs four times in Zech 4, but it always describes the components that make up a single lampstand in the vocalized MT (4.3, 12, 13, 14),[46] although it is not always clear precisely what the components are, especially in 4.12 (צנתרות). There is no example of 'two lampstands' in the MT, the OG/LXX, or in the Qumran corpus. The material seems to represent John's innovation.

This expansion ('and the two lampstands') stands in apposition to the phrase that immediately precedes it – αἱ δύο ἐλαῖαι ('the two olive trees') – and explicates the identity of the two witnesses introduced in Rev 11.3.[47] John explains a locution from Zech 4.14 by expanding his presentation of the reused material beyond the lexical material present in the source text. This expansion takes the form of an appositional locution that explains its parallel co-locution, although the logic behind the author's coordination of 'two olive trees' and 'two lampstands' is not immediately obvious.

Additionally, Rev 11.4 omits a single word from Zech 4.14: no Greek equivalent for כל is represented as John writes 'the Lord of the earth', not 'the Lord of *all* the earth'.

Beyond quantitative differences, Rev 11.4 alters the wording of Zech 4.14 in a way that is sensitive to the co-texts of the quoted text. John altered the phrase בני-היצהר ('sons of oil') to ἐλαῖαι ('olive trees'). This alteration is a reversion back to the narrator's question in Zech 4.11: 'what are these two *olive trees* (זיתים)?'[48] John reworked this locution by regressing to the original question that generated the response from the *angelus interpres* recorded in 4.14. This alteration signals that John was not entirely oblivious to the immediate co-texts of the locutions from which he drew linguistic material.

---

[46] The OG/LXX uses forms of λυχνία four times. There is never a reference to 'two lampstands'. The OG/LXX follows the vocalization preserved in the MT here.

[47] So Mounce, *Revelation*, 224 and Charles, *Revelation*, 1.282. A similar conglomeration of lexemes relating to the temple vessels (including 'oils' and 'candlesticks') occurs in *Ma'aseh De-R. Yeh. b. Levi* 8.7.

[48] The seer's question in Zech 4.11 is presupposed by the vision of 'two olive trees' in Zech 4.3. The opaque Hebrew text of Zech 4.12 (מה שתי שבלי הזיתים אשר ביד שני צנתרות הזהב) may also have influenced identification of the two witnesses as 'lampstands' and 'olive trees'.

The force of the preceding evidence signifies that the reference to Zech 4.14 in Rev 11.4 is a *quotation*. The locutions share a significant level of lexical and linguistic features, presented in a nearly identical serial arrangement. Some quantitative divergences are present, but the addition (καὶ αἱ δύο λυχνίαι) can be explained as the condensing of linguistic material from elsewhere in Zech 4 into the locution preserved in Zech 4.14. These locutions are nearly identical representations of each other and, if the text of Rev 11.4 was substituted for the text of Zech 4^OG, one would suggest that it was a rendering that differed quantitatively, but which ultimately retained a level of fidelity to its *Vorlage*. Moreover, Rev 11.4 is discreet from its surrounding co-texts, as linguistic markers demarcate this locution from its co-texts. The demonstrative pronoun οὗτοί, which refers back to the anaphoric article in v. 3 (τοῖς δυσὶν μάρτυσίν μου), delimits Rev 11.4 as an explanatory aside.[49] Although οὗτοί is properly a translation of אלה, the lemma's clear explicative and almost gloss-like function creates a level of logical discreetness from the surrounding material. Additionally, John's serial presentation delimits the locution. The placement of ἑστῶτες at the end of the locution functions in two directions. First, it creates noticeable syntactic dissonance between source text and target text, emphasizing the discreetness of the locution in the narrative environment in which it is embedded. Second, the location of the verb at the end of the locution creates a sense of finality that creates a narrative break with the following locution. The beginning of Rev 11.5, 'and if someone' (καὶ εἴ τις), also creates a bracketing effect on the back end of the locution. The narrative tersely moves on from the explanatory comment. The high level of linguistic and lexical correspondence between Rev 11.4 and Zech 4.14 and the discreetness of Rev 11.4 from its co-texts, set off by the use of linguistic and narrative markers, suggests that Rev 11.4 quotes Zech 4.14.

Some features of John's techniques of reuse offer insight into his reading habits. The first feature that accomplishes this is the locution καὶ αἱ δύο λυχνίαι, an expansion that does not correspond to any known reading in the MT, the OG/LXX tradition, the NT, or

---

[49] For more on the function of anaphoric articles, see David Aune, 'Apocalypse Renewed: An Intertextual Reading of the Apocalypse of John', in *The Reality of the Apocalypse: Rhetoric and Politics in the Book of Revelation* (Symposium 39; ed. D. L. Barr; Atlanta: SBL, 2006), 45–46.

any other Second Temple Jewish literature. The *two* lampstands in Rev 11.4 are, seemingly, John's invention. Every version and manuscript tradition of Zech 4 witnesses a single lampstand, including the reading tradition preserved in the MT. Most commentators imply that John has been inventive, suggesting that this phrase has been included because the two witnesses (Rev 11.3) symbolize churches in concert with the symbolism of seven lampstands as seven churches in Rev 1–3.[50] By this reasoning, the expansion is motivated by John's ecclesiological concerns. According to Charles, this theological expansion forced John to depart 'widely from both the text and the ideas' of Zech 4.[51] In contrast, Aune suggests that 'the mentions of *two* menorahs . . . when only *one* is found in Zech 4, may indicate the presence of an exegetical tradition upon which John is dependent'.[52] With Aune, I would argue that John's description of two lampstands derived from a reading sensitive to the syntax and logical structure of Zech 4, particularly vv. 2 and 12.

It is well documented that Zech 4.2, 12ᴾᴹ contains numerous syntactic and semantic ambiguities.[53] The opaque nature of the chapter provided John with the possibility to *equate* the two olive trees of Zech 4.3, 11 (זיתים) with *two* lampstands, based on the correlation of graphically similar lexemes in Zech 4.2, 12.

First, it is once again likely that John's reading tradition of Zech 4.2 differed from the tradition preserved in the MT. The word מנורת (Zech 4.2) can be read as a plural noun rather than a singular noun in construct

---

[50] See specifically, Rev 1.20. Beale, *Revelation*, 576–579; Jauhiainen, *The Use*, 92–3; Kiddle, *Revelation*, 181; Beasley-Murray, *Revelation*, 184; Sweet, *Revelation*, 185; Caird, *The Revelation*, 134–135; Boxall, *The Revelation*, 163–165; Mounce, *Revelation*, 224; Swete, *Apocalypse*, 135; Osborne, *Revelation*, 420–422; Morris, *Revelation*, 148; Boring, *Revelation*, 145; Bauckham, *Climax*, 165–166.

[51] Charles, *Revelation*, 1.282.

[52] Aune, *Revelation*, 2.612.

[53] See Mark Cameron Love, *Zechariah 1–8 and the Frustrated Reader* (JSOTsup 296; Sheffield: Sheffield Academic Press, 1999), 57 and Sweeney, *The Twelve*, 614. Al Wolters, 'The Meaning of Ṣanṭĕrôt (Zech 4:12)', *JHS* 12 (2012): 1 notes that Zech 4.12 and 'its immediate context are bristling with exegetical difficulties'. Meyers and Meyers, *Haggai*, 274 suggest that 'the information in verse 12 about the two branches of the olive trees with golden conduits comes as a surprise'. Importantly, they also note that 'the MT is less explicit and detailed than the versions' with reference to צנתרות (257). Referring to the text of Zech 4.2, Meyers and Meyers note that 'textual irregularities associated with the menorah's description are indicated' (229). This ambiguity in the consonantal text provided the ideal opportunity for the author of Revelation to correlate this difficult locution with a parallel locution that shares syntactic and visual characteristics.

(=MT). The only difference between these forms is the placement of the *waw*, a grapheme that lends itself to various readings through metathesis or a difference of reading tradition. John may have read מנורת (Zech 4.2) as a defective spelling of the plural construct state.[54]

However, some problems remain. If John read מנורת as plural, one needs to account for the string of third-person feminine singular affixatives attached to כלה ('all of it [referring to מנורת]') and ראשה ('its top'). The following reconstruction of John's reading tradition, alongside the reading tradition preserved in the MT, clarifies this issue (see Table 4.3).[55]

The reconstruction that I have offered explains the 'expansion' present in Rev 11.4 (αἱ δύο λυχνίαι); specifically, it identifies the reason that John describes multiple (two) lampstands, a reality that allowed him to connect them to the *two* olive trees. If מנורת is read as plural, it is natural for הנה to be understood as a third-person feminine plural pronoun ('they [are]'), instead of as the interjection preserved in the MT. This particular re-vocalization is not absolutely necessary for the argument, but it provides a further syntactic opportunity for John to read מנורת as a plural feminine noun. Moreover, if כלה is read adverbially ('completely'),[56] *not* as כל with a third-person feminine singular pronominal suffix, no number confusion remains between the purported suffix and its antecedent. An adjustment to the reading tradition of the following word, גלה, is also feasible. גל"ה in *piel* followed by על occurs in Lam 2.14 and 4.22 meaning 'to make known concerning'.[57] The semantics of this reconstruction correspond to the reconstructed reading tradition of ראשה. When the ה of ראשה is read as a feminine singular pronominal suffix, it requires that the antecedent of the suffix refer either to the גֻלָה ('bowl') or to מנורת read as a singular. Zech 4.7 offers an alternative reading, with the locution האבן הראשה ('the top stone') providing a graphically similar

---

[54] Love, *Frustrated*, 108–110 notes that orthographic practices are inconsistent within Zechariah[MT].

[55] I have reconstructed John's reading tradition using the Tiberian vocalization system because most modern readers of biblical Hebrew are familiar with this system. My presentation of this reconstruction is strictly heuristic.

[56] See BDB, 478. Cf. Gen 18.21; Exod 11.1. כָּלָה usually refers to 'complete destruction' or 'annihilation', and my construal of this word as an adverb is tentative here. Another possibility is that John read כָּלֶה ('firm' or 'rugged'). This option is theoretically possible as ח | ה confusion is common.

[57] BDB, 163. *Lev. Rab.* 32.8 contains an interesting discourse about the vocalization of גלה. A verbal form is not offered, but numerous other options are presented and the ambiguity of the lexemes is largely embraced: *guleh* ('bowl'); *golah* ('exile'); *goalah* ('redeemer'). A similar note is found in *Song. Rab.* 51.1 E-G.

Table 4.3 *MT and John's reading of Zech 4.2*

MT	Reconstruction
וַיֹּאמֶר אֵלַי מָה אַתָּה רֹאֶה וַיֹּאמֶר רָאִיתִי וְהִנֵּה מְנוֹרַת זָהָב כֻּלָּהּ וְגֻלָּהּ עַל־רֹאשָׁהּ וְשִׁבְעָה נֵרֹתֶיהָ עָלֶיהָ שִׁבְעָה וְשִׁבְעָה מוּצָקוֹת לַנֵּרוֹת אֲשֶׁר עַל־רֹאשָׁהּ	וַיֹּאמֶר אֵלַי מָה אַתָּה רֹאֶה וַיֹּאמֶר רָאִיתִי וְהִנֵּה מְנוֹרֹת זָהָב כֻּלָּה וְגִלָּה עַל רֹאשָׁה וְשִׁבְעָה נֵרֹתֶיהָ עָלֶיהָ שִׁבְעָה וְשִׁבְעָה מוּצָקוֹת לַנֵּרוֹת אֲשֶׁר עַל רֹאשָׁה
And he said to me, 'what are you seeing?' And I said,[2] 'I see and behold a lampstand of gold, all of it[3] and a bowl upon its[4] top and its[5] seven lamps upon its[6] seven and seven pipes to the lamps which are upon its[7] top.'	And he said to me, 'what are you seeing?' And he said,[8] 'I see and they are lampstands of gold, completely.' And he made known concerning the top (stone)[9] and its[10] seven lamps upon its[11] seven and seven pipes to the lamps which are towards the top (stone).

[1] Or, perhaps, מְנֹרוֹת.
[2] Reading with the *Qere*.
[3] Referring to the lampstand.
[4] Referring to the lampstand.
[5] Referring to the bowl.
[6] Referring to the bowl.
[7] Referring to the bowl.
[8] Reading with the *Ketib*.
[9] Cf. Zech 4.7.
[10] Referring to the top stone.
[11] Referring to the top stone.

co-text that potentially informs the reading of both instances of ראשה in Zech 4.2. The inclusion of האבן in 4.7 explicates the consonantally identical word that appears twice in Zech 4.2: the ראשה of 4.2 is a 'top stone', which is part of the lampstand apparatus, a reality not fully revealed until Zech 4.7.

This reconstructed reading tradition offers an explanation for John's inclusion of multiple lampstands (Rev 11.4), providing a grammatically coherent way to read מנורת as plural. The expansion is triggered by John's reading habits, combined with his deployment of certain exegetical resources. In this case, John read Zech 4.2 in light of the structure and semantic value of co-texts in Zech 4. The word ראשה was understood in coordination with a similar collocation in 4.7 (האבן הראשה), an intratextual connection that clarified the ambiguous description of the lampstands. The inherently polysemic nature of the consonantal Hebrew text, coupled with the abstruse grammar of this description, led to John's reading of this text and his internal coordination of its textual features.[58]

It remains, however, to be explained how John arrived at exactly *two* lampstands, as Zech 4.2–3 does not delimit the number of lampstands, only indicating that the seer saw more than one. I suggest that the semantic ambiguity of צנתרות (Zech 4.12), a *hapax legomenon*, coupled with its partial overlap of consonants with and visual similarity to מנרות, led John to correlate the collocation (שני צנתרות הזהב) with the syntactically parallel phrase in 4.2 (והנה מנורת זהב). The visual similarity between the two main words in these phrases, the semantic ambiguity of צנתרות, the shared designation of these items as gold (זהב), and the inclusion of שני in 4.12 provided an opportunity to equate these locutions. Their syntactic equation led John also to equate their meaning, because his reading strategy suggested that these locutions both described the same apparatus presented in the vision.

This textual relationship requires further explanation. First, the word צנתרות (Zech 4.12) is semantically opaque, but part of a clause that is syntactically parallel to a co-text (4.2), a relationship that helped to decode its meaning. Al Wolters has highlighted the problems associated with understanding the word and identified thirty-one different translations and/or interpretations of צנתרות in its reception history.[59] I suggest that John handled the semantic opacity of צנתרות by correlating this clause with a syntactically and graphically similar clause, a coordination that explains John's identification of two lampstands in Rev 11.4:

| Zech 4.2 | והנה מנורת זהב |
| Zech 4.12 | שני צנתרות הזהב |

The connections between these clauses are numerous, and especially obvious if מנורת is read as plural, as is unambiguously the case with

[58] Barr, '"Guessing"', 35–36 notes that a similar type of sustained divergence in reading tradition between MT and a translating Greek text is present in Ps 90(89). The application of a particular vocalization forces the translator to make a cascading array of decisions in order to produce a textual segment that is cohesive with the *initial* choice of vocalization. The implicit vocalization choice for one morpheme limits the vocalization options of trailing morphemes.

[59] Wolters, 'The Meaning', 13–15; cf. Tiemeyer, *Zechariah*, 165–167; Tigchelaar, *Prophets of Old*, 26.

צנתרות. Both locutions are modified by a form of זהב, suggesting that both of these words may describe the same or, at least, a visually similar apparatus. Their graphic similarity also raises the possibility that John intentionally correlated them on graphic grounds.[60] The coordination of these features is not without parallel in early Jewish literature. Teeter notes that

> rather than the fixed and rigid notion of lexical, verbal, or textual identity assumed by modern philological or text-critical mindsets, within this ancient Jewish scribal mentality words (as semantic entities) and even letters (as graphic signs) within the text were conceptualized as connected to others with similar features. This relationship, this mutual 'participation,' is an inherent resource – a latent potential – that can be actualized within the text-exegetical process when necessary and where permitted by the *Vorlage*.[61]

John's correlation of these locutions allowed him to explain a semantic difficulty in his Hebrew source (Zech 4.12) by correlating the phrase with another morphologically obscure, but semantically sure locution (Zech 4.2). This co-referential reading, an exegetical resource authorized and controlled by the textual similarities of the locutions, allowed him to solve perceived ambiguities in both locutions.[62]

This exegetical choice explains John's description of two lampstands in Rev 11.4 on linguistic grounds. Relying upon a particular reading tradition and exegetical choices, John's presentation of reused material, including the phrase αἱ δύο λυχνίαι, reflects his reading of Zech 4[PM]. The semantic, graphic, and syntactic ambiguity of his source text stimulated his identification of the בני־היצהר ('sons of oil') with the subjects of the seer's two questions in Zech 4.11–12 (what are the שני הזיתים and שני צנתרות [=הנה מנורת]?), the second of which had been coordinated with Zech 4.2 (הנה מנורת). The expansion in Rev 11.4 is, therefore, the result of John's habits of reading a complex Hebrew tradition.

---

[60] See Samely, *Rabbinic Interpretation*, 378.

[61] Teeter, *Scribal Laws*, 181.

[62] Samely, *Rabbinic Interpretation*, 47 notes that the Mishnaic authors/editors also made use of 'syntactic ambiguity of the consonantal text' in interpreting scripture (see *m. Mak* 3.10 and Deut 25.2–3).

A final notable feature of John's reuse, which confirms that he was acutely aware of the co-texts of his reused locutions, is the presentation of בני־היצהר ('sons of oil') as ἐλαῖαι ('olive trees'). The collapsing of this construct phrase into a single lexeme is the result of a reversion back to the antecedent of בני־היצהר. In v. 11 the seer asks his angelic guide 'what are these two olive trees (זיתים)?', and the angel's answer is recorded in Zech 4.14: they are 'sons of oil' (בני־היצהר). This reversion suggests that John paid close attention to the discourse of Zech 4, considering the textual details of his source *and* its broader narrative structure. The exegetical procedure that John employs here is word substitution based on coordinated material from an immediate co-text.

John's habits of reading Zech 4 betray a desire to condense as much co-textual linguistic material as possible into a reused locution, a desire for terse semantic representation also witnessed to a lesser degree in Rev 5.6. He played with the graphic value of his source and employed a reading tradition that differs in places from the tradition preserved in the MT, decoding difficult lexemes by correlating obscure locutions with graphically and syntactically parallel co-texts. John also reworked Zech 4.14 by reverting lexemes to their immediate discourse antecedent. The numerous resources that John utilized in the process of reusing Zech 4 are part of a broad exegetical repertoire employed in coordination with his habits of reading. Individual parts of the broader discourse are decoded based on intuited connections, and the broader discourse of Zech 4 is represented in his presentation of 4.14 in Rev 11.4. The judiciousness of John's reading of Zech 4 and his skill as an exegete are both readily apparent in this example of reuse.

The literary goal of this example of reuse is not to disclose John's close reading of Zech 4 or even his technical proficiency as a scribal exegete. Although both of these features are accessible through close engagement with John's use of scriptural traditions, Zechariah traditions are employed among numerous other scriptural traditions that together are indispensable for making sense of the two witnesses narrative. John's presentation of Zechariah material is only literarily relevant insofar as it is a part of John's collection of scriptural traditions. Understanding this complex process of reading Zech 4 adds very little substance to an already literarily dense narrative in Rev 11. However, considering the processes that stand behind John's use of Zechariah traditions helps us to understand his relationship to his broader textual culture. It is likely that readers would have comprehended the clear allusion to Zech 4.14 even without recourse to John's private exegetical strategies. The main item to take from this example is that John's exegetical strategies are not always related to his communicative strategy, although the surface of his work is shaped by these underlying stratagems.

4.4.6 Revelation 19.11–16 and Zechariah 1.8; 6.1–6

Rev 19.11–16   And I saw heaven opened (Καὶ εἶδον τὸν οὐρανὸν ἠνεῳγμένον) and behold a white horse (ἵππος λευκός) and the one sitting on it was called faithful and true and in righteousness he judges and makes war. And his eyes are as a burning flame and on his head are many diadems, having a name written which no one knows except him. And he has been clothed in a garment that had been dipped in blood and his name is called the word of God. And the armies which are in heaven follow him on white horses (Καὶ τὰ στρατεύματα τὰ ἐν τῷ οὐρανῷ ἠκολούθει αὐτῷ ἐφ' ἵπποις λευκοῖς), clothed in pure clean linen. And from his mouth comes a sharp sword, so that with it he can smite the nations and he shatters them with an iron rod and he tramples the winepress of the wrath of the anger of God Almighty

Zech 1.8; 6.1–6ᴾᴹ   I saw in the night and behold a man riding on a red horse (על־סוס אדם) and he was standing between myrtles which were in a glen and after him: horses red (סוסים אדמים), light green (שרקים) and white (לבנים) . . . And I turned and I lifted up my eyes and I saw and behold four chariots (ארבע מרכבות) coming from between two mountains and the mountains were mountains of bronze. With the first chariot red horses (סוסים אדמים) and with the second chariot black horses (סוסים שחרים) and with the third chariot white horses (סוסים לבנים) and with the fourth chariot strong spotted horses (סוסים ברדים אמצים). And I answered and I said to the angel speaking with me, 'what are these, my lord?' And the angel answered and he said to me, 'these are the four winds of heaven going out from being stationed before the Lord of all the earth.' And the black horses went to the land of the north and the white ones when behind them (והלבנים יצאו אל־אחריהם) and the spotted ones went to the land of the south

As noted in the parallel section of the previous chapter (Section 3.2.6), Rev 19.11–16 is a pastiche of scriptural material. The linguistic substance that constitutes this passage includes material from external traditional texts (including Zechariah) as well as material from within Revelation itself (particularly, the depiction of the 'one like a son of man' in Rev 1.12–16).[63] The compositional skill with which these traditions have been interwoven need not detain us here, although the author's ability to combine texts into a new coherent whole is skilful. The primary objective of this section is first to catalogue the author's techniques of reuse in reference to Zech 1.8; 6.15 alone, and then to explore the broader composition of the pericope.

Rev 19.11–16 contains numerous points of connection to Zechariah's horse visions. First, the phrase καὶ εἶδον τὸν οὐρανὸν ἠνεῳγμένον καὶ ἰδού (Rev 19.11; cf. Ezek 1.1) is similar to the locutions that introduce the visions in Zech 1.8 (ראיתי הלילה והנה) and 6.1 (ואשב ואשא עיני ואראה והנה). While the Hebrew equivalents to the phrase τὸν οὐρανὸν ἠνεῳγμένον are not present in Zech 1.8; 6.1PM, the angel's answer to the seer in Zech 6.5 identifies the horses as the 'four winds of *heaven*' (אלה ארבע רחות השמים). Furthermore, the phrase 'and I lifted up my eyes' (ואשא עיני) from Zech 6.1 might also have led John to explicate the origin of these riders as coming from τὸν οὐρανόν.

Second, the description of the accompanying 'armies of heaven' (τὰ στρατεύματα τὰ ἐν τῷ οὐρανῷ ἠκολούθει αὐτῷ ἐφ᾽ ἵπποις λευκοῖς)[64] described in Rev 19.14 parallels language located in both Rev 6.8 (ὁ ᾅδης ἠκολούθει μετ᾽ αὐτοῦ καὶ ἐδόθη αὐτοῖς ἐξουσία ἐπὶ τὸ τέταρτον τῆς γῆς) and Zech 6.6 (והלבנים יצאו אל ארץ אחרים). The language of 'following' or 'going out after' is another feature that is consistent across the horse visions of Revelation and Zechariah.

Finally, it remains possible that הלילה (Zech 1.8) was substituted for the locution τὸν οὐρανὸν ἠνεῳγμένον (Rev 19.11). This Greek locution stands in the same syntactic slot as הלילה in Zech 1.8 and, although there is no example of any form of ליל underlying any form of the lexemes in Rev 19.11, this may be an exegetical or explicative alteration. If so, it would constitute a further example of logical extension or synonymous substitution.

Embedded within Rev 19.11–16 are *implicit allusions* to Zechariah's horse visions. Most notably, vv. 11 and 14 contain points of connection to linguistic features in Zech 1.8; 6.1–5, although the level of discreetness of these reused locutions is minimal. While both are

---

[63] See Moyise, *Old Testament*, 37–44.
[64] See also Rev 9.15–16.

introduced with καί, there is no linguistic marker that delineates the end of the reused locutions from the lexemes that follow, lexemes that have no concrete connection to material in Zechariah. The combination of antecedent traditions in this pericope obfuscates further the boundaries of the reused locutions. Numerous other scriptural traditions are alluded to within this passage (notably Ezek 1.1), and the re-formation of these traditions creates an allusive pastiche in which Zechariah plays but a part.[65] First, the phrase τὸν οὐρανὸν ἠνεῳγμένον (Rev 19.11) expands John's purview beyond Zechariah's horse visions. The remainder of the introductory formula, Καὶ εἶδον . . . καὶ ἰδοὺ ἵππος λευκός, is similar to the pattern set forth in Zech 1.8 (ראיתי הלילה והנה) and 6.1 (ואשב ואשא עיני וארא והנה). It is possible that the impetus for this expansion exists in the text of Zechariah's horse visions. The seer's lifting of his eyes to see angelic horsemen (Zech 6.1) might have led John to conclude that the seer saw an open heaven (cf. Rev 4.1). However, numerous commentators suggest that the expansion (τὸν οὐρανὸν ἠνεῳγμένον) derives from Ezek 1.1, the description of the prophet's vision of the open heavens (ἠνοίχθησαν οἱ οὐρανοί | נפתחו השמים) and

---

[65] This includes the following texts: **Rev 19.12** (οἱ δὲ ὀφθαλμοὶ αὐτοῦ [ὡς] φλὸξ πυρός, καὶ ἐπὶ τὴν κεφαλὴν αὐτοῦ διαδήματα πολλά, ἔχων ὄνομα γεγραμμένον ὃ οὐδεὶς οἶδεν εἰ μὴ αὐτός), which is drawn from Rev 1.14b (καὶ οἱ ὀφθαλμοὶ αὐτοῦ ὡς φλὸξ πυρός); Rev 2.17b (ἐπὶ τὴν ψῆφον ὄνομα καινὸν γεγραμμένον ὃ οὐδεὶς οἶδεν εἰ μὴ ὁ λαμβάνων); Rev 12.3; 13.1 (ἑπτὰ διαδήματα; δέκα διαδήματα). **Rev 19.15** (καὶ ἐκ τοῦ στόματος αὐτοῦ ἐκπορεύεται ῥομφαία ὀξεῖα, ἵνα ἐν αὐτῇ πατάξῃ τὰ ἔθνη, καὶ αὐτὸς ποιμανεῖ αὐτοὺς ἐν ῥάβδῳ σιδηρᾷ, καὶ αὐτὸς πατεῖ τὴν ληνὸν τοῦ οἴνου τοῦ θυμοῦ τῆς ὀργῆς τοῦ θεοῦ τοῦ παντοκράτορος), which includes material coordinate with Rev 1.16b (καὶ ἐκ τοῦ στόματος αὐτοῦ ῥομφαία δίστομος ὀξεῖα ἐκπορευομένη); Rev 12.5 (cf. Ps 2.9; Isa 11.4; 49.2; 63.2–6; Beale, *Revelation*, 961–963) (καὶ ἔτεκεν υἱὸν ἄρσεν, ὃς μέλλει ποιμαίνειν πάντα τὰ ἔθνη ἐν ῥάβδῳ σιδηρᾷ; Rev 14.19b (καὶ ἔβαλεν εἰς τὴν ληνὸν τοῦ θυμοῦ τοῦ θεοῦ τὸν μέγαν). Also, **Rev 19.16** (καὶ ἔχει ἐπὶ τὸ ἱμάτιον καὶ ἐπὶ τὸν μηρὸν αὐτοῦ ὄνομα γεγραμμένον· Βασιλεὺς βασιλέων καὶ κύριος κυρίων), which is similar to Rev 17.14 (cf. Dan 4.37^OG: ὅτι αὐτός ἐστι θεὸς τῶν θεῶν καὶ κύριος τῶν κυρίων καὶ βασιλεὺς τῶν βασιλέων) (οὗτοι μετὰ τοῦ ἀρνίου πολεμήσουσιν καὶ τὸ ἀρνίον νικήσει αὐτούς, ὅτι κύριος κυρίων ἐστὶν καὶ βασιλεὺς βασιλέων καὶ οἱ μετ᾿ αὐτοῦ κλητοὶ καὶ ἐκλεκτοὶ καὶ πιστοί). Syntactic and lexical overlap also exists between Rev 19.11–16 and the description of the horses in Rev 9.17–19. Additionally, Kowalski, *Die Rezeption*, 208–210 argues that Rev 19.11 is, at least in part, a reworking of Ezek 1.1; 23.6, 12; 39.20 because of the presence of the 'open heaven' and horse motifs. Her case that material from Ezek 1.1 has been reused is stronger than the influence she detects from Ezek 23; 39. Numerous other commentators note the connection to Ezek 1.1 (Beale, *Revelation*, 949; Harrington, *Revelation* 190; Osborne, *Revelation*, 679 to name a few). See also Lear, 'Inscribed Thigh', 280–285.

visions of God.[66] This perspective is strengthened by a tradition preserved in *Targum Jonathan* that correlates the creatures in Ezek 1.4–14 with Zechariah's horses.[67] John seems to have composed his own horse vision within this tradition, combining elements from both Zechariah and Ezekiel's visions. Ezekiel's detailed depiction of *four* angelic beings (1.4–14) corresponds to Zechariah's depiction (6.1–5) of *four* angelic riders. In this instance, John followed an interpretative tradition also preserved in *Targum Jonathan* (cf. Section 5.6). The exegetical resource employed here is conflation with external scriptural traditions. Multiple traditional strands have been combined to form a new composite locution. The underlying reading habit that authorized this exegetical move is a broader intertextual approach to scriptural texts.[68] John made a connection between logically similar episodes preserved in different prophetic works, and conflated them on the grounds of their similarity of subject.

Another feature of Rev 19.11–16 that demonstrates John's awareness of other scriptural traditions external to Zech 1.8; 6.1–5 is the detailed description of the rider on the white horse and his army. Rev 19:11b-13 extensively describes the first rider, mimicking material from Rev 1.12–16. The first rider's entourage, the trailing angelic host (τὰ στρατεύματα τὰ ἐν τῷ οὐρανῷ), is described similarly in Rev 19.14b-15. These descriptions are not derived from any Zechariah tradition; instead, their portrayals are drawn from external scriptural parallels. The portrayal of the single rider on the white horse is drawn from Rev 1, a passage that alludes to other scriptural sources. The description of the rider's army (vv. 14b–15) is composed, in part, of references to scriptural sources including Ps 2.9; Isa 11.4; 49.2; 63.2; Dan 7.9. The combination of these traditions is inspired by their logical connections and lexical overlap. For example, Ps 2.9–12[OG] shares numerous lexemes, and a common theme – divine kingship through judgement – with Rev 19.15c-16 (see Table 4.4).

Likewise, material from Dan 7.9b[OG] (καὶ τὸ τρίχωμα τῆς κεφαλῆς αὐτοῦ ὡσεὶ ἔριον λευκὸν καθαρόν), used to describe the hair of the Ancient of Days, is deployed to describe the garments of the heavenly army (ἐνδεδυμένοι βύσσινον λευκὸν καθαρόν) in Rev 19.14. Isa

---

[66] Kowalski, *Die Rezeption*, 208–210; Smalley, *The Revelation*, 487; Blount, *Revelation*, 350; Maier, *Die Offenbarung*, 2.348; Sweet, *Revelation*, 282; Swete, *The Apocalypse*, 250; Prigent, *L'Apocalypse*, 415 (cf. also *1 En.* 4.1; 11.18; 2 Bar 22.1); Harrington, *Revelation*, 190; Beale, *Revelation*, 949; Aune, *Revelation 17–22*, 1052; Osborne, *Revelation*, 679.

[67] See Tooman, 'Will of Their Master', 229–230.

[68] See Teeter, *Scribal Laws*, 192–199.

Table 4.4 *Lexical overlap between Rev 19.15c–16 and Ps 2.9–12*

Rev 19.15c–16	Ps 2.9–12
ποιμανεῖ αὐτοὺς ἐν ῥάβδῳ σιδηρᾷ	ποιμανεῖς αὐτοὺς ἐν ῥάβδῳ σιδηρᾷ
Βασιλεὺς βασιλέων καὶ κύριος κυρίων	βασιλεῖς
τὴν ληνὸν τοῦ οἴνου τοῦ θυμοῦ	μήποτε ὀργισθῇ κύριος ... ὁ θυμὸς
τῆς ὀργῆς τοῦ θεοῦ τοῦ	αὐτοῦ
παντοκράτορος (cf. Isa 63.2)	

49.2a (καὶ ἔθηκεν τὸ στόμα μου ὡσεὶ μάχαιραν ὀξεῖαν | וישם פי כחרב
חדה) preserves significant lexical overlap with Rev 19.15a (καὶ ἐκ
τοῦ στόματος αὐτοῦ ἐκπορεύεται ῥομφαία ὀξεῖα), and material from
Isa 11.4 (καὶ πατάξει γῆν τῷ λόγῳ τοῦ στόματος αὐτοῦ καὶ ἐν
πνεύματι διὰ χειλέων ἀνελεῖ ἀσεβῆ; ושפט בצדק דלים והוכיח במישור לעני
ארץ והכה ארץ בשבט פיו וברוח שפתיו ימית רשע) also reappears in Rev
19.15ab (καὶ ἐκ τοῦ στόματος αὐτοῦ ἐκπορεύεται ῥομφαία ὀξεῖα,
ἵνα ἐν αὐτῇ πατάξῃ τὰ ἔθνη). John's allusive network forged from
diverse texts, the majority of which reflect heavenly court scenes,
produced this composite picture of the heavenly armies. In an
effort to recast a vision of the heavenly host, John conflated material from numerous similar scriptural scenes. The habit of reading
that underlies this reworking of scriptural texts is *equation*. John
equated logically similar episodes that describe the workings of
the heavenly court, absorbing material from these visions into
his own depiction of that setting. John is not only attentive to
the immediate co-texts of the locutions he reused, but also to a
broader scriptural tradition of related scenes, the implication of
which are determined by the character of individual texts as part
of the scriptural whole.

The exegetical resource that produced his presentation of reused
scriptural texts in Rev 19.11–16 is the conflation of various scriptural sources based on their thematic and lexical similarities. In this
segment, John illustrates a preoccupation with heavenly court depictions in the HB and its early Greek versions. The breadth of John's
exegetical encounter with scripture extends well beyond the boundaries of Zechariah; he read these in conjunction with similar segments of his scriptural tradition.

4.4.7 Revelation 19–22 and Zechariah 14

Rev 19.6

Καὶ ἤκουσα ὡς φωνὴν ὄχλου πολλοῦ καὶ ὡς φωνὴν ὑδάτων πολλῶν καὶ ὡς φωνὴν βροντῶν ἰσχυρῶν λεγόντων· ἀλληλουϊά, ὅτι ἐβασίλευσεν κύριος ὁ θεὸς [ἡμῶν] ὁ παντοκράτωρ

And I heard a sound like a great crowd and a sound like many waters and a sound like loud thunder saying, 'Alleluia, for the Lord our God, the almighty reigns'

Zech 14.9ᴾᴹ

והיה יהוה למלך על־כל־הארץ ביום ההוא יהיה יהוה אחד ושמו אחד

And YHWH will be king over all the land in that day. YHWH will be one, his name one

Rev 21.25

καὶ οἱ πυλῶνες αὐτῆς οὐ μὴ κλεισθῶσιν ἡμέρας, νὺξ γὰρ οὐκ ἔσται ἐκεῖ

And her gates will never be shut by day, for there will not be night there

Rev 22.5

καὶ νὺξ οὐκ ἔσται ἔτι καὶ οὐκ ἔχουσιν χρείαν φωτὸς λύχνου καὶ φωτὸς ἡλίου, ὅτι κύριος ὁ θεὸς φωτίσει ἐπ᾽ αὐτούς, καὶ βασιλεύσουσιν εἰς τοὺς αἰῶνας τῶν αἰώνων

And there will not be night again and they will not have need of the light of a lamp of the light of the sun, because the Lord God will shine upon them, and they will rule forever and ever

Zech 14.7ᴾᴹ

והיה יום־אחד הוא יודע ליהוה לא־יום ולא־לילה והיה לעת־ערב יהיה־אור

And it will be one day (so knows YHWH) that there will be neither day nor night, and it will be that there will be light in the evening

Rev 22.3

καὶ πᾶν κατάθεμα οὐκ ἔσται ἔτι. καὶ ὁ θρόνος τοῦ θεοῦ καὶ τοῦ ἀρνίου ἐν αὐτῇ ἔσται, καὶ οἱ δοῦλοι αὐτοῦ λατρεύσουσιν αὐτῷ

And every curse will be no more and the throne of God and the lamb will be in her [Jerusalem], and his servants will worship him

Zech 14.11ᴾᴹ

וישבו בה וחרם לא יהיה־עוד וישבה ירושלם לבטח

And they will dwell in her [Jerusalem] and an accursed thing will not be again, and Jerusalem will dwell in security

The final example to review here is located in numerous texts from Rev 19–22 that use material from Zech 14.7–11. This series of allusions to Zechariah is a part of John's larger use of traditions of divine judgement collected in the final chapters of his work. The allusive nature of these references creates difficulty in discussing techniques of reuse and reading habits. However, two points derived from the discussion in the previous chapter (Section 3.2.7) are relevant.

First, it seems clear to me that John was aware of a fairly substantial textual segment of Zechariah, at least by the standards of many of the reused locutions in Revelation. Unlike his awareness of Zech 4, which is only implied in his presentation of material in Rev 5.6b and 11.4, the author used wording from each verse in Zech 14.7–11 with the exception of v. 10. This speaks to the social realities of his scriptural reuse, a question to which we will return (Section 6.2), suggesting that John had access to a Hebrew manuscript of Zechariah. *Testimonia* or *excerpta* theories cannot adequately account for the breadth of scriptural traditions alluded to in Revelation, nor can appeals to memory explain the interpretative engagement with these traditions. The quantitatively large section of Zech 14 embedded in the last three chapters of the Apocalypse supports the assertion that the reuse of this text was predicated upon a textual encounter and that John read (at least) this portion of Zechariah as a whole.[69]

Second, John's utilization of Zech 14.7–11, like his use of the horse visions in Rev 19.11–16, is combined with resonances from numerous of the scriptural works. His use of Zechariah is not the primary cog in the compositional machine that creates meaning, but it is subordinated to and in conversation with similar texts, similar both in terms of lexical stock and thematic content, that comprise John's eschatological description. For example, in Rev 21.25 and 22.5 John drew upon language drawn from Zech 14.7, in combination with material from Isa 60, correlating these traditions based upon their common lexical (language of day and night) and thematic threads (open city motif). The author exploited the interconnectedness of Jewish scriptural texts, creating a network of allusions that supports the literary intentions of the work. This mode of composition is not too distant from that preserved in Zech 14 itself, a text that alludes incessantly to antecedent scriptural traditions.[70] A hearer of the Apocalypse would not necessarily need to be aware of this network of associations to make sense of Rev 19–22, however, since the cumulative effect of scriptural reuse in these chapters and their interconnection is the factor that controls meaning. The ability to identify individual

---

[69] Cf. J. P. M. Sweet, 'Maintaining the Testimony of Jesus: The Suffering of Christians in the Revelation of John', in *Suffering and Martyrdom in the New Testament* (ed. W. Horbury and B. McNeil; Cambridge: Cambridge University Press, 1981), 111–112.

[70] Cf. Konrad R. Schaefer, 'Zechariah 14: A Study in Allusion', *CBQ* 57 (1995): 66–91.

traditions may well deepen the meaning already contained in the whole, but the rhetorical and literary force of Rev 19–22 does not depend on the hearers' ability to understand John's own scriptural engagement – few would have been in the position to do so, and even fewer would have disagreed with John's exegetical movements – even though John's conceptions and presentation of scriptural wording, themes, and images are indicative of his own past encounters with scripture. The goal of these passages is not to highlight the exegetical prowess of the author, but to call the community to worship (Rev 22.9), even though sophisticated exegesis and habits of reading stand behind the author's use of scripture.

4.5 Concluding Reflections

This exploration of John's techniques of reuse, exegetical resources, and habits of reading leads to a number of important observations. First, John's use of Zechariah provides a clear picture of his techniques of reuse, although boundaries between these categories are somewhat fluid. In terms of John's use of Zech 4 in Rev 5.6b, 11.4, which are quotations, we can speak of various styles of expansion, omission, and alteration.

- *Addition of supplementary description*:[71] the addition of material beyond that witnessed in the source text. Theoretically, this might include features like expanded narrative framework, expanded descriptions, and expanded discourse features such as formulaic introductions, etc. See Rev 11.4 ‖ Zech 4.14.
- *Selective omission of linguistic material from source texts*: the omissions of small-scale linguistic information not presented in the target text vis-à-vis its source. See Rev 11.4 ‖ Zech 4.14.
- *Discourse sensitivity to the narrative of the target text*: stylistic changes to a source text that allow borrowed material to be incorporated in the new

---

[71] This phenomenon is a prevalent feature of Pseudo-Philo's rewriting of Genesis in *LAB* 1–8. See Howard Jacobson, 'Biblical Interpretation in Pseudo-Philo's *Liber Antiquitatum Biblicarum*', in *CBIEJ*, 180–182.

composition in a grammatically cohesive manner.[72] See Rev 5.6b || Zech 4.10b.

• *Lexical alteration or substitution*: the lexical value of a word (or a cluster of words within a larger locution) does not correspond to the lexical value of the borrowed locution. See Rev 5.6b || Zech 4.10b; Rev 11.4 || Zech 4.14.

• *Syntactical alteration*: alterations to the syntax or serial presentation of a reused locution in which the underlying syntactic pattern is still discernible in the target text, yet altered. See Rev 11.4 || Zech 4.14.

Each of these modes of reworking is broadly witnessed in textual culture of the Second Temple period. Although the sample size here is small, John's patterns of expansion and omission of material are restricted in scope, and instances of altering reused material in various ways are more prevalent.

Additionally, beyond quotation, John alluded to segments of Zechariah by creating various points of linguistic contact between the target composition and the antecedent text. Each allusion examined in this chapter retains a concrete lexical connection to a source tradition. Not all lexical connections are unique or lengthy, but they create an initial association. Often these lexical points of contact are conflated with other discernible traditional sources.[73] Moreover, John occasionally embeds lexical source material in a similar thematic context. For example, the vision of the four horsemen in Rev 6.1–8 borrows colour lexemes from Zechariah *and* evokes heavenly court motifs. John also mimics the syntactic structures of the source from which he borrows lexical material. The syntax and style of the opening of the vision in Rev 19.11 and the introduction of the following army in Rev 19.14 follow patterns set forth in Zech 1.8; 6.1 and 6.6 respectively. In addition, John creates additional points of contact with texts in Zechariah by preserving a lexeme that represents a visually similar word to the one that is present in the source text. This usually

---

[72] Wagner, *Reading*, 230 notes a similar strategy in the translator's *Übersetzungsweise* in Isa 1^{OG}. This discourse sensitivity can take the form of the inclusion of particles (especially in works or locutions translated from Hebrew/Aramaic to Greek).

[73] See Rev 7.1 || Zech 6.5 (Jer 49.36 [25.16]); Rev 19.11 || Zech 1.8; 6.1–5 (Ezek 1.1); Rev 19–22 || Zech 14.7–11 (cf. Section 3.2.7).

occurs through the interchange of graphically or audibly similar graphemes.[74]

Numerous conclusions can be deduced from these observations. Foremost among them is that John's exegetical repertoire is varied and supple. His modes of textual reworking and allusion are diverse. The techniques of reuse identified here are mostly consistent across Zechariah's various literary forms, including visions recorded in Zech 4.1–14 (Rev 5.6b; 11.4) and 1.8; 6.1–5 (Rev 6.1–8; 7.1; 19.11–16), pre-existing exegetical traditions associated with Jesus traditions (Rev 1.7; 11.2), and eschatologically oriented oracles (Zech 14.7–11). The question of genre is not a deciding factor in the mechanics of reuse.

The author's deployment of exegetical resources also highlights the fact that multiple revisionary impulses are witnessed even within the reuse of a single locution or pericope. For example, in Rev 11.4, John simultaneously omits a word from his source (כל) and expands the borrowed locution by including an explicatory appositional phrase (καὶ αἱ δύο λυχνίαι). Likewise, he selectively alters the morphological, syntactic, or lexical value of his sources.

Moreover, John reused multiple characteristics of his Hebrew and Greek source traditions to craft allusions. He not only borrowed lexical material, but also mimicked the syntactic structure and thematic content of his sources. John's employment of multiple techniques of reuse suggests that he exploited the tools available to him in response to features of each of the source texts that he reused. Put differently, the techniques of reuse employed in each of these examples reflect John's *reading* and/or *interpretation* of his source text. Moshe Bernstein refers to these alterations in his discussion of the *Genesis Apocryphon* as 'triggered', because the motivation for alteration can be traced back to a certain feature (or constellations of features) present in its textual source.[75]

Another significant conclusion to be drawn from the multiplicity of techniques of reuse employed by John is that these techniques are widely witnessed in a broad variety of Second Temple Jewish

---

[74] The interchange of graphemes in Hebrew or Aramaic is common in the OG/LXX tradition (for example, see Num 16.15; Hos 10.12; Ps 9.6 [catalogued by Tov, *Text-Critical Use*, 100–101]). See also Tov, *The Greek and Hebrew Bible: Collected Essays on the Septuagint* (VTsup 72; Atlanta: SBL, 1999), 301–311.

[75] Bernstein, '*Genesis Apocryphon*', 168.

literature. Parallels between these examples of reuse and interpretative techniques retained in Zechariah's early are especially relevant, particularly in cases where John translated a Hebrew text. Every technique in the 'expansion', 'omission', and 'alteration' categories is broadly witnessed in the OG/LXX and Targumic traditions. These techniques of reuse are also observable in the vast corpus of Jewish literature of this period that preserves residues of scriptural interpretation, including material from within the HB, pre-SP, Qumran works, NT writings, *1 Enoch*, *Jubilees*, Josephus, Philo, and other works subsumed under the (less-than-satisfactory) title 'Old Testament Pseudepigrapha'. John wrests meaning from the oft-intractable Hebrew text of Zechariah (in addition to his reformulation of existing Greek exegetical traditions) using similar techniques witnessed in other exegetical material from the late Second Temple period. In this way, John acts as a scribe, allowing the NT to speak as a witness to the handling of Jewish scripture in early Judaism. I will not comprehensively explore these parallels in this study, but it must be noted that, in terms of reworking and reusing scriptural traditions, John is very much at home in the textual culture of early Judaism. Access to the author's reading and interpretation of scriptural texts is mediated through techniques of reuse that are eminently scribal in this sense.

Furthermore, while John used the consonantal text of Zechariah in some examples, he did not always adhere to the Masoretic reading tradition. Even if the evidence suggests that John referenced a Hebrew text, as it does in some of the examples examined here, one cannot assume that John's reading tradition reflects the tradition preserved in Codex Leningradensis, the Aleppo Codex, or modern editions of the MT. Certainly, the reading traditions of the MT often reflect early vocalization patterns, but it is hazardous to assume that authors were aware of or adhered to *all* these traditional readings. John consistently plays with the consonantal text in a way that differs from the levelling of linguistic ambiguities imposed by the affixing of a graphic paratextual reading tradition.[76]

John's presentation of reused locutions also articulates implicit textual connections between the reused locution and its original co-texts. He consistently condenses sense contours and linguistic material from the broader context of his reused locutions, revealing an awareness of the broader discourse and features of his source

---

[76] See also Lear, 'Inscribed Thigh', 284.

traditions.[77] He demonstrates awareness of a specific source text and, additionally, establishes cognizance of the broader context of a locution by incorporating textual features present in the locutions' co-textual environment. Isomorphic accuracy to the wording of sources is sacrificed in favour of the terse presentation of the deep structure of a broader passage. John preserved antecedent traditions in a way that implicitly facilitated an interpretative encounter with the reused source tradition.

Expanding the previous point, the underlying structure of the reuse of Zechariah in Revelation betrays John's sustained attention to the similar scenes preserved in the broader scriptural tradition. As each of the preceding examples illustrated, John's presentation of material from Zechariah arose not only from the sense of the broader context of these locutions, but also from disparate scriptural accounts. John's exegetical target is the broader scriptural tradition. He read 'scripture' in the widest sense, and his presentation of reused material from Zechariah expands the horizon of intertextual discourse beyond the immediate reused locution. The literary force of reused material from Zechariah in the Apocalypse is only mediated through its connection to other scriptural words, locution, or themes in its new co-textual environment. In other words, John's conflation of Zechariah with other scriptural texts regulates the contribution of Zechariah material to John's meaning.

Finally, John employed a number of exegetical resources (word substitution, conflation, textual equation, inversion, co-referentiality) based on his habits of reading, habits that are undergirded by a number of assumptions. Although the wording of scriptural text was not immutable for John, neither was it amenable to arbitrary or whimsical change. He assumed that Zechariah was coherent and consistent, and employed particular traditions of reading that highlighted and, in some cases, created a heightened sense of cohesion (grammatical clarity) and coherence (consistency of meaning) in his sources. John's examples of reuse seem to

> *assume* the sanctity of the text and its meaning, though not – or rather, though only in a specific way – its wording. The wording, the surface structure of the text, does nonetheless

---

[77] See also parallel examples in Rom 9.25, 33; 10.6–8; 1 Cor 14.21 (Stanley, *Language of Scripture*, 263).

play a crucial role in facilitating changes authorized in some sense by the deep structure of the text.[78]

John also assumed that the broader scriptural tradition was consistent with the meaning of Zechariah. His conflation of like traditions from various discrete textual entities demonstrates his awareness of broader scriptural tradition. John employs the habits of a careful reader of both the internal discourse of a particular pericope and the scriptural tradition as a whole. He is conscious of the minute textual details of his sources and endeavours to understand these features in a way that often resolves their internal tensions. The author of Revelation is an attentive reader of scripture, a scriptural tradition that is unchangeable in its meaning, but malleable in its wording, but only insofar as the new wording accurately reflected the implied reality of its underlying meaning. For John, the surface structure of a scriptural work remains ductile inasmuch as it coheres with his perception the meaning of the text's deep structure.

---

[78] Norton, *Contours*, 200–201.

5

READING ZECHARIAH IN EARLY JUDAISM

5.1 Introduction

The preceding discussion has determined that John embedded material derived from different forms and sources of Zechariah, including Hebrew texts from manuscripts and Greek forms taken from existing exegetical traditions. This identification, in turn, has illuminated the exegetical procedures by which John's reuse was accomplished, as well as his underlying reading of Zechariah, suggesting that his modes of reuse and composition reflect scribal attitudes operative in early Judaism. The present chapter provides numerous examples parallel to the reuse of Zechariah in Revelation by analysing the reuse of Zechariah in early Jewish literature, emphasizing the reception of similar locutions in Zechariah that John reused. These ancient examples of reuse provide a control to the techniques of reuse, habits of reading, and exegetical resources observed in Revelation. The historical boundaries of these comparative examples are loosely set by the earliest translations of Zechariah: the OG (third to second century BCE)[1] and Aramaic Zechariah preserved in *Targum Jonathan* (second century CE).[2] Utilizing these two translations as loosely defined

---

[1] E. Tov, 'The Septuagint', in *Mikra*, 162. Pola, 'Sach 9,9–17^LXX', 238–251 argues that the Book of the Twelve was translated during the Maccabean period (ca. 165 BCE).

[2] P. S. Alexander, 'Jewish Aramaic Translations of Hebrew Scriptures', in *Mikra*, 247 notes, based on the Aramaic dialect of the official Babylonian Targumim, that 'it is highly unlikely that Onk and Yon could have originated before 135 CE'. See also Paul V. M. Flesher and Bruce Chilton, *The Targums: A Critical Introduction* (Waco: Baylor University Press, 2011), 181, 211. Alexander also notes that the translation of the Hebrew scriptures into Aramaic began in the Second Temple period and that the impetus to codify these 'official' Targumim lies in the belief that these translations preserved antique interpretations. Dogniez, 'Some Similarities', 90 notes that some traditions preserved in the Targumim can be traced back as early as the second century BCE. Beyond *TJ*, the only Targumic witness to the prophets is a Palestinian

chronological frames provides a convenient method of limiting the scope of the investigation, and ensures that each locution from Zechariah that John reused finds a parallel, at least in translation. This discussion is far from exhaustive, and I explore only a selection of many potential examples. A full treatment of the reuse of material from Zechariah in Jewish antiquity would surely necessitate its own study. This selective analysis is a microcosm of the two preceding chapters. First, I determine the textual form of Zechariah that was reused.[3] Second, I examine the textual points of connection between the borrowing and borrowed traditions, leading to an analysis of the borrowing tradition's techniques of reuse. Finally, I inspect the deep structure of the reference based on the analysis of its surface features. This chapter highlights the high level of coherence between interpretative traditions and techniques of reuse witnessed in the literature of early Judaism and the book of Revelation, demonstrating that the author of Revelation is part of an ambient mode of scribal literary composition and text handling.

5.2 Zechariah 4.10 and 2 Chronicles 16.9[4]

This first example places tension on the early end of the chronological framework, since 1–2 Chronicles was likely composed

---

Tosefta preserved in Codex Reuchlinianus which contains about eighty passages from the Former and Latter Prophets. Moreover, I. Himbaza, 'Le *Targum Pseudo-Jonathan* témoin de l'époque du Second Temple', in *The Targums in Light of the Traditions of the Second Temple Period* (JSJsup 167; ed. T. Legrand and J. Joosten; Leiden: Brill, 2014), 173–187 has made clear that interpretative traditions in certain Targumim are derivative of antecedent traditions from the Second Temple period. Using Zech[OG] and *TJ* Zech as a framework to analyse the reuse of Zechariah is appropriate both chronologically and in terms of the shared features of these traditions. Dogniez, 'Some Similarities', 89–102 notes that, despite numerous differences, these translations of Zechariah share numerous features including shared 'converse translations' (Zech 2.10; 5.3), the use of shared derogatory expressions (13.2), shared interpretations of their Hebrew *Vorlage* (9.9; 11.16; 12.5), and the tempering of some 'improper expressions' (13.3).

[3] This question is not consequential in every case, particularly if the language of the target composition is Hebrew.

[4] The formulation in 4Q368 (4QApocryphal Pentateuch A) X 4 may have also been influenced by Zech 4.10, but it is difficult to establish direct dependence. See Ariel Feldman and Liora Goldman, *Scripture and Interpretation: Qumran Texts that Rework the Bible* (BZAW 449; ed. D. Dimant; Berlin: De Gruyter, 2014), 185.

before the translation of the Torah into Greek. A broad range of dates exists for the composition of the books of Chronicles: from 520–515 BCE to a *terminus ante quem* in the Maccabean era (ca. 160 BCE; cf. Ben Sira 47.9–10).[5] A date in the fourth–third centuries BCE is likely, although this is difficult to determine with certainty.[6] Although this date lies outside our chronological frame, it places 1–2 Chronicles firmly within the Second Temple period. This dating also suggests that Chronicles was composed *after* Zechariah, even though Zechariah, especially the oracular portions, is difficult to date.[7]

5.2.1 Issues of Directionality

Zech 4.10b שבעה־אלה עיני יהוה המה משוטטים בכל־הארץ

These seven are the eyes of YHWH, they go eagerly
about in all the earth

2 Chr 16.9 כי יהוה עיניו משטטות בכל־הארץ להתחזק עם־לבבם שלם אליו
נסכלת על־זאת כי מעתה יש עמך מלחמות

For the eyes of YHWH go eagerly about in all the earth
in order to strengthen those whose hearts are perfect
towards him. You have acted foolishly about this for
from now on there will be wars[8] with you

Issues of direction of dependence are notoriously difficult to determine,[9] yet helpful criteria exist that aid in establishing the direction

---

[5] Ralph W. Klein, *1 Chronicles: A Commentary* (Hermeneia; Minneapolis: Fortress, 2006), 13. The *terminus ante quem* is further substantiated by the work of Eupolemos, who knows Chronicles in Greek.

[6] Ibid., 13–16. For appraisals of the dating of Chronicles, see Kai Peltonen, 'A Jigsaw without a Model? The Date of Chronicles', in *Did Moses Speak Attic? Jewish Historiography and Scripture in the Hellenistic Period* (JSOTsup 317; ed. L. L. Grabbe; London: Continuum, 2001), 225–271 and Isaac Kalimi, 'Die Abfassungszeit der Chronik: Forschungsstand und Perspektiven', *ZAW* 105 no 2 (1993): 223–233.

[7] The proposed date of 520 BCE is based on the date formulae within in Zech 1.1, 7; 7.1 and the sociohistorical context of the Persian Yehud in the aftermath of Cyrus' edict (538 BCE; see Ezra 1.1–4; 6.1–5; 2 Chr 36.22–23). See Meyers and Meyers, *Haggai*, xxxi–xliv; Chary, *Aggée-Zacharie*, 37–38; Wilhelm Rudolph, *Haggai; Sacharja 1–8; Sacharja 9–14; Maleachi* (KAT 13.4; Gütersloh: Mohn, 1976), 61; Sweeney, *The Twelve*, 2.561–563.

[8] Cf. 2 Chr 14.6.

[9] See, for example, S. R. Driver, *Introduction to the Literature of the Old Testament* (9th edn; Edinburgh: T&T Clark, 1913), 383: 'In the case of two similar passages, the

of reuse.[10] In addition to the likelihood that 2 Chronicles was composed after Zechariah (a fact advocating that it is the borrowing text), scholarly opinion is firmly entrenched in the position that 2 Chr 16.9 quotes Zech 4.10b, not vice versa.[11] Moreover, several features of 2 Chr 16.9 point towards this text as the borrower. First, the use of the particle כי signals a discursive intrusion into the narrative from outside material. In this case, כי introduces the reused material and replaces the awkwardly inverted phrase that introduces Zech 4.10b (שבעה־אלה). Second, the text of 2 Chr 16.9 levels the rutted grammatical texture of Zech 4.10b, correcting the grammatical gender of משוטטים to accurately reflect the gender of its subject (עין = fem.): משוטטות.[12] Third, 2 Chr 16.9 is expansive vis-à-vis Zech 4.10b, in that the borrowed locution is immediately followed by additional oracular material. Carr notes that, when two texts share verbal parallels, the text that includes substantial quantitative additions

difficulty of determining which is the one that is dependent on the other, *when we have no other clue to guide us*, is practically insuperable' (italics original).

[10] See Tooman, *Gog of Magog*, 31–35; Michael A. Lyons, *From Law to Prophecy: Ezekiel's Use of the Holiness Code* (LHBOTS 507; London: T&T Clark, 2009), 59–67; David Carr, 'Method in Determination of Direction of Dependence: An Empirical Test of Criteria Applied to Exodus 34,11–26 and its Parallels', in *Gottes Volk am Sinai. Untersuchungen zu Ex 32–34 und Dtn 9–10* (ed. M. Köckert and E. Blum; Gütersloh: Gütersloh, 2001), 109–110; Molly Zahn, 'Reexamining Empirical Models: The Case of Exodus 13', in *Das Deuteronomium zwischen Pentateuch und Deuteronomistischem Geschichtswerk* (FRLANT 206; ed. E. Otto and R. Achenbach; Göttingen: Vandenhoeck & Ruprecht, 2004), 36–55.

[11] H. G. M. Williamson, *1 and 2 Chronicles* (NCB; Grand Rapids: Eerdmans, 1982), 274; Christine Mitchell, 'Chronicles and Ben Sira: Questions of Genre', in *Rewriting Biblical History: Essays on Chronicles and Ben Sira in Honor of Pancratius C. Beentjes* (DCLS 7; ed. J. Corley and H. van Grol; Berlin: De Gruyter, 2011), 5; Paul K. Hooker, *First and Second Chronicles* (WeBC; Louisville: WJK, 2001), 196; Steven L. McKenzie, *1–2 Chronicles* (AOTC; Nashville: Abingdon, 2004), 284; Steven S. Tuell, *First and Second Chronicles* (Interpretation; Louisville: John Knox, 2001), 174; Sara Japhet, *I & II Chronicles* (OTL; London: SCM, 1993), 735; Martin J. Selman, *2 Chronicles* (TOTC 10b; Downers Grove: IVP, 1994), 400; Edward Lewis Curtis, *A Critical and Exegetical Commentary on the Books of Chronicles* (ICC; Edinburgh: T&T Clark, 1910), 389; Jacob M. Myers, *II Chronicles* (AB 13; Garden City, NY: Doubleday, 1965), 94.I categorize this example as a quotation due to close linguistic relationship between traditions, and the discreetness of the locution, bordered by כי and an infinitive construct phrase (להתחזק) that expounds on the quotation.

[12] Lyons, *From Law*, 60 notes that, where two related textual traditions differ on details (gender, pronouns, etc.), the text that has a clear reason to alter a reading is the likely borrower.

(particularly in character speech) is likely the borrower.[13] All the evidence points towards 2 Chr 16.9 as the borrowing text.

5.2.2 Vorlage(n)

The lack of numerous demonstrable Hebrew textual forms of Zechariah suggests that the Chronicler (C) utilized the proto-MT as the *Vorlage* to construct this quotation. There is no evidence to suggest that C utilized a Greek translation, or a Hebrew textual form that varied significantly from proto-MT. Although there *may* have existed multiple literary editions of Hebrew 1–2 Chronicles,[14] in terms of inner-biblical reuse, the *Vorlage* of a reused text is more easily determined than when dealing with early Christian Greek literature. C likely quoted a form of Zechariah close to the proto-MT.

5.2.3 Techniques of Reuse

Because the reused material contains a level of discreetness from its co-texts, it is possible to describe their relationship in text-critical terms. First, the locution borrowed from Zech 4.10b is expanded in 2 Chr 16.9 by the phrase להתחזק עם לבבם שלם אליו נסכלת על־זאת כי מעתה יש עמך מלחמות. The clause 'in order to strengthen those whose hearts are perfect towards him' (להתחזק עם לבבם שלם אליו) is of particular interest, as it serves as the ground clause to the reused locution. This expansion explains and qualifies the activity of the eyes of YHWH: they edify those who are faithful to covenants and keep oaths.[15] This language of qualification is absent from the text in Zechariah, and the narrative ambiguity of Zech 4 (see Sections 4.4.2 and 4.4.5) could account for the employment of this expansion. The expansion connected to the locution, along with the tersely communicated consequences of

---

[13] Carr, 'Method', 126.

[14] See L. C. Allen, *The Greek Chronicles: The Relation of the Septuagint of I and II Chronicles to the Masoretic Text* (VTsup 25; vol. 1; Leiden: Brill, 1974), 213–216. This distinction is only made in 2 Chr 35–36 where it seems that the OG translator (or the *Vorlage* that undergirds this translation) attempted to collate parallels to 2 Kgs 23–24. No such impulse exists in 2 Chr 16.9, and the OG is a fairly literal rendering of the proto-MT.

[15] BDB, 1023–1024 notes that של"ם can have covenantal overtones. The covenantal implications of the expansion are also made clear by the contrast of Asa's covenant with YHWH (2 Chr 15.9) and the alliance he forges with Ben-Hadad (2 Chr 16.3).

Asa's actions (נסכלת על־זאת כי מעתה יש עמך מלחמות), suggest that C borrowed from Zech 4.10b.

Additionally, C omitted material from Zech 4.10, the first instance of which is the lack of an equivalent for the opening word of Zech 4.10b: שבעה. C may have omitted this lexeme because it lacks a clear referent or antecedent in Zech 4. Beside John's solution to the lack of antecedent (cf. Section 4.4.2), the only other grammatically cohesive antecedent of שבעה is אלה (4.5), a demonstrative that refers to the two olive trees (זיתים) in vv. 3–4 or, possibly, to the sevenfold components of the lampstands in v. 2 (שבעה מוצקות; שבעה; שבעה נרתיה). None of these options seem to have satisfied C. The phrase 'seven spirits', John's solution, is unattested until the book of Revelation, and no other grammatically cohesive antecedent options exist to deal with שבעה.

Another possible explanation for C's omission is the application of a reading tradition that differs from Zech 4.10b^MT, reading שִׁבְעָ֫ה, 'seven' (Zech 4.10^MT) as שְׁבֻעָה, 'oath, curse', although this reading creates grammatical issues since שְׁבֻעָה is singular and אלה plural. 'Oath' carries connotations of faithfulness and friendship similar to those in the expansion that follows the quotation. The purpose of an oath (שְׁבֻעָה) is to enforce an agreement between parties, and Hanani's imploring of Asa to remain faithful to YHWH (not Ben-Hadad; 2 Chr 16.2)[16] is located in a similar argumentative trajectory. If C read Zech 4.10b as 'this is the *oath* of YHWH', it coheres with the argumentation of the expansion discussed above: YHWH strengthens those who keep their oaths. Perhaps, the two options discussed here work hand in hand. The grammatical incohesion and discourse ambiguity caused by reading שִׁבְעָ֫ה caused C to implicitly vocalize the consonantal framework of this lexeme as שְׁבֻעָה. However, the lack of an immediate antecedent for this word in both Zech 4 and its new co-textual environment in 2 Chr 16 caused C to rework שְׁבֻעָה into a locution that is quantitatively expansive. The concern of discourse coherence motivated C to rework שְׁבֻעָה, perhaps, into להתחזק עם לבבם שלם אליו. This reworking makes clear that Asa's willingness to submit to Ben-Hadad is an affront to his relationship with YHWH. The way in which C rewrites the Deuteronomic History leads to the retrojection of post-exilic prophetic locutions into the mouth of a

---

[16] See also Asa's conduct in reference to trust in YHWH and warfare in 2 Chr 14.9–15.19.

pre-exilic prophet in the Judean court. C's reworking of a grammatically incongruous lexeme in Zech 4.10b (שְׁבְעָה) adds rhetorical force to this example of reuse.

The second omission in 2 Chr 16.9 is the relative pronoun המה,[17] referring to עיני יהוה. The inclusion of this pronoun necessitates that the locution be comprised of two clauses, and its omission in 2 Chr 16.9 allows the remaining reused material to comprise a single clause. This grammatical simplification is precisely the type of stylistic alteration one might expect C to make in the process of incorporating material into a new composition.

Numerous alterations are also present in 2 Chr 16.9 in comparison to Zech 4.10b. First, the locution is introduced with a different lexeme: כי as opposed to שבעה־אלה. This alteration reflects C's discourse sensitivity. Zech 4.10b is deployed here in order to support Hanani's assertion that Asa's previous military victories, despite the strength of the Ethiopians and the Libyans, were won because of his trust in YHWH's ability to fight for those faithful to him (על־יהוה ניתם בידך; 2 Chr 16.8). Introducing the reused locution with כי reinforces Hanani's claim and cements the locution's place within the discourse structure of the prophetic disputation. In this context, the formula 'these seven/oaths' (שבעה־אלה) would serve no rhetorical function.

Second, the serial arrangement of the phrase עיני יהוה (Zech 4.10b) has been inverted to יהוה עיניו (2 Chr 16.9). The collocation in 2 Chr 16.9 creates, perhaps, a more aesthetically pleasing turn of phrase in contrast to the construction preserved in Zech 4.10b. The addition of a *waw* engrains a more visually pleasing pattern of *yod* + consonant + *waw* etc. in this construction. Also, as has been noted elsewhere,[18] the inversion of elements, whether lexical or thematic, large-scale or small, is a common way to reference scriptural traditions in the Second Temple period. This small-scale inversion of elements mirrors the inversion of the demonstrative pronoun and adjective that open Zech 4.10b (שבעה־אלה), suggesting that perhaps C altered the serial structure of his source to make it cohere more closely with another syntactic pattern that C ultimately omitted. Although שבעה־אלה is no

---

[17] Translated thusly by Rudolph, *Haggai*, 103: 'Diese Siebenzahl bedeutet die Augen Jahwes, *die* über die ganze Erde schweifen' (emphasis added). Chary, *Aggée-Zacharie*, 88 breaks Zech 4.10b into two distinct clauses ('Ces sept-là sont les yeux de Yahwé. Ils circulent par toute la terre').

[18] See Tooman, *Gog of Magog*, 30–31.

longer present, the quotation retains the structural integrity of these elements.

Third, C altered the grammatical gender of משוטטים (masculine in Zech 4.10b) to reflect more accurately the feminine grammatical gender of its subject (משטטות). As noted above, the smoothing of rutted grammatical incohesion is the type of alteration one might expect C to make in the process of reusing antecedent material.

5.2.4 Exegetical Resources

Based on the numerous surface feature divergences catalogued above, a picture of C's exegetical resources emerges. First, motivated by the discourse and semantic ambiguity of Zech 4.10b, C included an additional locution (להתחזק עם לבבם שלם אליו) that is itself a thematic expansion of an omitted collocation (שבעה־אלה) that C perhaps read with a different tradition than that preserved in the MT. The final clause in 2 Chr 16.9 (נסכלת על־זאת כי מעתה יש עמך מלחמות) is a direct inversion of the situation brought about by Asa's previous faithfulness (2 Chr 14.6). Various exegetical tendencies are operative here. First, C's unpacking of שבעה־אלה in thematically related language appended to the end of the reused locution suggests a desire to elucidate the implied meaning of the source text. This is a common form of exegesis in Jewish antiquity.[19] Additionally, C's appropriation of reading tradition ambiguity of an unvocalized text (שבעה) allowed him to create grammatical cohesion in an episode in which the word שִׁבְעָה lacked a direct antecedent. Applying this reading tradition removed the need for שבעה to have an antecedent, thus ironing the rutted texture of Zech 4. C's 'change' was motivated by a desire to make sense of the narrative of a source text *and* cohered with the thrust of Hanani's prophetic indictment of Asa. The concluding clause of v. 9 (נסכלת על־זאת כי מעתה יש עמך מלחמות) firmly implants the reused locution in the broader context of C's discussion of Asa's reign. The expansion of the phrase 'this oath' to other thematically linked language[20] attached to the original locution is another example of explication, wherein an implicit meaning is made manifest via textual expansion.

---

[19] See Kugel, *Potiphar's House*, 247–251; Esther Menn, 'Inner-Biblical Exegesis in the Tanak', in *A History of Biblical Interpretation: The Ancient Period* (vol. 1; ed. A. J. Hauser and D. F. Watson; Cambridge: Eerdmans, 2003), 75.

[20] בכל־הארץ להתחזק עם־לבבם שלם אליו.

The remaining divergences in surface features are not necessarily explicable by exegetical procedure, but by appeal to grammatical norms. The correction of the gender of the main verb in each locution to correctly reflect the grammatical gender of its subject (משוטטים to משטטות) illustrates C's desire to produce a grammatically cohesive narrative. The serial inversion of 'the eyes of YHWH' (עיני יהוה to יהוה עיניו) makes no semantic difference, but perhaps reflects C's desire to produce a text that is graphically pleasing. Even when using a grammatically and stylistically difficult source, C attempts to create a cohesive narrative.[21]

5.2.5 Habits of Reading

C's reading of Zech 4.10b conveys multiple impulses. First, C's reading tradition differs in places from that preserved in the MT. Additionally, C assumed that Zech 4 was grammatically cohesive and coherent in message with the Deuteronomic History that he was rewriting. His correction of the gender of a participle that was borrowed from Zech 4.10b demonstrates his care for cohesion. C's perception of coherence allowed him to insert material from Zech 4.10b within the rewriting of the Asa narrative (1 Kgs 15.8–24//2 Chr 14.2–16.14); the meaning of Zech 4.10 is consistent with and supplements the message of the Asa story: as long as Asa kept covenant with YHWH, his kingdom was at peace (2 Chr 15.12). However, Asa's alliance with Ben-Hadad (16.2) violated the oath he made with YHWH (15.14–15). Hanani makes this point to Asa using language borrowed from Zech 4.10b, an oracle that results in the prophet's torture (16.10) and the severe disease in Asa's 'feet' that leads to his death. The logic of Zech 4.10b, as

---

[21] See Love's despairing evaluation of Zech 1–8's overall coherence and adherence to grammatical norms (*Evasive Text*, 229): 'This is a text in which the reader does not know which direction to take and does not know where to base her reading. There are no stable points in the text, as almost all of the textual elements are involved in a game of perpetual substitution . . . the book is "consistently inconsistent" and totally frustrating.' For Love, Zech 1–8 is 'unreadable'. See also Rashi's introduction to his *Commentary on Zechariah*: 'The prophecy of Zechariah is extremely enigmatic, because it contains visions resembling a dream that requires an interpretation. We cannot ascertain the truth of its interpretation until the teacher of righteousness comes.' Martin Luther also complained that 'here, in this chapter [Zech 14], I give up. For I am not sure what the prophet is talking about' (in *Lectures on Zechariah*, [1527]).

read by C, is appropriated nicely into this prophetic disputation. Understanding שבעה־אלה as 'this oath' (or, perhaps, 'these oaths') connects Zech 4.10b to Zech 5.3–4, where a flying scroll destroys those who steal *and those who swear falsely or make false oaths* (הנשבע בשמי לשקר). The severe punishment for those who make false oaths in Zech 5 parallels the punishment that Hanani proclaims to Asa ('you will have wars') and the terse narration of Asa's sickness and death that follows Hanani's torture. For C, the focus on oath-making and oath-keeping in Zech 4–5 served as the ideal corollary through which to accuse Asa, a king who breaks his oath with YHWH in order to build an alliance with a foreign ruler.[22] Furthermore, C's reuse of language from Zechariah also builds his reputation as a writer of scripture. The deployment of Zech 4.10 within the chronological veneer of a first-hand historical work parallel to the Deuteronomic History makes it appear as if it is the author of Zechariah that reused Hanani's prophetic oracle. C's borrowing of material from a post-exilic prophet lends authoritative weight to his work.

5.2.6 Summary

In terms of techniques of reuse, C reworked Zech 4.10b differently than John. John does not create quantitative differences between Zech 4.10b and Rev 5.6b, while C both adds an explanatory phrase to the end of the reused locution and omits certain elements, in order to create a more cohesive texture. John betrays his understanding of Zechariah through the word substitution of 'eyes' for 'spirits' without resorting to quantitative expansion.[23] Moreover, John and C repurpose the locution in Zech 4.10b to support their own narratives in very different ways. C deploys the locution in a prophetic disputation against an unfaithful king, while John positions this locution as part of a description of a slain-yet-standing lamb. Both of these redeployments are controlled by each authors' reading of Zech 4,

---

[22] See the binding power of oaths in Josephus, *Ant.* 5.54–57. It is also noteworthy that in the parallel account of Asa in the Deuteronomic History (1 Kgs 15.8–24), Asa's actions in making a covenant with Ben-Hadad are not viewed negatively: Asa is extolled as a king like his ancestor David (15.11). Hanani has no contact with Asa, but instead with Baasha, king of Israel (1 Kgs 16.1–4).

[23] See Section 4.4.2.

particularly how they understood the place of שבעה־אלה (4.10b) in the vision. For John, the antecedent of שבעה־אלה is ברוחי (Zech 4.6), which allows him to interchange 'eyes' and 'spirits'. C found no logical antecedent (likely reading ברוחי as singular); therefore, שבעה must not be understood as 'seven' but as 'oaths' (cf. Zech 5.3–4; 2 Chr 15.15). Both of these options for understanding שבעה־אלה are grammatically possible. Although C and John arrive at different conclusions for how to understand שבעה־אלה, they both identify an area of semantic and grammatical opacity relating to an important locution, and seek to clarify the ambiguity by incorporating the phrase into new situations.

Beyond identifying the same issue in need of explication, John and C both take full advantage of a consonantal Hebrew text. Although John's reading tradition does not differ from the MT in this case, he too at times read Hebrew consonants differently than the Tiberian Masoretes (see Section 5.3). C, too, employed reading traditions that differ from the MT, motivated at least in part by an assumption of intelligibility on the grammatical and narrative levels of discourse. Although C and John apply Zech 4.10b to different contexts in their target narratives, their underlying stratagem for reading Zech 4.10b was identical. Moreover, C's techniques of reuse mirror similar techniques used by John (although not necessarily in Rev 5.6b).[24] These authors share a common system of exegetical resources, suggesting a shared textual culture.

5.3 Zechariah 4.14 and 4QCommentary on Genesis C 4 2 (4Q254)

The next comparative example to reuse found in Revelation is located in 4Q254 4, a small (4.1 × 6.6 cm) fragment containing parts of at least fourteen words.[25] This fragment is situated within a collection of seventeen others, some of which (2–14) are loosely related to Gen

---

[24] These include the addition of supplementary description, selective omission of linguistic material from borrowed source texts, discourse sensitivity, syntactic alterations, and evidence of a critical reflection as to the options for the application of reading traditions.

[25] See DJD XXII, 217–223.

48–50.[26] This manuscript, as a whole, is preserved in poor condition, yet line 2 of fragment 4 preserves a clear reference to Zech 4.14.

Zech 4.14 אלה <u>שני בני־היצהר</u> העמדים על־אדון כל־הארץ

These are *the two sons of oil* standing before the Lord of all the earth

4Q254 frag. 4   [עם °° להם °]

[אשר <u>שני בני היצהר</u>]

[שומרי מצות אל]

[ל כיא אנשי הי[ח]ד המ[ה]

] to them . . . a people [. . .]

] *two sons oil* who (that) [. . .]

] the ones who keep the commands of God [. . .]

] for the men of the *Ya*[*h*]*ad*, th[ey . . .]

According to Brooke, 'the allusion [in line 2] to the highly distinctive phraseology of Zech 4.14 is certain'.[27] In numerous articles, Craig A. Evans has expressed this same sentiment, advancing the hypothesis that 4Q254 4 preserves a 'messianic' interpretation of Zech 4.14 for the following reasons:

(1)   The interpretation of Zech 4.14 as 'messianic' coheres with some interpretations in rabbinic literature.[28]

(2)   Frag. 4 may be related to Gen 49.8–12 because frags. 2–3, 5–7 are potentially related to Gen 48.11–49.11, 15–26.[29]

---

[26]   Evans, 'Early Evidence', 568.

[27]   See DJD XXII, 224. See also Evans, 'Early Evidence', 571; Evans, 'Qumran's Messiah: How Important is He?' in *Religion in the Dead Sea Scrolls* (ed. J. J. Collins and R. A. Kugler; Cambridge: Eerdmans, 2000), 136 n. 15, 142 n. 30; Evans, 'The Messiah in the Old and New Testaments: A Response', in *The Messiah in the Old and New Testaments* (ed. S. Porter; Cambridge: Eerdmans, 2007), 234–237; George J. Brooke, '4Q254 Fragments 1 and 4, and 4Q254a: Some Preliminary Comments', in *Proceedings of the Eleventh World Congress of Jewish Studies* (ed. D. Assaf; Jerusalem: World Union of Jewish Studies, 1994), 186–188.

[28]   See *Sifra* §97; *Sav* §18; *'Abot R. Nat.* A 34.4; *Num. Rab.* 14.13 (cf. Num 7.84); 18.16 (cf. Num 16.1; *Lam. Rab.* 1.16 §51).

[29]   Evans, 'Early Evidence', 571.

(3) This interpretation coheres with diarchic messianic traditions in other Qumran manuscripts.[30]

(4) Larger diarchic/messianic overtones are present in Zech 3–6.[31]

Numerous issues remain with the suggestion that 4Q254 4 2 preserves a messianic interpretation of Zech 4.14, and I have recently attempted to nuance this assertion with a more extensive argument that I will not rehearse here.[32] The evidence provided by the manuscript supports numerous possible understandings of this instance of scriptural reuse, including the messianic option. However, I have suggested that the preserved wording of fragment 4 suggests that Zech 4.14 was deployed to describe the privileged status of the community, perhaps regarding their access to divine revelation. Regardless of the function of this material in 4Q254, the task presently at hand is to describe what the form of the material discloses about the scribe's techniques of reuse and habits of reading. This task is complicated by the poor preservation of the manuscript, making it difficult to determine whether the borrowed material was quoted or embedded as an allusion. For this reason, I refrain from discussing this reference in the text-critical language of expansion and omission, opting instead to describe the extant points of contact between traditions.

The remnant lexemes on 4Q254 4 1, 3–4 do not preserve material from Zech 4.14, but the words of line 3 are 'based on the oft repeated שמו את מצות יהוה אלהיכם of the Deuteronomic editor'.[33] Additionally, although the letters of line 4 presented in DJD XXII are reconstructed or doubtful, they seem to reference the 'men of the Yaḥad'.[34]

---

[30] See CD XII 23–31 1; XIV 19; XIX 10–11; 20 1; 1QS IX 11; 1QSa II 11–21; 1QSb III 22–5 29; 4Q174 1–3 i 10–13; 4QpIsa[a] 7–10 iii 27–29; 4Q285 V 1–16. This interpretation is also operative in some Karaite literature. See N. Wieder, 'The Doctrine of Two Messiahs among the Karaites', *JJS* 6 no 1 (1955): 14–25.

[31] See esp. Zech 6.12–13 and the parallel visions/oracles relation to Joshua (3.1–10) and Zerubbabel (4.6b–10a).

[32] Garrick V. Allen, 'The Reuse of Scripture in 4QCommentary on Genesis C (4Q254) and "Messianic Interpretation" in the Dead Sea Scrolls', *RevQ* 27/106 (2015): 303–317. See also Al Wolters, 'The Messiah in the Qumran Documents', in *The Messiah of the Old and New Testaments* (ed. S. Porter; Cambridge: Eerdmans, 2007), 82.

[33] Brooke, '4Q254', 187. E.g. Exod 20:6; Deut 4:2; 5:10; 6:17; 7:9; 8:6; 10:13; 28:9; 2 Kgs 17:19; CD III 2.

[34] E.g. 1QS V 1, 2, 3, 15; VIII 11, 16; IX 5, 7, 10, 19; 1Q31 I 1; 4Q165 IX 3; 4Q177 5–6 1; 4Q252 V 5; 4Q256 XVIII 2; 4Q258 VIII 3; 4Q259 II 7; 4Q286 XX 4; 4Q288 I 1; CD XX 32.

The material from lines 3–4 suggests that the reference to Zech 4.14 served a specific (but ultimately irrecoverable) literary purpose, connected to the community's self-conception. The focus does not seem to be on Zechariah, but on a broader issue. 4Q254 4 contains an allusion to Zech 4.14, a form of a well-known Deuteronomic trope, and a potential self-reference to the community that produced the document. This conglomeration of snippets preserved on a single fragment coheres with other such literary creations at Qumran and in other Second Temple Jewish literature; numerous examples of conflation and other forms of reworking antecedent scriptural traditions exist.[35]

It is interesting, however, that 4Q254 does not seem to retain the second clause of Zech 4.14 (העמדים על אדון כל הארץ). The last extant word of line 2 is אשר, a word not present in Zech 4.14. The deployment of אשר instead of העמדים (or the entire clause?) indicates that the two enigmatic figures from Zech 4.14 required further explication. The use of אשר levels the grammatical texture of the locution, clarifying the relationship between שני בני היצהר and the wording that once followed it, particularly if אשר introduced additional material that further explicated the identification of the שני בנ היצהר. Unfortunately, the material that followed אשר is lost. Nonetheless, the placement of אשר following שני בני היצהר suggests that the producer of the manuscript was compelled to explain the identity or actions of the 'sons of oil'.

The image of the two 'sons of oil' lent itself to further explanation in antiquity. The author of Revelation (11.4) also provided more material for understanding the identity of the שני בני היצהר by expanding the reference with additional material.[36] As Evans and Brooke have pointed out, various rabbinic works utilized this abstruse locution to identify numerous individuals: messiahs, teachers of the Torah, or the 'sons of God' from Gen 6.2.[37] While it is difficult to determine why material from Zech 4.14 was reused in 4Q254, it is clear that the producer of this work stands within

---

[35] This is particularly true for works like *Jubilees* (e.g. van Ruiten, *Abraham in the Book of Jubilees*, esp. 55–64), 11QTemple (see Moshe J. Bernstein and Shlomo A. Koyfman, 'The Interpretation of Biblical Law in the Dead Sea Scrolls: Forms and Methods', in *Biblical Interpretation at Qumran* [ed. M. Henze; Cambridge: Eerdmans, 2005], 61–87), and the 4QReworked Pentateuch manuscripts (see Zahn, *Rethinking*, esp. 25–74).

[36] See Section 4.4.5.

[37] See also Alexander, 'Early Exegesis', 60–71.

a long tradition of Second Temple and Tannaitic authors that expended exegetical energy on this ambiguous, but apparently tantalizing locution. In comparison with Rev 11.4, the analysis is incomplete (due to the fragmentary state of preservation), but suggestive. Because it is impossible to determine the function of אשר in 4Q254 4 2,[38] it can only be noted that both John and the producer of 4Q254 presented Zech 4.14 in forms that differed from the source tradition, suggesting that these authors determined that the שני בני היצהר required explication of some sort. Moreover, while it is difficult to intuit reading habits on the part of the producer of 4Q254 that might account for the form of the material in line 2, the scribe's presentation suggests that he and John shared the same intuition when it came to Zech 4.14: it required and/or lent itself amenably to further explication or clarification. The impetus to redeploy material from Zech 4.14 in 4Q254 and Rev 11.4 seems to have been instigated by similar modes of reading, in combination with the textual features of Zech 4.

5.4 Zechariah 1.8; 6.1–5 in OG and Targum Jonathan

The ancient translations of Zechariah provide an interesting parallel for John's reuse of Zech 1.8; 6.1–5 in Rev 6.1–8. This parallel is particularly poignant with reference to the colour lexemes of the horses that each translator extrapolated from their shared *Vorlage*.[39] This section focuses on a specific aspect of reuse that is common to the presentation of Zechariah's horse visions in OG, *TJ*, and the book of Revelation: translation and the equivalencies of colour lexemes. This example allows us to measure the level of interpretation preserved in a translator's choice of equivalents for an identical class of Hebrew lexemes.

---

[38] These options, to my mind, include: (1) smoothing/clarification of grammatical texture that does not necessarily require quantitative divergence from Zech 4.14; and (2) introduction of material foreign to Zech 4.14, thus neutralizing the co-textual relationships that the שני בני היצהר share with their native environment (cf. *b. Sanh.* 24a). See also the inclusion of a relative pronominal prefix in *TJ*: אלין תרין בני רברביא דַקימִין קדם רבון כל ארעא.

[39] The *Vorlage* of Zechariah[OG] is close to the proto-MT (see Section 3.2.3). Likewise, it is universally acknowledged that the *Vorlage* of Targum Jonathan is the proto-MT. See Robert P. Gordon, *Studies in the Targum to the Twelve Prophets: From Nahum to Malachi* (VTsup 51; Leiden: Brill, 1994), 61–73.

Table 5.1 *Horse colours in Zech 1.8 and 6.2–3*

Proto-MT	OG
Red (אדמים) 1.8; 6.2	Red (πυρροί) 1.8; 6.2
Vine-tendril coloured (שרקים) 1.8	Dappled (ψαροί)
Spotted strong (ברדים אמצים) 6.3	Spotted (ποικίλοι) 1.8; 6.3
White (לבנים) 1.8; 6.3	White (λευκοί) 1.8; 6.3
Black (שחרים) 6.2	Black (μέλανες) 6.2

5.4.1 OG Translator

The Greek translation of Zechariah's horse visions indicates the translator's (G) two primary goals. First, G attempts to coordinate both of Zechariah's horse visions in terms of content: the colour/ number of horses and their visionary setting (see Table 5.1).

In Zech 1.8, G inserted an additional horse to correspond to his translation of ברדים אמצים in 6.3. The obscure Hebrew word שרקים (1.8) does not have an equivalent in the OG translation, and the two adjectives that describe the fourth horse in the second vision (6.3) fill the slot of שרקים in 1.8. With the exception of the black horses (6.2), the colours from 1.8 and 6.2–3 are consistent in the OG translation. This translation coordinates the details of both visions and allows G to avoid difficult words from both horse/chariot visions: שרקים (1.8) and אמצים (6.3), neither of which have direct equivalents in the OG translation. This translation implicitly conflates the 'vine-tendril coloured' and the 'spotted strong' horses in both visions, suggesting that they describe the same animal.

Another aspect of Zech 6.1–5 retrojected to Zech 1.8 in the OG is the backdrop upon which the riders are introduced. The rare word ההדסים ('myrtles') from 1.8 is replaced with the phrase τῶν δύο ὀρέων τῶν κατασκίων ('two overshadowing mountains') in the OG. The Greek phrase is influenced by the introduction of the vision in Zech 6.1 (ἐκπορευόμενα ἐκ μέσου δύο ὀρέων, καὶ τὰ ὄρη ἦν ὄρη χαλκᾶ//יצאות מבין שני ההרים וההרים הרי נחשת). Like the colour of the horses, G imposed the visionary context of the second horse vision (Zech 6.1–5) on to the first (Zech 1.8).

G's second translation strategy is, whenever possible, to maintain the identical syntactic slots of his Hebrew source. For example, because two adjectives describe the fourth horse in Zech 6.3ᴾᴹ, two adjectives are required in the target language. This goal, when coupled with the desire to coordinate the details of the horse visions, ironically requires the insertion of two adjectives into 1.8, thus breaking a literal adherence to syntactic slotting in 1.8, while retaining it in 6.3. Likewise, the inclusion of the longer phrase from Zech 6.1 into the first vision (1.8) draws the visionary accounts together syntactically, but disrupts the syntax of Zech 1.8ᴾᴹ. G prioritizes the longer horse vision (Zech 6.1–5).

This translation approach illustrates G's dual desire to represent his *Vorlage* literally while explicating difficult words and creating coherence between logically similar visions. However, the level and type of literalness in translation is variable. G is less literal in terms of quantitative omission and addition of elements (especially in Zech 1.8) but this particular lack of literality is motivated by his high level of literalness to narrative consistency. Overall, G equated the fourth horse in Zech 6.3 (ברדים אמצים) with the third horse in 1.8 (שרקים) via narrative equation, thereby sacrificing semantic fidelity for narrative harmony.

5.4.2 Targum Jonathan Translator(s)

A similar, but subtler, coordinating strategy of reading is present in *TJ* Zechariah. The investigation in this case is complicated by the presence of an inner-Targum corruption in Zech 1.8.[40] The manuscript evidence offers six different options for the colour of our difficult third horse (שרקים). Robert P. Gordon suggests that it is from one original reading, קרוחין, that all other manuscript corruptions arise.[41] The corruptions appear, in part, because the Aramaic equivalent chosen to represent שרקים is as oblique as its *Vorlage*. For the sake of this discussion, I adopt Gordon's reconstruction (see Table 5.3).

Like G, the scribe(s) of *TJ* (T) altered the semantic value of the third horse (שרקים) in Zech 1.8. Additionally, T's translation of the colour of the fourth horse in Zech 6.3 illustrates semantic diversion as well, translating the phrase 'strong spotted' (ברדים אמצים) as 'ash spotted' (פציחין קטמנין). Based on the translation of the colour

---

[40] See R. P. Gordon, 'An Inner-Targum Corruption (Zech. I 8)', *VT* 25 (1975): 216–221.

[41] Ibid., 219.

Table 5.2 *Horse colours in Zech 1.8; 6.2 and Rev 6.1–8*

Proto-MT	TJ
Red (אדמים) 1.8; 6.2	Red (סומקין) 1.8; 6.2
Vine-tendril coloured (שרקים) 1.8	White-spotted (קרוחין)[1] 1.8
Spotted strong (ברדים אמצים) 6.3	Ash spotted (פציחין קטמנין) 6.3
White (לבנים) 1.8; 6.3	White (חורין)[2] 1.8; 6.3
Black (שחרים) 6.2	Black (אוכמין) 6.2

[1] This is an emendation of the corrupt word קחחין in the main text of Sperber.
[2] Spelled חיורין in 1.8.

of the third horse in Zech 1.8, it seems that T's primary goal was to
render the translation in a manner that coordinated the details of
the visions through semantic adjustment, while remaining faithful
to the syntactic slotting and lexical presentation of the source text.
Again, like the OG, שרקים and אמצים are the words that have been
coordinated in *TJ* (albeit less forcefully). Both Aramaic equivalents
refer to a light colour ('white'; 'grey') and קרוחין (Zech 1.8) is graphically similar to קטמנין in Zech 6.3 ('ash'). T coordinated the third
horse from Zech 1.8 with the fourth horse from Zech 6.3 by select-
ing translation equivalents that share a semantic sense and graphic
characteristics. The translation of אמצים to קטמנין further strengthens
the connection between the two horse visions. T translated אמצים
('strong') as a colour ('grey'), equating the third horse of the vision
in Zech 1.8 with the fourth horse in 6.3: both are light coloured and
dappled in *TJ*.

T's technique is much less intrusive than G. T does not diverge
quantitatively from proto-MT, but works within the syntactic confines
of the source tradition. This literal adherence to the syntax of Hebrew
Zechariah forced T to utilize different adjectives to describe the two
horses, although the words are semantically and graphically similar.
The alteration of שרקים and אמצים to semantically similar but different
Aramaic equivalents strongly suggests that the translator read these
visions in a coordinating fashion similar to G and, working within the
confines of his *Vorlage*, used the translational resources at his disposal
to present this coordination. Although T's *Übersetzungsweise* differed
from G's, both translators demonstrate similar habits of reading,
intuiting an implied correlation between the horses described as שרקים
(Zech 1.8) and those described as ברדים אמצים (Zech 6.3). T sacrificed

the semantic fidelity of individual translation equivalents for the narrative harmony of two logically related episodes.

5.4.3 The Translations and the Book of Revelation

As previously discussed (Section 3.2.3), the problem of the fourth horse in Zech 6.3 is also present in Rev 6.8. Like these translators, John read Zechariah's horse visions in a way that created a higher level of consistency of detail between visions. This allowed him to solve two semantic difficulties and narrative inconsistencies within the proto-MT, inconsistencies that were also targeted for explication by G and T: שׂרקים in Zech 1.8 and ברדים אמצים in Zech 6.3.

While John coordinated both horse visions, his approach contrasts that of G, who gave precedence to the second horse vision (Zech 6.1–5) by altering the first vision (Zech 1.8) to cohere with the setting and description of the charioteers in Zech 6.1–5. Contrastingly, John's representation of שׂרקים (Zech 1.8) with χλωρός (Rev 6.8) suggests that he gave precedence to the first horse vision (Zech 1.8), equating the first horse in Zech 1.8 with the fourth horse in Zech 6.3. John read the visions together, but his use of exegetical resources prioritized the first vision.

John's approach is both similar to and different from that of T, as both traditions drew a connection between both visions. However, John does not display T's semantic subtlety, demonstrated by his careful adjustment of the semantic sense of the horse colours to draw both of Zechariah's visions into closer relationship. Contrastingly, John's description of the four coloured horses suggests that he imposed his translation of the third horse in Zech 1.8 (שׂר"ק) upon the fourth horse in Zech 6.3.

Overall, the differences between the coordination of scenes in Revelation and the early versions of Zechariah are closely related to the confines of the literary form of their compositions. Because the textual data from the coordinated sections can actually be compared, the translations give a broader picture of a scribe's reading habits. John's form of reuse (allusion) is selective by definition.

5.5 1 Maccabees 14.9 and Zechariah 8.4–5

Although John did not reuse material from Zech 8, this example is profitable because it allows us to examine the reuse of Zechariah in a composition preserved only in Greek. This example does not provide a direct comparison for an example of John's reuse, but it does allow us to compare issues of textual form, techniques of reuse, and habits of reading.

Zech 8.4-5^PM	Zech 8.4-5^OG	1 Macc 14.9	Retroversion
כה אמר יהוה צבאות עד ישבו זקנים וזקנות ברחבות ירושלם ואיש משענתו בידו מרב ימים ורחבות העיר ימלאו ילדים וילדות משחקים ברחבתיה	τάδε λέγει κύριος παντοκράτωρ Ἔτι καθήσονται πρεσβύτεροι καὶ πρεσβύτεραι ἐν ταῖς πλατείαις Ιερουσαλημ, ἕκαστος τὴν ῥάβδον αὐτοῦ ἔχων ἐν τῇ χειρὶ αὐτοῦ ἀπὸ πλήθους ἡμερῶν,καὶ αἱ πλατεῖαι τῆς πόλεως πλησθήσονται παιδαρίων καὶ κορασίων παιζόντων ἐν ταῖς πλατείαις αὐτῆς	πρεσβύτεροι ἐν ταῖς πλατείαις ἐκάθηντο, πάντες περὶ ἀγαθῶν ἐκοινολογοῦντο, καὶ οἱ νεανίσκοι ἐνεδύσαντο δόξας καὶ⁴² στολὰς πολέμου	זקנים ברחבות ישבו כל לטבים יחדו⁴³ וילדים⁴⁴ לבשו כבוד ובגדי מלחמה⁴⁵

[42] F.-M. Abel, *Les Livres des Maccabées* (Paris: Lecoffre, 1949), 251 suggests that this final clause ought to be negated reading και ου στολας μολεμου. This negation is present in some Latin versions, Greek manuscript 311, and SyI.

[43] Forms of κοινολογέομαι occur in the OG/LXX only in 1 Macc 14.9, 15.28 (nominalized in 2 Macc 14.22), where no Hebrew equivalents are present, and in Ps 54(55).15^Sym where it serves as an equivalent of יחד.

[44] I have chosen ילדים even though other options have a higher quantitative witness in the OG/LXX tradition, specifically, נער and בחור. It is difficult to arbitrate between these options. The fact that the semantics of these three Hebrew lexemes are often represented by forms of νεανίσκος in Greek translation and the semantic range of the Greek equivalent makes this decision tentative. The choice that I have offered is the same lexeme in Zech 8.4, which creates the illusion of closer lexical overlap between the proto-MT and this retroversion. ילדים is one of multiple possible options; there is not enough evidence to commit strongly in any direction.

[45] The collocation στολὰς πολέμου is not witnessed anywhere in the OG/LXX tradition outside 1 Maccabees.

Thus says	Thus says the Lord	Old men sat in the
YHWH: 'Again,	Almighty: 'Again	open places and
old men and	old men and old	took counsel
old women	women will sit	regarding the
will sit in the	in the open	good things and
open places of	places of	the young boys
Jerusalem and a	Jerusalem, each	put on glory
man his staff in	having his staff	and [not] robes
his hand from	in his hand from	of war
many days	many days	
And the open	And the open	
places of the	places of the	
city will be	city will be	
full of young	filled with	
boys and girls	young boys and	
laughing in her	girls playing in	
open places'	her open places'	

The prosperous depiction of life in Judah under Simon (1 Macc 14.4–15), following his expulsion of gentile overlords (13.41–42), destruction of idols (13.47), cleansing of the temple (13.50), and celebration of victory (13.51–52), is partially crafted using language borrowed from Zech 8.4–5, particularly in 1 Macc 14.9.[46] The reused material alludes to agricultural blessing, peace and security, and a general sense of rest and prosperity.[47] The analysis of this pericope is encumbered, however, by the fact that the Greek text of 1 Maccabees is likely a translation of a Hebrew (or Aramaic) original.[48] The lost Hebrew *Vorlage* to 1 Maccabees both complicates and simplifies this analysis. What we are interested in presently is how the author of the Hebrew text of 1

---

[46] See also Zech 3.10; Mic 4.4; 1 Kgs 4.25 in Macc 14.12.

[47] 1 Macc 14.8 also retains similarities to Zech 8.12. However, both clauses in 1 Macc 14.8 are more closely related to Lev 26.4, 6 and Ezek 34.27 (see also Ezek 1.24; 31.4, 5, 15; 39.10). The author of Zech 8.12 also made use of these traditions in Leviticus and Ezekiel, but 1 Maccabees independently uses these same traditions. See Klaus-Dietrich Schunck, *1. Makkabäerbuch* (JSHZ 1.4; Gütersloh: Mohn, 1980), 357.

[48] See 1 Macc 3.37; 9.2 and 14.27, which are often pointed to as evidence that the Greek text is a translation of a Semitic original. For those who hold the view that 1 Maccabees was originally composed in a Semitic language, see Jonathan A. Goldstein, *1 Maccabees* (AB 41; Garden City: Doubleday, 1977), 14; Robert Doran, '1 Maccabees', in *The New Interpreter's Bible* (vol. 4; Nashville: Abingdon, 1996), 20; John J. Collins, *Daniel, First Maccabees, Second Maccabees with an Excursus on the Apocalyptic Genre* (OTM 16; Wilmington, DE: Michael Glazier, 1981), 149; Schunck, '1. Makkabäerbuch', 298; Abel, *Les Livres*, iv; J. C. Dancy, *A Commentary on 1*

Maccabees (M) reused Zechariah; this must be done through the lens of the Greek text and by careful retroversion of this Greek text into Hebrew. However, the search for the textual form of Zechariah that M referenced is relatively straightforward since the work was initially composed in Hebrew, suggesting a Hebrew *Vorlage*.[49] Whatever the textual situation, the extant Greek text of 1 Macc 14.9, 12 alludes to Zechariah.

5.5.1 *Vorlage* and Points of Connection

The *Vorlage* of Zech 8.4–5[OG] is a literal representation of Zech 8.4–5[PM50] and, additionally, most commentators note that 1 Macc 14.9 alludes to Zech 8.4–5.[51] Numerous linguistic connections exist between the two texts. First, the phrase זקנים ברחבות ישבו (1 Macc 14.9) corresponds closely to the Hebrew עד ישבו זקנים וזקנות ברחבות ירושלם of Zech 8.4.[52] Second, similar wording to ברחבות //πλατείαις (1 Macc 14.9) is located also in Zech 8.5 (ברחבתיה//πλατείαις αὐτῆς). ילדים//παιδαρίων (Zech 8.5) also corresponds to ילדים//νεανίσκοι (1 Macc 14.9). These instances of linguistic overlap suggest a direct connection between the traditions (see Table 5.3).

Maccabees (Oxford: Blackwell, 1954), 8–9; John R. Bartlett, *The First and Second Books of the Maccabees* (Cambridge: Cambridge University Press, 1973), 14–15; Bartlett, *1 Maccabees* (GAP; Sheffield: Sheffield Academic Press, 1998), 17–19; Paul Joüon, 'Quelques hebraïsmes de syntaxte dans le 1er livre des Maccabées', *Biblica* 3 (1922): 204–206; Charles C. Torrey, 'Three Troublesome Proper Names in First Maccabees', *JBL* 53 (1934): 31–33; Torrey, 'Schweizer's "Remains of a Hebrew Text of 1 Maccabees"', *JBL* 22 (1903): 51–59; Torrey, 'Maccabees (Books)', in *Encyclopaedia Biblica* (Vol. 3; ed. T. K. Cheyne and J. S. Black; London: Adam and Charles Black, 1902), 2857–2859. Josephus, Origen, and (possibly) Jerome knew the Hebrew original.

[49] M's use of non-scriptural source material (see 1 Macc 12.6–18) suggests that it is possible that M was multilingual. It is plausible that M could allude to Greek forms of scripture, representing this material in Hebrew, but this is ultimately unlikely.

[50] The close relationship between the OG and proto-MT of Zechariah, coupled with the fact that the Hebrew of 1 Macc 14.9 has been retroverted directly from the Greek text, necessitates that any observations made at the Hebrew level correspond to textual relationships of the Greek text as well.

[51] Schunck, '1 Makkabäerbuch', 357; Abel, *Les Livres*, 251; Dancy, *1 Maccabees*, 181; Collins, *Daniel*, 240; Bartlett, *Maccabees*, 190; Bartlett, *1 Maccabees*, 32; Doran, '1 Maccabees', 159; Goldstein, *1 Maccabees*, 491.

[52] The same is true for the Greek texts: πρεσβύτεροι ἐν ταῖς πλατείαις ἐκάθηντο (1 Macc 14.9)// Ἔτι καθήσονται πρεσβύτεροι καὶ πρεσβύτεραι ἐν ταῖς πλατείαις Ιερουσαλημ (Zech 8.4).

Table 5.3 *Linguistic connections between Zech 8.4–5 and 1 Macc 14.9*

Zech 8.4–5	1 Macc 14.9
//עד ישבו זקנים וזקנות ברחבות ירושלם Ἔτι καθήσονται πρεσβύτεροι καὶ πρεσβύτεραι ἐν ταῖς πλατείαις Ιερουσαλημ	//זקנים ברחבות ישבו כל לטבים יחדו πρεσβύτεροι ἐν ταῖς πλατείαις ἐκάθηντο, πάντες περὶ ἀγαθῶν ἐκοινολογοῦντο
//וילדים משחקים ברחבתיה παιδαρίων καὶ κορασίων παιζόντων ἐν ταῖς πλατείαις αὐτῆς	//וילדים לבשו כבוד ובגדי מלחמה, καὶ οἱ νεανίσκοι ἐνεδύσαντο δόξας καὶ στολὰς πολέμου.

Moreover, these traditions also share certain themes. Zech 8 is a collection of terse oracles relating to YHWH's future return to Zion (8.3), the resulting prosperity of the land and its inhabitants (8.4–6, 10–14), and the gathering of many people to Jerusalem (8.7–9, 20–23). Similarly, 1 Macc 14.4–15 is a eulogy for Simon the high priest that details his positive deeds and their results for Israel. During all the days of Simon the land had rest (14.4), the borders of the nation were expanded (14.5–6), foreign captives were gathered (14.7), the people lived in peace and agricultural abundance (14.8–14), and the glory and wealth of the sanctuary in Jerusalem was increased (14.15). The eulogy is presented as, at least partially, a fulfilment of the peace and prosperity expected in Zech 8. There is no explicit assertion that YHWH has returned to Jerusalem as Zech 8 expects, but the similar conditions of life in the land imply as much. 1 Macc 14 also references other antecedent traditions that adhere to the theme that, if the people and their leaders are faithful, prosperity and peace will follow.[53] Therefore, 1 Macc 14.9 almost certainly alludes to Zech 8.4–5.

Other features of 1 Macc 14.9 are traceable to a particular reading of Zech 8. First, the clause πάντες περὶ ἀγαθῶν ἐκοινολογοῦντο, and the idea that old men gather together to sit in council, is not foreign to Zech 8. Beyond the depiction of old men and women congregating in the plazas of Jerusalem (Zech 8.4), 8.16–17 enumerates a set of ethical demands. People will speak truth to their neighbours, judge peacefully within the city gates, and detest lies and evil designs. In particular, the command to judge peace within their gates suggests some sort of communal council.[54] While the

---

53 See Exod 34.24; Lev 26.4; Ezek 34.20–31; 1 Kgs 5.5; Mic 4.4; Zech 3.10.
54 See Ruth 4.1–12; Dan 2.49; Esth 2.19, 21; *Ahiqar* 9–10.

wording of this locution is not borrowed from Zechariah, its presence in 1 Macc 14.9 may be a response to the meaning of Zech 8.4, 16–17. Like John, M demonstrates an awareness of the co-texts of reused locutions.

An additional clause from 1 Macc 14.9 (οἱ νεανίσκοι ἐνεδύσαντο δόξας καὶ στολὰς πολέμου) shares some wording with Zech 8.5 (ילדים ~ παιδαρίων), but the remainder of the clause is logically awkward. The narrator repeatedly intimates that Simon's tenure as high priest brings about a situation in which there is no need for men of war (14.7–8, 10–13). If a negation is included in the final clause (καὶ οἱ νεανίσκοι ἐνεδύσαντο δόξας καὶ οὐ στολὰς πολέμου),[55] the locution restates Zech 8.5 in an inferential manner: the plazas of the city are filled with young men laughing (Zech 8.5), because they have no need to dress for war. This idea is expounded in 1 Macc 14. The land and its people are at peace as a result of Simon's reign. Ultimately, this reconstruction of interpretative events is uncertain; however, in light of the allusion to Zech 8.4 in the first clause of 1 Macc 14.9, it is suggestive.

5.5.2 Reading Habits

The cumulative force of M's allusion to Zech 8.4–5 suggests that M made a distinct effort to understand the oracle in Zech 8.4–5 within the context of his depiction of the rest, peace, and prosperity brought about by Simon's rule. In this way, the attention to the wording, thematic contours, and other features of Zech 8 in 1 Macc 14.9 presents, at least temporarily, a fulfilment of the prophetic thrust of Zech 8. The portions of Zechariah's oracles that relate to M's primary theme are represented in the text of 1 Macc 14.9. M was aware of the internal discourse and textual details of his source, and his process of reading created coherence from the oracle of Zech 8.4–5. This allusion illustrates M's sensitivity for the co-texts of a borrowed locution, a trait that he shared with John. Both illustrate an awareness of the minute textual details of their Hebrew sources, the inherent semantic, syntactic, and lexical ambiguity therein, and sensitivity for how material from these locutions ought to best be incorporated into their new compositions. Attention is given to the source tradition itself *and* its interpretation and presentation in the target composition.

---

55 Attested in some Latin witnesses, 311 SyI. See Abel, *Les Livres*, 251.

5.6 Zechariah 6.5 in Targum Jonathan

Although Zech 6.5 was not directly addressed in the preceding chapters, the handling of this text in *TJ* is of interest for the broader
concerns of this study. The 'four winds' tradition was widespread
in antiquity and located also in Rev 7.1, a text that may also allude
to Zech 6.5 among other traditions (see Appendix 1). Despite the
questionable use of Zech 6.5 in Rev 7.1, the following example provides an informative parallel to John's reuse of scriptural traditions
elsewhere. The breadth of the four winds tradition in Jewish and
Christian literature makes it difficult to determine that any specific
instance of this tradition can be retraced solely to Zech 6.5. In order
to determine an example of reuse, other linguistic material that ties
a reference to Zechariah must also be present. To ease the burden of
proof involved in suggesting that another tradition referenced Zech
6.5, I examine the preservation of this locution in *Targum Jonathan*.

Zech 6.5^{pM}	ויען המלאך ויאמר אלי אלה ארבע רחות השמים יוצאות מהתיצב על־ אדון כל־הארץ
	And the angel answered and he said to me, 'these are four winds of heaven sent out from presenting themselves before the lord of all the earth'
Zech 6.5^{TJ}	ואתיב מלאכא ואמר לי אלין ארבע מלכוון דאנין כארבע רוחי שמיא גלין מלאתעתדא קדם רבון כל ארעא
	The angel turned and said to me, 'these are four kingdoms which are like the four winds of heaven going forth after presenting themselves before the lord of all the earth'

The text of *TJ* in this locution, with the exception of the expansion
ארבע מלכוון דאנין כ, is a very literal translation of the proto-MT. The
quantity and order of lexemes are identical, as are the syntactic
and morphological structures of both locutions. The only difference between traditions is the expansion (ארבע מלכוון דאנין כ), which
itself does not break the syntactic integrity of the source. T maintained a very literal and readily identifiable relationship with his
Vorlage. The expansion is the natural point of departure for this
discussion.

First, the level of craft with which this expansion is introduced is
high. T utilized the exegetical resource *Wiederaufnahme* to incorporate the expansion: the same word that resumes the translation
introduces the insertion itself (ארבע). The syntactic slots of the

proto-MT are expanded, but not otherwise disturbed; thus the expansion is accomplished with surgical precision.[56]

Second, the expanded material is not original, but derives from another Aramaic tradition: Dan 7.2, 17.

Dan 7.2, 17

עָנֵה דָנִיֵּאל וְאָמַר חָזֵה הֲוֵית בְּחֶזְוִי עִם לֵילְיָא
<u>וַאֲרוּ אַרְבַּע רוּחֵי שְׁמַיָּא</u> מְגִיחָן לְיַמָּא רַבָּא
אִלֵּין חֵיוָתָא רַבְרְבָתָא דִּי <u>אַנִּין אַרְבַּע אַרְבְּעָה</u>
<u>מַלְכִין</u> יְקוּמוּן מִן אַרְעָא

Answering Daniel said, 'Seeing, I beheld in my vision I saw in the night and behold, the four winds of heaven breaking forth over the great water'

These four great beasts are four kings who will rise from the earth.

Zech 6.5[TJ]

וְאָתִיב מַלְאֲכָא וְאָמַר לִי אִלֵּין אַרְבַּע מַלְכְוָן
דְּאִנִּין כְּאַרְבַּע רוּחֵי שְׁמַיָּא גָּלִין מִלְאִתְעַתָּדָא
קֳדָם רִבּוֹן כֹּל אַרְעָא

The angel turned and said to me, 'these are four kingdoms which they are like the four winds of heaven going forth after presenting themselves before the lord of all the earth'

Based on the linguistic coherence between Zech 6.5ᴾᴹ (אלה ארבע רחות השמים) and Dan 7.2 (וארו ארבע רוחי שמיא), T coordinated these traditions by inserting material from Daniel that interprets the four beasts (Dan 7.16; פשר), which are introduced by the four winds in Dan 7.2. T spun a complicated web of tradition and interpreted the four winds of Zech 6.5 in light of the internal interpretation of the four beasts in Dan 7. This coordination of traditions has drastic implications for how the chariots and their horses (Zech 6.1–4) are understood. These implications are especially relevant to our discussion, as John uses the 'four winds' tradition to explain, in part, how the four horsemen (Rev 6.1–8) ought to be conceptualized. The expansion in T's translation suggests that he conflated the four winds in Dan 7.2 with the four beasts that immediately follow in v. 3. Thus, T coordinated the subjects in the following clauses:

---

[56] See Flesher and Chilton, *The Targums*, 40: 'when a Targum adds material into the translation, it integrates the addition smoothly so as not to interrupt its flow'.

Dan 7.2[57]   ואדו ארבע **רוחי** שמיא מגיחן ל<u>ימא רבא</u>

Dan 7.3   ו<u>ארבע **חיון** רברבן</u> סלקן מן <u>ימא</u>

The lexical sharing of each clause, as well as the graphic similarity of the bolded words led T to intuit that the winds and beasts refer to similar phenomena. The winds 'break forth' (גיח) from the 'great sea' in a similar manner to the 'great beasts arising' (סלק) from the sea. Additionally, the inclusion of the preposition כ before the resumption of the translation in *TJ* Zech 6.5 suggests that T's coordination is limited by analogy, and that he did not collapse the winds and beasts described in Daniel into a single entity. Yet, by referring to the interpretation of the four beasts,[58] T implicitly conflates the four winds and the four beasts in Dan 7.2–3. This move invites his readers to connect these traditions and illustrates T's broad sensitivity to the details of the breadth of the scriptural tradition. This type of traditional conflation is common, particularly in the Targumim,[59] and provides yet another example of a Zechariah/Daniel exegetical tradition.

The expansion in *TJ* Zech 6.5 also provides a clue as to how T conceptualized the activity of the horses and chariots in Zech 6.1–4. The coordination of the tradition of Zechariah's horsemen with the four malicious and threatening beasts suggests that T understood Zechariah's chariots to be a menacing cosmic force. In fact, the same locution that describes the location of the charioteers before YHWH (מהתיצב על אדון כל הארץ) is nearly identical to phraseology that describes the position of the בני אלהים and the שטן before YHWH in Job 1.6 (להתיצב על יהוה).

This reading of Zech 6.1–5 coheres with John's employment of the heavenly chariot tradition, whether or not his depiction is directly dependent on Zech 6.5. First, four angels restrain the four winds in Rev 7.1 so that the 144,000 can be sealed. G. B. Caird has suggested that the fact that these winds require restraint is an 'indication of their rebellious and demonic character',[60] which coheres loosely with the characteristics of the four beasts in Dan 7.2–17. The four winds

---

[57] Lexical parallels are underscored and coordinated pairs of different lexical value are highlighted. The coordinated subjects are in bold.
[58] 'These four great beasts are four kings that will arise from the earth' (Dan 7.17).
[59] See, for example, Tooman, 'Will of Their Master', 221–233.
[60] Caird, *The Revelation*, 94.

in Rev 7, much like the four winds in *TJ* Zech 6.5, are conceived of as instruments of harm or judgement upon the earth. If the four winds in Rev 7.1 refer internally back to the four horsemen in Rev 6.1–8,[61] this point becomes even sharper. Each horseman carries destructive implements or is granted authority to create havoc on the earth. The first horseman carries a bow and goes out to conquer (6.2); the second takes peace from the earth and carries a large sword (6.4); the third carries a scale, implying economic disruption (6.6); the final horseman is named Death, laying waste a fourth of the earth with sword, famine, and wild beasts (6.8). The depiction of the four horsemen in Revelation is an interpretation of material from Zech 6.1–5, wherein Zechariah's charioteers are understood as the instruments of judgement that come from the heavenly court. T makes an identical interpretation, but does so explicitly by appealing to the interpretation of the vision of the four beasts in Dan 7.17, seemingly because this vision is introduced with a similar locution found in Zech 6.5 (cf. Dan 7.2). Due to the nature of the translation process, T was constrained in the exegetical resources available to him to explicate his reading of Zech 6.1–5. The inclusion of a small textual expansion from an external tradition allowed T simultaneously to stay within the confines of his broader enterprise and to explicate his understanding of the pericope at hand. John, whose literary form does not come with the restrictions attached to that of T's, retains greater freedom to represent material from his source texts.

Overall, T's interpretation of Zech 6.1–5 and John's use of a 'four winds' tradition (Rev 7.1) are similar. T inserted an expansion, using *Wiederaufnahme*, comprising material from Dan 7, drawing an analogy between the four winds and charioteers in Zech 6.1–5 and the four winds and beasts in Dan 7.2–17. John interpreted Zechariah's charioteers to be instruments of judgement by ascribing to each of his riders acts of mayhem or by depicting them as carrying various weapons (Rev 6.1–8). Most importantly, the coordinating of the patrolling horses in Zechariah with the beasts from Daniel corresponds to John's habit of combining scriptural texts from diverse traditions based on their internal similarities, and his practice of using pre-existing Zechariah/Daniel exegetical traditions. Although the literary form and genre of the Targumim differs significantly from that of Revelation, the scribal experts responsible for the composition

---

[61] See Osborne, *Revelation*, 305; Beasley-Murray, *Revelation*, 142; Beale, *Revelation*, 406.

of these works drew from a common well of interpretative impulses based on their reading of scriptural texts and the network of connections that pervades the corpus.

5.7 Zechariah 12.3, 10 in Early Judaism[62]

The final section of this chapter briefly explores the reception of the texts from deutero-Zechariah reused in the book of Revelation. Zech 12.3 and 10, both texts that John accessed through existing exegetical traditions preserved also in the Gospels and other early Christian texts (see Sections 3.2.1 and 3.2.4), were only rarely referenced in early Judaism, perhaps owing to their association with the emerging Christian exegetical tradition associated with Jesus' messiahship (esp. 12.10). Nonetheless, there are some allusive examples of engagement with these texts apart from their rendering in their early versions. For example, a portion of the Enochic Book of Parables (ca. 40 BCE–50 CE), alludes to Zech 12.3 (*1 En.* 56.7).

Zech 12.3[OG/LXX]   καὶ ἔσται ἐν τῇ ἡμέρᾳ ἐκείνῃ θήσομαι τὴν Ιερουσαλημ λίθον καταπατούμενον πᾶσιν τοῖς ἔθνεσιν, πᾶς ὁ καταπατῶν αὐτὴν ἐμπαίζων ἐμπαίξεται, καὶ ἐπισυναχθήσονται [θ: πᾶς ὁ βαστάζων αὐτὸν σπαρασσόμενος ἀμυχθήσεται] ἐπ᾽ αὐτὴν πάντα τὰ ἔθνη τῆς γῆς

And it will be in that day, I will set Jerusalem a stone trampled by all the nations, all those who trample her will surely mock [θ: all those who bear it, shaking, will be scarred] and all the nations of the earth will be gathered to her

Zech 12.3[PM]   ‫והיה ביום־ההוא אשים את־ירושלם אבן מעמסה לכל־העמים כל־‬
‫עמסיה שרוט ישרטו ונאספו עליה כל גויי הארץ‬

And it will be in that day, I will set Jerusalem a stone of burden to all the peoples, all those who bear her will surely be lacerated and all the nations of the earth will be gathered to her

---

[62] It is difficult to discern an example of direct textual engagement with Zech 14.7–11 in early Judaism, as even the versions provide a fairly straightforward correspondence with the proto-MT. Parts of Zech 14.4–9 find potential parallels in *T. Naph.* 5.1 and *3 En.* 48A.10, but the connection is uncertain and *3 Enoch* likely dates from a period outside the scope of the current study.

Zech 12.3[TJ]   ויהי בעידנא ההוא אשוי ית ירושלם אבן תקלא לכל עממיא כל
אנסהא אתבזזא יתבזזון ויתכנשון עלה כל מלכי ארעא
And it will be in that time I will set Jerusalem stumbling
stone to all the people; all those who oppress her will
certainly be plundered and all the kings (var. peoples)
of the earth will be gathered to her

1 En. 56.6–7[63]   They will go out and trample the land of my chosen
ones, and the land of my chosen ones will be before
them like a threshing floor and a beaten path; [7] but
the city of my righteous ones will be a hindrance to
their horses. They will begin (to make) war among
themselves, and their right hand will be strong against
them, a man will not acknowledge his brother, nor a
son, his father or his mother

1 En. 56.5–57.3 comprises the end of the second parable that begins
in 45.1, and it narrates an eschatological conflict couched in the language of angelic warfare. *1 En.* 56.6–7a steps away from this simile
and spells out the reality of the conflict – it will take place on earth
and be recognizable in the form of a great battle. Armies will be so
massive that they will beat flat the ground when they move. The turning point in the description of destruction is found in v. 7a, where it is
pronounced that 'the city of my righteous ones will be a hindrance to
their horses'. This line is likely an allusion to Zech 12.3 where, in the
proto-MT and revising Greek stream, Jerusalem injures those who
mock or oppress her.[64] The reference to the trampling armies in *1 En.*
56.6 also corresponds to the description of Jerusalem as a stone trampled (λίθον καταπατούμενον; in contrast to the 'stone of burden' in the
proto-MT, אבן מעמסה) in the OG/LXX tradition. These observations
suggest either that the Enochic text reflects the semantic stream best
represented by a revising Greek tradition (like the exegetical combination in Rev 11.2), or that the composer of this tradition interpreted
the Hebrew text in a similar way to its early version. The rendering

---

[63] Translation taken from George W. E. Nickelsburg and James C. VanderKam,
1 Enoch 2: A Commentary on the Book of 1 Enoch Chapters 37–82 (Hermeneia;
Minneapolis: Fortress, 2012). This portion of *1 Enoch* is not preserved in Aramaic
or Greek, represented only a tertiary Ethiopic tradition. It is hazardous to undertake a close textual analysis similar to other examples based on the linguistic distance
between the present exemplars and the original Aramaic tradition. The comments on
1 Enoch here are more general.
[64] So also ibid., 212.

of Zech 12.3 in *Targum Jonathan* also preserves the tradition that Jerusalem is both a trampled stone (אבן תקלא) and an aggressor, a plunderer (בזז). Each tradition that engaged with Zech 12.3, with the exception of the OG, portrays Jerusalem threatened, signified by its description as a stone of trampling, and as an aggressor against enemies, either scarring (θ), lacerating (proto-MT), plundering (*TJ*), or hindering its opponents (*1 En.* 56.7). The prominent role of angels in *1 En.* 56.5–6 also corresponds to the defeat of Sennacherib's destruction before Jerusalem at the hand of an angel of YHWH (2 Kgs 19.35//2 Chr 32.20–23; Isa 37.36), echoing a tradition of Jerusalem's angelic protection.[65] It is within this broader tradition that material from Zech 12.3 was deployed.

The conception of this tradition in *1 Enoch* and the versions shows some marked similarities to the deployment of Zech 12.3 (in connection with Dan 8) in Rev 11.2. Both Revelation and these other Jewish tradition associate Zech 12.3 within a broader interpretative framework. In Revelation, the author adopted an exegetical tradition, encoded in a revising Greek form of Zechariah associated with the Greek tradition(s) of Dan 8.10–14, texts that were combined based on their shared language of trampling. In Rev 11.2, the holy city is trampled for forty-two months, a period corresponding to the prophetic ministries of the two witnesses and their exaltation and the judgement of the city (11.12–13). The allusion in *1 Enoch* is associated with other traditions of threats to Jerusalem and divine judgement, namely the Sennacherib/Hezekiah novella. The traditions that Zech 12.3 is associated with in both examples of reuse differ, but the greater similarity between the use of this verse in Revelation and *1 Enoch* is that Zech 12.3 in not read in isolation from the broader scriptural tradition in both instantiations. Moreover, the reuse of Zech 12.3 in Revelation corresponds to the pattern of the city's threat and aggression preserved in the versional witnesses (except OG) and *1 Enoch*: Jerusalem is trampled by the nations (it is 'given over'), but ultimately 7,000 of its inhabitants die as a result of a great earthquake, and the survivors worship the God of heaven (11.13). The way in which Zech 12.3 was reused in Revelation (and in the exegetical tradition that John adopted) corresponds to the trends of reuse in other early Jewish sources. The text is associated with

---

[65] See Christopher L. Mearns, 'Dating the Similitudes of Enoch', *NTS* 25 no 3 (1979): 360–369 (here 362).

other remote scriptural traditions and the city is portrayed as in danger, but ultimately lethal to the enemies of God's people.

Zech 12.10 was also rarely explicitly engaged with in Jewish tradition, apart from its popularity in early Christianity (see Section 3.2.1). Once again, the most interesting interpretative rendering of this verse (cf. Rev 1.7) is located in *Targum Jonathan*.[66]

Zech 12.10[TJ]	ואשפוך על בית דויד ועל יתבי ירושלם רוח חסד ורחמין ויבעון מן קדמי על דאטלטלו ויספדון שלוהי כמא דספדין על יחידא וימרון עלוהי כמא דממרן על בוכרא

And I will pour out on the house of David (var. Judah) and those who dwell in Jerusalem a spirit of mercy and compassion, and they will ask me about their going into exile; and they will mourn for him like one mourns for an only son and they will lament for him like one laments for a firstborn

Zech 12.10[PM]	ושפכתי על־בית דויד ועל יושב ירושלם רוח חן ותחנונים והביטו אלי את אשר־דקרו וספדו עליו כמספד על־היחיד והמר עליו כהמר על־הבכור

And I will pour out over (the) house of David and over the inhabitants of a Jerusalem a spirit of grace and supplication, and they will look to me, to the one they pierced, and they will wail over him like a lament over something of value and become bitter over him like the bitterness for a firstborn

On the one hand, the translation in *TJ* is faithful in terms of grammatical imitation, preserving some of the awkward construction from the proto-MT. For example, the Aramaic translation retains the structure of the grammatically awkward phrase (ויבעון מן קדמי על דאטלטלו והביטו אלי את אשר־דקרו). Additionally, the translation (like the OG) preserves the string of antecedent-less third-person masculine pronouns in the second part of the verse. On the other hand, however, the Aramaic translation makes some interpretative adjustments, avoiding the construction that includes verb 'to pierce' (דקר) or 'to dance' (רקד), if one follows the *V*OG. Instead

---

[66] The vision of the man from the sea and his stand-off with men from the four corners of the earth in the sixth vision of 4 Ezra (13.1–11) may also echo material from Zech 12.10 (along also with material from Dan 7.14), but the linguistic resemblance is minimal at best.

of 'they will look to me, the one they pierced' (והביטו אלי את אשר־דקרו), the translation transforms the locution into a reference to exile: 'they will ask me about their going into exile' (ויבעון מן קדמי על דאטלטלו).[67] The main feature of this translation to note is the change from 'looking' or 'beholding' in the proto-MT to 'asking' in *TJ*, in connection to the reference to exile. The Aramaic locution creates a more condensed utterance that includes a clear topic (exile) without varying quantitatively in terms of word count.

Interestingly, this alteration occurs at precisely the point where the author of Revelation adopts this text (intertwined with text from Dan 7.13), indicating that the Aramaic tradition's interpretation of this locution differed from Revelation's. This translation of דקר ('to pierce') with טלטל ('scatter; go into exile') is unique in *TJ*, and it ties YHWH's pouring out of mercy and compassion to the return from exile. The author of Revelation adopts the wording from the Greek revising tradition, connecting the piercing of the anonymous, but possibly divine figure in Zech 12.10 with Jesus. Both interpretations ultimately hang on the same word (דקר /ἐκκεντέω), but speak to the differing eschatologically oriented ideologies of the communities that produced these works. Interestingly, both the author of the Revelation and the anonymous scribes of *TJ* identified the same part of the locution as key to their method of comprehension, even though they diverged in how they handled this weighty lexeme. This phenomenon is also witnessed in the revision of דקר in the proto-Hexaplaric traditions and possibly the text represented by 8HevXIIgr.

An extensive Aramaic marginal note from Codex Reuchlinianus (early twelfth century CE), probably preserving a much older tradition, sheds further light on the interpretation of this text.

> And I shall cause to rest upon the house of David and upon the inhabitants of Jerusalem the spirit of prophecy and true prayer. And afterwards the Messiah son of Ephraim will go out to do battle with Gog, and Gog will slay him in front of the gate of Jerusalem. And they shall look to me and shall inquire of me (ויבעון) why the nations pierced (דקרו) the messiah son of Ephraim.

[67] Kevin J. Cathcart and Robert P. Gordon, *The Targum of the Minor Prophets* (The Aramaic Bible 15; Minneapolis: Liturgical Press, 1989), 218 render the clause 'and they shall entreat me because they were exiled'.

This note is revealing for two reasons. First, the last clause is interesting because it simultaneously preserves the semantic contours of the proto-MT ('look to me whom they pierced') and the dominant Aramaic tradition ('they shall inquire of me').

Both of these variants are preserved here in a single utterance, illustrating that the creator of this tradition was interested both in the preservation of the meaning of the proto-MT and in the interpretative rendering of the tradition in his received tradition. Some of John's scriptural references preserve a similar tendency to preserve (at least partially) the wording of a source tradition, and to alter the wording of this tradition in a way that implicitly demonstrates his interpretation of the source text. His use of Zech 4 (cf. Rev 5.6b and 11.4) best illustrates this impulse. The mechanics of this impulse differ between *TJ* and Revelation due to the form of the works, one being primarily a translation and the other a literary work, but similar text-exegetical practices pervade both traditions, namely a desire to preserve (and perhaps exploit) the various contours that a passage offers in connection with the received interpretative traditions of a given locution.

Second, the reference to Gog represents another intertwining of Ezekiel and Zechariah traditions preserved in *TJ* Zechariah, most notably Ezek 38–39 (cf. also Rev 19.17–20; 20.7–10).[68] Although Gog is here depicted as triumphant over an anointed figure ('messiah bar Ephraim'), a picture that is perhaps influenced by the failure of the Bar Kochba revolt[69] and quite distinct from his utter defeat in Ezekiel, this marginal note draws upon scriptural traditions pertaining to enemies of the faithful community. Similarly, the author of Revelation adopted an exegetical tradition that read Zech 12.10 in light of a different prophetic tradition (Dan 8.10–14). Although these traditions connect Zech 12.10 with different prophetic texts, they share a common habit of reading insofar as the contextual scope of Zechariah is extended beyond the work to the broader prophetic corpus. A potential solution for understanding a grammatically and conceptually complicated locution like Zech 12.10 was found in reading the text within the context of its related scriptural works. Although different communities (certain early Christian communities and Babylonian Judaism) adopted different exegetical traditions,

---

[68] For more on the relationship between Gog/Magog traditions and Revelation, see Bøe, *Gog*.

[69] So ibid., 197.

both used Zech 12.10 in their own messianic discourses in connection with other scriptural texts.

Although the interpretation of Zech 12.10 that John adopted differs from the related traditions in *TJ*, the mechanics of conflation and boundaries of reading preserved in both traditions are similar. Comparable exegetical strategies often arrive at differing interpretations. One need look no further than modern historical-critical interpretation. The correspondences between the use of Zech 12.10 in Revelation and the Aramaic tradition strongly suggests that John's use of scripture is part of a widely attested ambient mode of composition.

5.8 The Use of Zechariah in Early Judaism

The preceding discussion of the reuse of Zechariah in early Jewish traditions highlights the similarities on a number of issues between these authors and John, the author of Revelation. First, in each of these examples, the Hebrew textual form of Zechariah is the target of exegetical attention. For texts originally composed in Hebrew (2 Chronicles, 4Q254, 1 Maccabees) this fact is unremarkable; particularly for 2 Chronicles, which was likely composed before Zechariah[OG] was produced. In the case of 1 Maccabees, the extant Greek text refrained from highlighting its *Vorlage*'s use of Zech 8.4–5 by creating a heightened lexical coherence with Zechariah[OG]. For *1 Enoch,* which is only fully preserved in a translation of a translation, the question of textual form is difficult to answer. Likewise, as expected, the scribes responsible for *TJ* and the OG utilized Hebrew Zechariah. The similarity in choice of *Vorlage* was necessitated by the lack of a clear alternative Hebrew form. If other texts from the NT or other Hellenistic Jewish works were explored here, the evidence would probably be quite different. Unfortunately, these works rarely reused identifiable material from Zechariah.[70] None of the authors who composed the texts analysed in this chapter had a form of Greek

---

[70] Zech 9.9, however, is cited in each of the Synoptic Gospels in a form that most scholars suggest corresponds to OG Zechariah, at least in Matthew. See D. Instone-Brewer, 'The Two Asses of Zechariah 9:9 in Matthew 21', *TB* (2003): 87–98; Menken, *Matthew's Bible*, 106–113. In contrast, Robert Gundry, *The Use of the Old Testament in St. Matthew's Gospel. With Special Reference to the Messianic Hope* (Leiden: Brill, 1967), 198 suggests that Matthew used a Hebrew form of Zech 9.9.

Zechariah at their disposal,[71] although this certainly does not rule out the influence of Zechariah's Greek versions in this period or suggest that the Hebrew text was somehow considered exceptional over and against other languages. The predominance of a Hebrew form of Zechariah is likely due to chance, based on the sample texts selected.

Second, the authors of these texts share in common with John certain techniques of reuse. The techniques preserved in the works that directly quote or translate Zechariah are best described in text-critical language. In these examples, the authors demonstrate the following techniques of reuse:

- *Addition of supplementary description*: the addition of material beyond that witnessed explicitly in the source text. Zech 1.8^{OG}; 2 Chr 16.9.
- *Addition of material from other discernible traditional sources*: conflation of multiple textual sources inherently leads to the addition of each of the antecedent traditions that have been combined in the target composition. *TJ* Zech 6.5; 12.10.
- *Omission of material due to harmonization*: the harmonization of two literary accounts necessitates the omission of material from one or both accounts in question. Zech 1.8$^{OG.}$
- *Selective omission of linguistic material from borrowed source texts*: these omissions consist of details or other small-scale linguistic information not presented in the target text vis-à-vis its source. 2 Chr 16.9.
- *Discourse sensitivity to the narrative of the target text*: stylistic changes to a source text that allow borrowed material to be cohesively incorporated in the new composition. Zech 1.8^{OG}; 2 Chr 16.9.
- *Syntactical alteration*: alterations to the syntax of a reused locution in which the underlying syntactic pattern is still discernible in the target text. 2 Chr 16.9.

---

[71] Brooke, *Dead Sea Scrolls and the New Testament*, 92–93 notes that 'some Qumran and New Testament quotations of scriptural passages clearly represent the same text form, even though the former is in Hebrew and the latter in Greek' (see Amos 9.11 in 4Q174, CD VII 16, Acts 15.16). It should not be surprising that John and other Jewish authors using Zechariah might have both used Hebrew forms.

These techniques provide obvious parallels to similar modes of reuse witnessed in John's quotations of Zech 4 (see Sections 4.4.2 and 4.4.5). John and those situated within his textual culture utilized similar sets of resources to explicitly reference locutions from antecedent material. Evidently, these authors, including John, privileged the (implied) meaning of Zechariah over its exact wording. The wording of quotations and translations was malleable inasmuch as the new wording endorsed or enhanced the meaning of the original. John's techniques of reuse draw him into a close relationship with other scribal text producers located in his milieu.

Additionally, John's mode of crafting allusions is similar to the implicit reuses of Zechariah located in 1 Macc 14.9 and 4Q254 4. Both of these locutions maintain concrete, small-scale (in terms of quantity) lexical connections to particular texts in Zechariah. Orbiting around these anchoring lexical correspondences are other features that reflect a particular reading of certain features of the source text. The presentation of syntactic structures and the choice of thematic motifs, for example, often reflect inferences of the meaning of the source text.

Moreover, the presentation of reused material seems to be motivated by a desire to explicate the meaning that the various authors intuited to be latent in Zechariah (2 Chr 16.9; 1 Macc 14.9; 4Q254[?]; *TJ* Zech 6.5; 12.10; *1 En.* 56.6–7), suggesting a broad similarity in habits of reading. This impetus to explicate suggests that ancient authors assumed that Zechariah provided a coherent narrative, although some felt the need to clarify its surface features and grammatical form. The awareness of grammatical issues is especially prevalent in 2 Chr 16.9, where C adjusted the syntax and morphological value of Zech 4.10b to create a greater level of grammatical cohesion.

Many of these authors also illustrate an awareness of the broader co-textual environment of Zechariah (2 Chr 16.9 [cf. Zech 3, 5]; OG and *TJ* Zech 1.8; 6.1–5) and an awareness of similar traditions external to Zechariah (*TJ* Zech 6.5; 12.10; 1 Macc 14). In this way, these authors conflated similar traditions in a way that is commensurate with examples witnessed throughout the Apocalypse. All of this clearly demonstrates that Zechariah was read and reused in conversation with the larger scriptural tradition.

This brief exploration of the use of Zechariah in early Judaism suggests that John's reading and reuse of scripture is situated within the broader ambient textual culture of this period. This analysis also confirms findings from previous chapters. The same techniques that I previously identified are readily found in other works that make use of or translate scriptural traditions. Even in the narrow case of Zechariah, the same texts, techniques of reuse, modes of allusion, and reading habits are operative across diverse examples of Jewish literature. John's detailed attention to his *Vorlagen* and the scriptural tradition is paralleled in exegetical encounters preserved in multiple literatures of the same period. This analysis highlights the similarities of scriptural reuse in the NT and early Judaism more generally. John is a scribe insofar as his practices of scriptural reading and reuse are paralleled in numerous other Jewish works that handle Zechariah.

6

'THESE WORDS ARE FAITHFUL AND TRUE' (REV 22.6)

6.1 Summary

The book of Revelation is the product of a multifaceted and complex literary process. Its author, although an exegetically erudite reader of Jewish scripture, did not leave any explicit traces or statements regarding the principles or suppositions that underlie the construction of this work and his engagement with scriptural traditions. This unacknowledged interaction with Jewish scripture is the norm for scribal tradents and text producers in this period. A foundational facet of the construction of the Apocalypse is the reuse of antecedent scriptural traditions. John composed his work in a textual culture in which multiple forms of Jewish scriptural works circulated concurrently, a culture that privileged scriptural reuse as a dominant mode of literary composition, and a culture that he shared with other early Jewish and Christian scribes and literati.

I have attempted to highlight the textual complexity of the first centuries BCE and CE and gesture towards the importance of textual culture as a matrix for understanding John's reuse of scripture. Textual pluriformity – witnessed in the physical manuscript evidence and in reused material embedded in the quotations and allusions to Jewish scripture in other works – is a pre-eminent aspect of Jewish textual culture with which NT scholarship has not yet fully engaged. While this characteristic of early Jewish textual culture has been a dominant feature of scholarship related to the Dead Sea Scrolls, HB, and the OG/LXX in the past fifty years, NT scholarship is only beginning to explore the complexities involved in analysing the NT as a product of early Jewish textual culture, as well as the consequences of this investigation for understandings of the social make-up of early Christian communities and their theologies. Grappling with the reality of a pluriform scriptural tradition should receive a greater share of critical attention in NT studies. This approach has the potential to shed new light on old problems associated with early Christian interpretations of scripture. It is now clear that the NT cannot be studied in isolation from parallel disciplines. Textual criticism, early reception history, material philology, inner-biblical exegesis, Septuagint studies, and the scrolls (among other disciplines) are inextricable and foundationally valuable to the study of early Christian writings. Despite lamentations that the quantity of secondary literature in NT studies has become insurmountable (and it has), there remains much fertile ground to till in the ongoing study of the earliest Christian writings.

Relating to John specifically, he had access to numerous forms of Zechariah, and the evidence suggests that he drew material from Hebrew Zechariah traditions *and* exegetical traditions linked to Zechariah encoded in Greek. Whether John's use of particular forms was a process of selection or an accident of access, his use of Zechariah traditions is indebted to the pluriform textual culture that defined textual transmission as well as composition in this period.

In terms of techniques of reuse, John employed processes of alteration and created textual connections via allusion in ways commensurate with those employed by other ancient authors or scribes that reused Zechariah, utilizing techniques of reuse operative in his broader textual culture. Moreover, his textual changes and examples of reuse are almost always explicable by some internal exegetical logic based on the textual triggers (graphic, thematic, semantic, grammatical, lexical, etc.) of his source texts, but almost always in connection with the substance of the broader scriptural tradition. The reuse of Zechariah in Revelation is built on the foundation of various text-exegetical procedures, interacting with the minute textual features of particular forms of Zechariah and the perceived boundaries of the author's scriptural tradition. Contexts near and remote to the reused locution influenced John's presentation of material. These characteristics of John's textual engagement are the result of his participation in an ambient mode of early Jewish literary composition.

John's presentation of his source material was motivated by these habits of reading scriptural works. His reuse consistently illustrates care for his conception of the meaning of the textual details and internal discourse of his scriptural sources. Grammatical opacity, discourse incoherence, and ambiguous lexical items that preserved in his source traditions motivated textual change. Semantic considerations trumped text-critical concerns for precise fidelity to source traditions. When using Hebrew traditions, John tended to employ reading traditions that solve these issues, traditions that differ in places from the Tiberian tradition preserved in the MT. This desire to read source traditions coherently and holistically is shared, by and large, by the parallel examples we examined, but the logic of these readings is not always clear or at least clearly reconstructible based on the extant evidence.

6.2 Findings

This discussion culminates in the following findings pertaining to the reuse of scripture in Revelation in the context of early Jewish textual culture, many of which I have hinted at throughout the preceding discussion.

1. *The book of Revelation was composed in a pluriform textual culture, both in terms of the substance of scriptural works and the mediums in which they were available.* John made copious references to antecedent literature within a textual culture in which multiple forms of Jewish scriptural works (in both Hebrew and Greek) circulated concurrently, and which he shared with numerous other antique Jewish and Christian text producers. Within this culture, text producers maintained access to scriptural traditions via a pluriformity of mediums (both oral/aural and textual), and it is the combination of these mediums that shaped scriptural encounters and the presentation of these scriptural encounters in works like Revelation. Some of the preceding examples (e.g. Rev 6.1–8 and John's presentation of Zech 4 [Rev 5.6; 11.4]) intimate that John had access to a Hebrew form of Zechariah through an immediate encounter with a textual artefact. The detail of the engagements, focusing at times on particular lexemes and their relationship to other textual segments in terms of reading tradition, indicates that John had the ability and means to access manuscripts of Zechariah. And likely this manuscript contained the whole of Zechariah since his reuse of Zech 4, for instance, relies on his ability to access or recall the remainder of the chapter in detail. Also, John would have needed to have recourse to both of Zechariah's disparately located horse visions. It would make little sense to excerpt these lengthy texts on a wax tablet or some other medium, especially since Zechariah traditions play a rather limited role in Revelation compared to omnipresent traditions from Isaiah, Daniel, Ezekiel, and the Psalter among others.

Even though an immediate textual encounter lies behind these examples, it does not follow that aural experience or memory played no role in John's conceptions of these texts. Past aural experiences of Hebrew (and potentially Greek or Aramaic) Zechariah and conversations regarding this text shaped his conceptions of it at the time of inscription. John's encounters with textual artefacts stimulated the cultivation of memory that offered the space to reimagine Zechariah's vision in a new literary context. His skill with Jewish scriptural texts, as well as his participation in early Christian literary circles, all but guarantees that interpretative communities helped to shape his perceptions of Zechariah. In this way, John's scriptural reuse is both scribal (insofar as it related to the composition of a work that relied heavily on the idiom of Jewish scripture) and communal (insofar as he was aware of exegetical traditions preserved in both Jewish and Christian sources). This aspect of scriptural reuse in Revelation is often ignored, but one would do well to keep the communal aspect of exegetical appropriation in mind. John's textual culture was pluriform because multiple forms of scriptural works circulated concurrently in a single milieu, and because these forms were accessible through a number of mediums, both physical and oral/aural.

The communal aspect of John's scriptural reuse applies also to his recourse to exegetical traditions of Zechariah (combined with material from Daniel) that circulated in Greek in early Christianity. John's use of Zech 12 in Rev 1.7, in light of the use of similar traditions in many early Christian works (cf. Matt 24.30; John 19.37; *Barn.* 7.9; *Apoc. Pet.* 6; Justin, *Dia.* 14.8; *1 Apol.* 52.12), demonstrates that John was also able to access scriptural traditions through the medium of Greek exegetical traditions. Again, John's access to this tradition was likely mediated through both aural and textual encounters. The wide currency of this particular tradition implies that it was inscribed at an early stage, using Matthew's Gospel as a *terminus ante quem*. We can assume that this utterance enjoyed a long oral tradition as well, and it seems counterproductive to polarize these two options. Instead, acknowledging that his textual culture was predominantly oral but also adept at creating and transmitting textual artefacts, it seems likely that John's aural encounters with this tradition and his potential textual encounters complemented one another, leading ultimately to his presentation in Rev 1.7.

So what is one to make of the complexity of John's scriptural encounter in the context of the mechanics of text production? Should we envision him working like a modern text critic, his desk covered with scrolls and other documents, sifting readings and shifting between manuscripts? Or should we imagine a lonely monastic-esque cave dweller sitting alone with his thoughts, composing as he feels led and using material as memory allows? Neither the hypertextualized image of John among a mound of papyri and parchment, nor the persona of the lonely aesthetic adequately explains the social reality of John's detailed scriptural engagement. Although the lack of historical information does not allow for the construction of a detailed sociohistorical reconstruction of John's access and handling of scriptural works, the evidence internal to John's reuse of Zechariah suggests a spectrum of aural/textual encounters. Ross Wagner's summary of the social reality of Paul's scriptural encounters is not too distant from how we ought to understand John's practices:

> Rather than posing the question in terms of mutually exclusive alternatives – *either* memorization *or* use of written texts and anthologies of excerpts – we should imagine Paul interacting with scripture in a *variety* of modes, including meditation on memorized passages, hearing of spoken texts, personal reading of written texts, and collection of and reflection on excerpts from larger texts. Such a multifaceted approach, though it may require a less 'rigorous' methodology in the study of Paul's appropriations of scripture, is absolutely necessary to capture the complex reality of books and readers in the first century.[1]

Even though John did not function as a text critic, collecting and reappropriating various lexemes selected from multiple possible manuscripts and textual forms, it is not implausible that he had access to textual artefacts at different points in the process of composition. If John was familiar with the communities to which the Apocalypse is addressed, it is possible that he may have accessed artefacts in these cities, either in contacts with synagogues, with private libraries associated with members of the Christian community, or through the good graces of patrons.[2] It is not that he always must have had

---

[1] Wagner, *Heralds*, 25–26.
[2] On potential locations of access to textual artefacts, see Hezser, *Literacy*, 145–168.

immediate recourse to a cumbersome library, as Penley suggests those who argue for textual encounters must necessarily construct;[3] occasional access to written artefacts is not diametrically opposed to oral transmission. Penley also omits consideration of patronage as a powerful social tool that enabled the production of literary works and provided the tools needed to create such a work.[4]

John's possibly sporadic access to textual artefacts indicates that his memory of the shape of scriptural texts played a significant role in his reuse of scripture. The combination of various mediums – inscribed, remembered, and aurally experienced – formed a network of mediums that contributed to and constituted John's scriptural experiences. One cannot be prioritized against another, since textual artefacts aided the refinement of one's memory and controlled the substance of aural encounters. Additionally, memory remains an unavoidable feature of reading generally and of allusion and quotation in particular. If John read a manuscript of Zechariah at some point in the process of composing Revelation – a scenario that I find quite plausible – his turning from this artefact to a writing surface requires the faculties of memory. Artefact and memory are inextricable.

In all this, I still find the assumption that John made exclusive use of excerpta collections or *testimonia* unconvincing, the example of Rev 1.7 notwithstanding. The sheer quantity of allusions in Revelation seems to militate against this, making an excerpta collection that included all the antecedent traditions that John engaged with more cumbersome than working directly from scrolls. The cumbrousness of such an object would surely mitigate its expediency. Although, this is not to say that he never saw such an artefact.

---

[3] Penley, *Common Tradition*, 44–45.

[4] Kim Haines-Eitzen, *Guardians of Letters: Literacy, Power, and the Transmitters of Early Christian Literature* (Oxford: Oxford University Press, 2000), 5 notes that 'throughout antiquity, poets, novelists, and commentators relied upon the system of patronage for financial support; patrons provided writers the freedom to devote themselves to their craft'. Although the book of Revelation does not explicitly name a patron, it is not inconceivable that patronage played a role in the composition of Revelation and potentially provided its author with access to textual artefacts – textual production and transmission were closely related to social networks in antiquity. See Harry Y. Gamble, 'The Book Trade in the Roman Empire', in *The Early Text of the New Testament* (ed. C. H. Hill and M. J. Kruger; Oxford: Oxford University Press, 2012), 23–36 (esp. 30–33). There is much more to be said on the question of the Apocalypse and patronage, but this simple statement will suffice in this context.

The social realities of John's scriptural reuse are also strongly connected to his linguistic capabilities. Charles's dictum that John thinks in Hebrew but writes in Greek is valid insofar as it seems that the author was a native of Palestine and only became familiar with Greek secondarily. The multilingual capabilities of the author allowed him to access Zechariah traditions in both Hebrew and Greek. Linguistic ability, access to texts, memory, community interpretation, and oral transmission each contributed to shape the way that the author of Revelation interacted with Jewish scripture, thus significantly influencing the composition of the Apocalypse.

2. *John is aware of and references Hebrew textual traditions.* To highlight this point further, when John used Hebrew from of Zechariah, his translation choices often differ from those preserved in the OG/LXX, but they retain a general semblance. It is no longer sufficient in scholarly discourse to simply assert that John 'used the LXX' or 'proto-Theodotion'. This observation also points to the fact that quotations and allusions in the book of Revelation (and the NT generally) are independent witnesses to the shape of the text of Jewish scripture (usually in Greek, but also in Hebrew). These examples of reuse are valuable and underdeveloped text-critical resources.

3. *The manner in which John reused scripture is comparable to procedures preserved in Second Temple literature.* The textual differences between source text and target text, and the points of connection to antecedent traditions constructed by allusions provide the necessary evidence for this process. If John's references to scripture are examined in light of contemporary practices of reuse in Second Temple Jewish works, his allusive tendencies become demythologized. Teeter notes that the form of textual changes to and the reuse of scribal laws in the Second Temple period were implicit: 'one of the most salient features of the interpretive mode represented by all of these variants is its non-explicit quality.'[5] Instances of reuse are rarely explicitly signalled.

When examined within the literary context of the NT the book of Revelation is an anomaly. John does not make use of explicit introductory formulae and there is little effort to present source

---

[5] Teeter, *Scribal Laws*, 175.

material verbatim. This is a disorienting practice when considered in comparison to the explicit quotations and more mimetic uses of scripture found in the Gospels or portions of NT epistolary literature. However, when compared to the broader body of Second Temple literature, it is the Gospels and NT epistles that do not cohere with patterns of reuse operative in this milieu. Allusions and implicit examples of reuse are certainly still present in these works, but not in the ubiquitous quantity witnessed in Revelation. John's reuse of scripture is commensurate not only with other NT works, but to a higher degree with the literature of the Second Temple period. This holds true for techniques of reuse and the identification of textual features of source texts that require explication. Revelation is probably one of the latest written piece that was eventually included in the collection of writings known as the NT, but the literary forms of other NT works did not exert much influence on the form of Revelation or its author's practices of reuse.

The textual differences present in John's allusions betray important information about him and his reading of scriptural traditions. Just because an allusion does not reproduce source traditions verbatim and does not explicitly state its source does not mean that it is not valuable to the analysis of how ancient authors read and reused their scriptural texts; it just means that the work of recovering ancient reading habits becomes more arduous and less certain. The allusive networks that John builds, drawing related lexical, thematic, and structural threads from across Jewish scripture, implies literary intent, intent that is likewise found ubiquitously in the Jewish literature of the late Second Temple period.

4. *John made textual changes to Zechariah based on a particular conceptualization of its meaning, using a system of text-exegetical resources.* Strands of NT scholarship have a tendency to pivot towards theological motivations as a means to explain textual divergence between source text and target text.[6] This move is not entirely misguided. NT writers were concerned to pass on their theological beliefs and convictions, and John's theology directly impacts the world that he creates within the Apocalypse, a world

---

[6] See e.g. Ellis, 'Biblical Interpretation', 710–725; Beale, *Revelation*, 86–99.

where the dominating world power is personified evil, and where disassociation from the beast in the world of the text creates drastic real-world consequences for the work's hearers. Yet, this concern does not universally explain the textual differences between certain forms of Jewish scripture and references in the NT. John's alteration of his source traditions, for instance, created various points of contact with antecedent traditions. These alterations explicate John's perception of their latent meaning. This meaning may be theological or support his theological perspective, but the changes are not firstly motivated by theology. Instead, John's scriptural understanding informs the world that the Apocalypse embodies. The explication of ambiguous source traditions naturally leads to the author's given theological convictions, but the procedures that underlie his instances of reuse are immanently textual. Teeter makes a similar observation regarding changes in legal texts in the Second Temple period, noting that

> the evidence points unambiguously toward the reality of *a textual approach based upon a system of exegetical resources or interpretive norms* – which is to say, toward the operation of an accepted *exegetical method* of sorts within textual transmission.[7]

Claiming that the form and presentation of John's reuse of scripture is motivated by theological concerns does not by itself validate the assumption that all textual differences are disingenuous or uncontrolled. John's arrangement of the wording of his quotations and allusions is authorized by his understanding of the implied deep structure of the reused segment, relating it to its near co-texts and remotely located segments in the broader scriptural tradition and in the broader reservoir of pre-existent exegetical traditions. The form of John's reuse is underwritten by the implied meaning of a locution in conversation with analogous scriptural segments, analogies that were drawn based on syntactic, lexical, thematic, and/or structural similarities. One cannot pivot towards a theological explanation for textual change without first exhausting the multilayered possibilities for textual change offered by contemporary textual culture, and without understanding that theology and textual transmission are integrally linked. The textual changes and points of connection to antecedent texts witnessed in John's

---

[7] Teeter, *Scribal Laws*, 178 (emphasis original).

reuse of Zechariah almost always clarify ambiguities in the source text (interpretation), even if we cannot decide with certainty that these interpretative decisions belong to John himself. This goes to show that exegetical engagement with Jewish scripture stood at the centre of John's textual culture, and was a central feature of literary composition. This process of interpretation is not distinct from the author's theological understanding, but, instead, reading and interpretation are the underlying building blocks of theological perception.

5. *Communication strategies and the stratified 'audience' of the Apocalypse.* Scholarship is divided on the social and educational disposition of early Christian communities in the Greek-speaking world. On the one hand, Christopher Stanley, continuing his 'audience-centred' approach to Pauline literature, has argued that Paul's largely gentile original audiences were unfamiliar with the details of Jewish scripture, and thus oblivious to the detailed exegetical procedures that stand behind Paul's explicit quotations, although a few scripturally literature experts would have been resident in these communities along with a small number of moderately educated hearers.[8] On the other hand, Jan Fekkes has described the seven churches in western Asia Minor as 'biblically oriented conventicles' in which 'all that is needed are a few key words of an OT passage to trigger associations and remind the hearers of themes and biblical topoi with which they are probably already familiar'.[9] According to this argument, because the Apocalypse is a nearly endless string of allusion, the initial hearers of the text must have been immediately able to comprehend its full literary and theological richness. Fekkes oversteps what is known about the social make-up of these communities, and one cannot expect the audience to have been able to reconstruct John's allusive style of composition nor his play with Hebrew lexemes that Fekkes himself identifies (e.g. Rev 3.14a//Isa 65.16; Rev 21.21//Isa 54.12).[10]

Stanley's initial attempt to create a stratified audience, consisting of an 'informed audience' (familiar with the referenced passage and its original context), a 'competent audience' (familiar with the general contours of the reused material), and a 'minimal audience'

---

[8] Stanley, *Arguing with Scripture*, 38–61 (esp. 60–61). See also the appraisal of Jewish literacy abilities in Hezser, *Literacy*, 496–504.

[9] Fekkes, *Isaiah*, 287.

[10] Ibid., 137–140, 241–244.

(familiar only with the general contours of the best-known scriptural episodes), is a welcome first step that allows scholars to make sense of the entire process of reuse, including the part the audience plays in creating meaning.[11] His analysis underlines the reality that the detailed exegetical encounters with scriptural texts that undergird the composition of these works (Pauline or otherwise) were not always intended to be acknowledged by the audience, and that reconstructing these features of literary construction was not always central to the message of the work, even when quotations are explicitly signalled. That said, the literary sophistication of the works of the NT and the book of Revelation indicates that they were not intended for the uninitiated or for the lowest-common-denominator reader/hearer. Just as the advanced student of Greek at a modern university cannot fully grasp the depth of the intertextual texture of Revelation in a first reading, so too first-time hearers in antiquity would not have been able to grapple with the Apocalypse's complex argumentation and weaving of traditions, even though the text was composed in their native language. Comprehending these works through numerous encounters was as essential in antiquity as it is today.

The variety of literary ability encapsulated in early Christian communities would have made the details and significance of reuse more accessible to some community members than others. While the Apocalypse, for example, is anxious to address the whole of the community and to dissuade the faithful from blasphemous cooperation with Roman imperial power, the plenitude of significance embedded in John's engagement with Zechariah and other traditions would only have been comprehended by those who belonged to his own peer group – scribal experts familiar with existing exegetical traditions and attuned to the processes of literary composition that John embodies. The paucity of angelic intermediaries that directly interpret Revelation's visionary

---

[11] See also Sean Michael Ryan's portrayal of variable education levels in early Christianity in the context of understanding the cosmology of Revelation in *Hearing at the Boundaries of Vision: Education Informing Cosmology in Revelation 9* (LNTS 448; London: T&T Clark, 2012). Additionally, using Josephus and Philo as examples of highly educated Jewish literati, Ryan (pp. 27–37) makes the point that high educational levels were often associated with priestly circles and the élite ruling class (e.g. Josephus, *Ant.* 12.4.6–7), suggesting that John may have been privy to the informal forms of education, based largely on the study of Jewish scriptural works, common to the upper echelons of Roman-Palestinian society.

material (like those in the proto-Zechariah, *4 Ezra*, *2 Baruch*, and other works) also indicates that John composed with other experts in mind.[12] The book of Revelation is insider literature on two fronts. First, it is addressed to particular communities, urging them to withdraw (to varying degrees) from cooperation with features of Roman society and to lead a distinctive life under the auspices of a ruler more powerful than the Caesars. It is written for Christian communities. Second, the book is composed in such a way that it appeals to the scribal expert with high literary sensibilities, likely one with a background, be it formal or informal, in Jewish scriptural texts. However, another layer of the 'implied audience' takes us beyond the seven churches and the 'original audience' of the Apocalypse. The Apocalypse's awareness of its own physicality as a book to be transmitted, a point recently emphasized by Hans-Georg Gradl,[13] and the presence of the famous *Sicherungsformel* of Rev 22.18–19,[14] suggests that the book was composed with an eye to future circulation. It is difficult to describe exactly how John imagined the literary capabilities of this broader audience. However, if one (like Fekkes) is wont to argue that the sophistication of John's scriptural reuse must correspond to the literary skill of his audience, then perhaps this future audience is the one that John imagined would be able to engage in the details of his work as faithful communities continued to transmit and engage with the work beyond their initial hearing.

If John's literary sophistication, a sophistication accentuated by the complexity of his exegetical engagement with scripture, did not correspond to the literary erudition of the majority his actual audience, how can the Apocalypse be considered effective communication? And how can complex literary entities such as Revelation be considered effective at all if the majority of early Christians were only minimally literate?[15] These vexing questions can be answered in

---

[12] Cf. Dochhorn, *Prophetie*, 66: 'Es ist kein Zufall, daß Erläuterungen zu den Visionen, in anderen Offenbarungsbüchern wie etwa dem 4. Esra und dem 2. Baruch gewöhnlich die Aufgabe eines Angelus interpres, in der Apc Joh nur eine untergeordnete Rolle spielen . . . Der Leser soll offenbar die Deutung selbst vornehmen, indem er die Visionen auf ihre alttestamentlichen Hindergrundtexte hin dechiffriert.'

[13] *Buch und Offenbarung: Medien und Medialität der Johannesoffenbarung* (Wien: Herder, 2014), esp. 123–131.

[14] See also Haines-Eitzen, *Guardians*, 107–110.

[15] This question becomes even more poignant when one notices that the audience is expected to actively take part in the interpretation of the text (e.g. Rev 13.18). Additionally, referring to rabbinic Judaism, Willem Smelik notes, 'it is clear that most

a number of ways. First, as I have argued at length, the composition of the Apocalypse and John's practices of scriptural reuse correspond to an ambient form of literary construction present across early Jewish and early Christian literature. In this sense, the Apocalypse is effective communication because it resembles other forms of literature familiar to his initial hearers *and* because the producers of other texts would have recognized John as one of their own. The book of Revelation is effective communication inasmuch as the ideal or maximal audience is John's literary peer group of scribal experts. Additionally, the Apocalypse communicates effectively to the remainder of the gradation of the audience that was present in the seven churches inasmuch as the overall message of the Apocalypse is quite clear even without recourse to scriptural traditions, even if the details of some episodes would not have been entirely accessible. The clarion call to 'come out of her my people' (Rev 18.3) and John's encounter with a mighty angel culminating in a command to 'worship God' (19.9) clarify to those with only a cursory knowledge of Jewish scripture the overriding message that they are being encouraged to inhabit.

Moreover, as Steven Friesen has convincingly argued, the book of Revelation communicates its anti-imperial message quite clearly to gentile and Jewish audiences (of all literary competencies) by subverting and reappropriating numerous key features of imperial cults and other Greco-Roman civic and social organizations. The temporal and geographic emphases of imperial institutions, for example – organized around Rome and important dates in the lives of the Emperors – are subverted by John, for whom the heavenly realm and Jesus Christ are the organizing principles of reality.[16] In this sense, the churches belong to a different kingdom, presided over by a different king whose supremacy supersedes the deception and attractiveness of imperial power. Revelation's appeal to its hearers to disavow the ubiquitous symbols of Roman imperial power communicates its message even to those with a limited knowledge of Jewish scriptural

---

Jews would not have been able to read a complex literary text' ('Code-switching: The Public Reading of the Bible in Hebrew, Aramaic and Greek', in *Was ist ein Text? Alttestamentliche, ägytologische und altorientalistische Perspektiven* [BZAW 362; ed. L. Morenz and S. Schorch; Berlin: De Gruyter, 2007], 125). I see no reason to suggest that the literary ability of the majority of community members in the seven churches would have been much different.

[16] Cf. Friesen, *Imperial Cults*, 152–166.

traditions. Even so, Jewish scriptural traditions are the medium through which the systems of Roman power are reinterpreted.

What then does John's pervasive use of scriptural traditions accomplish? On a surface level, the embodiment of scriptural language based on exegetical engagement witnessed in Revelation contributes to John's authority as a prophet and accentuates the continuity of his work with the message of Jewish scripture.[17] John's compositional technique provides a veneer of clout for his own work as authoritative, a claim that is further supported by his exposition of visionary experiences and assertion of access to privileged revelation from God and Jesus (Rev 1.1). The reuse of scripture in Revelation also cements John's status as a literary elite, one who has control of both the broad narratives and detailed textual features of Jewish scriptural works; it ensures that the compositional characteristics of his work are commensurate with other forms of Jewish literary formation and scriptural engagement in this period. The message of the Apocalypse – most obviously, its high Christology – differs markedly from other Jewish works that engage Zechariah, but the ways in which John presented his scriptural reading stands in the same stream of composition as numerous other Jewish traditions, both 'apocalyptic' and 'non-apocalyptic' works.[18] John's reuse of scriptural texts offers an opportunity to display his literary skill and to embed layers of meaning within the textual surface of the Apocalypse.

6.3 Broader Considerations

This study has also identified some areas in need of further examination. First, the NT as a witness to the HB in antiquity: only rarely do those who analyse the reuse of scripture in the book of Revelation do so with an eye towards text-critical issues. Revelation and other NT works were composed at a crucial time for the text of the HB. The proto-MT was becoming the dominant Hebrew textual form in opposition to the acutely pluriform traditions preserved at Qumran.

---

[17] See Fekkes, *Prophetic Traditions*, 22–58 for further perspectives on John as prophet.

[18] Scholars often draw special parallels between Revelation and works like *1 Enoch*, Tobit, *4 Ezra*, and *2 Baruch*, and rightly so. However, the mode of composition witnesses in John's reuse of scripture extends well beyond the confines of these works that share some generic markers with the Apocalypse. This mode of scriptural engagement is ambient in this broader textual culture.

Before the late first century CE there is little evidence that readers and authors paid much attention to the issue of textual form and that, although Jewish sectarianism already existed, the disagreements of various sects never devolved to the textual level. It is not until the end of the first century CE and into the second century that particular groups begin to adopt specific textual forms: rabbinic Judaism (proto-MT), early Christianity (OG/LXX), and Samaritans (pre-SP). These divisions of textual forms are not absolute, but are eventually adopted by the majority of practitioners in these communities. The use of scripture in the book of Revelation – one of the latest written document in the NT – can serve as a valuable resource to determine the timeframe in which these various adoptions took place. The evidence in this study suggests that the sectarian adoption of particular textual forms had not yet taken place, at least in the community in which Revelation was composed, although John's access to Jesus traditions was mediated through Greek. This reality reveals that the NT is an underdeveloped resource for measuring the reception and transmission of the HB in antiquity. A methodical examination of the form of John's scriptural references as vessel of reception for early Jewish textual culture and scriptural reuse/rewriting is a point of consideration for future study.

Second, translation as a facet of scriptural reuse creates an additional level of textual analysis and reconstruction that must take place in an examination of an ancient author's reuse of scripture, particularly in a NT work. A specific examination of the role that translation plays in reuse, which this study has explored as part of the larger phenomenon, remains a *desideratum*.

Finally, due to the heterogeneity of techniques and methods of reuse in NT works, it is difficult to speak of a unified NT or early Christian approach to the reuse of scripture. Certainly, all authors, at least tacitly, partook in the textual culture of early Judaism, but the book of Revelation stands apart from other NT works and closer to the literature of the Second Temple period. It would be valuable to define and compare the techniques of reuse preserved within the NT to determine if a consistent (sectarian) Christian approach to scripture existed at an early stage. I suspect that such a study would find a multiplicity of approaches to Jewish scripture.

This study has highlighted the complex textual and historical issues that revolve around scriptural reuse in early Christianity and emphasized foundational issues that are often neglected in similar studies. It has also situated the author of Revelation in one of his primary context: the textual culture of early Judaism. John is a scribal exegete insofar as his scriptural engagement was designed to aid in the production of a new literary work. His engagements with scripture embody the ethos of reading embedded in the textual culture of which he was a part. Zechariah, for John, was an important (although not dominant) partner in the process of literary composition. Certain texts in Revelation (e.g. 5.6; 11.4) are more reliant upon the text of Zechariah than others (e.g. 19.11–16), where Zechariah stands in combination with and in subordination to a collage of other traditions. Nonetheless, John's engagement with Zechariah traditions underlines his role as a scribal exegete, as a literary producer that is fully of aware of the detailed features of scriptural texts (from multiple sources and in many languages) and their interconnectedness with breadth of early Jewish scripture. Whether or not his initial audiences would have comprehended the plenitude of meaning embedded in John's examples of scriptural reuse, exegetical attention to the sacred writings of Judaism formed the core of John's literary engagement.

Appendix 1

TEXTS INFLUENCED BY ZECHARIAH

Beyond the texts analysed in this body of this study, other passages in Revelation bear a resemblance to features of Zechariah. These passages were not included in the main text because the direct evidence linking these texts is weak. John may have borrowed traditional or thematic material that is present in Zechariah, but not unique to this specific tradition. The following texts are included in this appendix for one or a combination of the following reasons:

(1) The text in Revelation shares linguistic parallels with a text in Zechariah that are not uniquely attributable to Zechariah.

(2) The text in Revelation shares thematic or structural parallels with Zechariah that are not directly attributable to the specific features of a form of Zechariah.

(3) Other scholars suggest that the author of Revelation alluded to a certain text, but no linguistic data necessitates such a link.

The Seven Spirits (Rev 1.4; 3.1; 4.4–5) and Zech 4.10b

Rev 1.4 Ἰωάννης ταῖς ἑπτὰ ἐκκλησίαις ταῖς ἐν τῇ Ἀσίᾳ· χάρις ὑμῖν καὶ εἰρήνη ἀπὸ ὁ ὢν καὶ ὁ ἦν καὶ ὁ ἐρχόμενος καὶ ἀπὸ τῶν ἑπτὰ πνευμάτων ἃ ἐνώπιον τοῦ θρόνου αὐτοῦ

Rev 3.1 Τάδε λέγει ὁ ἔχων τὰ ἑπτὰ πνεύματα τοῦ θεοῦ καὶ τοὺς ἑπτὰ ἀστέρας· οἶδά σου τὰ ἔργα ὅτι ὄνομα ἔχεις ὅτι ζῇς, καὶ νεκρὸς εἶ

Rev 4.4–5 Καὶ κυκλόθεν τοῦ θρόνου θρόνους εἴκοσι τέσσαρες, καὶ ἐπὶ τοὺς θρόνους εἴκοσι τέσσαρας πρεσβυτέρους καθημένους περιβεβλημένους ἐν ἱματίοις λευκοῖς καὶ ἐπὶ τὰς

κεφαλὰς αὐτῶν στεφάνους χρυσοῦς. Καὶ ἐκ τοῦ θρόνου
ἐκπορεύονται ἀστραπαὶ καὶ φωναὶ καὶ βρονταί, καὶ ἑπτὰ
λαμπάδες πυρὸς καιόμεναι ἐνώπιον τοῦ θρόνου, ἅ εἰσιν τὰ
ἑπτὰ πνεύματα τοῦ θεοῦ

Zech 4.10b^{pM} שבעה־אלה עיני יהוה המה משוטטים בכל־הארץ

Zech 4.10b^{OG} ἑπτὰ οὗτοι ὀφθαλμοὶ κυρίου εἰσὶν οἱ ἐπιβλέποντες
ἐπὶ πᾶσαν τὴν γῆν

The reference to the seven spirits in Rev 5.6b was analysed in the
body of this discussion because it contained an explanatory locution not present in the other three references: ἀπεσταλμένοι εἰς πᾶσαν
τὴν γῆν. Rev 5.6b is the fourth and final reference to the seven spirits, and the references to the seven spirits in Rev 1.4; 3.1; 4.5 have
no distinguishing textual features that connect them to Zech 4.10b
that are not also present in Rev 5.6b. The exercise is largely redundant. The collocations στεφάνους χρυσοῦς and ἱματίοις λευκοῖς in Rev
4.4 do loosely correspond to linguistic material in Zech 6.11 and 3.5
respectively.

Revelation 2.17 and Zechariah 3.9; 4.7; 4.10a

Rev 2.17 Τῷ νικῶντι δώσω αὐτῷ τοῦ μάννα τοῦ κεκρυμμένου
καὶ δώσω αὐτῷ ψῆφον λευκήν, καὶ ἐπὶ τὴν ψῆφον ὄνομα
καινὸν γεγραμμένον ὃ οὐδεὶς οἶδεν εἰ μὴ ὁ λαμβάνων

Zech 3.9 כי הנה האבן אשר נתתי לפני יהושע על אבן אחת שבעה עינים
הנני מפתח פתחה נאם יהוה צבאות ומשתי את־עון הארץ־ההיא ביום אחד
διότι ὁ λίθος, ὃν ἔδωκα πρὸ προσώπου Ἰησοῦ, ἐπὶ τὸν λίθον
τὸν ἕνα ἑπτὰ ὀφθαλμοί εἰσιν, ἰδοὺ ἐγὼ ὀρύσσω βόθρον, λέγει
κύριος παντοκράτωρ, καὶ ψηλαφήσω πᾶσαν τὴν ἀδικίαν τῆς
γῆς ἐκείνης ἐν ἡμέρᾳ μιᾷ

Zech 4.7 מי־אתה הר־הגדול לפני זרבבל למישר והוציא את־האבן הראשה
תשאות חן חן לה
τίς εἶ σύ, τὸ ὄρος τὸ μέγα, πρὸ προσώπου Ζοροβαβελ τοῦ
κατορθῶσαι; καὶ ἐξοίσω τὸν λίθον τῆς κληρονομίας ἰσότητα
χάριτος χάριτα αὐτῆς

Zech 4.10a כי מי בז ליום קטנות ושמחו וראו את־האבן הבדיל
διότι τίς ἐξουδένωσεν εἰς ἡμέρας μικράς; καὶ χαροῦνται καὶ
ὄψονται τὸν λίθον τὸν κασσιτέρινον ἐν χειρὶ Ζοροβαβελ

Rogers suggests that the white stone (ψῆφον λευκήν) in Rev 2.17
may be a 'remote allusion' to Zech 3.9 and other stone imagery in

Zechariah.[1] However, as Jauhiainen observes,[2] the connection is unlikely. First, there is no lexical overlap between Rev 2.7 and Zech 3.9; 4.7; 4.10a[OG]. Second, ψῆφος never serves as a translation equivalent for אבן in the OG/LXX tradition, and the only possible connections between λευκήν and the Zechariah texts are a misreading of the consonantal text of 3.9 (לאבן for על אבן) and an equivocation of הבדיל with the root בָּדָל ('earlobe'[?]). This word is translated with λοβός in Amos 3.12, a medical term that can mean 'white part' or 'liver'.[3] These possible connections are hardly convincing. Moreover, the connection between Rev 2.17 and Zech 3.9 is further weakened by the fact that forms of γράφω (γεγραμμένον) never serve as a translation equivalent for פתח or מוש. Jauhiainen also notes the lack of thematic or contextual correspondence between Rev 2.7 and the Zecharian stone passages.[4]

White Garments: Revelation 3.4–5 and Zechariah 3.3–5

Rev 3.4–5 ἀλλὰ ἔχεις ὀλίγα ὀνόματα ἐν Σάρδεσιν ἃ οὐκ ἐμόλυναν τὰ ἱμάτια αὐτῶν, καὶ περιπατήσουσιν μετ' ἐμοῦ ἐν λευκοῖς, ὅτι ἄξιοί εἰσιν. Ὁ νικῶν οὕτως περιβαλεῖται ἐν ἱματίοις λευκοῖς καὶ οὐ μὴ ἐξαλείψω τὸ ὄνομα αὐτοῦ ἐκ τῆς βίβλου τῆς ζωῆς καὶ ὁμολογήσω τὸ ὄνομα αὐτοῦ ἐνώπιον τοῦ πατρός μου καὶ ἐνώπιον τῶν ἀγγέλων αὐτοῦ

Zech 3.3–5 ויהושע היה לבש בגדים צואים ועמד לפני המלאך ויען ויאמר אל־העמדים לפניו לאמר הסירו הבגדים הצאים מעליו ויאמר אליו ראה העברתי מעליך עונך והלבש אתך מחלצות ואמר ישימו צניף טהור על־ ראשו וישימו הצניף הטהור על־ראשו וילבשהו בגדים ומלאך יהוה עמד καὶ Ἰησοῦς ἦν ἐνδεδυμένος ἱμάτια ῥυπαρὰ καὶ εἱστήκει πρὸ προσώπου τοῦ ἀγγέλου. καὶ ἀπεκρίθη καὶ εἶπεν πρὸς τοὺς ἑστηκότας πρὸ προσώπου αὐτοῦ λέγων Ἀφέλετε τὰ ἱμάτια τὰ ῥυπαρὰ ἀπ' αὐτοῦ. καὶ εἶπεν πρὸς αὐτόν Ἰδοὺ ἀφῄρηκα τὰς ἀνομίας σου, καὶ ἐνδύσατε αὐτὸν ποδήρη καὶ ἐπίθετε κίδαριν καθαρὰν ἐπὶ τὴν κεφαλὴν αὐτοῦ. καὶ περιέβαλον αὐτὸν ἱμάτια καὶ ἐπέθηκαν κίδαριν καθαρὰν ἐπὶ τὴν κεφαλὴν αὐτοῦ, καὶ ὁ ἄγγελος κυρίου εἱστήκει

---

[1] Rogers, 'Exegetical Analysis', 89–91.
[2] Jauhiainen, *The Use*, 82–83.
[3] LSJ, 1055.
[4] Jauhiainen, *The Use*, 83. Cf. Ernst Sellin, 'Der Stein des Sacharja', *JBL* 50 no 4 (1931): 242–249.

The connections between these texts are weak. Garments are mentioned in both accounts, but the adjectives used to describe them are different. The final three words of Zech 3.5ᴾᴹ (ומלאך יהוה עמד) are similar to the final locution of Rev 3.5 (καὶ ἐνώπιον τῶν ἀγγέλων αὐτοῦ), but beyond the reference to 'angel(s)', the locutions share no lexical items. Another possible textual connection relies on a misreading of the consonantal Hebrew text of Zech 3.3. The text reads לפני המלאך and it is possible that John 'misread' a form of מָלֵא ('full') for מלאך ('angel'). In Gen 23.9 and 1 Chr 21.22, 24 מָלֵא is translated with a form of ἄξιος ('worthy'), a word that appears in Rev 3.4 (ὅτι ἄξιοί εἰσιν). While theoretically possible, this connection is unlikely as the referent is different in each text and there is no explanation for the omission of a final ך. There is not enough linguistic correlation to confirm that John referenced Zech 3.3–5 in this passage.

Jauhiainen notes that this imagery in Rev 3 is similar to the depiction of the wise in Dan 11–12 and suggests that these texts are linked thematically. However, he too notes that 'this appropriation of existing motifs, or coherence and correspondence with earlier prophetic material, does not require an allusion to one or more background passages to be present.'[5]

Scrolls and Flying Scrolls: Revelation 5.1 and Zech 5.1–4

Rev 5.1 Καὶ εἶδον ἐπὶ τὴν δεξιὰν τοῦ καθημένου ἐπὶ τοῦ θρόνου βιβλίον γεγραμμένον ἔσωθεν καὶ ὄπισθεν κατεσφραγισμένον σφραγῖσιν ἑπτά

Zech 5.1–4ᴾᴹ ואשוב ואשא עיני ואראה הנה מגלה עפה
ויאמר אלי מה אתה ראה ואמר אני ראה מגלה עפה ארכה עשרים באמה
ורחבה עשר באמה ויאמר אלי זאת האלה היוצאת על־פני כל־הארץ כי
כל־הגנב מזה כמוה נקה וכל הנשבע מזה כמוה נקה הוצאתיה נאם יהיה
צבאות ובאה אל בית הגנב ואל־בית הנשבע בשמי לשקר ולנה בתוך ביתו
וכלתו ואת עציו ואת אבניו

Zech 5.1–4ᴼᴳ Καὶ ἐπέστρεψα καὶ ἦρα τοὺς ὀφθαλμούς μου καὶ εἶδον καὶ ἰδοὺ δρέπανον πετόμενον. καὶ εἶπεν πρός με Τί σὺ βλέπεις; καὶ εἶπα Ἐγὼ ὁρῶ δρέπανον πετόμενον μῆκος πήχεων εἴκοσι καὶ πλάτος πήχεων δέκα. καὶ εἶπεν πρός με Αὕτη ἡ ἀρὰ ἡ ἐκπορευομένη ἐπὶ πρόσωπον πάσης τῆς γῆς,

---

5 Jauhiainen, *The Use*, 82. See also Beale, *Revelation*, 276–278.

διότι πᾶς ὁ κλέπτης ἐκ τούτου ἕως θανάτου ἐκδικηθήσεται,
καὶ πᾶς ὁ ἐπίορκος ἐκ τούτου ἕως θανάτου ἐκδικηθήσεται,
καὶ ἐξοίσω αὐτό, λέγει κύριος παντοκράτωρ, καὶ εἰσελεύσεται
εἰς τὸν οἶκον τοῦ κλέπτου καὶ εἰς τὸν οἶκον τοῦ ὀμνύοντος
τῷ ὀνόματί μου ἐπὶ ψεύδει καὶ καταλύσει ἐν μέσῳ τοῦ οἴκου
αὐτοῦ καὶ συντελέσει αὐτὸν καὶ τὰ ξύλα αὐτοῦ καὶ τοὺς
λίθους αὐτοῦ

A few scholars have advanced the argument that John referenced
Zechariah's flying scroll (Zech 5.1–4) in his description of the
opisthographic seven-sealed scroll (Rev 5.1).[6] This is unlikely for
multiple reasons. First, the *Vorlage* of John's source text cannot
be the OG/LXX as the Greek tradition is unified in its translation
of מגלה עפה ('flying scroll') as δρέπανον πετόμενον ('flying sickle').
The OG translator read מגלה as מגל which is translated by forms of
δρέπανον in Joel 3(4).10 and Jer 27(50).16. The absence of a reference to a βιβλίον in the OG/LXX eliminates this textual form as a
possible source text.

Beyond the Greek tradition, there is also little evidence that necessitates a link between Zech 5.1–4[pM] and Rev 5.1. Beyond the connection between מגלה (Zech 5.1) and βιβλίον (Rev 5.1),[7] there is no lexical
correlation between these texts. Inconclusive thematic parallels are
present – Zechariah's flying scroll punishes those who swear falsely
and those who steal while John's four horsemen serve as instruments
of judgement – but these themes are certainly not unique to these
two passages. The linguistic correlation between Rev 5.1 and Ezek
2.9–10 is much stronger and the connection more logical.[8] Jauhiainen
confirms this analysis arguing that 'despite this thematic parallelism
however, there is nothing else that these scrolls or respective contexts
have in common'.[9] Overall, there is not enough conclusive linguistic
or thematic evidence to necessitate a direct link between Rev 5.1 and
Zech 5.1–4.

---

[6] Namely Shea, 'Zechariah's Flying Scroll', 95–99 and Hultberg, 'Messianic
Exegesis', 251–252. Although, Hultberg does ultimately suggest that Ezek 2.9–10 is
the likely 'subtext' (252) behind John's description of an opisthographic scroll in Rev
5.1. Kowalski, *Die Rezeption*, 118–120 follows Hultberg's conclusion.

[7] Cf. Jer 43(36).14, 20, 25, 29[OG].

[8] See Kowalski, *Die Rezeption*, 118–120.

[9] Jauhiainen, *The Use*, 95.

The Martyrs under the Altar: Revelation 6.9–11 and Zechariah 1.12–14[10]

Although I think that this example of reuse is quite probable, I discuss it in the context of the appendix because the data is ultimately inconclusive and the scholarly opinion thoroughly mixed.

Rev 6.9–11	And when he opened the fifth seal, I saw under the altar the souls of those who had been slain because of the word of God (τὸν λόγον τοῦ θεοῦ) and because of the witness which they had. And they cried out in a loud voice saying, 'Until when (ἕως πότε), holy and true master, will you not judge and avenge our blood from those dwelling on the earth?' And He gave to each of them a white robe and it was spoken to them that they might rest a short time until also their fellow servants and their brothers who are about to be killed are fulfilled like them also.
Zech 1.12–14[OG]	And the angel of the Lord answered and said: 'Lord Almighty, why have you, for a time (ἕως τίνος), not comforted Jerusalem and the cities of Judah, which you disregarded these seventy years?' And Lord Almighty answered the angel who was speaking with me good words and comforting words (ῥήματα καλὰ καὶ λόγους παρακλητικούς). And the angel who was speaking with said to me: 'Cry out saying: Thus says Lord Almighty: I have had zeal for Jerusalem and Zion great zeal.

[10] Those who argue for reuse in this instance include Beale, *Revelation*, 393; Thompson, *Revelation*, 104; Boxall, *The Revelation*, 114. Osborne, *Revelation*, 286; Kiddle, *The Revelation*, 119; Caird, *The Revelation*, 84; Smalley, *The Revelation*, 160; Harrington, *Revelation*, 93; Maier, *Die Offenbarung*, 332; Blount, *Revelation*, 134; Sweet, *Revelation*, 142 notes a *possible* connection between Rev 6.9–11 and Zech 1.12 (among many other texts). The point of contact between the texts noted by these commentators is the martyrs' cry from under the altar ('how long?'; Zech 1.12; Rev 6.10). They do not attempt to argue that John directly reused Zech 1.12–14 but tacitly suggest that his depiction of the martyrs under the altar is part of a broader traditional stream. The majority of commentators do not make mention of Zechariah in their exposition of the fifth seal.

Zech 1.12–14ᴾᴹ   And the angel of YHWH answered and he said: 'YHWH of Hosts, until when (עד־מתי) will you not comfort Jerusalem and the cities (witnesses) of Judah (ערי יהודה) to which you were indignant these seventy years?' And YHWH answered the angel who was speaking with me good words, comforting words (דברים טובים דברים נחמים). And the angel who was speaking with me said to me: 'Call saying: thus says YHWH of Hosts: I am zealous for Jerusalem and Zion with great zeal.'

First, the *Vorlage* of Zech 1.12–14ᴼᴳ is the same consonantal Hebrew text that was later adopted by the Masoretes (proto-MT), and the translation preserves an identical reading tradition to the MT. In this pericope, the translator carefully retained identical serial fidelity, and none of the translations' equivalents are unique in the OG/LXX tradition. In terms of vocabulary and syntax, the translation is a straightforward representation of the proto-MT.

Despite this concordance, two small additions are present in the OG. First, the translation preserves an additional adjective to describe God in 1.13: παντοκράτωρ, a word that usually stands as an equivalent of the Hebrew צבאות, which occurs commonly in Zech 1–8 in the divine title of יהוה צבאות ('YHWH of Hosts'). In Zechariahᴼᴳ, this phrase is commonly translated as κύριος παντοκράτωρ ('Lord Almighty').[11] This descriptor is also added in Zech 1.16; 8.2, 8.17ᴼᴳ where it has no representation in any Hebrew witness. Some tendencies to revise away from the inclusion of παντοκράτωρ are present, however, in the Greek tradition (B 8HevXIIgr).

A second addition in Zech 1.12–14ᴼᴳ is the word καί in the phrase ῥήματα καλὰ καὶ λόγους παρακλητικούς (1.13).[12] The proto-MT does not include a conjunctive ו in the corresponding phrase דברים טובים דברים נחמים. The inclusion of καί in Zech 1.13ᴼᴳ smooths the texture of the locution, and is a logical inclusion even in a translation that tends towards literality.[13]

---

[11] See Zech 1.3, 4, 6, 12, 13, 14, 16, 17; 2.8, 9, 11; 3.8, 10; 4.9; 5.4; 6.12, 15; 7.3, 9, 12, 13; 8.1, 2, 3, 4, 6, 7, 9, 11, 14, 17, 18, 19, 20, 21, 22, 23.

[12] The καί is likely omitted in 8HevXIIgr, reading ῥήματα] ἀγα[θά λόγους παρακλητικούς.

[13] The inclusion of καί is a fairly common addition to the OG. Daniel M. O'Hare, *'Have you Seen, Son of Man?' A Study in the Translation and Vorlage of LXX Ezekiel 40–48* (SCS 57; Atlanta: SBL, 2010), 36 notes six instances in Ezek 40–48 (Ezek 41.19; 42.20; 43.10; 45.13, 21, 25).

Neither of these small additions into the OG – both of which were subsequently corrected in 8HevXIIgr and other LXX traditions – suggests an alternate Hebrew *Vorlage* beside the proto-MT. There is no manuscript evidence pointing towards a different textual form that underlies this pericope, and the alterations are minor in light of the larger syntactic and semantic coherence between proto-MT and OG. The OG is not an isomorphic translation but it is difficult to isolate a different Hebrew *Vorlage* for Zech 1.12–14^{OG}.

How then do these forms of Zechariah relate to Rev 6.9–11? In my estimation, the linguistic connections between Rev 6.9–11 and Zech 1.12–14 rely on John's use of the consonantal Hebrew text. First, the initial cry from those under the altar, ἕως πότε (Rev 6.10; 'how long?'), is a common translation of the Hebrew locution עד־מתי.[14] The OG/LXX tradition of Zech 1.12 is consistent in witnessing the locution ἕως τίνος ('for a time'), a phrase that is also not an uncommon translation of עד־מתי. The subtle semantic difference between Zech 1.12^{OG} and Rev 6.10 suggests that the Greek tradition is not John's source in this instance.

It must be noted, however, that this locution is not unique to Zechariah and that the language may have been drawn from elsewhere.[15] Nonetheless, the fact that this locution occurs as the introduction of a negative rhetorical question in which God is addressed strengthens the case that this locution is drawn from Zech 1.12.[16] This verbal correspondence serves as an entry point into further analysis of the pericope.

The second potential verbal correlation between the two texts in question is the phrase τὸν λόγον τοῦ θεοῦ (Rev 6.9) and the locution דברים טובים דברים נחמים (Zech 1.13). The linguistic connection is minor: λόγον as a translation of דברים is the only direct verbal correspondence between these locutions. There is no example in the OG/LXX tradition of θεοῦ as a translation equivalent of a form of טובים or נחמים or visually similar graphemes. However, there is evidence that the 'word of God', for which the martyrs were slain in Rev 6.9, is related to the message which YHWH relays to his angel in Zech 1.13. It is logical that the 'word of God' – a collocation that is not explicated in Rev 6.9–11 – may be associated with a divine

---

[14] See 1 Sam 1.14; 16.1; 2 Sam 2.26; 1 Kgs 18.21; Neh 2.6; Isa 6.11; Jer 4.14, 21; 12.4; 23.26; 31(38).22; Dan 8.13; 12.6.

[15] See Exod 10.3, 7; Num 14.27; Prov 6.9; Hos 8.5.

[16] So Beale, *Revelation*, 393 and Harrington, *Revelation*, 93.

utterance that is only secondarily reported in Zechariah. The verbal connection is not entirely conclusive, but the *potential* of the correspondence increases the possibility that Rev 6.9–11 references Zech 1.12–14.

A final possible verbal connection between these texts is also inconclusive, as it relies on John's misreading of a Hebrew grapheme. Zech 1.12 reads עד־מתי אתה לא תרחם את־ירושלם ואת ערי יהודה ('until when will you not comfort Jerusalem and the cities of Judah'). However, if ערי ('cities') is read as עדי ('witnesses'), there is a further verbal correlation between Zech 1.12–14ᴾᴹ and Rev 6.9–11. Forms of μαρτυρία (Rev 6.9) often stand as translation equivalents for forms of עד.[17] And the misreading or interchange of visually similar Hebrew radicals – especially *dalet* and *resh* – is not uncommon in ancient translations.

In this instance, the textual data is not entirely conclusive in terms of confirming that Rev 6.9–11 reused material from Zech 1.12–14. However, the corresponding features between Zech 1.12–14ᴾᴹ and Rev 6.9–11 are suggestive. Beyond lexical and textual considerations, the context of both passages is similar. Jauhiainen notes that 'the proximity of the horsemen [Rev 6.1–8] in both visions and the perceived similarities between their contexts is considered to tip the balance in favour of a direct allusion to Zechariah.'[18] Jauhiainen's positive assessment of the data is based primarily on the narrative and contextual similarities between Rev 6.9–11 and Zech 1.12–14, and he notes *only* the verbal connection between עד־מתי and ἕως πότε. The other two verbal connections that I have identified strengthen his case. If Rev 6.9–11 does reuse material from Zech 1.12–14, John used a Hebrew tradition similar to the proto-MT.

In Rev 6.9–11, John *implicitly alluded*, at most, to Zech 1.12–14. Direct linguistic connections, while present, are minimal. This lexical connection establishes a baseline relationship between texts, a connection that is strengthened by the possibility of palaeographic play and logical extension. But there is no attempt in the target composition to set apart the allusion from its co-texts. The reused portions of Zech 1.12–14 are completely embedded in a new literary context, and no discreetness is evident.

---

[17] Cf. Gen 31.44; Mic 1.2; Isa 55.4.

[18] Jauhiainen, *The Use*, 66. Beale, *Revelation*, 393 also directly connects Rev 6.9–11 to Zech 1.12–14.

The Four Winds: Revelation 7.1 and Zechariah 6.5

The relationship between Zech 6.5 and Rev 7.1 is debated.[19] Although I suspect that Rev 7.1 does primarily allude to Zech 6.5, the evidence is not entirely clear. The following textual analysis, and the location of Rev 7.1 in proximity to John's extended reference to Zechariah's horse visions (Rev 6.1–11), indicates that the reference to the 'four winds of the earth' in Rev 7.1 is likely (but not conclusively) an allusion to Zech 6.5.

Rev 7.1

Μετὰ τοῦτο εἶδον τέσσαρας ἀγγέλους ἑστῶτας ἐπὶ τὰς τέσσαρας γωνίας τῆς γῆς, κρατοῦντας τοὺς τέσσαρας ἀνέμους τῆς γῆς ἵνα μὴ πνέῃ ἄνεμος ἐπὶ τῆς γῆς μήτε ἐπὶ τῆς θαλάσσης μήτε ἐπὶ πᾶν δένδρον

Zech 6.5^{OG}

καὶ ἀπεκρίθη ὁ ἄγγελος ὁ λαλῶν ἐν ἐμοὶ καὶ εἶπε Ταῦτά ἐστιν οἱ τέσσαρες ἄνεμοι τοῦ οὐρανοῦ, ἐκπορεύονται παραστῆναι τῷ κυρίῳ πάσης τῆς γῆς

Zech 6.5^{PM}

ויען המלאך ויאמר אלי אלה ארבע רחות
השמים יוצאות מהתיצב על־אדון כל־הארץ

[19] Aune, *Revelation*, 450–451; Holtz, *Die Offenbarung*, 73; Maier, *Die Offenbarung*, 351; and Harrington, *Revelation*, 98 appeal to a general tradition of the four winds representing the cardinal direction in the ancient world without suggesting a specific textual connect, although they mention both Zech 2.6 and 6.5. They also note that these 'four winds' are often thought of in terms of angelic powers. Blount, *Revelation*, 141 notes that Rev 7.1 may refer to Zech 6.5 but that the connection is not certain. Boxall, *The Revelation*, 121 and Smalley, *The Revelation*, 179 suggest that a more general tradition might lie behind the reference. Jauhiainen, *The Use*, 70–72 is more forceful in his objection to this proposed scriptural reference, arguing that the 'four winds of the earth' (Rev 7.1) cannot be conflated with the four horsemen in Zech 6.5 because the 'presence of an allusion to Zech 2.6; 6.5 tend[s] to confuse and complicate the exegesis of the pericope' and because the adjective describing the 'four winds' in each account is different. He concludes that 1. 'there are no indicators in ch. 7 that the four winds restrained by the four angels should be seen as . . . anything other than four winds; and 2. though there is a verbal connection to Zech 2:6; 6:5, "four winds", it is not unique' (72). Koester, *Revelation*, 414–415 follows this diagnosis. Osborne, *Revelation*, 305 mounts the strongest defence of Rev 7.1 as a reference to Zech 6.5. He suggests that the 'four winds of the earth' (Rev 7.1) may refer back to Zech 6.5, noting that 'the closest parallel to our text is probably Zech. 6:5, the same passage behind the four horsemen of Rev. 6:1–8. The "four winds of heaven" take their place

The verbal parallel between Rev 7.1 and Zech 6.5 is clear: both reference 'the four winds of heaven/earth', a common trope in ancient literature including the Hebrew Jewish scriptures and their early Greek versions (Jer 49.36 [26.16^{OG}]; Ezek 37.9; Dan 8.8; 11.4; and Zech 2.10; 6.5).[20] In each of these locutions a reference to 'the four winds of the *earth*' is never present. This inclusion of the modifier 'earth' in Revelation connects the four winds to the 'four corners of the earth' (τὰς τέσσαρας γωνίας τῆς γῆς) that immediately precede the description of the winds. The substitution of 'earth' for 'heaven(s)' also ties the locution more closely to Zech 6.5 as the 'four winds of heaven' go out from before the 'Lord of all the *earth*' (ארץ/γῆς).

The fact that this phrase occurs in other Jewish scriptural works complicates the identification process. I will take each option in turn. First, Rev 7.1 likely did not reuse material from Ezek 7.2 or 37.9; neither the proto-MT nor OG/LXX qualifies Ezekiel's 'four winds' with an adjective. It is possible that Rev 7.1 is a *Mischanspielung*, which partially uses material from Ezekiel.[21] Likewise Jer 49.36 (25.16^{OG}) refers not to the 'four winds of heaven', but to the 'four corners of heaven' whence the 'four winds' come. Jer 25.16^{OG} employs ἄκρων

in front of each of the chariot horses and lead them in the four directions of the compass. For this reason several (e.g. Farrer, Caird, Morris, Beasley-Murray, Johnson, Beale) believe that the four winds are identical with the four horsemen, a very real possibility in light of the retrospective look of this scene.' Other commentators, beyond those mentioned by Osborne, notice a connection between Rev 7.1 and Zech 6.5: Roloff, *Revelation*, 96; Müller, *Die Offenbarung*, 166; Kraft, *Die Offenbarung*, 125; Akira Satake, *Die Offenbarung des Johannes* (KEKNT 16; Göttingen: Vandenhoeck & Ruprecht, 2008), 228.

[20] Cf. *1 En.* 69.22 for example. Loren T. Stuckenbruck and Mark D. Matthews, 'The Apocalypse of John, 1 Enoch, and the Question of Influence', in *Die Johannesapokalypse* (WUNT 287; ed. J. Frey, J. A. Kelhoffer, and F. Tóth; Tübingen: Mohr Siebeck, 2012), 208 notes further reference to the 'four winds' in Jewish literature, including 4 Ezra 13.5 (2 Esdras 13.5), Josephus. *J.W.* 6.300; *Vit. Ad. Et Ev.* 38.3; Mark 13.27//Matt 24.31. This tradition can also be discerned in *Seder Gan 'Eden* 4.7; *Gedulat Moshe* 4.6; *The Cave of Treasures* 22.8; *Massekhet Kelim* §XII; *Principle of the Selendromion of David the Prophet and His Son Solomon* 3; *Adam Octipartite* (both the Latin and Slavonic traditions); Josephus, *Ant.* 10.271; and possibly *The Latin Vision of Ezra* 19. A similar collocation is also witnessed in *1 En.* 18.2 and multiple documents from Qumran: 3Q15; 4Q223; 4Q381; 4Q385; 4Q386; 4Q448; 4Q491; 11Q19. See Aune, *Revelation 6–16*, 450–451 for further comment on this tradition.

[21] As Kowalski, *Rezeption*, 130–132 argues, suggesting that Ezek 7.2 is the primary source, not Zech 6.5.

while Rev 7.1 preserves γωνίας for 'corners'. Jer 49.36ᴾᴹ witnesses קצות which in the OG/LXX tradition is never rendered by a form of γωνία. No version of the Jeremiah locution corresponds closely with Rev 7.1. In the Danielic 'four winds' locutions (8.8; 11.4), the phrase illustrates the downfall of world empires. The great horn of the male goat (Dan 8.8) is broken, and four small horns sprout in its place 'towards the four winds of heaven'. In this case, the four winds represent the geographic totality of Alexander's fractured kingdom, alluding to the rise of the *Diadochi*.[22] Likewise, Dan 11.4 foretells of the eventual downfall of the Persian Empire, which will be 'divided towards the four winds of heaven'. The phrase is geographic in Rev 7.1 as well, but it does not carry the political implications present in the employment of this collocation in Daniel. The logic of Dan 8.8; 11.4 does not fit well into the framework of Rev 7, and there are no unique linguistic links that indicate that John referenced these traditions over and above Zech 6.5. The inexact verbal parallels of Ezek 37.9 and Jer 49.36, the contextual difficulties of the Danielic texts, and their lack of further verbal connection to the vision in Rev 7, intimate that Zech 6.5 is likely referred to in Rev 7.1. However, it is not clear that Zechariah is the controlling tradition in this locution or that John has engaged with Zechariah's four wind traditions in an interpretative manner.

Nonetheless, the proximity of Rev 7.1 to John's depiction of the four horsemen suggests a connection to Zech 6. The extended, vivid imagery of the coloured horses only nine verses previously and the allusion to Zech 1.12–14 in Rev 6.9–10 connects Rev 6.1–11 and Rev 7.1. Beale agrees, proposing that 'the Zechariah context would still be hovering in the author's mind so soon after he had expounded on [Rev 6.1–11].'[23] While Beale's explanation is somewhat imprecise, he recognizes that Rev 6.1–7.1 contains a highly concentrated cluster of allusions to Zechariah. Labahn has also noted a compositional tendency to reuse scriptural texts in clusters or complexes in Revelation.[24] The reference to the 'four winds' in Rev 7.1 connects this new vision (introduced with Μετὰ τοῦτο εἶδον) with the preceding vision (Rev 6.1–17) and creates narrative consistency in these

[22] So Marvin A. Sweeney, *The Twelve Prophets* (BO; Vol. 2; Collegeville, MN: Liturgical Press, 2000), 626.

[23] Beale, *Revelation*, 406.

[24] M. Labahn, 'Die Macht', 356. See also Bøe, *Gog*, 26–27.

seemingly disparate visions.[25] John's use of Zechariah in Rev 6.1–11 strengthens the case that the reference to the 'four winds' (Rev 7.1) refers to the same work.

The assertion that the 'four winds' are borrowed from Zechariah is further supported by the fact that John often references the *angelus interpres*' answers to the seer in Zechariah. Rev 5.6b reuses Zech 4.10b precisely where the angelic messenger answers the prophet's question from Zech 4.4. Again, Rev 11.4 alludes to Zech 4.14 at the point where the angel answers the prophet's questions posed in Zech 4.11–12. Compositionally, the reference in Rev 7.1 corresponds with other examples of John's reuse of Zechariah.

The verbal correspondence between Zech 6.5 and Rev 7.1 is obvious. Both the proto-MT and OG preserve the phrase 'these are the four winds of heaven', which corresponds closely to the description of the four angels in Rev 7.1 who are 'holding the four winds of the earth'. The case of the 'four winds' differs in Rev 7.1 and Zech 6.5[OG], but the difference is stylistic and contextual. Further evidence of reuse exists in the fact that two of the three areas upon which the wind blows in Rev 7.1 (γῆς and θαλάσσης) parallel Hebrew words in Zech 6.6.[26] The close verbal correspondence between these locutions, in concert with the preceding compositional evidence, suggests that the 'four winds' of Rev 7.1 refer to Zech 6.5.

The short length of this locution both simplifies and complicates the identification of the textual form of the source text. The compact locution in Zech 6.5, and its close verbal correspondence to Rev 7.1, quickly eliminates many of the proposed textual options. As mentioned above, Zech 6.5[OG] differs slightly from the proto-MT. Nonetheless, the *Vorlage* of Zech 6.5[OG] is very close to the text of the proto-MT. Also, there are no proto-Hexaplaric variants or any other LXX witnesses to Zech 6.5 that alter the locution in question.[27] This lack of variation in the manuscript evidence, and agreement between proto-MT and *V*OG, eliminates options 2, 5, 6. Also, the close verbal agreement between the source and target text eliminates options 9 and 10 (see Section 2.7).

---

[25] Farrer, *The Revelation*, 104 notes that 'the insertion of a chapter-division between vi. 17 and vii. 1 is particularly unfortunate, since it disguises the continuity between the three visions under the sixth seal.' In contrast to Farrer's observation, Giesen, *Die Offenbarung*, 191 notes that the locution Μετὰ τοῦτο εἶδον creates narrative dissonance between Rev 6 and 7.

[26] See תימן ('south'), which is translated as a form of θαλάσσα in Num 10.6.

[27] 8HevXIIgr does not witness Zech 6.5 and its reconstruction (Appendix 2) does not evidence any recensional activity from OG towards proto-MT in Zech 6.5.

The remaining textual options are the proto-MT, OG, proto-MT with adaptations, and OG with adaptations. The text of Zech 6.5 in the OG and Hebrew tradition share a common textual stream and the lack of differentiation between these versions does not permit us to make conclusive claims regarding the *Vorlage* of this reference, but the textual analysis *limits* the possible textual options to which John referred.

Unclean Spirits and Frogs: Revelation 16.13 and Zechariah 13.2–6

Rev 16:13 Καὶ εἶδον ἐκ τοῦ στόματος τοῦ δράκοντος καὶ ἐκ τοῦ στόματος τοῦ θηρίου καὶ ἐκ τοῦ στόματος τοῦ ψευδοπροφήτου πνεύματα τρία ἀκάθαρτα ὡς βάτραχοι [ἐκπορεύεσθαι P47 051 א*]

Zech 13.2ᵖᴹ והיה ביום ההוא נאם יהוה צבאות אכרית את־שמות העצבים מן־הארץ ולא יזכרו עוד וגם את־הנביאים ואת־רוח הטמאה אעביר מן־הארץ

Zech 13.2ᴼᴳ καὶ ἔσται ἐν τῇ ἡμέρᾳ ἐκείνῃ, λέγει κύριος, ἐξολεθρεύσω τὰ ὀνόματα τῶν εἰδώλων ἀπὸ τῆς γῆς, καὶ οὐκέτι ἔσται αὐτῶν μνεία, καὶ τοὺς ψευδοπροφήτας καὶ τὸ πνεῦμα τὸ ἀκάθαρτον ἐξαρῶ ἀπὸ τῆς γῆς

Rev 16.13–16 narrates the gathering of the nations for war, a mustering of force undertaken by three unclean spirits (πνεύματα τρία ἀκάθαρτα) that descend from the mouths of the dragon, beast, and false prophet (ψευδοπροφήτου). The wording in this passage, especially in v. 13, corresponds to similar language used in Zech 13.2 to describe YHWH Sebaoth's destruction of idolatry and false prophecy (καὶ τοὺς ψευδοπροφήτας καὶ τὸ πνεῦμα τὸ ἀκάθαρτον) from the land 'in that day'. The description of the destruction of false prophets in Zechariah blends into the terse pronouncements of judgement and reconciliation that close the chapter (13.3–9).

While certain lexemes are shared between these texts, a connection that is particularly obvious in the OG translation, there are serious incongruities between the texts that suggest that there is no interpretative engagement with Zechariah. The false prophet in Rev 16.13 is an eschatological adversary that eventually succumbs to judgement (cf. Rev 19.20; 20.10), while the false prophets in Zechariah seem to refer to the unfaithful leaders of the people who masquerade as faithful servants of YHWH (cf. Jer 6.13; 33[26].7–8, 11, 16). Although ψευδοπροφήτης, πνεῦμα, and ἀκάθαρος are found clustered only in Zech 13.2 in the OG/

LXX (which in this instance represents a fairly straightforward translation of the proto-MT), there seems to be no direct exegetical pay-off
in the language's reuse here in Revelation. It is possible that the author
of Revelation drew a cluster of lexemes from Zechariah to depict the
gathering of the nations for an eschatological battle (themes that forms
a significant undercurrent in Zech 9.9–17; 10.5–7; 12.2–14; 13.7–14.21),
but I cannot ascertain any interpretative engagement with Zechariah
traditions. In fact, description of the spirits as 'like frogs' (ὡς βάτραχοι) is
the clearest allusion in this locution. The term βάτραχος (and its underlying Hebrew equivalent צפרדע) is only used in the OG/LXX in various
versions of the Exodus plague accounts (Exod 8.2–13; Pss 77(78).45;
104(105).30; Wis. 19.10), suggesting that the gathering of the wicked
army initiated in Rev 16.13 is a type of anti-exodus.[28]

---

[28] See Beale, *Revelation*, 832–833 who gives a full treatment of the potential significance of the frogs and their symbolic value.

Appendix 2

RECONSTRUCTIONS OF 8HEVXIIGR

In this appendix, I reconstruct the text of Zechariah (for the locutions that John reused) as they might have appeared in 8HevXIIgr. Zech 1.4a-3.7a; 8.18–9.7 are the only portions of the work that are witnessed in the manuscript, and most of these segments are very fragmentary.[1] The editors of DJD VIII have reconstructed large parts of these fragmentary extant portions. The relevant texts are reconstructed based on the indices of DJD VIII, 'A Hebrew-Greek Index to 8HevXIIgr', and any relevant readings preserved in Hexaplaric traditions (esp. when the Hexaplaric readings are unified against a OG reading).[2] For each example, the text of the proto-MT and Ziegler's OG are given followed by my reconstruction of 8HevXIIgr.

Sigla

[. . .] indicates that the contained words are reproductions of the OG, since no such equivalency exists in the extant portions of 8HevXIIgr. That is, no Greek word in 8HevXIIgr that stands as a translation equivalent of the Hebrew word present in Zechariah[PM]. Words outwith brackets indicate that enough data within 8HevXIIgr exists to compare translation equivalents and revising tendencies.

Italicized words indicate that my reconstruction differs from the text preserved in the OG. Support for this reconstruction is given in the notes.
ᵀ marks an omission in 8HevXIIgr vis-à-vis OG.

Zech 1.12–14

ויען מלאך־יהוה ויאמר יהוה צבאות עד־מתי אתה לא תרחם את־ירושלם ואת
ערי יהודה אשר זעמתה זה שבעים שנה ויען יהוה את־המלאך הדבר בי
דברים טובים דברים נחמים ויאמר אלי המלאך הדבר בי קרא לאמר כה
אמר יהוה צבאות קנאתי לירושלם ולציון קנאה גדולה

---

[1] See DJD VIII, 66–77.
[2] De Crom, Verbeke, Ceulemans, 'Hebrew-Greek', 331–349.

OG: καὶ ἀπεκρίθη ὁ ἄγγελος κυρίου καὶ εἶπεν Κύριε παντοκράτωρ, ἕως τίνος οὐ μὴ ἐλεήσῃς τὴν Ιερουσαλημ καὶ τὰς πόλεις Ιουδα, ἃς ὑπερεῖδες τοῦτο ἑβδομηκοστὸν ἔτος; καὶ ἀπεκρίθη κύριος παντοκράτωρ τῷ ἀγγέλῳ τῷ λαλοῦντι ἐν ἐμοὶ ῥήματα καλὰ καὶ λόγους παρακλητικούς. καὶ εἶπεν πρός με ὁ ἄγγελος ὁ λαλῶν ἐν ἐμοὶ Ἀνάκραγε λέγων Τάδε λέγει κύριος παντοκράτωρ Ἐζήλωκα τὴν Ιερουσαλημ καὶ τὴν Σιων ζῆλον μέγαν

Reconstruction: καὶ ἀπεκρίθη ᵀ³ ἄγγελος 𐤉𐤄𐤅𐤄 καὶ εἶπεν 𐤉𐤄𐤅𐤄 δυναμεων⁴ [ἕως τίνος] οὐ μὴ [ἐλεήσῃς] Ιερουσαλημ [τὰς πόλεις] Ιουδα ἃς [ὑπερεῖδες]⁵ τοῦτο ἑβδομηκοστὸν [ἔτος]⁶ καὶ ἀπεκρίθη 𐤉𐤄𐤅𐤄 τῷ ἀγγέλῳ τῷ λαλοῦντι ἐν ἐμοὶ ῥήματα *ἀγαθά*⁷ λόγους παρακλητικούς. καὶ εἶπεν πρός με ὁ ἄγγελος ὁ λαλῶν ἐν ἐμοὶ Ἀνάκραγε λέγων Τάδε λέγει 𐤉𐤄𐤅𐤄 δυναμεων Ἐζήλωκα τὴν Ιερουσαλημ καὶ τὴν *σειων*⁸ ζῆλον μέγαν.

Zech 4.10b

שבעה־אלה עיני יהוה המה משוטטים בכל־הארץ

OG: ἑπτὰ οὗτοι ὀφθαλμοὶ κυρίου εἰσὶν οἱ ἐπιβλέποντες ἐπὶ πᾶσαν τὴν γῆν

Reconstruction: ἑπτὰ⁹ οὗτοι¹⁰ [ὀφθαλμοὶ] 𐤉𐤄𐤅𐤄 εἰσὶν¹¹ [οἱ ἐπιβλέποντες] εἰς¹² πᾶσαν τὴν γῆν

Zech 4.14

אלה שני בני־היצהר העמדים על־אדון כל־הארץ

---

³ It is possible that the definite article is included locution in 8HevXIIgr, but Zech 3.5 in this manuscript likely omits the article before the phrase ἄγγελος 𐤉𐤄𐤅𐤄 .

⁴ See Mic 4.4; Hab 2.13; Zech 1.3, 4; 3.7; 8.20 in 8HevXIIgr.

⁵ The noun form of עׁד is witnessed in Hab 3.12 in 8HevXIIgr. It is adjusted towards the proto-MT from the OG, but no verbal form of this root is present in the manuscript. I have chosen to reproduce the OG reading.

⁶ Verses 13–14 are reconstructed identically to DJD VIII, 69.

⁷ The first three letters of this word are visible in the manuscript.

⁸ ΣΕ are visible in the manuscript.

⁹ Cf. Mic 5.4(5) in 8HevXIIgr.

¹⁰ There is no revisionary impulse in 8HevXIIgr in reference to near or far demonstrative pronouns.

¹¹ OG occasionally includes forms of εἰμί which are implicit in the Hebrew text, and there is no revisionary impulse in 8HevXIIgr to substantiate the omission of this word vis-à-vis the OG (cf. Zech 1.19[2.1]).

¹² This preposition represents the Hebrew preposition ב consistently in the manuscript (with the exception of Mic 5.4[5]). 8HevXIIgr also witnesses revisionary tendencies with ב as it revises to εἰς from other Greek prepositions on six occasions (see Mic 5.4[5], 5[6]; Hab 2.4, 17; Zeph 1.5).

OG: Οὗτοι οἱ δύο υἱοὶ τῆς πιότητος παρεστήκασιν τῷ κυρίῳ πάσης τῆς γῆς.

Reconstruction: Οὗτοι[13] οἱ [δύο] υἱοὶ[14] [τῆς πιότητος][15] παρεστήκασιν[16] [τῷ] 𝕌𝕌𝕌 πάσης τῆς γῆς

Zech 6.5

ויען המלאך ויאמר אלי אלה ארבע רחות השמים יוצאות מהתיצב על־אדון כל־הארץ

OG: καὶ ἀπεκρίθη ὁ ἄγγελος ὁ λαλῶν ἐν ἐμοὶ καὶ εἶπεν Ταῦτά ἐστιν οἱ τέσσαρες ἄνεμοι τοῦ οὐρανοῦ, ἐκπορεύονται παραστῆναι τῷ κυρίῳ πάσης τῆς γῆς

Reconstruction: καὶ ἀπεκρίθη ὁ ἄγγελος ὁ λαλῶν ἐν ἐμοὶ[17] καὶ εἶπεν Ταῦτά ἐστιν[18] οἱ τέσσαρες ἄνεμοι[19] οὐρανοῦ[20] ἐκπορεύονται[21] στηλωναι[22] [τῷ 𝕌𝕌𝕌][23] πάσης τῆς γῆς

[13] See n. 11.

[14] See Zeph 1.1; Zech 1.1.

[15] Neither πιότητος, nor its Hebrew equivalent (יצהר) occurs in the extant portions of 8HevXIIgr. This word received significant revisionary attention in the Hexaplaric evidence (see Fields, *Hexaplorum*, 2.1040) as each of 'the Three' offer alternatives that differ from the OG and each other: στιλπνότητος (Aquila), ἐλαίου (Symmachus), λαμπρότητος (Theodotion). Each of these equivalents is related in some manner to the semantics of oil and the Aquilanic and Theodontic revisions preserve morphological and phonological similarities to the OG equivalent. Based on the intense revising of this word in later LXX traditions, it is possible that the tradition of 8HevXIIgr also targeted this word for revision. However, even with this manuscript's relationship to later revisions (see Barthélemy, *Les Devanciers*), it is difficult to determine which possible form this intuited revision might take. Due to the difficulties in determining the shape of the revisions, I have tentatively reproduced the OG reading here.

[16] There is no revisionary pattern in reference to the Hebrew verbal form עמד in 8HevXIIgr (see Mic 5.3(4); Nah 2.9; Hab 2.1). The only difference between the OG and 8HevXIIgr in these examples is in Nah 2.9. The alteration is not lexical, but morphological. I have preserved the OG reading here.

[17] The phrase ὁ ἄγγελος ὁ λαλῶν ἐν ἐμοὶ is preserved by the editors of DJD VIII in Zech 1.14. I have also preserved it here.

[18] See n. 11.

[19] The only two equivalents of רוח in 8HevXIIgr occur in Hab 1.11; 2.19. In both instances, forms of πνεῦμα serve as equivalents in agreement with OG. There is not enough evidence to substantiate a reconstruction that differs from OG here.

[20] Cf. Zeph 1.3, 5 in 8HevXIIgr.

[21] A form of ἐκπορεύομαι is preserved in Mic 1.3, and there is no revision of any translation equivalents of forms of יצא in 8HevXIIgr (see also Mic 5.1[2]; Hab 1.7).

[22] The only instance of יצב (in *hithpael*) in 8HevXIIgr is in Hab 2.1. The reading in this manuscript (στηλωσομαι [partially reconstructed]) does not agree with OG (ἐπιβήσομαι). Forms of στηλόω ('to stand firm; devote oneself to another' [LSJ, 1644]) also serve as translation equivalents for יצב (in *hithpael*) in 1 Sam 17.16; 2 Sam 18.30; 23.12[OG]. The only available evidence from 8HevXIIgr points in the direct of alteration, although it is difficult to establish a pattern of revision based on one example.

[23] על does not have a direct equivalent in OG, but is expressed with the dative case. Similarly, translation equivalents that have אדון as a Hebrew antecedent are

Zech 12.10

ושפכתי על־בית דויד ועל יושב ירושלם רוח חן ותחנונים והביטו אלי את

³¹ אשר־דקרו וספדו עליו כמספד על־היחיד והמר עליו כהמר על־הבכור

καὶ ἐκχεῶ ἐπὶ τὸν οἶκον Δαυιδ καὶ ἐπὶ τοὺς κατοικοῦντας

Ιερουσαλημ πνεῦμα χάριτος καὶ οἰκτιρμοῦ, καὶ ἐπιβλέψονται

πρός με ἀνθ ὧν κατωρχήσαντο καὶ κόψονται ἐπ' αὐτὸν κοπετὸν

ὡς ἐπ' ἀγαπητὸν καὶ ὀδυνηθήσονται ὀδύνην ὡς ἐπὶ πρωτοτόκῳ

Reconstruction: καὶ [ἐκχεῶ]²⁴ ἐπὶ ᵀ²⁵ οἶκον Δαυιδ καὶ

ἐπὶ τοὺς κατοικοῦντας Ιερουσαλημ πνεῦμα χάριτος

καὶ [οἰκτιρμοῦ]²⁶ καὶ²⁷ ἐπιβλέψονται²⁸ πρός με²⁹ [εἰς ὅν

ἐξεκέντησαν]³⁰ καὶ [κόψονται]³¹ ᵀ³² αὐτὸν ὡς κοπετόν³³ [ἐπ'

not present in in 8HevXIIgr. No forms of κύριος are witnessed in 8HevXIIgr as the Tetragrammaton stands is written in a palaeo-Hebrew script in this Greek manuscript twenty-four times in the preserved sections (See DJD VIII, 16). It is difficult to determine how the scribes of 8HevXIIgr would have handled אדון. Θεός is an option, but it consistently translated אלהים in the manuscript (see Jon 3.8, 9, 19; Mic 4.5; 5.3(4); Nah 1.14; Zech 8.23). I find it more likely that the scribes who produced 8HevXIIgr likely understood אדון in this verse as a reference to יהוה, thus I have inserted 𐤉𐤄𐤅𐤄 here. They may also have responded to the presence of κυρίῳ in the OG and revised this word to 𐤉𐤄𐤅𐤄 without reference to the Hebrew. This is a tenuous reconstruction.

²⁴ This word (שפך) does not find an equivalent in 8HevXIIgr, but no alternative reading to ἐκχεῶ is witnessed here in the rest of the Greek tradition.

²⁵ I tentatively omit the article here for three reasons: (1) the article is not present in the Hebrew; (2) manuscript 130 likewise omits the article; (3) 8HevXIIgr omits an article present in the OG to bring the text into greater alignment with proto-MT (= no article) in eight places (Hab 1.11, 14; 2.2, 4, 19; Mic 1.2; Nah 2.9; 3.8).

²⁶ This word is not measurable against a parallel reading in 8HevXIIgr, but there is no evidence of other variation in the Greek tradition.

²⁷ Manuscript 130 omits this καί.

²⁸ There is no evidence of a revising tendency regarding נבט (see Jon 2.5; Hab 2.15), although ὄψονται is the reading witnessed in Matt 24.30, John 19.37, *and* Rev 1.7 (in א 2351 1611, otherwise in a different morphological form ὄψεται).

²⁹ In Zech 1.4 and 8.21, 8HevXIIgr presents πρός as an equivalent for אל contra OG.

³⁰ Although there is no evidence internal to 8HevXIIgr that might suggest such a reading (hence the square brackets), the weight of the tradition, especially in the Hexaplaric tradition, suggests that an early revising version might preserve a similar reading. Reading דקרו, instead of the reading preserved in the OG (κατωρχήσαντο = רקדו), ἐξεκέντησαν makes perfect sense, since it is preserved in each of the Hexaplaric witnesses (ἐπεξεκέντησαν in Symm.; cf. also Rev 1.7; John 19.37; Cyril of Alexandria *Comm. Zach.* 2.493; Justin Martyr *Dial.* 14.8; *1. Apol.* 52.12). W also preserves κατηχησαντο diverging from the OG reading. Additionally, the correspondence with the Justin text signals that 8HevXIIgr might also preserve this reading.

³¹ S* 919 preserve οψονται (cf. John 19.37).

³² None of the Hexaplaric traditions witness the preposition here.

³³ I have transposed these words because 8HevXIIgr shows a slight tendency to stylistic transposition to the serial order of Hebrew elements. See DJD VIII, 140.

ἀγαπητὸν]³⁴ καὶ [ὀδυνηθήσονται] ἐπ᾽αὐτόν³⁵ ὡς [ὀδύνην] ἐπὶ [πρωτοτόκῳ]³⁶

---

³⁴ There is no direct comparison to יחד in 8HevXIIgr; however, this collocation in brackets does exhibit variation in the rest of the Greek tradition, particularly the choice of preposition and the corresponding case of the noun. See esp. W among other witnesses.

³⁵ Different preposition/pronoun combinations are employed to create this plus, but I have chosen the one that corresponds to other equivalencies of עליו (an equivalent for which is not present in OG) in this verse. There is no direct evidence for this plus in 8HevXIIgr, but in other locations (Jon 2.4; Zeph 1.4) prepositions are included against the OG in alignment with the proto-MT.

³⁶ The Greek tradition has a tendency to present this word in different morphological arrangements, in agreement with the deployment of similar pronouns (like ἐν in 538).

BIBLIOGRAPHY

Abegg, Martin G. '1QIsaᵃ and 1QIsaᵇ: A Rematch'. Pages 221–228 in *The Bible as Book: The Hebrew Bible and the Judean Desert Discoveries*. Edited by E. D. Herbert and E. Tov. London: British Library, 2002.

Abel, F.-M. *Les Livres des Maccabées*. Paris: Lecoffre, 1949.

Aharoni, Y. 'Expedition B – The Cave of Horror'. *IEJ* 12 no 3/4 (1961): 186–199.

Ahearne-Kroll, Patricia. 'LXX/OG Zechariah 1–6 and the Portrayal of Joshua Centuries after the Restoration of the Temple'. Pages 179–192 in *Septuagint Research: Issues and Challenges in the Study of the Greek Jewish Scriptures*. SCS 53. Edited by W. Kraus and R. G. Wooden. Atlanta: SBL, 2006.

Albl, M. C. *'And Scripture Cannot be Broken': The Form and Function of Early Christian Testimonia Collections*. NTsup 96. Leiden: Brill, 1999.

Alexander, P. S. 'The Targumim and Early Exegesis of "the Sons of God" in Genesis 6'. *JJS* 23 (1972): 60–71.

Alexander, P. S. 'Jewish Aramaic Translations of Hebrew Scriptures'. Pages 217–251 in *Mikra: Text, Translation, Reading & Interpretation of the Hebrew Bible in Ancient Judaism & Early Christianity*. Edited by M. Mulder. Peabody, MA: Hendrickson, 1988.

Alexander, P. S. 'The Bible in Qumran and Early Judaism'. Pages 25–62 in *Text in Context: Essays by Members of the Society for Old Testament Study*. Edited by A. D. H. Mays. Oxford: Oxford University Press, 2000.

Alexander, P. S. 'Why no Textual Criticism in Rabbinic Midrash? Reflections on the Textual Culture of the Rabbis'. Pages 175–190 in *Jewish Ways of Reading the Bible*. JSSsup 11. Edited by G. J. Brooke. Oxford: Oxford University Press, 2000.

Allegro, J. M. with A. A. Anderson. *Qumran Cave 4.I (4Q158–4Q186)*. DJD V. Oxford: Clarendon, 1968.

Allen, Garrick V. 'Textual Pluriformity and Allusion in the Book of Revelation: The Text of Zechariah 4 in the Apocalypse'. *ZNW* 106 no 1 (2015): 136–145.

Allen, Garrick V. 'Techniques of Reuse: Reworking Scripture in the Apocalypse'. Pages 1–17 in *The Book of Revelation: Currents in British*

Research on the Apocalypse. WUNT 2.411. Edited by G. V. Allen, I. Paul, and S. P. Woodman. Tübingen: Mohr Siebeck, 2015.

Allen, Garrick V. 'The Reuse of Scripture in 4QCommentary on Genesis C (4Q254) and "Messianic Interpretation" in the Dead Sea Scrolls'. *RevQ*, 27/106 (2015): 303–317.

Allen, Garrick V. 'Scriptural Allusions in the Book of Revelation and the Contours of Textual Research 1900–2014: Retrospect and Prospects'. *CBR* 14 (2016): 319–339.

Allen, L. C. *The Greek Chronicles: The Relation of the Septuagint of I and II Chronicles to the Masoretic Text*. VTsup 25. Vol. 1. Leiden: Brill, 1974.

Anderson, Robert T. and Terry Giles. *The Samaritan Pentateuch: An Introduction to Its Origins, History, and Significance for Biblical Studies*. RBS 72. Atlanta: SBL, 2012.

Assmann, Jan. *Cultural Memory and Early Civilization: Writing, Remembrance, and Political Imagination*. Cambridge: Cambridge University Press, 2011.

Attridge, H. et al. *Qumran Cave 4.VIII: Parabiblical Texts, Part 1*. DJD XIII. Oxford: Clarendon, 1994.

Aune, David. *Revelation*. 3 vols. WBC 52a–c. Nashville: Thomas Nelson, 1997–1998.

Aune, David. *Apocalypticism, Prophecy and Magic in Early Christianity: Collected Essays*. WUNT 199. Tübingen: Mohr Siebeck, 2006.

Aune, David. 'Apocalypse Renewed: An Intertextual Reading of the Apocalypse of John'. Pages 43–70 in *The Reality of Apocalypse: Rhetoric and Politics in the Book of Revelation*. Symposium 39. Edited by D. L. Barr. Atlanta: SBL, 2006.

Baillet, M., J. T. Milik, and R. de Vaux. *Les 'petits grottes' de Qumran*. DJD III. Oxford: Clarendon, 1962.

Bakhtin, Mikhail. *The Dialogic Imagination: Four Essays*. Translated by C. Emerson and M. Holquist. London: University of Texas Press, 1981.

Barker, Margaret. *The Revelation of Jesus Christ*. Edinburgh: T&T Clark, 2000.

Barr, James. *The Typology of Literalism in Ancient Biblical Translations*. MSU 15. Göttingen: Vandenhoeck & Ruprecht, 1979.

Barr, James. 'Reading the Bible as Literature'. Pages 74–91 in *Bible and Interpretation The Collected Essays of James Barr*. Vol. 1. Edited by J. Barton. Oxford: Oxford University Press, 2013. Repr. from *Bulletin of the John Rylands Library* 56 (1973–1974): 10–33.

Barr, James. 'Hebrew עד, Especially at Job i.8 and Neh. vii.8'. Pages 596–609 in *Bible and Interpretation: The Collected Essays of James Barr*. Vol. 3. Edited by J. Barton. Oxford: Oxford University Press, 2014. Repr. from *JSS* 27 (1982): 177–188.

Barr, James. 'Ερίζω and Επειδω in the Septuagint: A Note Principally on Gen. xlix. 6'. Pages 115–129 in *Bible and Interpretation: The Collected Essays of*

James Barr. Vol. 3. Edited by J. Barton. Oxford: Oxford University Press, 2014. Repr. from *JSS* 19 (1974): 198–215.

Barr, James. 'Vocalization and the Analysis of Hebrew Among the Ancient Translators'. Pages 5–13 in *Bible and Interpretation: The Collected Essays of James Barr*. Vol. 3. Edited by J. Barton. Oxford: Oxford University Press, 2014. Repr. from *VT* 16 (1967): 1–11.

Barr, James. '"Guessing" in the Septuagint'. Pages 28–43 in *Bible and Interpretation: The Collected Essays of James Barr*. Vol. 3. Edited by J. Barton. Oxford: Oxford University Press, 2014. Repr. from *Studien zur Septuaginta: Robert Hanhard zu Ehren*. Abhandlungen der Akademie der Wissenschaften in Göttingen. Edited by D. Fraenkel et al. Göttingen: Vandenhoeck & Ruprecht, 1990, 19–34.

Barr, James. 'Translator's Handling of Verb Tense in Semantically Ambiguous Contexts'. Pages 190–205 in *Bible and Interpretation: The Collected Essays of James Barr*. Vol. 3. Edited by J. Barton. Oxford: Oxford University Press, 2014. Repr. from *LXX: VI Congress of the International Organization for Septuagint and Cognate Studies, Jerusalem 1986*. SCS 23. Edited by C. E. Cox. Atlanta: Scholars, 1987.

Barthélemy, D. 'Redécouverte d'un chaînon manquant de l'histoire de la Septante'. *RB* 60 no 1 (1953): 18–29.

Barthélemy, D. *Les Devanciers D'Aquila*. VTsup 10. Leiden: Brill, 1963.

Barthélemy, D. 'Histoire du texte Hébraïque de l'Ancien Testament'. Pages 341–364 in *Études d'histoire du texte de l'Ancient Testament*. OBO 21. Göttingen: Vandenhoeck & Ruprecht, 1978.

Barthélemy, D. *Critique Textuelle de l'Ancien Testament: Ézéchiel, Daniel et les 12 Prophètes*. Vol. 3. Göttingen: Vandenhoeck & Ruprecht, 1992.

Bartlett, John R. *The First and Second Books of the Maccabees*. Cambridge: Cambridge University Press, 1973.

Bartlett, John R. *1 Maccabees*. Guides to the Apocrypha & Pseudepigrapha. Sheffield: Sheffield Academic Press, 1998.

Barzilai, Gabriel. 'Incidental Biblical Exegesis in the Qumran Scrolls and its Importance for the Study of the Second Temple Period'. *DSD* 14 no 1 (2007): 1–22.

Bauckham, Richard. *The Climax of Prophecy: Studies on the Book of Revelation*. Edinburgh: T&T Clark, 1993.

Bauckham, Richard. *The Theology of the Book of Revelation*. Cambridge: Cambridge University Press, 1993.

Bauks, Michaela. 'Intertextuality in Ancient Literature in Light of Textlinguistics and Cultural Studies'. Pages 27–46 in *Between Text and Text: The Hermeneutics of Intertextuality in Ancient Culture and Their Afterlife in Medieval and Modern Times*. JAJsup 6. Edited by M. Bauks, W. Horowitz, and A. Lange. Göttingen: Vandenhoeck & Ruprecht, 2013.

Bautch, Kelley Coblentz. 'Putting Angels in Their Place: Developments in Second Temple Angelology'. Pages 174–188 in *With Wisdom as a*

Robe: Qumran and Other Jewish Studies in Honour of Ida Fröhlich. HBM 21. Edited by K. D. Dobos and M. Köszeghy. Sheffield: Sheffield Phoenix, 2009.

Beal, Lissa W. Wray. 'Blessing Lost: Intertextual Inversion in Hosea'. *Didaskalia* (2005): 17–39.

Beale, G. K. *The Use of Daniel in Jewish Apocalyptic Literature and in the Revelation of St. John.* London: University Press of America, 1984.

Beale, G. K. 'The Origins of the Title "King of Kings and Lord of Lords" in Revelation 17.14'. *NTS* 31 (1985): 618–620.

Beale, G. K. 'A Reconsideration of the Text of Daniel in the Apocalypse'. *Biblica* 67 (1986): 539–543.

Beale, G. K. *John's Use of the Old Testament in Revelation.* JSNTsup 166. Sheffield: Sheffield Academic Press, 1998.

Beale, G. K. *The Book of Revelation: A Commentary on the Greek Text.* New International Greek Testament Commentary. Cambridge: Eerdmans, 1999.

Beale, G. K. 'A Response to Jon Paulien on the Use of the Old Testament in Revelation'. *AUSS* 39 (2001): 23–34.

Beale, G. K. *Handbook on the New Testament Use of the Old Testament: Exegesis and Interpretation.* Grand Rapids: Baker, 2012.

Beasley-Murray, G. B. *The Book of Revelation.* NCB. London: Oliphants, 1974.

Beckwith, Isbon T. *The Apocalypse of John.* New York: Macmillan, 1919.

Ben-Porat, Ziva. 'The Poetics of Literary Allusion'. *PTL: A Journal for Descriptive Poetics and Theory of Literature* 1 (1976): 105–128.

Benoit, P., J. T. Milik, and R. de Vaux. *Les grottes de Murabba'at.* DJD II. Oxford: Clarendon, 1961.

Bernstein, Moshe J. 'Pesher Habakkuk'. Pages 647–650 in *EDSS.* Vol. 2. Edited by L. H. Schiffman and J. C. VanderKam. Oxford: Oxford University Press, 2000.

Bernstein, Moshe J. 'Interpretation of Scriptures'. Pages 376–383 in *EDSS.* Vol. 1. Edited by L. H. Schiffman and J. C. VanderKam. Oxford: Oxford University Press, 2000.

Bernstein, Moshe J. 'The Contribution of the Qumran Discoveries to the History of Early Biblical Interpretation'. Pages 215–238 in *The Idea of Biblical Interpretation: Essays in Honor of James L. Kugel.* Edited by H. Najman and J. H. Newman. Leiden: Brill, 2004.

Bernstein, Moshe J. 'The Genesis Apocryphon'. Pages 157–179 in *A Companion to Biblical Interpretation in Early Judaism.* Edited by M. Henze. Cambridge: Eerdmans, 2012.

Bernstein, Moshe J. and Shlomo A. Koyfman. 'The Interpretation of Biblical Law in the Dead Sea Scrolls'. Pages 61–87 in *Biblical Interpretation at Qumran.* Edited by M. Henze. Cambridge: Eerdmans, 2005.

Berrin, Shani L. 'Pesharim'. Pages 644–647 in *EDSS.* Vol. 2. Edited by L. H. Schiffman and J. C. VanderKam. Oxford: Oxford University Press, 2000.

Bissell, E. C. 'On Zech. vi. 1–7'. *Journal of the Society of Biblical Literature and Exegesis* 6 (1886): 117–118.

Bloom, Harold. *The Anxiety of Influence: A Theory of Poetry*, 2nd edn. Oxford: Oxford University Press, 1997.

Bloom, Harold. *The Shadow of a Great Rock: A Literary Appreciation of the King James Bible*. London: Yale University Press, 2011.

Bloomquist, L. Gregory. 'Methodological Criteria for Apocalyptic Rhetoric: A Suggestion for Expanded Use of Sociorhetorical Analysis'. Pages 181–203 in *Vision and Persuasion: Rhetorical Dimensions of Apocalyptic Discourse*. Edited by G. Carey and L. G. Bloomquist. St. Louis: Chalice: 1999.

Blount, Brian K. *Revelation: A Commentary*. NTL. Louisville: WJK, 2009.

Bocur, Bogdan G. *Angelomorphic Pneumatology: Clement of Alexandria and Other Early Christian Witnesses*. VCsup 95. Leiden: Brill, 2009.

Boda, Mark J. and Michael H. Floyd, eds. *Tradition in Transition: Haggai and Zechariah 1–8 in the Trajectory of Hebrew Theology*. New York: T&T Clark, 2008.

Bøe, Sverre. *Gog and Magog: Ezekiel 38–39 as Pre-text for Revelation 19,17–21 and 20,7–10*. WUNT 2.135. Tübingen: Mohr Siebeck, 2001.

Böhl, Eduard. *Die alttestamentlichen Zitate im Neuen Testament*. Vienna, 1878.

Böhler, Dieter. 'Abraham und Seine Kinder im Johannesprolog. Zur Vielgestaltigkeit des alttestamentlichen Textes bei Johannes'. Pages 15–29 in *L'Ecrit et l'Esprit: Etudes d'Histoire du Texte et de Théologie Biblique en Hommage à Adrian Schenker*. OBO 214. Edited by D. Böhler, I. Himbaza, and P. Hugo. Göttingen: Vandenhoeck & Ruprecht, 2005.

Boismard, M.-É. 'Rapprochements littéraires entre l'évangelie de Luc et l'Apocalypse'. Pages 53–63 in *Synoptische Studien: Festschrift A. Wikenhauser*. Edited by J. Schmid and A. Vöglte. Munich: Karl Zink, 1953.

Boring, Eugene M. *Revelation*. Interpretation. Louisville: John Knox, 1989.

Boring, Eugene M. *Mark: A Commentary*. NTL. London: WJK, 2006.

Boxall, Ian. *The Revelation of Saint John*. BNTC. London: Continuum, 2006.

Boxall, Ian. *Patmos in the Reception History of the Apocalypse*. OTRM. Oxford: Oxford University Press, 2013.

Brenner, Athalya. *Colour Terms in the Old Testament*. JSOTsup 21. Sheffield: Sheffield Academic Press, 1982.

Briggs, Charles A. 'The Use of רוח in the Old Testament'. *JBL* 19 no 1 (1900): 132–145.

Briggs, Robert A. *Jewish Temple Imagery in the Book of Revelation*. SB 10. New York: Peter Lang, 1999.

Brooke, George J. *Exegesis at Qumran: 4QFlorilegium in its Jewish Context*. JSOTsup 29. Sheffield: SBL, 1985.

Brooke, George J. '4Q254 Fragments 1 and 4, and 4Q254a: Some Preliminary Comments'. Pages 185–192 in *Proceedings of the Eleventh World Congress of Jewish Studies*. Edited by D. Assaf. Jerusalem: Word Union of Jewish Studies, 1994.

Brooke, George J. 'Rewritten Bible'. Pages 777–780 in *EDSS*. Vol. 2. Edited by L. H. Schiffman and J. C. VanderKam. Oxford: Oxford University Press, 2000.

Brooke, George J. 'The Rewritten Law, Prophets and Psalms: Issues for Understanding the Text of the Bible'. Pages 31–40 in *The Bible as Book: The Hebrew Bible and the Judean Desert Discoveries*. Edited by E. D. Herbert and E. Tov. London: British Library, 2002.

Brooke, George J. 'Deuteronomy 5–6 in the Phylacteries From Qumran Cave 4'. Pages 57–70 in *Emanuel: Studies in Hebrew Bible, Septuagint and Dead Sea Scrolls in Honor of Emanuel Tov*. VTsup 94. Edited by S. M. Paul et al. Leiden: Brill, 2003.

Brooke, George J. 'Thematic Commentaries on Prophetic Scripture'. Pages 134–157 in *Biblical Interpretation at Qumran*. Edited by M. Henze. Cambridge: Eerdmans, 2005.

Brooke, George J. *The Dead Sea Scrolls and the New Testament*. Minneapolis: Fortress, 2005.

Brooke, George J. 'Biblical Interpretation at Qumran'. Pages 287–319 in *The Bible and the Dead Sea Scrolls*. Vol. 1. Edited by J. H. Charlesworth. Waco: Baylor University Press, 2006.

Brooke, George J. 'The Twelve Minor Prophets and the Dead Sea Scrolls'. Pages 19–43 in *Congress Volume Leiden 2004*. VTsup 109. Edited by A. Lemaire. Leiden: Brill, 2006.

Brooke, George J. 'New Perspectives on the Bible and its Interpretation in the Dead Sea Scrolls'. Pages 19–37 in *The Dynamics of Language and Exegesis at Qumran*. FAT 2.35. Edited by D. Dimant and R. G. Kratz. Tübingen: Mohr Siebeck, 2009.

Brooke, George J. 'Aspects of Matthew's Use of Scripture in Light of the Dead Sea Scrolls'. Pages 821–838 in *A Teacher for All Generations: Essays in Honor of James C. VanderKam*. JSJsup 153.2. Edited by E. F. Mason. Leiden: Brill, 2012.

Brooke, George J. *Reading the Dead Sea Scrolls: Essays in Method*. EJL 39. Atlanta: SBL, 2013.

Brooke, George J. '2 Corinthians 6:14–7:1 Again: A Change in Perspective'. Pages 1–16 in *The Dead Sea Scrolls and Pauline Literature*. STDJ 102. Edited by J.-S. Rey. Leiden: Brill, 2014.

Brooke, G. J. et al. *Qumran Cave 4.XVII: Parabiblical Texts, Part 3*. DJD XXII. Oxford: Clarendon: 1996.

Brown, David. *Tradition & Imagination: Revelation & Change*. Oxford: Oxford University Press, 1999.

Brownlee, William H. 'Biblical Interpretation among the Sectaries of the Dead Sea Scrolls'. *The Biblical Archaeologist* 14 (1951): 54–76.

Bruehler, Bart B. 'Seeing Through the עינים of Zechariah: Understanding Zechariah 4'. *CBQ* 63 no 3 (2001): 430–443.

Bruno, Christopher R. 'The Deliverer From Zion: The Source(s) and Function of Paul's Citation in Romans 11:26–27'. *TB* 59 no 1 (2008): 119–134.

Bynum, Wm. Randolph. *The Fourth Gospel and the Scriptures: Illuminating the Form and Meaning of Scriptural Citation in John 19:37*. NTsup 144. Leiden: Brill, 2012.

Caird, G. B. *The Revelation of Saint John*. BNTC. Peabody, MA: Hendrickson, 1966.

Cambier, J. 'Les Images de l'Ancien Testament dans l'Apocalypse de saint Jean'. *NTR* 2 (1955): 113–122.

Campbell, Jonathan G. *The Use of Scripture in the Damascus Document 1–8, 19–20*. BZAW 228. Berlin: De Gruyter, 1995.

Carr, David M. 'Method in Determination of Direction of Dependence: An Empirical Test of Criteria Applied to Exodus 34,11–16 and its Parallels'. Pages 107–140 in *Gottes Volk am Sinai. Untersuchungen zu Ex 32–34 und Dtn 9–10*. Edited by M. Köckert and E. Blum. Gütersloh: Gütersloh Verlag, 2011.

Carr, David M. *Writing on the Tablet of the Heart: Origins of Scripture and Literature*. Oxford: Oxford University Press, 2005.

Carrell, Peter R. *Jesus and the Angels: Angelology and the Christology of the Apocalypse of John*. SNTSMS 95. Cambridge: Cambridge University Press, 1997.

Casey, Jay Smith. 'Exodus Typology in the Book of Revelation'. PhD diss., Southern Baptist Theological Seminary, 1981.

Cathcart, Kevin J. and Robert P. Gordon, eds. *The Targum of the Minor Prophets*. The Aramaic Bible 14. Minneapolis: Liturgical Press, 1989.

Caulley, Thomas Scott and Hermann Lichtenberger, eds. *Die Septuaginta und das frühe Christentum*. WUNT 277. Tübingen: Mohr Siebeck, 2011.

Charles, R. H. *The Greek Versions of the Testaments of the Twelve Patriarchs*. Oxford: Clarendon, 1908.

Charles, R. H. *A Critical and Exegetical Commentary on The Revelation of St. John*. 2 vols. ICC. Edinburgh: T&T Clark, 1920.

Chary, Théophane, *Aggée-Zacharie Malachie*. Sources Bibliques. Paris: Lecoffre, 1969.

Choat, Malcolm. 'The Unidentified Text in the Freer Minor Prophets Codex'. Pages 87–121 in *The Freer Biblical Manuscripts: Fresh Studies of an American Treasure Trove*. TCS 6. Edited by L. W. Hurtado. Leiden: Brill, 2006.

Clarke, Kent D. 'Paleography and Philanthropy: Charles Lang Freer and His Acquisitions of the "Freer Biblical Manuscripts"'. Pages 17–73 in *The Freer Biblical Manuscripts: Fresh Studies of an American Treasure Trove*. TCS 6. Edited by L. W. Hurtado. Leiden: Brill, 2006.

Clines, David J. A. 'What Remains of the Hebrew Bible? The Accuracy of the Text of the Hebrew Bible in Light of the Qumran Samuel (4QSam^a)'.

Pages 211–220 in *Studies on the Text and Versions of the Hebrew Bible in Honour of Robert Gordon*. VTsup 149. Edited by G. Kahn and D. Lipton. Leiden: Brill, 2012.

Collins, Adela Yarbro. *The Combat Myth in the Book of Revelation*. HDR 9. Missoula: Scholars, 1976.

Collins, John J. *Daniel, First Maccabees, Second Maccabees with an Excursus on the Apocalyptic Genre*. OTM 16. Wilmington, DE: Michael Glazier, 1981.

Collins, John J. *The Scepter and the Star: Messianism in Light of the Dead Sea Scrolls*. 2nd edn. Cambridge: Eerdmans, 2010.

Considine, J. S. 'The Rider on the White Horse'. *CBQ* 6 no 4 (1944): 406–422.

Crawford, Sidnie White. 'Reworked Pentateuch'. Pages 775–777 in *EDSS*. Vol. 2. Edited by L. H. Schiffman and J. C. VanderKam. Oxford: Oxford University Press, 2000.

Crawford, Sidnie White. *The Temple Scroll and Related Texts*. Sheffield: Sheffield Academic Press, 2000.

Crawford, Sidnie White. 'Reading Deuteronomy in the Second Temple Period'. Pages 127–140 in *Reading the Present in the Qumran Library: The Perception of the Contemporary by Means of Scriptural Interpretations*. Symposium 30. Edited by K. De Troyer and A. Lange. Atlanta: SBL, 2005.

Crawford, Sidnie White. *Rewriting Scripture in Second Temple Times*. Cambridge: Eerdmans, 2008.

Crawford, Sidnie White and Cecilia Wassen, eds. *The Dead Sea Scrolls at Qumran and the Concept of a Library*. STDJ 116; Leiden: Brill, 2016.

Cross, F. M. 'The Contribution of the Qumran Discoveries to the Study of the Biblical Text'. Pages 278–292 in *Qumran and the History of the Biblical Text*. Edited by F. M. Cross and S. Talmon. London: Harvard University Press, 1975.

Cross, F. M. 'The Biblical Scrolls from Qumran and the Canonical Text'. Pages 67–75 in *The Bible and the Dead Sea Scrolls*. Vol. 1. Edited by J. H. Charlesworth. Waco: Baylor University Press, 2006.

Curtis, Edward Lewis. *A Critical and Exegetical Commentary of the Books of Chronicles*. ICC. Edinburgh: T&T Clark, 1910.

Day, John. 'The Origin of Armageddon: Revelation 16:16 as an Interpretation of Zechariah 12:11'. Pages 315–326 in *Crossing the Boundaries: Essays in Biblical Interpretation in Honour of Michael D. Goulder*. Edited by S. E. Porter, P. Joyce, and D. E. Orton. Leiden: Brill, 1994.

Dancy, J. C. *A Commentary on 1 Maccabees*. Oxford: Blackwell, 1954.

Davis, R. Dean. *The Heavenly Court Judgment of Revelation 4–5*. London: University Press of America, 1992.

De Beaugrande, Robert and Wolfgang Dressler. *Introduction to Text Linguistics*. New York: Longman, 1981.

De Crom, Dries, Elke Verbeke, and Reinhart Ceulemans. 'A Hebrew-Greek Index to 8HevXIIgr'. *RevQ* 95 no 3 (2010): 331–349.

De Groote, Marc. *Oecumenii Commentarius in Apocalypsin*. Traditio Exegetica Graeca 8. Leuven: Peeters, 1999.

De Lagarde, Paul. *Anmerkungen zur griechischen Übersetzung der Proverbien*. Leipzig: Brockhaus, 1863.

De Moor, Johannes C., ed. *A Bilingual Concordance to the Targum of the Prophets*. 21 vols. Leiden: Brill, 1996–2003.

De Troyer, Kristin. *Rewriting the Sacred Text: What the Old Greek Tells Us about the Literary Growth of the Bible*. TCS 4. Leiden: Brill, 2004.

De Troyer, Kristin. 'The Freer Twelve Minor Prophets Codex – A Case Study: The Old Greek Text of Jonah, Its Revisions, and Its Corrections'. Pages 75–85 in *The Freer Biblical Manuscripts: Fresh Studies of an American Treasure Trove*. TCS 6. Edited by L. W. Hurtado. Leiden: Brill, 2006.

De Vries, Johannes. 'Ps 86^{MT}/Ps 85^{LXX} in Apk 15,4bß: Anmerkungen zum Text von Psalter und Johannesoffenbarung'. Pages 417–423 in *Von Der Septuaginta zum Neuen Testament: Textgeschichtliche Erörterungen*. ANTF 43. Edited by M. Karrer, S. Kreuzer, and M. Sigismund. Berlin: De Gruyter, 2010.

De Vries, Johannes and Martin Karrer, eds. *Textual History and the Reception of Scripture in Early Christianity*. SCS 60. Atlanta: SBL, 2013.

De Vries, Johannes and Martin Karrer. 'Early Christian Quotations and the Textual History of the Septuagint: A Summary of the Wuppertal Research Project and Introduction to the Volume'. Pages 3–19 in *Textual History and the Reception of Scripture in Early Christianity*. SCS 60. Edited by J. de Vries and M. Karrer. Atlanta: SBL, 2013.

De Waard, J. *A Comparative Study of the Old Testament Text in the Dead Sea Scrolls and in the New Testament*. STDJ 4. Leiden: Brill, 1975.

Debel, Hans. 'Greek "Variant Literary Editions" to the Hebrew Bible?' *JSJ* 42 (2010): 161–190.

Debel, Hans. 'Rewritten Bible, Variant Literary Editions and Original Text(s): Exploring the Implications of a Pluriform Outlook on the Scriptural Tradition'. Pages 65–91 in *Changes in Scripture: Rewriting and Interpreting Authoritative Traditions in the Second Temple Period*. BZAW 419. Edited by H. von Weissenberg et al. Berlin: De Gruyter, 2011.

Decock, Paul B. 'The Scriptures in the Book of Revelation'. *Neotestamentica* 33 (1999): 373–410.

Derrida, Jacques. *Of Grammatology*. Translated by G. C. Spivak. London: The Johns Hopkins University Press, 1998.

deSilva, David A. *Seeing Things John's Way: The Rhetoric of the Book of Revelation*. Louisville: WJK, 2009.

Docherty, Susan. 'The Text Form of the OT Citations in Hebrews Chapter 1 and the Implications for the Study of the Septuagint'. *NTS* 55 no 3 (2009): 355–365.

Docherty, Susan. *The Use of the Old Testament in Hebrews: A Case Study in Early Jewish Interpretation*. WUNT 2.260. Tübingen: Mohr Siebeck, 2009.

Dochhorn, Jan. *Schriftgelehrte Prophetie: Der eschatologische Teufelsfall in Apoc Joh 12 und seine Bedeutung für das Verständnis der Johannesoffenbarung*. WUNT 268. Tübingen: Mohr Siebeck, 2010.

Dodd, C. H. *According to the Scriptures: The Sub-Structure of New Testament Theology*. London: Nisbet & Co., 1952.

Doering, Lutz. '4QMMT and the Letter of Paul: Selected Aspects of Mutual Illumination'. Pages 69–87 in *The Dead Sea Scrolls and Pauline Literature*. STDJ 102. Edited by J.-S. Rey. Leiden: Brill, 2013.

Dogniez, Cecile. 'La Reconstruction du Temple selon al Septante de Zacharie'. Pages 45–64 in *Congress Volume Leiden 2004*. VTsup 109. Edited by A. Lemaire. Leiden: Brill, 2006.

Dogniez, Cecile. 'Some Similarities between the Septuagint and the Targum of Zechariah'. Pages 89–102 in *Translating a Translation: The LXX and its Modern Translations in the Context of Early Judaism*. BETL 213. Edited by H. Ausloos et al. Leuven: Peeters, 2008.

Doran, Robert. '1 Maccabees'. Pages 3–178 in *The New Interpreter's Bible*. Vol. 4. Nashville: Abingdon, 1996.

Driver, S. R. *Introduction to the Literature of the Old Testament*. 9th edn. Edinburgh: T&T Clark, 1913.

Dunn, James D. G. *Romans 9–16*. WBC 38b. Dallas: Word, 1988.

Ego, Beate et al., eds. *Minor Prophets*. BQ 3b. Leiden: Brill, 2005.

Ellinger, K. and W. Rudolph, eds. *Biblia Hebraica Stuttgartensia*. Stuttgart: Deutsche Bibelgesellschaft, 1983.

Elliott, J. K. *New Testament Textual Criticism: The Application of Thoroughgoing Principles: Essays on Manuscripts and Textual Variation*. NTsup 137. Leiden: Brill, 2010.

Ellis, E. Earle. 'Biblical Interpretation in the New Testament Church'. Pages 691–725 in *Mikra: Text, Translation, Reading & Interpretation of the Hebrew Bible in Ancient Judaism & Early Christianity*. Edited by M. Mulder. Peabody, MA: Hendrickson, 1988.

Elschenbroich, Julian and Johannes de Vries, eds. *Worte der Weissagung: Studien zu Septuaginta und Johannesoffenbarung*. ABG 47. Leipzig: Evangelische Verlagsanstalt, 2014.

Evans, Craig A. '"The Two Sons of Oil": Early Evidence of Messianic Interpretation of Zechariah 4:14 in 4Q254'. Pages 566–575 in *The Provo International Conference on the Dead Sea Scrolls: Technological Innovations, New Texts, and Reformulated Issues*. STDJ 30. Edited by D. W. Parry and E. Ulrich. Leiden: Brill, 1999.

Evans, Craig A. 'Qumran's Messiah: How Important is He?' Pages 135–149 in *Religion in the Dead Sea Scrolls*. Edited by. J. J. Collins and R. A. Kugler. Cambridge: Eerdmans, 2000.

Evans, Craig A. 'The Messiah in the Old and New Testaments: A Response'. Pages 230–248 in *The Messiah in the Old and New Testaments*. Edited by S. Porter. Cambridge: Eerdmans, 2007.

Ezell, Meredith Douglas. 'A Study of the Book of Revelation with Special Reference to its Jewish Literary Background'. PhD diss., Southwestern Baptist Theological Seminary, 1970.

Fabry, Heinz-Josef. 'The Reception of Nahum and Habakkuk in the Septuagint and Qumran'. Pages 241–256 in *Emanuel: Studies in Hebrew Bible, Septuagint and Dead Sea Scrolls in Honor of Emanuel Tov*. VTsup 94. Edited by S. M. Paul et al. Leiden: Brill, 2003.

Farmer, Ronald L. 'Undercurrents and Paradoxes: The Apocalypse of John in Process Hermeneutic'. Pages 109–118 in *Reading the Book of Revelation: A Resource for Students*. RBS 44. Edited by D. L. Barr. Atlanta: SBL, 2003.

Farrer, Austin. *The Revelation of St. John the Divine*. Oxford: Clarendon, 1964.

Fekkes, Jan. *Isaiah and Prophetic Traditions in the Book of Revelation: Visionary Antecedents and Their Development*. JSNTsup 93. Sheffield: Sheffield Academic Press, 1994.

Feldman, Ariel and Liora Goldman. *Scripture and Interpretation: Qumran Texts that Rework the Bible*. BZAW 449. Edited by D. Dimant. Berlin: De Gruyter, 2014.

Fernández Marcos, Natalio. *The Septuagint in Context: Introduction to the Greek Version of the Bible*. Translated by W. G. E. Watson. Leiden: Brill, 2001.

Fernández Marcos, Natalio. 'The Antiochene Edition in the Text History of the Greek Bible'. Pages 57–73 in *Der Antiochenische Text der Septuaginta in seiner Bezeugung und seiner Bedeutung*. DSI 4. Edited by S. Kreuzer and M. Sigismund. Göttingen: Vandenhoeck & Ruprecht, 2013.

Fields, F. *Origenis Hexaplorum*. 2 vols. Oxford: Benediction Classics, 2010.

Finamore, Stephen. *God, Order and Chaos: René Girard and the Apocalypse*. Paternoster Biblical Monographs. Milton Keynes: Paternoster, 2009.

Fishbane, Michael. *Biblical Interpretation in Ancient Israel*. Oxford: Clarendon, 1985.

Fishbane, Michael. 'Use, Authority and Interpretation of Mikra at Qumran'. Pages 339–377 in *Mikra: Text, Translation, Reading & Interpretation of the Hebrew Bible in Ancient Judaism & Early Christianity*. Edited by M. Mulder. Philadelphia: Fortress, 1988.

Fishbane, Michael. 'Inner-Biblical Exegesis'. Pages 33–48 in *HB/OT*. Vol. 1.1. Edited by M. Sæbø. Göttingen: Vandenhoeck & Ruprecht, 1996.

Fitzmyer, Joseph A. *The Gospel According to Luke*. 2 volumes. AB 28A. Garden City, NY: Doubleday, 1985.

Fitzmyer, Joseph A. *Romans*. AB 33. London: Doubleday, 1993.

Fitzmyer, Joseph A. *Tobit*. CEJL. Berlin: De Gruyter, 2003.

Flesher, Paul V. M. and Bruce Chilton. *The Targums: A Critical Introduction*. Waco: Baylor University Press, 2011.

Flint, Peter W., ed. *The Bible at Qumran: Text, Shape, and Interpretation*. Cambridge: Eerdmans, 2001.

Flint, Peter W., 'The Shape of the "Bible" at Qumran'. Pages 45–103 in *The Judaism of Qumran: A Systematic Reading of the Dead Sea Scrolls*. HdO 57.5.2. Edited by A. J. Avery-Peck, J. Neusner, and B. Chilton. Leiden: Brill, 2001.

Flint, Peter W., 'Scriptures in the Dead Sea Scrolls: The Evidence from Qumran'. Pages 269–304 in *Emanuel: Studies in Hebrew Bible, Septuagint and Dead Sea Scrolls in Honor of Emanuel Tov*. VTsup 94. Edited by S. M. Paul et al. Leiden: Brill, 2003.

Flint, Peter W., 'Psalms and Psalters in the Dead Sea Scrolls'. Pages 233–272 in *The Bible and the Dead Sea Scrolls*. Vol. 1. Edited by J. H. Charlesworth. Waco: Baylor University Press, 2006.

Ford, J. Massyngberde. *Revelation*. AB 38. Garden City, NY: Doubleday, 1975.

Frankel, Zacharias. *Ueber den Einfluss der palästinischen Exegese auf die alexandrinische Hermeneutik*. Leipzig: Verlag von Joh. Ambr. Barth, 1851.

Frey, Jörg. 'The Notion of "Flesh" in 4QInstruction and the Background of Pauline Usage'. Pages 197–226 in *Sapiential, Liturgical & Poetical Texts from Qumran: Proceedings of the Third Meeting of the International Organization for Qumran Studies, Published in Memory of Maurice Baillet*. STDJ 35. Edited by D. K. Falk, F. García Martínez, and E. M. Schuller. Leiden: Brill, 2000.

Frey, Jörg. 'Was Erwartet die Johannesapokalypse? Zur Eschatologie des letzten Buchs der Bibel'. Pages 473–551 in *Die Johannesapokalypse: Kontexte – Konzepte – Rezeption*. WUNT 287. Edited by J. Frey, J. A. Kelhoffer, and F. Tóth. Tübingen: Mohr Siebeck, 2012.

Frey, Jörg. 'Paul's View of the Spirit in the Light of Qumran'. Pages 237–260 in *The Dead Sea Scrolls and Pauline Literature*. STDJ 102. Edited by J.-S. Rey. Leiden: Brill, 2014.

Frey, Jörg. 'Das Corpus Johanneum und die Apokalypse des Johannes: Die Johanneslegende, die Problem der johanneischen Verfasserschaft und die Frage der Pseudonymität der Apokalypse'. Pages 71–133 in *Poetik und Intertextualität der Johannesapokalypse*. WUNT 346. Edited by S. Alkier, T. Hieke, and T. Nicklas. Tübingen: Mohr Siebeck, 2015.

Friesen, Steven J. *Imperial Cults and the Apocalypse of John: Reading Revelation in the Ruins*. Oxford: Oxford University Press, 2001.

Fuller, Russell E. 'The Minor Prophets Manuscripts from Qumran, Cave IV'. PhD diss., Harvard University, 1988.

Fuller, Russell E. 'Textual Traditions in the Book of Hosea and the Minor Prophets'. Pages 247–256 in *The Madrid Qumran Congress*. STDJ 11. Edited by J. Trebolle Barrera and L. Vegas Montaner. Leiden: Brill, 1992.

Fuller, Russell E. '4QMicah: A Small Fragment of a Manuscript of the Minor Prophets from Qumran, Cave IV'. *RevQ* 16 (1993): 193–202.

Fuller, Russell E. 'The Form and Formation of the Book of the Twelve: The Evidence from the Judean Desert'. Pages 86–101 in *Forming Prophetic Literature: Essays on Isaiah and the Twelve in Honor of John D. W. Watts*. JSOTsup 235. Edited by J. W. Watts and P. R. House. Sheffield: Sheffield Academic Press, 1996.

Fuller, Russell E. 'Minor Prophets'. Pages 554–557 in *EDSS*. Vol. 1. Edited by L. H. Schiffman and J. VanderKam. Oxford: Oxford University Press, 2000.

Fuller, Russell E. 'The Biblical Prophetic Manuscripts from the Judean Desert'. Pages 3–23 in *Prophecy after the Prophets? The Contribution of the Dead Sea Scrolls to the Understanding of Biblical and Extra-Biblical Prophecy*. CBET 52. Edited by K. De Troyer and A. Lange. Leuven: Peeters, 2009.

Fuller, Russell E. 'Some Thoughts on How the Dead Sea Scrolls Have Changed our Understanding of the Text of the Hebrew Bible and Its History and the Practice of Textual Criticism'. Pages 23–28 in *The Hebrew Bible in Light of the Dead Sea Scrolls*. FRLANT 239. Edited by N. Dávid et al. Göttingen: Vandenhoeck & Ruprecht, 2012.

Gallagher, Edmon L. *Hebrew Scripture in Patristic Biblical Theory: Canon, Language, Text*. VCsup 114. Leiden: Brill, 2012.

Gamble, Harry Y. 'The Book Trade in the Roman Empire'. Pages 23–36 in *The Early Text of the New Testament*. Edited by C. E. Hill and M. J. Kruger. Oxford: Oxford University Press, 2012.

García Martínez, Florentino. 'Temple Scroll'. Pages 927–933 in *EDSS*. Vol. 2. Edited by L. H. Schiffman and J. C. VanderKam. Oxford: Oxford University Press, 2000.

García Martínez, Florentino. 'Rethinking the Bible: Sixty Years of Dead Sea Scrolls Research and Beyond'. Pages 19–36 in *Authoritative Scriptures in Ancient Judaism*. JSJsup 141. Edited by M. Popović. Leiden: Brill, 2010.

García Martínez, Florentino. 'Galatians 3:10–14 in the Light of Qumran'. Pages 51–67 in *The Dead Sea Scrolls and Pauline Literature*. STDJ 102. Edited by J.-S. Rey. Leiden: Brill, 2013.

Geiger, Abraham. *Urschift in Übersetzungen der Bibel in ihrer Abhängigkeit von der inneren Entwicklung des Judentums. Zweite Auflage mit einer Einführung von Prof. Dr. Paul Kahle und einem Anhang enthaltend: Nachträge zur Urschrift, Verzeichnis der Bibelstellen und Bibliographie zusammengestellt und bearbeitet von Dr. Nachum Czortkowski*. 2nd edn. Frankfurt am Main: Verlag Madda, 1928. First edition: Breslau: Julius Hainauer, 1857.

Gelston, Anthony, ed. *The Twelve Minor Prophets*. BHQ 13. Stuttgart: Deutsche Bibelgesellschaft, 2010.

Genette, Gérard. *Narrative Discourse: An Essay in Method*. Translated by J. E. Lewin. Ithaca, NY: Cornell University Press, 1980.

Gesenius, W. *De Pentateuchi Samaritani origine, indole, et auctoritate commentation philoligo-critica*. Halle: Rengersche Buchhandlung, 1815.

Gheorghita, Radu. *The Role of the Septuagint in Hebrews: An Investigation of its Influence with Special Consideration to the Use of Hab 2:3–4 in Heb 10:37–38*. WUNT 2.160. Tübingen: Mohr Siebeck, 2003.

Gheorghita, Radu. 'The Minor Prophets in Hebrews'. Pages 115–133 in *The Minor Prophets in the New Testament*. LNTS 377. Edited by M. J. J. Menken and S. Moyise. London: T&T Clark, 2009.

Giesen, Heinz. *Die Offenbarung des Johannes*. RNT. Regensburg: Pustet, 1997.

Goldstein, Jonathan A. *1 Maccabees*. AB 41. Garden City, NY: Doubleday, 1977.

Gordon, R. P. 'An Inner-Targum Corruption (Zech. I 8)'. *VT* 25 (1975): 216–221.

Gordon, R. P. *Studies in the Targum to the Twelve Prophets: From Nahum to Malachi.* VTsup 51. Leiden: Brill, 1994.

Goshen-Gottstein, M. H. 'The Rise of the Tiberian Bible Text'. Pages 79–122 in *Biblical and Other Studies.* Edited by A. Altmann. Cambridge, MA: Harvard University Press, 1963.

Goulder, M. D. 'The Apocalypse as an Annual Cycle of Prophecies'. *NTS* 27 no 3 (1981): 342–367.

Gradl, Hans-Georg. *Buch und Offenbarung: Medien und Medialität der Johannesapokalypse.* Wien: Herder, 2014.

Gradwohl, Roland. *Die Farben im Alten Testament: Eine Terminologische Studie.* BZAW 83. Berlin: Töpelmann, 1963.

Green, Barbara. *Mikhail Bakhtin and Biblical Scholarship.* Semeia 38. Atlanta: SBL, 2000.

Greenspoon, Leonard. 'The Use and Abuse of the Term "LXX" and Related Terminology in Recent Scholarship'. *BIOSCS* 20 (1987): 21–29.

Gundry, Robert. *The Use of the Old Testament in St. Matthew's Gospel. With Special Reference to the Messianic Hope.* Leiden: Brill, 1967.

Hachlili, Rachel. *The Menorah, the Ancient Seven-Armed Candelabrum: Origin, Form and Significance.* JSJsup 68. Leiden: Brill, 2001.

Haines-Eitzen, Kim. *Guardians of Letters: Literacy, Power, and the Transmitters of Early Christian Literature.* Oxford: Oxford University Press, 2000.

Ham, Clay Alan. 'The Minor Prophets in Matthew's Gospel'. Pages 39–56 in *The Minor Prophets in the New Testament.* LNTS 377. Edited by M. J. J. Menken and S. Moyise. London: T&T Clark, 2009.

Hanhart, Robert. 'Introduction'. In *The Septuagint as Christian Scripture.* By Martin Hengel. Translated by M. E. Biddle. Edinburgh: T&T Clark, 2002.

Hare, D. R. A. 'The Lives of the Prophets: A New Translation and Introduction'. Pages 379–399 in *OTP.* Vol. 2. Edited by J. H. Charlesworth. Peabody, MA: Hendrickson, 1983.

Harmon, Matthew S. *She Must and Shall Go Free: Paul's Isaianic Gospel in Galatians.* BZNW 169. Berlin: De Gruyter, 2010.

Harrington, Wilfrid J. *Revelation.* SP 16. Collegeville, MN: Liturgical Press, 1993.

Harris, Rendel. *Testimonies.* 2 Volumes. Cambridge: Cambridge University Press, 1916–1920.

Hartley, John E. *The Semantics of Ancient Hebrew Colour Lexemes.* ANESsup 33. Leuven: Peeters, 2010.

Hatch, Edwin. *Essays in Biblical Greek.* Amsterdam: Philo, 1970.

Hatch, Edwin and Henry A. Redpath. *A Concordance to the Septuagint and the Other Greek Versions of the Old Testament.* 2nd edn. Grand Rapids: Baker, 1998.

Hauser, Alan J. and Duane F. Watson, eds. *A History of Biblical Interpretation.* Vol. 1. Cambridge: Eerdmans, 2003.

Hempel, Charlotte. 'The Social Matrix that Shaped the Hebrew Bible and Gave us the Dead Sea Scrolls'. Pages 221–237 in *Studies on the Text and Versions of the Hebrew Bible in Honour of Robert Gordon.* VTsup 149. Edited by G. Kahn and D. Lipton. Leiden: Brill, 2012.

Hengel, Martin. *Judaica, Hellenistica et Christiana.* WUNT 109. Tübingen: Mohr Siebeck, 1999.

Henze, Matthias, ed. *Biblical Interpretation at Qumran.* Cambridge: Eerdmans, 2005.

Henze, Matthias, *A Companion to Biblical Interpretation in Early Judaism.* Cambridge: Eerdmans, 2012.

Hernández, Jr., Juan. *Scribal Habits and Theological Influences in the Apocalypse.* WUNT 2.218. Tübingen: Mohr Siebeck, 2006.

Hernández, Jr., Juan. 'The Apocalypse in Codex Alexandrinus: Its Singular Readings and Scribal Habits'. Pages 341–358 in *Scripture and Traditions: Essays on Early Judaism and Christianity in Honor of Carl R. Holladay.* NTsup 129. Edited by P. Gray and G. R. O'Day. Leiden: Brill, 2009.

Hezser, Catherine. *Jewish Literacy in Roman Palestine.* TSAJ 81. Tübingen: Mohr Siebeck, 2001.

Hieke, Thomas. 'Die literarische und theologische Funktion des Alten Testaments in der Johannesoffenbarung'. Pages 271–290 in *Poetik und Intertextualität in der Johannesapokalypse.* WUNT 346. Edited by S. Alkier, T. Hieke, and T. Nicklas; Tübingen: Mohr Siebeck, 2015.

Himbaza, Innocent. 'Le *Targum Pseudo-Jonathan* témoin de l'époque du Second Temple'. Pages 174–187 in *The Targums in Light of the Traditions of the Second Temple Period.* JSJsup 167. Edited by T. Legrand and J. Joosten. Leiden: Brill, 2014.

Holladay, Carl R. *Fragments from Hellenistic Jewish Authors.* Vol. 3. Atlanta: SBL, 1995.

Hollander, John. *The Figure of Echo: A Mode of Allusion in Milton and After.* London: University of California Press, 1981.

Holtz, Traugott. 'Gott in der Apokalypse'. Pages 247–265 in *L'Apocalypse Johannique et l'Apocalypse dans le Nouveau Testament.* BETL 53. Edited by J. Lambrecht. Leuven: Leuven University Press, 1980.

Holtz, Traugott. *Die Offenbarung des Johannes.* NTD 11. Göttingen: Vandenhoeck & Ruprecht, 2008.

Hooker, Morna D. 'Isaiah in Mark's Gospel'. Pages 35–49 in *Isaiah in the New Testament.* Edited by S. Moyise and M. J. J. Menken. London: T&T Clark, 2005.

Hooker, Paul K. *First and Second Chronicles.* WBC. Louisville: WJK, 2001.

Hoskier, H. C. *Concerning the Text of the Apocalypse.* 2 vols. London: Quaritch, 1929.

Howard, George E. 'To the Reader of the Twelve Prophets'. Pages 777–781 in *A New English Translation of the Septuagint*. Edited by A. Pietersma and B. G. Wright. Oxford: Oxford University Press, 2007.

Hübner, Hans. *Gottes Ich und Israel: Zum Schriftgebrauch des Paulus in Römer 9–11*. FRLANT 135. Göttingen: Vandenhoeck & Ruprecht, 1984.

Hübner, Hans. 'New Testament Interpretation of the Old Testament'. Pages 332–372 in *HB/OT*. Vol. 1.1. Edited by M. Sæbø. Göttingen: Vandenhoeck & Ruprecht, 1996.

Hultberg, Alan David. 'Messianic Exegesis in the Apocalypse: The Significance of the Old Testament for the Christology of Revelation'. PhD diss., Trinity Evangelical Divinity School, 2001.

Hurtado, Larry W. 'Oral Fixation and New Testament Studies? "Orality", "Performance" and Reading Texts in Early Christianity'. *NTS* 60 no 3 (2014): 321–340.

Instone-Brewer, David. 'The Two Asses of Zechariah 9:9 in Matthew 21'. *TB* (2003): 87–98.

Irwin, Eleanor. *Colour Terms in Greek Poetry*. Toronto: Hakkert, 1974.

Jacobson, Howard. 'Biblical Interpretation in Pseudo-Philo's *Liber Antiquitatum Biblicarum*'. Pages 180–199 in *A Companion to Biblical Interpretation in Early Judaism*. Edited by M. Henze. Cambridge: Eerdmans, 2012.

Japhet, Sara. *I & II Chronicles*. OTL. London: SCM, 1993.

Jassen, Alex P. *Scripture and Law in the Dead Sea Scrolls*. Cambridge: Cambridge University Press, 2014.

Jauhiainen, Marko. *The Use of Zechariah in Revelation*. WUNT 2.199. Tübingen: Mohr Siebeck, 2005.

Jauhiainen, Marko. 'Revelation and Rewritten Prophecies'. Pages 177–197 in *Rewritten Bible Reconsidered: Proceedings of the Conference in Karkku, Finland August 24–26 2006*. SRB 1. Edited by A. Laato and J. van Ruiten. Winona Lake: Eisenbrauns, 2008.

Jauhiainen, Marko. 'The Minor Prophets in Revelation'. Pages 155–171 in *The Minor Prophets in the New Testament*. LNTS 377. Edited by M. J. J. Menken and S. Moyise. London: T&T Clark, 2009.

Jellicoe, Sidney. *The Septuagint and Modern Study*. Oxford: Clarendon, 1969.

Jenkins, Ferrell. *The Old Testament in the Book of Revelation*. Grand Rapids: Baker, 1972.

Jewett, Robert. *Romans*. Hermeneia. Minneapolis: Fortress, 2007.

Jobes, Karen H. 'The Septuagint Textual Tradition in 1 Peter'. Pages 311–333 in *Septuagint Research: Issues and Challenges in the Study of Greek Jewish Scriptures*. SCS 53. Edited by W. Kraus and R. G. Wooden. Leiden: Brill, 2006.

Jobes, Karen H. and Moisés Silva. *Invitation to the Septuagint*. Grand Rapids: Baker, 2000.

Jones, Barry Alan. *The Formation of the Book of the Twelve: A Study on Text and Canon*. SBLDiss 149. Atlanta: Scholars, 1995.

Joosten, Jan. 'A Septuagintal Translation Technique in the Minor Prophets: The Elimination of Verbal Repetitions'. Pages 217–223 in *Interpreting Translation: Studies on the LXX and Ezekiel in Honour of Johan Lust*. BETL 192. Edited by F. García Martínez and M. Vervenne. Leuven: Leuven University Press, 2005.

Joosten, Jan. *Collected Essays on the Septuagint: From Languages to Interpretation and Beyond*. FAT 83. Tübingen: Mohr Siebeck, 2012.

Joüon, Paul. 'Quelques hebraïsmes de syntaxe dans le 1er livre des Maccabées'. *Biblica* 3 (1922): 204–206.

Kahle, Paul. *The Cairo Geniza*. 2nd edn. Oxford: Blackwell, 1959.

Kalimi, Isaac. 'Die Abfassungszeit der Chronik: Forschungsstand und Perspektiven'. *ZAW* 105 no 2 (1993): 223–233.

Karrer, Martin. *Die Johannesoffenbarung als Brief: Studien zu ihrem literarischen, historischen und theologischen Ort*. FRLANT 140. Göttingen: Vandenhoeck & Ruprecht, 1986.

Karrer, Martin. 'Von der Apokalypse zu Ezechiel: Der Ezechieltext der Apokalypse'. Pages 84–120 in *Das Ezechielbuch in der Johannesoffenbarung*. BTS 76. Edited by D. Sänger. Neukirchen-Vluyn: Neukirchener, 2004.

Karrer, Martin. 'The Epistle to the Hebrews and the Septuagint'. Pages 335–353 in *Septuagint Research: Issues and Challenges in the Study of the Greek Jewish Scriptures*. SCS 53. Edited by W. Kraus and R. G. Wooden. Leiden: Brill, 2006.

Karrer, Martin. 'Der Text der Johannesoffenbarung – Varianten und Theologie'. *Neotestamentica* 42 no 2 (2009): 373–398.

Karrer, Martin. 'Ps 22 (MT 23): von der Septuaginta zur Eschatologisierung im frühen Christentum'. Pages 130–148 in *La Septante en Allemagne et en France*. OBO 238. Edited by W. Krause and O. Munnich. Göttingen: Vandenhoeck & Ruprecht, 2009.

Karrer, Martin. 'The Angels of the Congregations in Revelation – Textual History and Interpretation'. *JECH* 1 no 1 (2011): 57–84.

Karrer, Martin. 'Der Text der Johannesapokalypse'. Pages 43–78 in *Die Johannesapokalypse: Kontexte – Konzepte – Rezeption*. WUNT 287. Edited by J. Frey, J. A. Kelhoffer, and F. Tóth. Tübingen: Mohr Siebeck, 2012.

Karrer, Martin. 'Die Rezeption des Jesajabuches in der Johannesoffenbarung'. In *Überlieferung und Auslegung des Jesajabuches in intra- und interreligiösen Spannungsfeldern*. BETL. Edited by F. Wilk. Leuven: Peeters, forthcoming.

Karrer, Martin, Sigfried Kreuzer, and Marcus Sigismund, eds. *Von der Septuaginta zum Neuen Testament: Textgeschichtliche Erörterungen*. ANTF 43. Berlin: De Gruyter, 2010.

Keith, Chris. *Jesus' Literacy: Scribal Culture and the Teacher from Galilee*. LNTS 413. London: T&T Clark, 2011.

Kelber, Werner. *The Oral and Written Gospel: The Hermeneutics of Speaking and Writing in the Synoptic Tradition, Mark, Paul, and Q*. Philadelphia: Fortress, 1983.

Kelber, Werner. 'The History of the Closure of Biblical Texts'. Pages 71–99 in *The Interface of Orality and Writing: Speaking, Seeing, Writing in the Shaping of New Genres*. WUNT 260. Edited by A. Weissenrieder and R. B. Coote. Tübingen: Mohr Siebeck, 2010.

Kiddle, Martin. *The Revelation of St. John*. MNTC. London: Hodder and Stoughton, 1940.

Kim, Jong-Hoon. 'Zu den Textformen der neutestamentlichen Zitate aus dem Zwölfprophetenbuch'. Pages 163–178 in *Der Antiochenische Text der Septuaginta in seiner Bezeugung und seiner Bedeutung*. DSI 4. Edited by S. Kreuzer and M. Sigismund. Göttingen: Vandenhoeck & Ruprecht, 2013.

Kim, Jong-Hoon. 'Die hebräischen Textformen der hellenistische-frühjüdischen Zeit: Ausgehend vom Habakuk-Text der griechischen Zwölfprophetenrolle aus Nahal Hever (8HevXIIgr)'. Pages 347–357 in *Text – Textgeschichte – Textwirkung: Festschrift zum 65. Geburtstag von Sigfried Kreuzer*. Alter Orient und Altes Testament 419. Edited by T. Wagner, J. M. Robker, and F. Ueberschaer. Münster: Ugarit Verlag, 2014.

Klein, Ralph W. *1 Chronicles: A Commentary*. Hermeneia. Minneapolis: Fortress, 2006.

Knibb, Michael A. 'Reflections on the Status of the Early Enochic Writings'. Pages 143–154 in *Authoritative Scriptures in Ancient Judaism*. JSJsup 141. Edited by M. Popović. Leiden: Brill, 2010.

Knight, Jonathan. *Revelation*. Sheffield: Sheffield Academic Press, 1999.

Knohl, Israel. 'The Gabriel Revelation'. Pages 435–475 in *The Dead Sea Scrolls and Contemporary Culture: Proceedings of the International Conference held at the Israel Museum Jerusalem (July 6–8, 2008)*. STDJ 93. Edited by A. D. Roitman, L. H. Schiffman, and S. Tzoref. Leiden: Brill, 2011.

Knust, Jennifer Wright. 'Early Christian Re-Writing and the History of the Pericope Adulterae'. *JECS* 14 no 4 (2006): 485–536.

Koch, Dietrich-Alex. *Die Schrift als Zeuge des Evangeliums: Untersuchungen zur Wendung und zum Verständis der Schrift bei Paulus*. Beiträge zur historischen Theologie 69. Tübingen: Mohr Siebeck, 1986.

Koehler, L., W. Baumgartner, and J. J. Stamm, eds. *The Hebrew and Aramaic Lexicon of the Old Testament*. 2 vols. Leiden: Brill, 2001.

Koester, Craig R. *Revelation*. AYB 38A. London: Yale University Press, 2014.

Kohn, Samuel. *De Pentateucho Samaritano – Ejusque cum Versionibus Antiquis Nexu*. Leipzig: G. Kreysing, 1865.

Koller, Aaron. *Esther in Ancient Jewish Thought*. Cambridge: Cambridge University Press, 2014.

Köstenberger, Andreas J. *John*. BECNT. Grand Rapids: Baker, 2004.

Kovacs, Judith and Christopher Rowland. *Revelation: The Apocalypse of Jesus Christ*. BBC. Oxford: Blackwell, 2004.

Kowalski, Beate. *Die Rezeption des Propheten Ezechiel in der Offenbarung des Johannes*. SBB 52. Stuttgart: Katholisches Bibelwerk, 2004.

Kowalski, Beate. 'Zur Funktion der Schriftzitate in Röm 9,19–29'. Pages 713–732 in *The Letter to the Romans*. BETL 226. Edited by U. Schnelle. Leuven: Peeters, 2009.

Kowalski, Beate. 'Die Ezechielrezeption in der Offenbarung des Johannes und ihre Bedeutung für Textkritik'. *SNTU* 35 (2010): 51–77.

Kraft, Heinrich. *Die Offenbarung des Johannes*. HZNT 16a. Tübingen: Mohr Siebeck, 1974.

Kratz, Reinhard G. *Das Judentum im Zeitalter des zweiten Tempels: kleine Schriften*. 2nd edn. FAT 42. Tübingen: Mohr Siebeck, 2013.

Kreuzer, Sigfried. 'Der Antiochenische Text der Septuaginta Forschungsgeschichte und eine neue Perspektive'. Pages 23–56 in *Der Antiochenische Text der Septuaginta in seiner Bezeugung und seiner Bedeutung*. DSI 4. Edited by S. Kreuzer and M. Sigismund. Göttingen: Vandenhoeck & Ruprecht, 2013.

Kreuzer, Sigfried. 'Ursprüngliche Septuaginta (Old Greek) und hebraisierende Bearbeitung: Die Entwicklung der Septuaginta in ihrer Bedeutung für die Zitate und Anspielungen im Neuen Testament, untersucht anhand der Zitate aus dem Dodekapropheton'. Pages 17–55 in *Worte der Weissagung: Studien zu Septuaginta und Johannesoffenbarung*. ABG 47. Edited by J. Elschenbroich and J. de Vries. Leipzig: Evangelische Verlagsanstalt, 2014.

Kristeva, Julia. *Desire in Language: A Semiotic Approach to Literature and Art*. Oxford: Blackwell, 1980.

Kugel, James L. *In Potiphar's House: The Interpretive Life of Biblical Texts*. London: Harvard University Press, 1994.

Kugel, James L. *The Bible as it Was*. London: The Belknap Press of Harvard University Press, 1997.

Kugel, James L. 'The Beginnings of Biblical Interpretation'. Pages 3–23 in *A Companion to Biblical Interpretation in Early Judaism*. Edited by M. Henze. Cambridge: Eerdmans, 2012.

Kutscher, E. Y. *The Language and Linguistic Background of the Isaiah Scroll (1QIsaᵃ)*. STDJ 6. Leiden: Brill, 1974.

Labahn, Michael. 'Ausharren im Leben, um von Baum des Lebens zu Essen und Ewig zu Leben: Zur Textform und Auslegung der Paradiesgeschichte der Genesis in der Apokalypse des Johannes und deren Textgeschichte'. Pages 291–316 in *Florilegium Lovaniense: Studies in Septuagint and Textual Criticism in Honour of Florentino García Martínez*. BETL 224. Edited by H. Ausloos, B. Lemmelijn, and M. Vervenne. Leuven: Peeters, 2008.

Labahn, Michael. ' "Geschrieben in diesem Buch": Die "Anspielungen" der Johannesapokalypse im Spannungsfeld zwischen den Referenztexten und der handschriftlichen Überlieferung in den großen Bibelhandschriften'. Pages 339–383 in *Von der Septuaginta zum Neuen Testament: Textgeschichtliche Erörterungen*. ANTF 43. Edited by M. Karrer, S. Kreuzer, and M. Sigismund. Berlin: De Gruyter, 2010.

Labahn, Michael. 'Die Macht des Gedächtnisses. Überlegungen zu Möglichkeit und Grenzen des Einflusses hebräischer Texttradition auf die

Johannesapokalypse'. Pages 385–416 in *Von der Septuaginta zum Neuen Testament: Textgeschichtliche Erörterungen*. ANTF 43. Edited by M. Karrer, S. Kreuzer, and M. Sigismund. Berlin: De Gruyter, 2010.

Labahn, Michael. 'Die Septuaginta und die Johannesapokalypse: Möglichkeiten und Grenzen einer Verhältnisbestimmung im Spiegel von kreativer Intertextualität und Textentwicklung'. Pages 149–190 in *Die Johannesapokalypse: Kontexte – Konzepte – Rezeption*. WUNT 287. Edited by J. Frey, J. A. Kelhoffer, and F. Tóth. Tübingen: Mohr Siebeck, 2012.

Labahn, Michael. 'Die Schriftrezeption in den großen Kodizes der Johannesoffenbarung'. Pages 99–130 in *Die Johannesoffenbarung: Ihr Text und ihre Auslegung*. ABG 38. Edited by M. Labahn and M. Karrer. Leipzig: Evangelische Verlagsanstalt, 2012.

Labahn, Michael. 'Griechische Textformen in der Schriftrezeption der Johannesoffenbarung? Eine Problemanzeige zu Möglichkeiten und Grenzen ihrer Rekonstruktion anhand von Beispielen aus der Rezeption des Ezechielbuches'. Pages 529–560 in *Die Septuaginta – Entstehung, Sprache, Geschichte*. WUNT 286. Edited by S. Kreuzer, M. Meiser, and M. Sigismund. Tübingen: Mohr Siebeck, 2012.

Labahn, Michael and Martin Karrer, eds. *Die Johannesoffenbarung: Ihr Text und ihre Auslegung*. ABG 38. Leipzig: Evangelische Verlagsanstalt, 2012.

Ladd, George E. *A Commentary on the Revelation of John*. Grand Rapids: Eerdmans, 1972.

Lange, Armin. 'The Status of the Biblical Texts in the Qumran Corpus and the Canonical Process'. Pages 21–30 in *The Bible as Book: The Hebrew Bible and the Judean Desert Discoveries*. Edited by E. D. Herbert and E. Tov. London: British Library, 2002.

Lange, Armin. 'The Parabiblical Literature of the Qumran Library and the Canonical History of the Hebrew Bible'. Pages 305–321 in *Emanuel: Studies in Hebrew Bible, Septuagint and Dead Sea Scrolls in Honor of Emanuel Tov*. VTsup 94. Edited by S. M. Paul et al. Leiden: Brill 2003.

Lange, Armin. 'From Literature to Scripture: The Unity and Plurality of the Hebrew Scriptures in Light of the Qumran Library'. Pages 51–107 in *One Scripture or Many? Canon from Biblical, Theological, and Philosophical Perspectives*. Edited by C. Helmer and C. Landmesser. Oxford: Oxford University Press, 2004.

Lange, Armin. *Handbuch der Textfunde vom Toten Meer*. Volume 1. Tübingen: Mohr Siebeck, 2009.

Lange, Armin. '"They Confirmed the Reading" (*y. Ta'an* 4.68a): The Textual Standardization of the Jewish Scriptures'. Pages 29–80 in *From Qumran to Aleppo: A Discussion with Emanuel Tov about the Textual History of the Jewish Scriptures in Honor of his 65th Birthday*. FRLANT 230. Edited by A. Lange, M. Weigold, and J. Zsengellér. Göttingen: Vandenhoeck & Ruprecht, 2009.

Lange, Armin. 'The Textual Plurality of Jewish Scriptures in the Second Temple Period in Light of the Dead Sea Scrolls'. Pages 43–96 in *Qumran and the Bible: Studying Jewish and Christian Scriptures in Light of the Dead Sea Scrolls*. CBET 57. Edited by N. Dávid and A. Lange. Leuven: Peeters, 2010.

Lange, Armin and Matthias Weigold. *Biblical Quotations and Allusions in Second Temple Jewish Literature*. JAJsup 5. Göttingen: Vandenhoeck & Ruprecht, 2011.

Law, Timothy Michael. 'The Translation of Symmachus in 1 Kings (3 Kingdoms)'. Pages 227–292 in *XIII Congress of the International Organization for Septuagint and Cognate Studies Ljubljana, 2007*. SCS 55. Edited by M. K. H. Peters. Atlanta: SBL, 2008.

Law, Timothy Michael. *When God Spoke Greek: The Septuagint and the Making of the Christian Bible*. Oxford: Oxford University Press, 2013.

Lear, Sheree. 'Revelation 19.16's Inscribed Thigh: An Allusion to Gen 49.10b'. *NTS* 60 (2014): 280–285.

Lear, Sheree. 'Visions of Locusts: The Composition of Revelation 9.7–11'. Pages 169–182 in *'I Lifted my Eyes and Saw': Reading Dream and Visions Reports in the Hebrew Bible*. LHBOTS 584. Edited by. E. R. Hayes and L.-S. Tiemeyer. London: T&T Clark, 2014.

Lee, Pilchan. *The New Jerusalem in the Book of Revelation: A Study of Revelation 21–22 in the Light of its Background in Jewish Tradition*. WUNT 2.129; Tübingen: Mohr Siebeck, 2001.

Lembke, Markus. 'Beobachtungen zu den Handschriften der Apokalypse des Johannes'. Pages 19–69 in *Die Johannesoffenbarung: Ihr Text und ihre Auslegung*. ABG 38. Edited by M. Labahn and M. Karrer. Leipzig: Evangelische Verlagsanstalt, 2012.

Lichtenberger, Hermann. 'Die Schrift in der Offenbarung des Johannes'. Pages 382–390 in *Die Septuaginta und das frühe Christentum*. WUNT 277. Edited by T. S. Caulley and H. Lichtenberger. Tübingen: Mohr Siebeck, 2011.

Lichtenberger, Hermann. *Die Apokalypse*. TKZNT 23. Stuttgart: Kohlhammer, 2014.

Liebermann, Saul. *Hellenism in Jewish Palestine: Studies in the Literary Transmission, Beliefs and Manners of Palestine in the I Century B.C.E – IV Century C.E*. Texts and Studies of the Jewish Theological Seminary of America 18. New York: Jewish Theological Seminary of America, 1950.

Lifshitz, B. 'The Greek Documents from the Cave of Horror'. *IEJ* 12 no 3/4 (1961): 201–207.

Lim, Timothy H. *Holy Scripture in the Qumran Commentaries and Pauline Letters*. Oxford: Clarendon, 1997.

Lim, Timothy H. 'The Qumran Scrolls, Multilingualism, and Biblical Interpretation'. Pages 57–73 in *Religion in the Dead Sea Scrolls*. Edited by J. J. Collins and R. A. Kugler. Cambridge: Eerdmans, 2000.

Lim, Timothy H. 'Biblical Quotations in the Pesharim and the Text of the Bible'. Pages 71–79 in *The Bible as Book: The Hebrew Bible and the Judean Desert Discoveries*. Edited by E. D. Herbert and E. Tov. London: British Library, 2002.

Lincoln, Andrew T. *The Gospel According to Saint John*. BNTC. London: Continuum, 2005.

Lindars, Barnabas. *New Testament Apologetic: The Doctrinal Significance of the Old Testament Quotations*. London: SCM, 1961.

Linton, Gregory Leroy. 'Intertextuality in the Revelation of John'. PhD diss., Duke University, 1993.

Littman, Robert J. *Tobit: The Book of Tobit in Codex Sinaiticus*. SC. Leiden: Brill, 2008.

Lo, Wei. 'Ezekiel in Revelation: Literary and Hermeneutic Aspect'. PhD diss., University of Edinburgh, 1999.

Lohmeyer, Ernst. *Die Offenbarung des Johannes*. HZNT 16. Tübingen: Mohr Siebeck, 1927.

Lohse, Eduard. 'Die Alttestamentliche Sprache des Sehers Johannes'. *ZNW* 52 (1961): 122–126.

Love, Mark Cameron. *Zechariah 1–8 and the Frustrated Reader*. JSOTsup 296. Sheffield: Sheffield Academic Press, 1999.

Lupieri, Edmondo F. *A Commentary on the Apocalypse of John*. Translated by M. P. Johnson and A. Kamesar. Cambridge: Eerdmans, 2006.

Lyons, Michael A. *From Law to Prophecy: Ezekiel's Use of the Holiness Code*. LHBOTS 507. London: T&T Clark, 2009.

Macintosh, A. A. *Hosea*. ICC. Edinburgh: T&T Clark, 1997.

Maier, Gerhard. *Die Offenbarung des Johannes*. 2 vols. HTA. Witten: Brockhaus, 2009–2012.

Mann, C. S. *Mark*. AB 27. Garden City, NY: Doubleday, 1986.

Martin, Gary D. *Multiple Originals: New Approaches to Hebrew Bible Textual Criticism*. TCS 7. Atlanta: SBL, 2010.

Martone, Corrado. 'Qumran Readings in Agreement with the Septuagint Against the Masoretic Text Part Two: Joshua-Judges'. Pages 141–145 in *Flores Florentino: Dead Sea Scrolls and Other Early Jewish Studies in Honour of Florentino García Martínez*. JSJsup 122. Edited by A. Hilhorst et al. Leiden: Brill, 2007.

Mason, Rex. *The Books of Haggai, Zechariah and Malachi*. CBC. Cambridge: Cambridge University Press, 1977.

Mason, Rex. 'Some Echoes of the Preaching in the Second Temple: Tradition Elements in Zechariah 1–8'. *ZAW* 96 no 2 (1984): 221–235.

Mason, Steve. 'Josephus and His Twenty-Two Book Canon'. Pages 110–127 in *The Canon Debate*. Edited by L. M. McDonald and J. A. Sander. Peabody, MA: Hendrickson, 2002.

Mazzaferri, Frederick David. *The Genre of the Book of Revelation from a Source-Critical Perspective*. BZAW 54. Berlin: De Gruyter, 1989.

McComiskey, Thomas Edward. 'Alteration of OT Imagery in the Book of Revelation: Its Hermeneutical and Theological Significance'. *JETS* 36 no 3 (1993): 307–316.

McHardy, W. D. 'The Horses in Zechariah'. Pages 174–179 in *In Memoriam Paul Kahle*. Edited by M. Black and G. Fohrer. Berlin: Töpelmann, 1968.

McKenzie, Steven L. *1–2 Chronicles*. AOTC. Nashville: Abingdon, 2004.

McLay, R. Timothy. *The Use of the Septuagint in New Testament Research*. Cambridge: Eerdmans, 2003.

McLay, R. Timothy. 'Biblical Texts and the Scriptures for the New Testament Church'. Pages 38–58 in *Hearing the Old Testament in the New Testament*. Edited by S. E. Porter. Cambridge: Eerdmans, 2006.

McLean, John Andrew. *The Seventieth Week of Daniel 9:27 as a Literary Key for Understanding the Structure of the Apocalypse of John*. Queenston: Mellen, 1996.

Mearns, Christopher L. 'Dating the Similitudes of Enoch'. *NTS* 25 no 3 (1979): 360–369.

Meiser, Martin. 'Antiochenische Textformen in neutestamentlichen Psalmzitaten in der Rezeption der christlichen Antike – eine textkritische Spurensuche'. Pages 179–196 in *Der Antiochenische Text der Septuaginta in seiner Bezeugung und seiner Bedeutung*. DSI 4. Edited by S. Kreuzer and M. Sigismund. Göttingen: Vandenhoeck & Ruprecht, 2013.

Menken, Maarten J. J. 'The Textual Form and the Meaning of the Quotation of Zech 12:10 in John 19:37'. *CBQ* (1993): 494–509.

Menken, Maarten J. J. *Old Testament Quotations in the Fourth Gospel: Studies in Textual Form*. CBET 15. Kampen: Kok Pharos, 1996.

Menken, Maarten J. J. 'The Quotation From Jeremiah 31(38).15 in Matthew 2.18: A Study of Matthew's Scriptural Text'. Pages 106–125 in *The Old Testament in the New Testament: Essays in Honour of J. L. North*. JSNTsup 189. Edited by S. Moyise. Sheffield: Sheffield Academic Press, 2000.

Menken, Maarten J. J. *Matthew's Bible: The Old Testament Text of the Evangelist*. BETL 173. Leuven: Leuven University Press, 2004.

Menken, Maarten J. J. 'The Minor Prophets in John's Gospel'. Pages 79–96 in *The Minor Prophets in the New Testament*. LNTS 377. Edited by M. J. J. Menken and S. Moyise. London: T&T Clark, 2009.

Menn, Esther. 'Inner-Biblical Exegesis in the Tanak'. Pages 55–79 in *A History of Biblical Interpretation: The Ancient Period*. Vol. 1. Edited by A. J. Hauser and D. F. Watson. Cambridge: Eerdmans, 2003.

Metzger, Bruce M. *A Textual Commentary on the Greek New Testament*. Stuttgart: UBS, 1971.

Meyers, Carol L., and Eric M. Meyers. *Haggai, Zechariah 1–8*. AB 25b. Garden City, NY: Doubleday, 1987.

Meyers, Carol L., and Eric M. Meyers. *Zechariah 9–14*. AB 25c. Garden City, NY: Doubleday, 1993.

Mez, Adam. *Die Bibel des Josephus: untersucht für Buch V–VII de Archäologie.* Basel: Jaeger & Kober, 1895.

Michaels, J. Ramsey. *The Gospel of John.* NICNT. Cambridge: Eerdmans, 2010.

Miller, Merrill P. 'Targum, Midrash and the Use of the Old Testament in the New Testament'. *JSJ* 2 (1971): 29–82.

Mitchell, Christine. 'Chronicles and Ben Sira: Questions of Genre'. Pages 1–25 in *Rewriting Biblical History: Essays on Chronicles and Ben Sira in Honor of Pancratius C. Beentjes.* DCLS 7. Edited by J. Corley and H. van Grol. Berlin: De Gruyter, 2011.

Mitchell, Hinckley G. *A Critical and Exegetical Commentary on Haggai and Zechariah.* ICC. Edinburgh: T&T Clark, 1912.

Moo, Douglas J. *The Epistle to the Romans.* NICNT. Cambridge: Eerdmans, 1996.

Morris, Leon. *Revelation.* TNTC 20. Grand Rapids: Eerdmans, 1984.

Moss, Charlene McAfee. *The Zechariah Tradition and the Gospel of Matthew.* BZNW 156. Berlin: De Gruyter, 2008.

Mounce, Robert H. *The Book of Revelation.* NICNT. Grand Rapids: Eerdmans, 1977.

Moyise, Steve. 'Does the NT Quote the OT out of Context?' *Anvil* 11 no 2 (1992): 133–143.

Moyise, Steve. *The Old Testament in the Book of Revelation.* JSNTsup 115. Sheffield: Sheffield Academic Press, 1995.

Moyise, Steve. 'The Language of the Old Testament in the Apocalypse'. *JSNT* 76 (1999): 97–113.

Moyise, Steve. 'Authorial Intention and the Book of Revelation'. *AUSS* 39 (2001): 35–40.

Moyise, Steve. 'The Psalms in the Book of Revelation'. Pages 231–246 in *The Psalms in the New Testament.* Edited by S. Moyise and M. J. J. Menken. London: T&T Clark, 2004.

Moyise, Steve. 'Matthew's Bible in the Infancy Narrative'. Pages 11–24 in *The Scriptures of Israel in Jewish and Christian Tradition: Essays in Honour of Maarten J. J. Menken.* NTsup 148. Leiden: Brill, 2013.

Moyise, Steve. 'A Response to Currents in British Research on the Apocalypse'. Pages 281–288 in *The Book of Revelation: Currents in British Research on the Apocalypse.* WUNT 2.411. Edited by G. V. Allen, I. Paul, and S. P. Woodman. Tübingen: Mohr Siebeck, 2015.

Mulder, Jan, ed. *Mikra: Text, Translation, Reading & Interpretation of the Hebrew Bible in Ancient Judaism & Early Christianity.* Assen: Van Gorcum, 1988.

Müller, Darius. 'Zitatmarkierungen und die Gegenwart der Schrift im Neuen Testament'. Pages 189–199 in *Textual History and the Reception of Scripture in Early Christianity.* SCS 60. Edited by J. de Vries and M. Karrer. Atlanta: SBL, 2013.

Müller, Ulrich B. *Die Offenbarung des Johannes.* OTKNT 19. Würzburg: Gütersloh, 1984.

Muraoka, T. 'Introduction aux Douze Petits Prophètes'. Pages I–XXIII in *Les Douze Prophètes: Osée*. La Bible d'Alexandrie 23.1. Edited by E. Bons, J. Joosten, and S. Kessler. Paris: Éditions du Cerf, 2002.

Muraoka, T. *A Greek-English Lexicon of the Septuagint*. Louvain: Peeters, 2009.

Myers, Jacob M. *II Chronicles*. AB 13. Garden City, NY: Doubleday, 1965.

Nickelsburg, George W. E. and James C. VanderKam. *1 Enoch 2: A Commentary on the Book of 1 Enoch Chapters 37–82*. Hermeneia. Minneapolis: Fortress, 2012.

Norton, Jonathan D. H. 'The Question of Scribal Exegesis at Qumran'. Pages 135–154 in *Northern Lights on the Dead Sea Scrolls: Proceedings of the Nordic Qumran Network 2003–2006*. STDJ 80. Edited by A. K. Petersen et al. Leiden: Brill, 2009.

Norton, Jonathan D. H. *Contours in the Text: Textual Variant in the Writing of Paul, Josephus, and the Yahad*. LNTS 430. London: T&T Clark, 2011.

O'Brien, Kelli S. *The Use of Scripture in the Markan Passion Narrative*. LNTS 384. London: T&T Clark, 2010.

O'Callaghan, J. '¿Papiros neotestamentarios en la cueva 7 de Qumran?' *Bib* 53 (1972): 91–100.

O'Hare, Daniel M. *'Have you Seen, Son of Man?' A Study in the Translation and Vorlage of LXX Ezekiel 40–48*. SCS 57. Atlanta: SBL, 2010.

Osborne, Grant R. *Revelation*. BECNT. Grand Rapids: Baker, 2002.

Ozanne, Charles Gordon. 'The Influence of the Text and Language of the Old Testament on the Book of Revelation'. PhD diss., University of Manchester, 1964.

Palmer, James K. ' "Not Made With Tracing Paper": Studies in the Septuagint of Zechariah'. *TB* 57 no 2 (2006): 317–320.

Parker, David C. *Codex Bezae: An Early Christian Manuscript and its Text*. Cambridge: Cambridge University Press, 1992.

Parker, David C. *The Living Text of the Gospels*. Cambridge: Cambridge University Press, 1997.

Parker, David C. *Textual Scholarship and the Making of the New Testament*. Oxford: Oxford University Press, 2012.

Parsons, Peter J. 'Scripts and Their Dates'. Pages 19–26 in DJD VII. Edited by E. Tov. Oxford: Clarendon, 1990.

Paul, Ian. 'The Use of the Old Testament in Revelation 12'. Pages 256–276 in *The Old Testament in the New Testament: Essays in Honor of J.L. North*. JSNTsup 189. Edited by S. Moyise. Sheffield: Sheffield Academic Press, 2000.

Paulien, Jon. 'Allusions, Exegetical Method, and the Interpretation of Revelation 8:7–12'. PhD diss., Andrews University, 1987.

Paulien, Jon. *Decoding Revelation's Trumpets: Literary Allusions and the Interpretation of Revelation 8:7–12*. AUSDDS 11. Berrien Springs, MI: Andrews University Press, 1987.

Paulien, Jon. 'Elusive Allusions: The Problematic Use of the Old Testament in Revelation'. *BR* 33 (1988): 37–53.

Paulien, Jon. 'Dreading the Whirlwind: Intertextuality and The Use of the Old Testament in Revelation'. *AUSS* 39 (2001): 5–22.

Peachey, Barry F. 'A Horse of a Different Colour: The Horses in Zechariah and Revelation'. *ET* 110 no 7 (1999): 214–216.

Pearson, Brook W. R. 'The Book of the Twelve, Aqiba's Messianic Interpretations, and the Refuge Caves of the Second Jewish Was'. Pages 221–239 in *The Scrolls and the Scriptures: Qumran After Fifty Years*. JSPsup 26. Edited by S. E. Porter and C. A. Evans. Sheffield: Sheffield Academic Press, 1997.

Peltonen, Kai. 'A Jigsaw without a Model? The Date of Chronicles'. Pages 225–271 in *Did Moses Speak Attic? Jewish Historiography and Scripture in the Hellenistic Period*. JSOTsup 317. Edited by L. L. Grabbe. London: Continuum, 2001.

Penley, Paul T. *The Common Tradition behind Synoptic Sayings of Judgment and John's Apocalypse: An Oral Interpretive Tradition of Old Testament Prophetic Material*. LNTS 424. London: T&T Clark, 2010.

Petersen, Anders Klostergaard. 'Rewritten Bible as a Borderline Phenomenon – Genre, Textual Strategy, or Canonical Anachronism'. Pages 285–306 in *Flores Florentino: Dead Sea Scrolls and Other Early Jewish Studies in Honour of Florentino García Martínez*. JSJsup 122. Edited by A. Hilhorst et al. Leiden: Brill, 2007.

Peuch, E. 'Les fragments non identifiés de 8KhXIIgr et le manuscrit grec des Douze Petites Prophètes'. *RB* 98 (1991): 161–169.

Peuch, E. 'Notes en marge de 8KhXIIgr'. *RevQ* 15 (1991–1992): 583–593.

Pola, Thomas. 'The Greek Text of Zechariah: A Document From Maccabean Jerusalem?' Pages 291–300 in *Tradition in Transition: Haggai and Zechariah 1–8 in the Trajectory of Hebrew Theology*. LHBOTS 475. Edited by M. Boda and M. Floyd. London: T&T Clark, 2008.

Pola, Thomas. 'Sach 9,9–17[LXX] – Indiz für die Entstehung des griechischen Dodekaprophetons im makkabäischen Jerusalem'. Pages 238–251 in *La Septante en Allemagne et en France: Textes de la Septante à Traduction Double ou à Traduction très Littérale*. OBO 238. Edited by W. Kraus and O. Munnich. Göttingen: Vandenhoeck & Ruprecht, 2009.

Porter, Stanley E., ed. *Hearing the Old Testament in the New Testament*. Cambridge: Eerdmans, 2006.

Preuss, H. D. 'זרע'. Pages 143–163 in *Theological Dictionary of the Old Testament*. Vol. 4. Edited by G. J. Botterweck and H. Ringgren. Translated by D. E. Green. Grand Rapids: Eerdmans, 1980.

Prigent, Pierre. *L'Apocalypse de Saint Jean*. Commentaire du Nouveau Testament XIV. Geneva: Labor et Fides, 2000.

Quell, Gottfried. 'σπέρμα'. Pages 536–547 in *Theological Dictionary of the New Testament*. Vol. 7. Edited by G. Friedrich. Translated by G. W. Bromiley. Grand Rapids: Eerdmans, 1971.

Rahlfs, Alfred, ed. *Psalmi cum Odis*. VTG 10. Göttingen: Vandenhoeck & Ruprecht, 1979.

Rey, Jean-Sébastian. 'Les manuscripts de la Mer Morte et l'Épître aux Galates: Quelques cas d'interdiscursivité'. Pages 17–49 in *The Dead Sea Scrolls and Pauline Literature*. STDJ 102. Edited by J.-S. Rey. Leiden: Brill, 2013.

Richter, Hans-Friedemann. 'Die Pferde in den Nachtgesichten des Sacharja'. *ZAW* 98 (1986): 96–100.

Riska, Magnus. 'The Temple Scroll – Is it More or Less Biblical?' Pages 607–613 in *Scripture in Transition: Essays on Septuagint, Hebrew Bible, and Dead Sea Scrolls in Honour of Raija Sollamo*. JSJsup 126. Edited by A. Voitila and J. Jokiranta. Leiden: Brill, 2008.

Rissi, Mathias. 'The Rider on the White Horse: A Study of Revelation 6:1–8'. *Interpretation* 18 no 4 (1964): 407–418.

Robbins, Vernon K. *Exploring the Texture of Texts: A Guide to Socio-Rhetorical Interpretation*. Valley Forge, PA: Trinity Press, 1996.

Rogers, R. R. 'An Exegetical Analysis of John's Use of Zechariah in the Book of Revelation: The Impact and Transformation of Zechariah's Text and Themes in the Apocalypse'. PhD diss., Southwestern Baptist Theological Seminary, 2002.

Roloff, Jürgen. *The Revelation of John*. Translated by J. E. Alsup. Minneapolis: Fortress, 1993.

Rösel, Martin. 'Translators as Interpreters: Scriptural Interpretation in the Septuagint'. Pages 64–91 in *A Companion to Biblical Interpretation in Early Judaism*. Edited by M. Henze. Cambridge: Eerdmans, 2012.

Rosenmüller, E. F. C. *Handbuch für die Literatur der biblischen Kritik und Exegese*. Göttingen: Vandenhoeck & Ruprecht, 1797.

Rudolph, Wilhelm. *Haggai; Sacharja 1–8; Sacharja 9–14; Maleachi*. KAT 13.4. Gütersloh: Mohn, 1976.

Ruiz, Jean-Pierre. *Ezekiel in the Apocalypse: The Transformation of Prophetic Language in Revelation 16:17–19:10*. Frankfurt: Lang, 1989.

Rüsen-Weinhold, Ulrich. *Der Septuagintapsalter im Neuen Testament: Eine textgeschichtliche Untersuchung*. Neukirchen-Vluyn: Neukirchener, 2004.

Ruzer, Serge. *Mapping the New Testament: Early Christian Writings as a Witness for Jewish Biblical Exegesis*. Jewish & Christian Perspectives 13. Leiden: Brill, 2007.

Ryan, Sean Michael. *Hearing at the Boundaries of Vision: Education Informing Cosmology in Revelation 9*. LNTS 448. London: T&T Clark, 2012.

Samely, Alexander. *Rabbinic Interpretation of Scripture in the Mishnah*. Oxford: Oxford University Press, 2002.

Samely, Alexander, in collaboration with Philip Alexander, Rocco Bernasconi, and Robert Hayward. *Profiling Jewish Literature in Antiquity: An Inventory, from Second Temple Texts to the Talmuds*. Oxford: Oxford University Press, 2013.

Sanders, Henry A. and Carl Schmidt. *The Minor Prophets in the Freer Collection and Berlin Fragment of Genesis*. UMSHS XXI. London: Macmillan and Company, 1928.

Sanders, James A. 'The Dead Sea Scrolls and Biblical Studies'. Pages 323–336 in *Sha'arei Talmon: Studies in the Bible, Qumran, and the Ancient Near East Presented to Shemaryahu Talmon*. Edited by M. Fishbane and E. Tov. Winona Lake, IN: Eisenbrauns, 1992.

Sanders, James A. 'Origen and the First Christian Testament'. Pages 134–142 in *Studies in the Hebrew Bible, Qumran, and the Septuagint Presented to Eugene Ulrich*. Edited by P. Flint, E. Tov, and J. VanderKam. Leiden: Brill, 2006.

Sanders, James A. 'The Impact of the Judean Desert Scrolls on Issues of Text and Canon of the Hebrew Bible'. Pages 25–36 in *The Bible and the Dead Sea Scrolls*. Edited by J. H. Charlesworth. Waco: Baylor University Press, 2006.

Satake, Akira. *Die Offenbarung des Johannes*. KEKNT 16. Göttingen: Vandenhoeck & Ruprecht, 2008.

Sauzeau, Pierre and André Sauzeau. 'Les chevaux colorés de l'Apocalypse: L'Apocalypse de Jean, Zacharie et les traditions de l'Iran'. *Revue de l'Histoire des Religions* 212 no 3 (1995): 259–298.

Schaefer, Konrad R. 'Zechariah 14: A Study in Allusion'. *CBQ* 57 (1995): 66–91.

Schechter, S. *Documents of Jewish Sectaries: Fragments of a Zadokite Work Edited from Hebrew Manuscripts in the Cairo Geniza Collection now in the Possession of the University Library, Cambridge*. Vol. 1. Cambridge: Cambridge University Press, 1910.

Schlatter, Adolf. *Das alte Testament in der johanneischen Apokalypse*. Gütersloh: Mohn, 1912.

Schmid, J. *Studien zur Geschichte des Griechischen Apokalypse-Textes*. 3 vols. Munich: Karl Zink, 1956.

Schofield, Alison. 'Between Center and Periphery: The *Yahad* in Context'. *DSD* 16 (2009): 330–350.

Schorch, Stefan. 'Die Rolle des Lesens für die Konstituierung alttestamentlicher Texte'. Pages 108–122 in *Was ist ein Text? Alttestentliche, ägyptologische und altorientalistische Perspektiven*. BZAW 362 Edited by L. Morenz and S. Schorch. Berlin: De Gruyter, 2007.

Schorch, Stefan. 'What Kind of Authority? The Authority of the Torah during the Hellenistic Period'. Pages 1–15 in *Scriptural Authority in Early Judaism and Ancient Christianity*. DCLS 16. Edited by I. Kalimi, T. Nicklas, and G. G. Xeravits. Berlin: De Gruyter, 2013.

Schorch, Stefan. 'Rewritten Bible and the Vocalization of the Biblical Text'. Pages 137–151 in *Rewritten Bible after Fifty Years: Text, Terms, or Techniques? A Last Dialogue with Geza Vermes*. JSJsup 166. Edited by J. Zsengellér. Leiden: Brill, 2014.

Schunk, Klaus-Dietrich. *1. Makkabäerbuch*. Jüdische Schriften aus hellenisitisch-römischer Zeit 1.4. Gütersloh: Mohn, 1980.

Schüssler Fiorenza, Elisabeth. *The Book of Revelation: Judgment and Justice*. Philadelphia: Fortress, 1985.

Segal, Michael. '4QReworked Pentateuch or 4QPentateuch?' Pages 391–399 in *The Dead Sea Scrolls Fifty Years After Their Discovery*. Edited by L. H. Schiffman, E. Tov, and J. VanderKam. Jerusalem: Israel Exploration Society, 2000.

Segal, Michael. 'Between Bible and Rewritten Bible'. Pages 10–28 in *Biblical Interpretation at Qumran*. Edited by M. Henze. Cambridge: Eerdmans, 2005.

Sellin, Ernst. 'Der Stein des Sacharja'. *JBL* 50 no 4 (1931): 242–249.

Selman, Martin J. *2 Chronicles*. TOTC 10b. Downers Grove: IVP, 1994.

Shea, William H. 'Zechariah's Flying Scroll and Revelation's Unsealed Scroll'. *Journal of Adventist Theological Society* 14 no 2 (2003): 95–99.

Shemesh, Aharon. 'Biblical Exegesis and Interpretation from Qumran to the Rabbis'. Pages 467–489 in *A Companion to Biblical Interpretation in Early Judaism*. Edited by M. Henze. Cambridge: Eerdmans, 2012.

Skehan, Patrick W. 'The Divine Name at Qumran, in the Masada Scroll, and in the Septuagint'. *BIOSCS* 13 (1980): 14–44.

Smalley, Stephen S. *The Revelation to John: A Commentary on the Greek Text of the Apocalypse*. Downers Grove: IVP, 2005.

Smelik, Willem. 'Code-switching: The Public Reading of the Bible in Hebrew, Aramaic and Greek'. Pages 123–151 in *Was ist ein Text? Alttestamentliche, ägyptologische und altorientalistische Perspektiven*. BZAW 362. Edited by L. Morenz and S. Schorch. Berlin: De Gruyter, 2007.

Sperber, Alexander, ed. *The Bible in Aramaic*. 3 vols. Leiden: Brill, 1963.

Spottorno, Victoria. 'Can Methodological Limits be Set in the Debate on the Identification of 7Q5?' *DSD* 6 (1999): 66–77.

Spottorno, Victoria. 'The Status of the Antiochene Text in the First Century A.D.: Josephus and the New Testament'. Pages 74–83 in in *Der Antiochenische Text der Septuaginta in seiner Bezeugung und seiner Bedeutung*. DSI 4. Edited by S. Kreuzer and M. Sigismund. Göttingen: Vandenhoeck & Ruprecht, 2013.

Stanley, Christopher D. *Paul and the Language of Scripture: Citation Technique in the Pauline Epistles and Contemporary Literature*. SNTSMS 69. Cambridge: Cambridge University Press, 1992.

Stanley, Christopher D. *Arguing with Scripture: The Rhetoric of Quotations in the Letters of Paul*. London: T&T Clark, 2004.

Stead, Michael R. *The Intertextuality of Zechariah 1–8*. LHBOTS 506. London: T&T Clark, 2009.

Stein, Robert H. *Mark*. BECNT. Grand Rapids: Baker, 2008.

Stendahl, Krister. *The School of St. Matthew and its Use of the Old Testament*. Philadelphia: Fortress, 1968.

Sternberg, Meir. 'Proteus in Quotation-Land: Mimesis and Forms of Reported Discourse'. *Poetics Today* 3 no 2 (1982): 107–156.

Stevenson, Gregory. *Power and Place: Temple and Identity in the Book of Revelation*. BZNW 107. Berlin: De Gruyter, 2001.

Steyn, Gert J. 'Which "LXX" are We Talking About in NT Scholarship'. Page 697–707 in *Die Septuaginta – Texte, Kontexte, Lebenswelten*. WUNT 219. Edited by M. Karrer and W. Kraus. Tübingen: Mohr Siebeck, 2008.

Steyn, Gert J. 'The Text Form of the Isaiah Quotations in the *Sondergut Matthäus* Compared to the Dead Sea Scrolls, Masoretic Text and Septuagint'. Pages 427–446 in *Text-Critical and Hermeneutical Studies in the Septuagint*. VTsup 157. Edited by J. Cook and H. Stipp. Leiden: Brill, 2012.

Stone, Michael E., ed. *Jewish Writings of the Second Temple Period: Apocrypha, Pseudepigrapha, Qumran Sectarian Writings, Philo, Josephus*. Assen: Van Gorcum, 1984.

Streett, Matthew. *Here Comes the Judge: Violent Pacifism in the Book of Revelation*. LNTS 462. London: T&T Clark, 2012.

Stuart, Moses. *A Commentary on the Apocalypse*. 2 vols. London: Wiley and Putnam, 1845.

Stuckenbruck, Loren T. 'The Formation and Re-Formation of Daniel in the Dead Sea Scrolls'. Pages 101–130 in *The Bible and the Dead Sea Scrolls*. Vol. 1. Edited by J. H. Charlesworth. Waco: Baylor University Press, 2006.

Stuckenbruck, Loren T. and Mark D. Matthews. 'The Apocalypse of John, 1 Enoch, and the Question of Influence'. Pages 191–234 in *Die Johannesap okalypse: Kontexte-Konzepte-Rezeption*. WUNT 287. Edited by J. Frey, J. A. Kelhoffer, and F. Tóth. Tübingen: Mohr Siebeck, 2012.

Sweeney, Marvin A. *The Twelve Prophets*. BO. 2 vols. Collegeville, MN: Liturgical Press, 2000.

Sweet, John P. M. *Revelation*. London: SCM, 1979.

Sweet, John P. M. 'Maintaining the Testimony of Jesus: The Suffering of Christians in the Revelation of John'. Pages 101–117 in *Suffering and Martyrdom in the New Testament*. Edited by W. Horbury and B. McNeil. Cambridge: Cambridge University Press, 1981.

Swete, H. B. *The Apocalypse of St John: The Greek Text with Introduction, Notes and Indices*. 3rd edn. London: Macmillan, 1911.

Talmon, Shemaryahu. 'The Old Testament Text'. Pages 1–41 in *Qumran and the History of the Biblical Text*. Edited by F. M. Cross and S. Talmon. London: Harvard University Press, 1975.

Talmon, Shemaryahu. 'Aspects of the Textual Transmission of the Bible in Light of Qumran Manuscripts'. Pages 95–132 in *Qumran and the History of the Biblical Text*. Edited by F. M. Cross and S. Talmon. London: Harvard University Press, 1975.

Talmon, Shemaryahu. 'Textual Criticism: The Ancient Versions'. Pages 141–166 in *Text in Context: Essays by Members of the Society for Old*

Testament Studies. Edited by A. D. H. Mayes. Oxford: Oxford University Press, 2000.

Talmon, Shemaryahu. 'The Transmission History of the Text of the Hebrew Bible in the Light of Biblical Manuscripts from Qumran and Other Sites in the Judean Desert'. Pages 40–50 in *The Dead Sea Scrolls Fifty Years After Their Discovery.* Edited by L. Schiffman, E. Tov, and J. VanderKam. Jerusalem: Israel Exploration Society, 2000.

Tanner, Cullen. 'Climbing the Lampstand-Witness-Trees: Revelation's use of Zechariah 4 in Light of Speech Act Theory'. *JPT* 20 no 1 (2011): 81–92.

Tauschev, Averky and Seraphim Rose. *The Apocalypse in the Teachings of Ancient Christianity.* 2nd edn. Platina, CA: St. Herman of Alaska Brotherhood, 1998.

Tavo, Felise. *Woman, Mother and Bride: An Exegetical Investigation into the 'Ecclesial' Notions of the Apocalypse.* BT 3. Leuven: Peeters, 2007.

Teeter, David Andrew. *Scribal Laws: Exegetical Variation in the Textual Transmission of Biblical Law in the Late Second Temple Period.* FAT 92. Tübingen: Mohr Siebeck, 2014.

Thackeray, H. St. J. *Jewish Antiquities Books I–III.* Reprint. LCL 242. Harvard: Harvard University Press, 2001.

Theocharous, Myrto. *Lexical Dependence and Intertextual Allusion in the Septuagint of the Twelve Prophets: Studies in Hosea, Amos, and Micah.* LHBOTS 570. London: T&T Clark, 2012.

Thomas, Kenneth J. 'Torah Citations in the Synoptics'. *NTS* 24 no 1 (1977): 85–96.

Thompson, Leonard L. *Revelation.* ANTC. Nashville: Abingdon, 1998.

Tiemeyer, Lena-Sofia. 'Zechariah's Spies and Ezekiel's Cherubim'. Pages 104–127 in *Tradition in Transition: Haggai and Zechariah 1–8 in the Trajectory of Hebrew Bible Theology.* LHBOTS 475. Edited by M. J. Boda and M. H. Floyd. London: T&T Clark, 2008.

Tiemeyer, Lena-Sofia. *Zechariah and His Visions: An Exegetical Study of Zechariah's Vision Report.* LHBOTS 605. London: T&T Clark, 2014.

Tigchelaar, Eibert J. C. *Prophets of Old and the Day of the End: Zechariah, the Book of Watchers and Apocalyptic.* OS 35. Leiden: Brill, 1996.

Tigchelaar, Eibert J. C. 'The Cave 4 Damascus Document Manuscripts and the Text of the Hebrew Bible'. Pages 93–111 in *The Bible as Book: The Hebrew Bible and the Judean Desert Discoveries.* Edited by E. D. Herbert and E. Tov. London: British Library, 2002.

Tigchelaar, Eibert J. C. 'Assessing Emanuel Tov's "Qumran Scribal Practice"'. Pages 173–205 in *The Dead Sea Scrolls: Transmission of Traditions and Production of Texts.* STDJ 92. Edited by N. Hilton et al. Leiden: Brill, 2010.

Tooman, William A. *Gog of Magog: Reuse of Scripture and Compositional Technique in Ezekiel 38–39.* FAT 2.52. Tübingen: Mohr Siebeck, 2011.

Tooman, William A. 'Between Imitation and Interpretation: Reuse of Scripture and Composition in *Hodayot* (1QH^a) 11:6–19'. *DSD* 18 (2011): 54–73.

Tooman, William A. '"To do the Will of Their Master": Re-envisioning the *ḤAYYÔT* in Targum Jonathan of Ezekiel'. Pages 221–233 in '*I Lifted my Eyes and Saw': Reading Dream and Vision Reports in the Hebrew Bible*. LHBOTS 584. Edited by E. Hayes and L.-S. Tiemeyer. London: T&T Clark, 2014.

Tooman, William A. 'The Hermeneutics of Scribal Rewriting in Targum Jonathan Ezekiel 1'. *JAJ* 5 no 3 (2014): 393–414.

Torrey, Charles C. 'Maccabees (Books)'. Pages 2857–2859 in *Encyclopaedia Biblica*. Vol. 3. Edited by T. K. Cheyne and J. S. Black. London: Adam and Charles Black, 1902.

Torrey, Charles C. 'Schweitzer's "Remains of a Hebrew Text of 1 Maccabees"'. *JBL* 22 (1903): 51–59.

Torrey, Charles C. 'Three Troublesome Proper Names in First Maccabees'. *JBL* 53 (1934): 31–33.

Tóth, Franz. 'Von der Vision zur Redaktion: Untersuchungen zur Komposition, Redaktion und Intention der Johannesapokalypse'. Pages 319–411 in *Die Johannesapokalypse: Kontexte-Konzepte-Rezeption*. WUNT 287. Edited by J. Frey, J. A. Kelhoffer, and F. Tóth. Tübingen: Mohr Siebeck, 2012.

Tov, Emanuel. 'Hebrew Bible Manuscripts from the Judaean Desert: Their Contribution to Textual Criticism'. *JJS* 38 (1988): 5–37.

Tov, Emanuel. 'The Septuagint'. Pages 161–188 in *Mikra: Text, Translation, Reading & Interpretation of the Hebrew Bible in Ancient Judaism & Early Christianity*. Edited by M. Mulder. Peabody, MA: Hendrickson, 1988.

Tov, Emanuel. *The Greek Minor Prophets Scroll from Nahal Hever (8HevXIIgr)*. DJD VIII. Oxford: Clarendon, 1990.

Tov, Emanuel. 'The History and Significance of a Standard Text of the Hebrew Bible'. Pages 49–66 in *HB/OT*. Vol. 1. Edited by M. Sæbø. Göttingen: Vandenhoeck & Ruprecht, 1996.

Tov, Emanuel. *The Text-Critical Use of the Septuagint in Biblical Research*. 2nd edn. Jerusalem: Simor, 1997.

Tov, Emanuel. *Hebrew Bible, Greek Bible and Qumran*. TSAJ 121. Tübingen: Mohr Siebeck, 1999.

Tov, Emanuel. *The Greek and Hebrew Bible: Collected Essays on the Septuagint*. VTsup 72. Atlanta: SBL, 1999.

Tov, Emanuel. 'Scriptures: Texts'. Pages 832–836 in *EDSS*. Vol. 2. Edited by L. H. Schiffman and J. C. VanderKam. Oxford: Oxford University Press, 2000.

Tov, Emanuel. 'The Biblical Text from the Judean Desert – An Overview and Analysis of the Published Texts'. Pages 139–166 in *The Bible as Book: The Hebrew Bible and the Judean Desert Discoveries*. Edited by E. D. Herbert and E. Tov. London: British Library, 2002.

Tov, Emanuel. *The Text from the Judaean Desert: Indices and an Introduction to the Discoveries in the Judaean Desert Series*. DJD XXXIX. Oxford: Clarendon, 2002.

Tov, Emanuel. *Scribal Practices and Approaches Reflected in the Texts Found in the Judean Desert*. STDJ 54. Leiden: Brill, 2004.

Tov, Emanuel. 'The Many Forms of Hebrew Scripture: Reflections in Light of the LXX and 4QReworked Pentateuch'. Pages 11–28 in *From Qumran to Aleppo: A Discussion with Emanuel Tov about the Textual History of the Jewish Scriptures in Honor of his 65th Birthday*. FRLANT 230. Edited by A. Lange, M. Weigold, and J. Zsengellér. Göttingen: Vandenhoeck & Ruprecht, 2009.

Tov, Emanuel. 'Some Thoughts about the Diffusion of Biblical Manuscripts in Antiquity'. Pages 151–172 in *The Dead Sea Scrolls: Transmission of Traditions and Production of Texts*. STDJ 92. Edited by N. Hilton et al. Leiden: Brill, 2010.

Tov, Emanuel. 'From 4QReworked Pentateuch to 4QPentateuch (?)'. Pages 73–91 in *Authoritative Scriptures in Ancient Judaism*. JSJsup 141. Edited by M. Popović. Leiden: Brill, 2010.

Tov, Emanuel. 'The Dead Sea Scrolls and the Textual History of the Masoretic Bible'. Pages 41–53 in *The Hebrew Bible in Light of the Dead Sea Scrolls*. FRLANT 239. Edited by N. Dávid et al. Göttingen: Vandenhoeck & Ruprecht, 2012.

Tov, Emanuel. *Textual Criticism of the Hebrew Bible*. 3rd edn. Minneapolis: Fortress, 2012.

Tov, Emanuel. 'The Myth of the Stabilization of the Text of Hebrew Scripture'. Pages 37–45 in *The Text of the Hebrew Bible: From the Rabbis to the Masoretes*. JAJsup 13. Edited by E. Martín-Contreras and L. Miralles-Maciá. Göttingen: Vandenhoeck & Ruprecht, 2014.

Toy, Crawford Howell. *Judaism and Christianity: A Sketch of the Progress of Thought From Old Testament to New Testament*. Boston: Little, Brown, and Company, 1892.

Trebilco, Paul R. *Jewish Communities in Asia Minor*. SNTSMS 69. Cambridge: Cambridge University Press, 1991.

Trebolle, Julio. 'A "Canon Within a Canon": Two Series of Old Testament Books Differently Transmitted, Interpreted and Authorized'. *RevQ* 75 no 19 (2000): 383–399.

Trever, John C. 'The Isaiah Scroll'. Pages xiii–xviii in *The Dead Sea Scrolls of St. Mark's Monastery VI: The Isaiah Manuscript and Habakkuk Commentary*. Edited by M. Burrows and J. C. Trever. New Haven, CT: American Schools of Oriental Research, 1950.

Trever, John C. *The Untold Story of Qumran*. Westwood, NJ: Revell, 1965.

Tripaldi, Daniele. '"Discrepat evangelista et Septuaginta nostraque translatio" (*Hieronymus*, Briefe 57,7,5): Bemerkungen zur Textvorlage des Sacharja-Zitats in Offb 1,7'. Pages 131–143 in *Die Johannesoffenbarung: Ihr Text und ihre Auslegung*. ABG 38. Edited by M. Labahn and M. Karrer. Leipzig: Evangelische Verlagsanstalt, 2012.

Troxel, Ronald L. *LXX-Isaiah as Translation and Interpretation: The Strategies of the Translator of the Septuagint of Isaiah*. JSJsup 124. Leiden: Brill, 2008.

Trudinger, Leonhard Paul. 'The Text of the Old Testament in the Book of Revelation'. PhD diss., Boston University, 1963.

Tsai-Chen, Jenny Jingling. 'The Use of Zechariah 14 in the Book of Revelation'. PhD diss., Dallas Theological Seminary, 2004.

Tuell, Steven S. *First and Second Chronicles*. Interpretation. Louisville: John Knox, 2001.

Turpie, David McCalman. *The Old Testament in the New: A Contribution to Biblical Criticism and Interpretation*. Edinburgh: Williams and Norgate, 1868.

Tzoref, Shani. 'The Use of Scripture in the Community Rule'. Pages 203–234 in *A Companion to Biblical Interpretation in Early Judaism*. Edited by M. Henze. Cambridge: Eerdmans, 2012.

Ulrich, Eugene. 'Pluriformity in the Biblical Text, Text Groups, and Questions of Canon'. Pages 23–41 in *The Madrid Qumran Congress*. STDJ 11. Edited by J. Trebolle Barrera and L. Vegas Montaner. Leiden: Brill, 1992.

Ulrich, Eugene. *The Dead Sea Scrolls and the Origins of the Bible*. Cambridge: Eerdmans, 1999.

Ulrich, Eugene. 'The Absence of "Sectarian Variants" in the Jewish Scriptural Scrolls Found at Qumran'. Pages 179–195 in *The Bible as Book: The Hebrew Bible and the Judean Desert Discoveries*. Edited by E. D. Herbert and E. Tov. London: British Library, 2002.

Ulrich, Eugene. 'The Dead Sea Scrolls and the Hebrew Scriptural Texts'. Pages 77–99 in *The Bible and the Dead Sea Scrolls*. Vol. 1. Edited by J. H. Charlesworth. Waco: Baylor University Press, 2006.

Ulrich, Eugene. 'Light from 1QIsa^a on the Translation Technique of the Old Greek Translator of Isaiah'. Pages 193–204 in *Scripture in Transition: Essays on Septuagint, Hebrew Bible, and Dead Sea Scrolls on Honour of Raija Sollamo*. JSJsup 126. Edited by A. Voitila and J. Jokiranta. Leiden: Brill, 2008.

Ulrich, Eugene. 'The Jewish Scriptures: Texts, Versions and Canons'. Pages 97–119 in *The Eerdmans Dictionary of Early Judaism*. Edited by J. J. Collins and D. C. Harlow. Grand Rapids: Eerdmans, 2010.

Ulrich, Eugene. *The Biblical Qumran Scrolls: Transcriptions and Textual Variations*. VTsup 134. Leiden: Brill, 2010.

Ulrich, Eugene. 'The Evolutionary Production and Transmission of the Scriptural Books'. Pages 47–64 in *Changes in Scripture: Rewriting and Interpreting Authoritative Traditions in the Second Temple Period*. BZAW 419. Edited by H. von Weissenberg et al. Berlin: De Gruyter, 2011.

Ulrich, E. et al. *Qumran Cave 4.X: The Prophets*. DJD XV. Oxford: Clarendon, 1997.

Ureña, Lourdes García. 'Colour Adjectives in the New Testament'. *NTS* 61 (2015): 219–238.

Van de Sandt, Huub. 'The Minor Prophets in Luke-Acts'. Pages 57–77 in *The Minor Prophets in the New Testament*. LNTS 377. Edited by M. J. J. Menken and S. Moyise. London: T&T Clark, 2009.

van der Bergh, Ronald H. 'Differences Between the MT and LXX Contexts of Old Testaments Quotation in the New Testament: Isaiah 45:18–25 as a Case Study'. Pages 159–176 in *Septuagint and Reception*. VTsup 127. Edited by J. Cook. Leiden: Brill, 2009.

van der Bergh, Ronald H. 'The Textual Tradition of Explicit Quotations in Codex Bezae Cantabrigiensis of the Acts of the Apostles'. PhD diss., University of Pretoria, 2013.

van der Kooij, Arie. 'The Textual Criticism of the Hebrew Bible Before and After the Qumran Discoveries'. Pages 167–177 in *The Bible as Book: The Hebrew Bible and the Judean Desert Discoveries*. Edited by E. D. Herbert and E. Tov. London: British Library, 2002.

van der Kooij, Arie. 'The Septuagint of Zechariah as Witness to an Early Interpretation of the Book'. Pages 53–64 in *The Book of Zechariah and its Influence*. Edited by C. Tuckett. Hampshire, UK: Ashgate, 2003.

van der Woude, Adam S. 'Pluriformity and Uniformity: Reflections on the Transmission of the Text of the Old Testament'. Pages 151–169 in *Sacred History and Sacred Texts in Judaism*. CBET 5. Edited by J. N. Bremmer and F. García Martínez. Kampen: Kok Pharos, 1992.

van Henten, Jan Willem. 'The Intertextual Nexus of Revelation and Greco-Roman Literature'. Pages 395–422 in *Poetik und Intertextualität in der Johannesapokalypse*. WUNT 346. Edited by S. Alkier, T. Hieke, and T. Nicklas. Tübingen: Mohr Siebeck, 2015.

van Ruiten, Jacques T. A. G. M. *Abraham in the Book of Jubilees: The Rewriting of Genesis 11:26–25:10 in the Book of Jubilees 11:14–23:8*. JSJsup 161. Leiden: Brill, 2012.

van Ruiten, Jacques T. A. G. M. 'Biblical Interpretation in the Book of Jubilees'. Pages 121–156 in *A Companion to Biblical Interpretation in Early Judaism*. Edited by M. Henze. Cambridge: Eerdmans, 2012.

Van Seters, John. 'Did the *Sopherim* Create a Standard Edition of the Hebrew Scriptures?' Pages 47–61 in *The Text of the Hebrew Bible: From the Rabbis to the Masoretes*. JAJsup 13. Edited by E. Martín-Contreras and L. Miralles-Maciá. Göttingen: Vandenhoeck & Ruprecht, 2014.

VanderKam, James. '1 Enoch, Enochic Motifs, and Enoch in Early Christian Literature'. Pages 33–101 in *The Jewish Apocalyptic Heritage in Early Christianity*. CRINT 3.4. Edited by J. C. VanderKam and W. Adler. Assen: Van Gorcum, 1996.

VanderKam, James. 'The Wording of Biblical Citations in Some Rewritten Scriptural Works'. Pages 41–56 in *The Bible as Book: The Hebrew Bible and the Judean Desert Discoveries*. Edited by E. D. Herbert and E. Tov. London: British Library, 2002.

VanderKam, James and Peter Flint. *The Meaning of the Dead Sea Scrolls: Their Significance for Understanding the Bible, Judaism, Jesus, and Christianity*. New York: HarperCollins, 2002.

Vanhoye, Albert. 'L'utilisation du livre d'Ézéchiel dans l'Apocalypse'. *Biblica* 43 (1962): 436–476.

Vanni, Ugo. 'The Apocalypse and the Gospel of Luke'. Pages 9–25 in *Luke and Acts*. Translated by M. J. O'Connell. Edited by G. O'Collins and G. Marconi. New York: Paulist, 1993.

Vermes, Geza. *Scripture and Tradition in Judaism: Haggadic Studies*. SPB 4. Leiden: Brill, 1961.

Vermes, Geza. 'Biblical Proof-Texts in Qumran Literature'. *JSS* 34 no 2 (1989): 493–508.

Vogelgesang, Jeffrey Marshall. 'The Interpretation of Ezekiel in the Book of Revelation'. PhD diss., Harvard University, 1985.

Volohonsky, Henri. 'Is the Color of That Horse Really Pale?' *International Journal of Transpersonal Studies* 18 no 2 (1999): 167–168.

Von Weissenberg, Hanne. 'Changing Scripture? Scribal Corrections in MS 4QXIIᶜ'. Pages 247–271 in *Changes in Scripture: Rewriting and Interpreting Authoritative Traditions in the Second Temple Period*. BZAW 419. Edited by H. von Weissenberg et al. Berlin: De Gruyter, 2011.

Vos, Louis A. *The Synoptic Traditions in the Apocalypse*. Kampen: Kok, 1965.

Voß, Jens. *Die Menora: Gestalt und Funktion des Leuchters im Tempel zu Jerusalem*. OBO 128. Göttingen: Vandenhoeck & Ruprecht, 1993.

Wagner, J. Ross. *Heralds of the Good News: Isaiah and Paul 'in Concert' in the Letter to the Romans*. NTsup 101. Leiden: Brill, 2002.

Wagner, J. Ross. 'Isaiah in Romans and Galatians'. Pages 117–132 in *Isaiah in the New Testament*. Edited by S. Moyise and M. J. J. Menken. London: T&T Clark, 2005.

Wagner, J. Ross. *Reading the Sealed Book: Old Greek Isaiah and the Problem of Septuagint Hermeneutics*. Waco: Baylor University Press, 2013.

Walser, Georg. *Old Testament Quotations in Hebrews: Studies in Their Textual and Contextual Background*. WUNT 2.356. Tübingen: Mohr Siebeck, 2013.

Watts, Rikki E. *Isaiah's New Exodus and Mark*. WUNT 2.88. Tübingen: Mohr Siebeck, 1997.

Weiss, D. B. *Die Johannes-Apokalypse: Textkritische Untersuchungen und Textherstellung*. Leipzig: J. C. Hinrichs'sche, 1891.

Wernberg-Møller, Preben. 'The Contribution of the Hodayot to Biblical Textual Criticism'. *Text* 4 (1964): 133–175.

Wevers, John William. 'The Interpretive Character and Significance of the Septuagint Version'. Pages 84–107 in *HB/OT*. Vol. 1.1. Edited by M. Sæbø. Göttingen: Vandenhoeck & Ruprecht, 1996.

Whittaker, John. 'The Value of Indirect Tradition in the Establishment of Greek Philosophical Texts or the Art of Misquotation'. Pages 63–95 in

Editing Greek and Latin Texts: Papers given at the Twenty-Third Annual Conference on Editorial Problems University of Toronto 6–7 November 1987. Edited by J. N. Grant. New York: AMS, 1987.

Wieder, N. 'The Doctrine of Two Messiahs among the Karaites'. *JJS* 6 no 1 (1955): 14–25.

Wikenhauser, Alfred. *Die Offenbarung des Johannes.* RNT 9. Regensburg: Pustet, 1959.

Wilcox, Max. 'Text Form'. Pages 193–204 in *It is Written: Scripture Citing Scripture.* Edited by. D. A. Carson and H. G. M. Williamson. Cambridge: Cambridge University Press, 1988.

Wilk, Florian. *Die Bedeutung des Jesajabuches für Paulus.* FRLANT 179. Göttingen: Vandenhoeck & Ruprecht, 1998.

Wilk, Florian and J. Ross Wagner, eds. *Gospel and Election: Explorations in the Interpretation of Romans 9–11.* WUNT 257. Tübingen: Mohr Siebeck, 2010.

Williamson, H. G. M. *1 and 2 Chronicles.* NCB. Grand Rapids: Eerdmans, 1982.

Witherington III, Ben. *Revelation.* NCBC. Cambridge: Cambridge University Press, 2003.

Wolters, Albert M. 'Word Play in Zechariah'. Pages 223–230 in *Puns and Pundits: Word Play in the Hebrew Bible and Ancient Near Eastern Literature.* Edited by S. B. Noegel. Bethesda, MD: CDL Press, 2000.

Wolters, Albert M. 'The Messiah in the Qumran Documents'. Pages 75–89 in *The Messiah in the Old and New Testaments.* Edited by S. Porter. Cambridge: Eerdmans, 2007.

Wolters, Albert M. 'The Meaning of Ṣantĕrôt (Zech 4:12)'. *JHS* 12 (2012).

Wolters, Albert M. *Zechariah.* Historical Commentary on the Old Testament. Leuven: Peeters, 2014.

Young, Ian. 'The Stabilization of the Biblical Text in the Light of Qumran and Masada: A Challenge for Conventional Qumran Chronology?' *DSD* 9 no 3 (2002): 364–390.

Zahn, Molly M. 'Reexamining Empirical Models: The Case of Exodus 13'. Pages 36–55 in *Das Deuteronomium zwischen Pentateuch und Deuteronoistischem Geschichtswerk.* FRLANT 206. Edited by E. Otto and R. Achenbach. Göttingen: Vandenhoeck & Ruprecht, 2004.

Zahn, Molly M. *Rethinking Rewritten Scripture: Composition and Exegesis in the 4QReworked Pentateuch Manuscripts.* STDJ 95. Leiden: Brill, 2011.

Zakovitch, Yair. 'Through the Looking Glass: Reflections/Inversions of Genesis Stories in the Bible'. *Biblical Interpretation* 1 no 2 (1993): 139–152.

Zakovitch, Yair. 'Inner-Biblical Interpretation'. Pages 27–63 in *A Companion to Biblical Interpretation in Early Judaism.* Edited by M. Henze. Cambridge: Eerdmans, 2012.

Ziegler, Joseph, ed. *Isaias.* VTG 14. Göttingen: Vandenhoeck & Ruprecht, 1939.

Ziegler, Joseph, *Duodecim Prophetae.* VTG 13. Göttingen: Vandenhoeck & Ruprecht, 1943.

SUBJECT INDEX

INDEX OF MODERN AUTHORS

INDEX OF ANCIENT SOURCES

Other Early Jewish Literature